MAKERS OF
WORLD
HISTORY

Volume 2

SECOND EDITION

MAKERS OF WORLD HISTORY

Volume 2

SECOND EDITION

J. Kelley Sowards, editor

Wichita State University

St. Martin's Press

New York

Editor: Louise H. Waller
Managing editor: Patricia Mansfield-Phelan
Project editor: Alda D. Trabucchi
Production supervisor: Joe Ford
Photo research: Elnora Bode
Cover design: Eileen Burke

Library of Congress Catalog Card Number: 94-65217

Manufactured in the United States of America.

9 8 7 6 5
f e d c b a

For information, write:
St. Martin's Press, Inc.
175 Fifth Avenue
New York, NY 10010

ISBN: 0-312-09651-8

CT
104
.M295
1995
V 2
July 1998

Acknowledgments

Suleiman: From *The Life and Letters of Ogier Ghiselin de Busbecq* by C. T. Forster and F. A. B.
Daniell. Copyright © 1971 Editions Slatkine, Geneva.
From *Suleiman the Magnificent, 1529–1566* by Roger B. Merriman.
From *The Ottoman Empire: The Classical Age 1300–1804* by Halil Inalcik, trans. by Norman
Itzkowitz and Colin Imber, pp. 35–38, 41. (London: Weidenfeld & Nicolson Ltd., 1973).
Reprinted by permission of George Weidenfeld & Nicolson Ltd.

Acknowledgments and copyrights are continued at the back of the book on pages
318–319, which constitute an extension of the copyright page.

To my dear daughters-in-law Cindy and Jane

Preface

Are men and women able to force change upon history by their skill and wits, their nerve and daring? Are they capable of altering history's course by their actions? Or are they hopelessly caught in the grinding process of great, impersonal forces over which they have no real control?

Historians—like theologians, philosophers, and scientists—have long been fascinated by this question. People of every age have recognized great forces at work in their affairs, whether they perceived those forces as supernatural and divine, climatological, ecological, sociological, or economic. Yet obviously at least a few individuals—Alexander, Suleiman—were able to seize the opportunity their times offered and compel the great forces of history to change course. Still others—Confucius, Muhammad, Gandhi—were able, solely by the power of their thoughts or their visions, to shape the history of their periods and of all later times even more profoundly than conquerors or military heroes.

The purpose of *Makers of World History* is to examine the careers and the impact of a number of figures who have significantly influenced world history or embodied much that is significant about the periods in which they lived. At the same time the book introduces students to the chief varieties of historical interpretation. Few personalities or events stand without comment in the historical record; contemporary accounts and documents, the so-called original sources, no less than later studies, are written by people with a distinct point of view and interpretation of what they see. Problems of interpretation are inseparable from the effort to achieve historical understanding.

The basic skeleton of all history is political history, and the "names" that occur most often are those of rulers, political figures, and other kinds of "movers and shakers." Hence, the figures loom large in the historical narrative, a fact that is reflected in the contents of *Makers of World History*.

The readings in this book have been chosen for their inherent interest and their particular way of treating their subjects. Typically, three selections are devoted to each figure. The first selection is usually an autobiographical or contemporary biographical account; in a few instances, differing assessments by contemporaries are included. Next, a more or less orthodox interpretation is presented; it is often a selection from the "standard work" on the figure in question. The final selection offers a more recent view, which may reinforce the standard interpretation, revise it in light of new evidence, or dissent from it completely. In some cases, two very different recent views are set side by side.

A book of this size cannot hope to include full-length biographies of all the individuals studied. Instead, each chapter focuses on an important interpretive issue. In some chapters the figure's relative historical importance is at issue; in others the significance of a major point revealed in the sources is discussed; in still others the general meaning of the figure's career, as debated in a spread of interpretive positions, is weighed. In every chapter the question examined is interesting and basic to an understanding of the figure's place in history.

Makers of World History is an alternative version of an earlier book, *Makers of the Western Tradition,* and has been adapted for use in World History, as opposed to Western Civilization, courses. The breakpoint between the two volumes lies in the late sixteenth/early seventeenth centuries, a fairly common dividing line between the two terms of World History courses. Each volume contains fourteen chapters; thus each fits into the fifteen weeks of a typical college semester. Each volume is also divided equally between Western and non-Western figures. This, I believe, reflects the usual subject emphasis of World History courses.

An effort was made to represent a spread of regional civilizations, resulting in three Chinese, three Indian, three Middle Eastern, two Japanese, two African, and one Native American among the non-Western figures. There is also a spread among subject areas—twenty political leaders, four philosophers or religious leaders, two literary figures, one explorer, and one scientist.

This revised second edition was prepared in response to suggestions from users of the first edition. We have eleven new figures in the second edition of this text—Hammurabi, Sappho, Cleopatra, Genghis Khan, Joan of Arc, Christopher Columbus, Clive of India, Catherine the Great, Simón Bolívar, Gandhi, and Golda Meir. We have retained the Review and Study Questions for each chapter, and have updated all the chapter bibliographies.

The second edition of *Makers of World History* is based on responses to a questionnaire by colleagues across the country who used the first

edition in their classes. Their suggestions about which historical fig-
ures ought to be deleted and which added were extremely helpful in
the revision. The author would especially like to thank: Norman R.
Bennett, Boston University; John B. Guarino, Northern Essex Com-
munity College; Ellwood B. Hannum, University of South Alabama;
Joseph P. Huffman, Westmont College; Karen L. Jolly, University of
Hawaii at Manoa; Irving A. Kelter, University of St. Thomas; Lisa M.
Lane, Mira Costa College; Stephen Morillo, Wabash College; Elsa
Nystrom, Kennesaw State College; Joseph R. Peden, CUNY, Baruch
College; Thomas D. Reins, California State University at Fullerton;
Gary W. Shanafelt, McMurray University; J. Lee Shneidman, Adelphi
University; and Lawrence Squeri, East Stroudsburg University.

J. K. S.

Contents

GOLDA MEIR: MOTHER OF ISRAEL 271

JOMO KENYATTA: "THE BURNING SPEAR" 295

MAKERS OF WORLD HISTORY

Volume 2

SECOND EDITION

SULEIMAN THE MAGNIFICENT: GOD'S SLAVE AND SULTAN OF THIS WORLD

1494	Born
1520	Became Ottoman sultan
1521	Turks take Belgrade
1522	Surrender of Rhodes
1526	Battle of Mohács
1529	Siege of Vienna
1534–55	Campaigns against Persia
1560	Naval victory of Djerba
1566	Died

In the year 1520 Suleiman came to the throne of the Ottoman Empire, the only surviving son and successor of the Sultan Selim I. Thus began a reign that would last for forty-six years, during the course of which the Ottomans would reach the apex of their history. The accomplishments of Suleiman would outweigh even those of Muhammad II, the conqueror of Constantinople. To his Turkish subjects Suleiman was known as Kanuni, the Lawgiver, the second Solomon. To the West he was known as the Magnificent. This latter title, so ruefully granted to the sultan by his western contemporaries, reflects his great military career, particularly his campaigns and conquests in Europe. Those conquests were to establish the Turks as a presence in Europe for the next three hundred years, intruding "the Turkish question" into virtually every matter of international politics until the twentieth century.

Suleiman's two predecessors, Bayazid II (1481–1512) and his father Selim I (1512–1520), had been concerned mainly with the Asiatic portions of the Ottoman Empire. But Suleiman was to be preoccupied with the conquest of the West.

One of his first acts was to mount a campaign against the Balkan

1

fortress city of Belgrade, which fell to his armies in 1521. At nearly the same time, his naval forces blockaded the island of Rhodes, the last crusading stronghold in the Near East, held by the Knights of St. John. In 1522 it fell. In 1526 he mounted another massive campaign in the Balkans that culminated in the decisive defeat of the Hungarians at Mohács and the death of their king, Louis II. Three years later his armies stood before Vienna. The siege of Vienna was to be the high-water mark of Suleiman's conquests in Europe.

That the main line of Suleiman's imperial policy was the conquest of Europe was the conclusion of the greatest of all European authorities on the Ottoman Empire, the nineteenth-century Austrian historian Josef von Hammer-Purgsdahl. "We recall," he wrote, "the thirteen campaigns that he conducted in person, his numerous battles and conquests: Rhodes and Belgrade, those two roads to empire on land and sea, opened at the beginning of his reign," and "the Ottoman banners planted before the walls of Vienna. . . . He extended the frontier of his empire" to the fortress of Gran, "to the foot of Mount Semmering and the mountains of Styria. . . . In the Mediterranean the fleets, led by Khäreddin-Barbarossa and Torghoud, carried their conquests and their depredations to the Greek islands, Apulia and Calabria, Sicily and Corsica, making Rome tremble, and advancing to the mouth of the Rhone where they besieged Marseille. . . . The designation of a great ruler incontestably belongs to him."[1]

---

[1] The translation of this passage is made from the superior, updated French edition of the work, J. De Hammer, *Histoire de l'Empire Ottoman*, tr. J.-J. Hellert (Paris: Bellizard, 1836), VI, pp. 287–89.

Suleiman: The Last Years

OGIER GHISELIN DE BUSBECQ

There are many contemporary accounts of the Sultan Suleiman. He himself kept a detailed diary; there are accounts and descriptions by court figures and official Turkish historians; and there are reports of European diplomats at the Porte.[2] For the purpose of revealing the character and motives of the sultan the Turkish sources are limited. Suleiman's diary is prosaic and factual and not very revealing of the man who wrote it. The accounts of courtiers and official chroniclers are marred by excessive adulation of the sultan and hence unreliable. Western diplomats' accounts, while sometimes useful, are more often too closely related to their own policy ends. An exception is the account of Ogier Ghiselin de Busbecq.

Busbecq was a noble Fleming, born in 1522, who spent most of his life as a professional diplomat, much of it in the service of King Ferdinand, the brother of the Hapsburg Emperor Charles V, Charles's regent for the eastern Hapsburg lands and his successor as Holy Roman Emperor. Busbecq was hastily summoned back to Vienna in 1554 from London, where he had represented Ferdinand at the marriage of Queen Mary Tudor and Prince Philip of Spain. Relations with the Turks had taken a turn for the worse. Since the Turkish siege of Vienna had failed in 1529, Turkish relations with the Hungarians and Hapsburgs had swung between truce and open warfare, with first one and then the other gaining a momentary advantage, the preponderance usually on the side of the Turks. Ferdinand had succeeded in 1551 in taking Transylvania. Suleiman was furious, accusing Ferdinand of bad faith and duplicity, and threatened full-scale war. The only hope Ferdinand had of preserving the precarious position he held in Hungary lay in the skill and tact of his diplomats. He asked Busbecq to go to Constantinople as his ambassador; Busbecq agreed. It was not an enviable assignment. His immediate predecessor, Giovanni Maria Malvezzi, had spent the last two years locked in a Turkish prison, under threat of torture and mutilation in punishment for his king's perfidy.

Busbecq went to Constantinople, where he was to spend most of

---

[2]The seat of Ottoman government, "The Sublime Porte" was the sultan's palace in Constantinople, named after its gate (port).—Ed.

3

the next eight years, with occasional journeys back to Vienna to consult with his government. The substance of his mission and the account of the sights and people he saw—including the sultan—are all contained in a series of "Turkish Letters" that he wrote to an old friend, fellow diplomat, and fellow Fleming Nicolas Michault, Lord of Indeveldt. Busbecq's account is extremely candid and perceptive. It reveals that Suleiman saw himself not only as a participant in European affairs but as the prime participant, the arbiter of Europe's destiny, as of Asia's. It also reveals a man used to the exercise of absolute power, impatient with the delays and disappointments of diplomacy and the deceitfulness of diplomats and their political masters—a man nearing the end of his reign and his life, and uncertain about his place in history.

In his account Busbecq has already described the long and harrowing trip to the East. Now he has arrived and been summoned to see the sultan at Amasia, the capital of Cappadocia.

On our arrival at Amasia we were taken to call on Achmet Pasha (the chief Vizier) and the other pashas—for the Sultan himself was not then in the town—and commenced our negotiations with them touching the business entrusted to us by King Ferdinand. The Pashas, on their part, apparently wishing to avoid any semblance of being prejudiced with regard to these questions, did not offer any strong opposition to the views we expressed, and told us that the whole matter depended on the Sultan's pleasure. On his arrival we were admitted to an audience; but the manner and spirit in which he listened to our address, our arguments, and our message, was by no means favourable.

The Sultan was seated on a very low ottoman, not more than a foot from the ground, which was covered with a quantity of costly rugs and cushions of exquisite workmanship; near him lay his bow and arrows. His air, as I said, was by no means gracious, and his face wore a stern, though dignified, expression.

On entering we were separately conducted into the royal presence by the chamberlains, who grasped our arms. This has been the Turkish fashion of admitting people to the Sovereign ever since a Croat, in order to avenge the death of his master, Marcus, Despot of Servia, asked Amurath[3] for an audience, and took advantage of it to slay him. After having gone through a pretence of kissing his hand, we were conducted backwards to the wall opposite his seat, care being taken

---

[3]Amurath is a variant spelling of Murad I (1360–1389). The incident referred to never actually occurred.—Ed.

that we should never turn our backs on him. The Sultan then listened to what I had to say; but the language I held was not at all to his taste, for the demands of his Majesty breathed a spirit of independence and dignity, which was by no means acceptable to one who deemed that his wish was law; and so he made no answer beyond saying in a tetchy way, 'Giusel, giusel,' i.e. well, well. After this we were dismissed to our quarters. . . .

By May 10 the Persian Ambassador had arrived, bringing with him a number of handsome presents, carpets from famous looms, Babylonian tents, the inner sides of which were covered with coloured tapestries, trappings and housings of exquisite workmanship, jewelled scimitars from Damascus, and shields most tastefully designed; but the chief present of all was a copy of the Koran, a gift highly prized among the Turks; it is a book containing the laws and rites enacted by Mahomet, which they suppose to be inspired.

Terms of peace were immediately granted to the Persian Ambassador with the intention of putting greater pressure on us, who seemed likely to be the more troublesome of the two; and in order to convince us of the reality of the peace, honours were showered on the representative of the Shah. . . .

Peace having been concluded with the Persian, as I have already told you, it was impossible for us to obtain any decent terms from the Turk; all we could accomplish was to arrange a six months' truce to give time for a reply to reach Vienna, and for the answer to come back.

I had come to fill the position of ambassador in ordinary; but inasmuch as nothing had been as yet settled as to a peace, the Pashas determined that I should return to my master with Solyman's letter, and bring back an answer, if it pleased the King to send one. Accordingly I had another interview with the Sultan. . . . Having received the Sultan's letter, which was sealed up in a wrapper of cloth of gold, I took my leave; the gentlemen among my attendants were also allowed to enter and make their bow to him. Then having paid my respects in the same way to the Pashas I left Amasia with my colleagues on June 2. . . .

You will probably wish me to give you my impressions of Solyman.

His years are just beginning to tell on him, but his majestic bearing and indeed his whole demeanour are such as beseem the lord of so vast an empire. He has always had the character of being a careful and temperate man; even in his early days, when, according to the Turkish rule, sin would have been venial, his life was blameless; for not even in youth did he either indulge in wine or commit those unnatural crimes which are common among the Turks; nor could those who were disposed to put the most unfavourable construction on his acts bring anything worse against him than his excessive devotion to his wife, and the precipitate way in which, by her influence, he was induced to put Mustapha to death; for it is commonly believed that it was by her philtres and witchcraft that he was led to commit this act. As regards herself, it is a well-known fact that from the time he made her his lawful wife he has been perfectly faithful to her, although there was nothing in the laws to prevent his having mistresses as well.[4] As an upholder of his religion and its rites he is most strict, being quite as anxious to extend his faith as to extend his empire. Considering his years (for he is now getting on for sixty) he enjoys good health, though it may be that his bad complexion arises from some lurking malady. There is a notion current that he has an incurable ulcer or cancer on his thigh. When he is anxious to impress an ambassador, who is leaving, with a favourable idea of the state of his health, he conceals the bad complexion of his face under a coat of rouge, his notion being that foreign powers will fear him more if they think that he is strong and well. I detected unmistakable signs of this practice of his; for I observed his face when he gave me a farewell audience, and found it was much altered from what it was when he received me on my arrival. . . .

> This was only the first of several journeys back to Vienna between 1554 and 1562. Busbecq finally departed Constantinople for good in August of 1562.

I commenced my wished-for journey, bringing with me as the fruit of eight years' exertions a truce for eight years, which however it will be easy to get extended for as long as we wish, unless some remarkable change should occur. . . .

> The truce Busbecq had negotiated entailed, on Austria's part, the recognition of all Ottoman conquests and the independence of Translyvania under Ottoman suzerainty. Ferdinand was also obliged to continue to pay tribute. But it was a peace that spared Hungary the agony of yet another Turkish invasion and spared the strapped Austrian monarchy the need to mount yet another expensive military defense. Busbecq's account of his successful negotiation is followed by his judicious assessment of the situation between Suleiman and Ferdinand.

---

[4]Suleiman was indeed devoted to Roxelana, who enjoyed the unusual status of his lawful wife and lived not in the harem but in the imperial palace. She did exercise a baneful influence over the sultan and may even have influenced his decision to execute his eldest son Mustapha, who had rebelled against him. However, deep suspicion of a sultan's sons and even their murder by their father was a common occurrence among the Ottoman rulers. All of Suleiman's brothers, for example, had been killed by Selim.—Ed.

Against us stands Solyman, that foe whom his own and his ancestors' exploits have made so terrible; he tramples the soil of Hungary with 200,000 horse, he is at the very gates of Austria, threatens the rest of Germany, and brings in his train all the nations that extend from our borders to those of Persia. The army he leads is equipped with the wealth of many kingdoms. Of the three regions, into which the world is divided, there is not one that does not contribute its share towards our destruction. Like a thunderbolt he strikes, shivers, and destroys everything in his way. The troops he leads are trained veterans, accustomed to his command; he fills the world with the terror of his name. . . . Nevertheless, the heroic Ferdinand with undaunted courage keeps his stand on the same spot, does not desert his post, and stirs not an inch from the position he has taken up. He would desire to have such strength that he could, without being charged with madness and only at his own personal risk, stake everything on the chance of a battle; but his generous impulses are moderated by prudence. He sees what ruin to his own most faithful subjects and, indeed, to the whole of Christendom would attend any failure in so important an enterprise, and thinks it wrong to gratify his private inclination at the price of a disaster ruinous to the state. He reflects what an unequal contest it would be, if 25,000 or 30,000 infantry with the addition of a small body of cavalry should be pitted against 200,000 cavalry supported by veteran infantry. The result to be expected from such a contest is shown him only too plainly by the examples of former times, the routs of Nicopolis and Varna, and the plains of Mohacz, still white with the bones of slaughtered Christians. . . .

It is forty years, more or less, since Solyman at the beginning of his reign, after taking Belgrade, crushing Hungary, and slaying King Louis, made sure of obtaining not only that province but also those beyond; in this hope he besieged Vienna, and renewing the war reduced Güns, and threatened Vienna again, but that time from a distance. Yet what has he accomplished with his mighty array of arms, his boundless resources and innumerable soldiery? Why, he has not made one single step in Hungary in advance of his original conquest. He, who used to make an end of powerful kingdoms in a single campaign, has won, as the reward of his invasions, ill-fortified castles or inconsiderable villages, and has paid a heavy price for whatever fragments he has gradually torn off from the vast bulk of Hungary. Vienna he has certainly seen once, but as it was for the first, so it was for the last time.

Three things Solyman is said to have set his heart on, namely, to see the building of his mosque finished (which is indeed a costly and beautiful work), by restoring the ancient aqueducts to give Constantinople an abundant supply of water, and to take Vienna. In two of these things his wishes have been accomplished, in the third he has been stopped, and I hope will be stopped. Vienna he is wont to call by no other name than his disgrace and shame.

The Young Suleiman

ROGER B. MERRIMAN

From the foregoing account of an ailing and world-weary Suleiman at the end of his reign, with his ambitions for the conquest of Europe thwarted, we turn back to the beginning of his reign and the bright promise which that conquest seemed to hold. The account is by the American scholar Roger B. Merriman.

Merriman is best known for his massive four-volume work *The Rise of the Spanish Empire in the Old World and in the New,* published between 1911 and 1934. It remains the preeminent work on its subject. In the course of his research for that book, Merriman became interested in not only the Spanish but the Austrian Hapsburgs, and their imperial problems, not the least of which was the Turks. Then, in the early 1940s, he undertook to finish a book on Suleiman the Magnificent that had been left unfinished by a close friend and Harvard colleague, Archibald Coolidge, on his death. Merriman updated the research, reworked parts of the manuscript, and rewrote other parts entirely. The result is his *Suleiman the Magnificent 1520–1566,* which appeared in 1944 and which is still the most comprehensive and authoritative biography of Suleiman in English.

After sketching in the background of Suleiman's reign, dealing with his boyhood, youth, and accession to the throne, and his first two major campaigns against Belgrade and Rhodes, Merriman takes up the story of the campaign of Mohács and Vienna, between 1526 and 1529, the culminating events of Suleiman's assault on Europe.

On Monday (reckoned a lucky day) the twenty-third of April, 1526, Suleiman, accompanied by Ibrahim[5] and two other vizirs, left Con-

---

[5]Ibrahim Pasha was an early favorite of Suleiman whom he had rapidly advanced to the office of Grand Vizier and to whom he granted extraordinary powers. Ibrahim's personal ambition, however, finally became a threat even to the sultan and, encouraged by Roxelana, Suleiman had him put to death in 1536.—Ed.

stantinople at the head of more than 100,000 men with 300 cannon. The Sultan's diary gives many details of the advance, which continued for more than eighty days before contact was established with the enemy. . . .

The two middle weeks of August were the really critical period of the campaign. The Hungarian king, council, magnates, and generals had been wrangling at Buda and Tolna over the question of the defence of the realm; while Tömöri,[6] from across the Danube, kept sending them messages of the continued advance of the Turks which he was impotent to impede. The obvious thing for the Hungarians to do was, of course, to move southward and defend the strong line of the Drave, but petty jealousies prevented this. The most they would consent to do was to advance to the plain of Mohács, on the west side of the Danube, some thirty miles to the north of the point where the Drave unites with it. The inhabitants of Esseg, on the south bank of the Drave, realized that they had been abandoned, and made haste to send the keys of their town to the Sultan, in token of submission, as he slowly approached in a driving rain. When Suleiman reached the Drave, he could scarcely believe his eyes when he found that its northern bank had been left undefended, but he was prompt to avail himself of a God-given opportunity. On August 15 he "gave orders to throw a bridge of boats across this river and personally supervised the work." As the Turkish historian Kemal Pasha Zadeh rapturously declares, "They set to work without delay to get together the materials necessary for this enterprise. All the people expert in such matters thought that the construction of such a bridge would take at least three months, but yet, thanks to the skilful arrangements and the intelligent zeal of the Grand Vizir, it was finished in the space of three days." (The Sultan's diary makes it five.) After the army had crossed over, Esseg was burned and the bridge destroyed. It was a bold step to take; for though the invaders were thereby partially protected from the arrival of Hungarian reënforcements from Croatia, they were also deprived of all means of escape in case of defeat by their Christian foes. . . .

Meantime the Hungarians were slowly assembling on the plain of Mohács. King Louis had a bare 4,000 men with him when he arrived there; but fresh detachments came continually dribbling in, and others were known to be rapidly approaching. But they were a motley host, whose mutual jealousies made it wellnigh impossible for them effectively to combine. There was much difficulty over the choice of a

---

[6]Paul Tömöri, the Archbishop of Kalocsa, was a warlike cleric who had been assigned the task of defending the Turkish frontier and who was the most experienced of the Hungarian commanders.—ED.

commander-in-chief. King Louis was obviously unequal to the task; the Palatine Stephen Báthory had the gout; and so it was finally decided to give the place to Archbishop Tömöri, the memory of whose past successes in border warfare against the Moslems was enough to stifle his own protestations that he was not the man for the task. Soon after his appointment, and when the Turks had already crossed the Drave, the Hungarians held a council of war to determine the strategy most expedient for them to adopt. The more cautious of them advocated a retreat toward Buda-Pesth; then the Turks would have no choice but to follow, for Buda was their announced objective and they were staking everything on success. Every day's march forward would take them further from their base, while the Hungarians if they retired would be sure to be joined by reënforcements. John Zápolya[7] was but a few days distant with 15,000 to 20,000 men; John Frangipani was coming up from Croatia; the Bohemian contingent, 16,000 strong, was already on the western frontier of the realm. But unfortunately the bulk of the Hungarians, including Tömöri himself, refused to listen to such reasoning as this. They were filled with an insane overconfidence. The gallant but rash and turbulent Magyar nobility clamored for an immediate fight. They distrusted the king. Many of them were hostile to Zápolya, and unwilling to have him share in the glory of the victory which they believed certain. It was accordingly decided to give battle at once; and the Hungarians, who could choose their own ground, elected to remain on the plain of Mohács, in a place which would give them full play for their cavalry. Apparently they forgot that the enemy, whose horsemen were much more numerous than their own, would derive even greater advantage from the position they had chosen.

The relative size of the two armies which were about to encounter one another has been a fertile source of discussion ever since. One thing only is certain; the contemporaneous estimates on both sides are ridiculously exaggerated. Tömöri told King Louis, on the eve of the battle, that the Sultan had perhaps 300,000 men; but that there was no reason to be frightened by this figure, since most of the Turks were cowardly rabble, and their picked fighting-men numbered only 70,000! Even if we accept the statement that Suleiman left Constantinople at the head of 100,000 men, we must remember that less than one-half of them were troops of the line. It seems likely that his losses through skirmishing and bad weather, as he advanced, must have more than counterbalanced his gains through reënforcements re-

---

[7]John Zápolya was the ruler of Transylvania and sometime claimant to the Hungarian throne.—ED.

ceived along the route. If we put the Janissaries[8] at 8,000, the regular cavalry of the bodyguard at 7,000, the Asiatic feudal cavalry at 10,000, the European at 15,000, and the miscellaneous levies at 5,000, we get a total of 45,000 Turkish fighting troops, besides the irregular and lightly armed akinji,[9] possibly 10,000 to 20,000, who hovered about the battlefield but were never expected to stand the charge of regular soldiers. It is also very doubtful if Suleiman still had anywhere near the 300 cannon with which he is said to have left Constantinople in the previous April.

The actual size of the Hungarian army is almost equally difficult to estimate—principally because of the reënforcements which continued to arrive until the day of the fight. In the grandiloquent letter which the Sultan despatched a few days after the battle to announce his victory to the heads of his different provinces, he puts the number of his Christian foes at approximately 150,000, but it seems probable that the true figures were less than one-fifth as large: perhaps 25,000 to 28,000 men, about equally divided between cavalry and infantry, and 80 guns. Part of these troops were well drilled professional soldiers, many of them Germans, Poles, and Bohemians; there was also the Hungarian national cavalry, made up of the brave but utterly undisciplined nobles. And they had, besides, large numbers of heavy-armored wagons, which could be chained together to make rough fortifications, or even pushed forward, like the modern tank, to pave the way for an infantry or a cavalry charge. . . .

The plain of Mohács, some six miles in length, is bounded on the east by the Danube. At the northern end is the town, while to the south and west there is a line of low hills, then covered with woods, which furnished an admirable screen for the Turkish advance. Apparently neither side expected a combat till well after noon of the day on which it occurred, and actual fighting did not begin till after three. The story of the details of the battle itself varies widely in the different contemporaneous accounts that have come down to us, but the main outlines seem reasonably clear. The combat opened with a tremendous charge of the heavy-armed Hungarian cavalry against the centre of the Turkish line emerging from the woods. It pierced the opposing ranks, and soon after appeared to be so decisively successful that orders were given for a general advance of all the Hungarian forces. But the Turkish centre had been withdrawn on purpose, in

---

[8]The Janissaries were the primary infantry force of the Ottomans, made up of Christian boys raised as Moslems in strict military discipline.—ED.

[9]Akinji were irregular cavalry forces.—ED.

order to lure their enemies on to their destruction. By the time they had reached the Janissaries and the Sultan's standard, they were held up. There were furious hand-to-hand combats between the Christian leaders and the members of Suleiman's bodyguard; at one moment Suleiman himself was in grave danger. But the Turkish artillery was far more skilfully handled than that of their opponents; the Hungarians were mowed down in droves; most important of all, the concentration of the Christians in the centre gave their numerous foes a splendid opportunity, of which they were prompt to take advantage, to outflank their enemies, particularly on the westward. Within an hour and a half, the fate of the battle had been decided. The Hungarians fled in wild disorder to the north and east. Such, apparently, are the principal facts. But as we are following the story of the battle from the Turkish standpoint, it will be worth while to supplement these data by a few passages from the history of Kemal Pasha. He gives Ibrahim all the credit for the feint by which the Christians were enticed to disaster. "The young lion," he declares, "no matter how brave, should remember the wisdom and experience of the old wolf. . . . When the Grand Vizir seized his redoubtable sword, ready to enter the lists, he looked like the sun, which sheds its rays on the universe. In combat, he was a youth, ardent as the springtime: in council, he was an old man, as experienced as Fortune in numerous vicissitudes." When the battle began, he continues, "the air was rent with the wind of the fury of the combatants; the standards shone forth in the distance; the drums sounded like thunder, and swords flashed like the lightning. . . . While the faces of the miserable infidels grew pale and withered before they felt the flame of the blades . . . the cheeks of our heroes, drunk with lust for combat, were tinged with the color of roses. . . . With all these murderous swords stretched out to lay hold on the garment of life, the plain seemed like a fiend with a thousand arms; with all these pointed lances, eager to catch the bird of life in the midst of slaughter, the battlefield resembled a dragon with a thousand heads." And then, when the rout began, he concludes: "At the order of the Sultan the fusiliers of the Janissaries, directing their blows against the cruel panthers who opposed us, caused hundreds, or rather thousands of them, in the space of a moment, to descend into the depths of Hell."

The slaughter which followed the battle was indeed fearful. The Turks took no prisoners, and few of the defeated escaped. The Sultan's diary is even more than usually laconic. For August 31 it reads "The Emperor, seated on a golden throne, receives the homage of the vizirs and the beys: massacre of 2000 prisoners: the rain falls in torrents"; and for September 2: "Rest at Mohács; 20,000 Hungarian infantry and 4000 of their cavalry are buried." On this occasion his figures seem to be corroborated, in round numbers at least, by the Christian accounts of the disaster. Mohács indeed was the "tombeau de la nation hongroise";[10] never has a single battle proved so fatal to the life of a people. In addition to the annihilation of its army, almost all of its leaders had perished. King Louis, after fighting bravely, turned to flee when all was lost, but his horse, in trying to climb the steep bank of a small stream, fell backwards into the waters below and buried his rider under him. Tömöri and his second in command were also killed, together with two archbishops, five bishops, many magnates, and the greater part of the Hungarian aristocracy; the flower of the nation, both lay and clerical, had been sacrificed on the fatal day. Suleiman's announcement of his victory to his governors is couched in more expansive language than is his diary, but the impression conveyed in the following sentences from it is substantially correct, as seen from the standpoint of the Turks. "Thanks be to the Most High! The banners of Islam have been victorious, and the enemies of the doctrine of the Lord of Mankind have been driven from their country and overwhelmed. Thus God's grace has granted my glorious armies a triumph, such as was never equalled by any illustrious Sultan, all-powerful Khan, or even by the companions of the Prophet. What was left of the nation of impious men has been extirpated! Praise be to God, the Master of Worlds!"

After Mohács organized resistance practically ceased. On the day following the battle John Zápolya with his army reached the left bank of the Danube; but he made haste to withdraw as soon as he learned of the catastrophe. On September third the Ottoman army resumed its advance; on the tenth it entered Buda. Apparently the keys of the town had been sent out in advance to Suleiman in token of submission by those who had been unable to flee (Kemal Pasha assures us that only "humble folk" had remained within the walls), and the Sultan, in return promised them that they should be spared the horrors of a sack. But his troops got out of hand, and he was unable to keep his word. As his diary tersely puts it (September 14), "A fire breaks out in Buda, despite the efforts of the Sultan: the Grand Vizir seeks in vain to extinguish it": as a matter of fact the entire city was burnt to the ground with the exception of the royal castle, where Suleiman himself had taken up his residence. There the Sultan found many treasures which he carried back with him to Constantinople. . . .

In the midst of the celebrations of his victory he was seriously considering the question of the disposition he should make of the prize that he had won. . . . On the whole it seemed wiser to be satis-

---

[10]"Tomb of the Hungarian nation."—Ed.

fied with what had already been achieved. To quote Kemal again, "The time when this province should be annexed to the possessions of Islam had not yet arrived, nor the day come when the heroes of the Holy War should honor the rebel plains with their presence. The matter was therefore postponed to a more suitable occasion, and heed was given to the sage advice; 'When thou wouldst enter, think first how thou wilt get out again.' "

On September 13, accordingly, the Sultan ordered the construction of a bridge of boats across the Danube from Buda to Pesth, and seven days later the vanguard of the Turkish army passed across it. On the night of the twenty-third the bridge apparently broke into three parts, two of which were swept away, so that the last detachments had to be ferried over in boats. The next day Pesth was burnt, and on the morrow the Ottoman army started homeward. . . .

In the year following his return from Mohács, his chief immediate care was the suppression of two insurrections in Asia Minor. The first, in Cilicia, was put down by the local authorities. The second, in Karamania and the districts to the east of it, was more serious; and Ibrahim had to be despatched with a force of Janissaries to insure the final defeat of the rebels in June, 1527. Meantime the Sultan had remained at Constantinople; partly, perhaps, because he did not wish to lower his own prestige in the eyes of his subjects by seeming to be obliged to deal personally with revolts; but more probably because he was principally interested in the course of events in Hungary. . . .

By midsummer of 1528 . . . it must have been reasonably clear that Suleiman soon intended to launch a third great expedition up the Danube, this time as the ally, or perhaps better the protector, of Zápolya, against Ferdinand and the power of the House of Hapsburg. There is no reason to be surprised that he delayed his departure until the following year. The season was already too late to embark on an enterprise whose ultimate goal, Vienna, was so remote. Moreover the Sultan fully realized that in challenging Ferdinand he was also indirectly bidding defiance to the Emperor Charles V. On May 10, 1529, however, he left Constantinople, at the head of a much larger army than that of 1526. The Christian chroniclers talk vaguely of 250,000 to 300,000, though it is doubtful if there were more than 75,000 fighting men, and it seems clear that four-fifths of them were cavalry. Ibrahim was again seraskier,[11] and the artillery is given, as before, at 300 guns. The rains, which in the preceding campaign had been a nuisance, were this year so continuous and torrential that they seriously affected the outcome of the campaign. Suleiman did not reach

---

[11]The title of the Turkish Minister of War, who was also the army commander.—ED.

Vienna till a month later than he expected, and that month may well have made just the difference between failure and success. The Sultan's comments on the bad weather in his diary are constant and bitter. At Mohács, on August 18, he had been joined by Zápolya, whose prospects had speedily revived when it became known that he had won the favor of Suleiman. He brought with him 6,000 men. The Sultan received him with great pomp, and presented him with four robes of honor and three horses caparisoned with gold. But Suleiman, in his diary, takes great pains to point out that he regarded him merely as a vassal. He explains that the gifts were only bestowed in recognition of the voivode's[12] homage; and he emphasizes the fact that Zápolya twice kissed his hand. At Buda a feeble resistance was offered by a few hundred Austrian mercenaries; but they soon surrendered after a promise of good treatment, which was shamefully violated by the Janissaries. Zápolya was permitted to make a royal entrance there on September 14; but he was obviously dominated and controlled by the Turkish soldiers and officials who escorted him. . . . September 18 the akinji swarmed across the Austrian frontier, and swept like a hurricane through the open country. On the twenty-seventh the Sultan himself arrived before Vienna. Two days later the investment was complete.

The siege of Vienna appeals strongly to the imagination. Never since the battle of Tours, almost precisely eight centuries before, had Christian Europe been so direfully threatened by Mohammedan Asia and Africa. Had the verdict on either occasion been reversed, the whole history of the world might have been changed. And the cause of the Moslem defeat in both cases was fundamentally the same; the invaders had outrun their communications. This is well demonstrated in the case of Vienna by the fact that the long distances and heavy rains had forced the Turks to leave behind them the bulk of their heavy artillery, which had been such a decisive factor in the siege of Rhodes. The lighter cannon, which was almost all that they succeeded in bringing with them, could make little impression on the city walls. Only by mining operations could they hope to open a breach for a general assault. . . .

The Sultan's headquarters were his splendid red tent, pitched on a hill, three or four miles away. Mining and countermining operations were vigorously pushed during the early days of October. Several times the besiegers were encouraged to launch assaults, which were invariably repulsed. On the other hand, the constant sorties of the garrison were generally unsuccessful. October 12 was the critical day

---

[12]A Slavic word denoting the military commander or governor of a territory.—Ed.

of the siege. On that morning the walls had been breached by mines, and the Turks had delivered the most furious of their attacks. Only with great difficulty had it been beaten off, and the garrison was deeply discouraged; that very afternoon it despatched the most pressing of its messages to hasten the arrival of relief. But the Turks were in even worse case. At the Divan which they held that same day, the preponderance of opinion was in favor of withdrawal. The season was ominously late; supplies were getting short; the Janissaries were murmuring; powerful Christian reënforcements were known to be at hand. Ibrahim besought his master to go home. One more last attack was launched on October 14; but despite the unprecedented rewards that had been offered in case it should be successful, it was delivered in such half-hearted fashion that it was foredoomed to failure from the first. That night the Turks massacred some 2000 of the prisoners that they had taken from the Austrian countryside; they burnt their own encampment; on the fifteenth they began to retire. Their retreat was cruelly harassed by enemy cavalry, and truly horrible weather pursued them all the way to Constantinople. It was cold comfort that Zápolya came out from Buda as the Sultan passed by to compliment his master on his "successful campaign." All that the Sultan had "succeeded" in doing was to expel Ferdinand from his Hungarian dominions; and we need not take too seriously the statement in his diary that since he had learned that the archduke was not in Vienna, he had lost all interest in capturing the place! The fundamental fact remained that Suleiman had been beaten back before the walls of the Austrian capital by a force a third the size of his own, or perhaps less. His prestige, about which, like all Orientals, he was abnormally sensitive, had suffered a serious blow.

Suleiman the Statesman: An Overview

HALIL INALCIK

Despite the best efforts of Merriman, in the previous selection, to write his account "from the Turkish standpoint," it is inescapably Eurocentric, as was that of Busbecq. Fortunately, we have an assessment of Suleiman and his achievements by "the leading Turkish historian of the Balkans today,"[13] Halil Inalcik, from his *The Ottoman Empire, The Classical Age 1300–1600*. Inalcik is not only familiar with the works of Turkish historians and what he calls the "unusually rich" Ottoman archives, but with the standard western accounts of the wars and politics of the Reformation. For the first time, he weaves together the two traditions and shows us the extent to which Suleiman was regarded not only as a dangerous scourge by the West but as a counter in the western concept of the balance of power. He also shows us the extent to which Suleiman himself was aware of western politics and how that awareness affected his policies. It is a brilliant achievement of historical synthesis.

In 1519 the Habsburg Charles V and Francis I of France were candidates for the crown of the Holy Roman Empire, and both promised to mobilize all the forces of Europe against the Ottomans. The Electors considered Charles V more suited to the task, and shortly after the election, in March 1521, these two European rulers were at war with each other. Europe, to the great advantage of the Ottomans, was divided, and Süleymân I chose this time to march against Belgrade, the gateway to central Europe. Belgrade fell on 29 August 1521. On 21 January 1522 he captured Rhodes, the key to the eastern Mediterranean, from the Knights of St. John.

When Charles V took Francis prisoner at Pavia in 1525, the French, as a last resort, sought aid from the Ottomans. Francis later informed the Venetian ambassador that he considered the Ottoman Empire the only power capable of guaranteeing the existence of the European states against Charles V. The Ottomans too saw the French alliance as a means of preventing a single power dominating Europe. Francis I's ambassador told the sultan in February 1526 that if Francis accepted Charles' conditions, the Holy Roman Emperor would become 'ruler of the world'.

In the following year Süleymân advanced against Hungary with a large army. The Ottoman victory at Mohács on 28 August 1526, and the occupation of Buda, threatened the Habsburgs from the rear. The Ottomans withdrew from Hungary, occupying only Srem, and the Hungarian Diet elected John Zapolya as King. At first the Ottomans wished to make Hungary a vassal state, like Moldavia, since it was considered too difficult and too expensive to establish direct Ottoman rule in a completely foreign country on the far side of the Danube. But the Hungarian partisans of the Habsburgs elected

---

[13]Peter F. Sugar, *Southeastern Europe under Ottoman Rule, 1354–1804* (Seattle and London: University of Washington Press, 1977), p. 305.

Charles V's brother, Archduke Ferdinand, King of Hungary, and in the following year he occupied Buda and expelled Zapolya. Süleymân again invaded Hungary, and on 8 September 1529 again enthroned Zapolya in Buda as an Ottoman vassal. Zapolya agreed to pay an annual tribute and accepted a Janissary garrison in the citadel. Although the campaigning season was over, Süleymân continued his advance as far as Vienna, the Habsburg capital. After a three-week siege, he withdrew.

In 1531 Ferdinand again entered Hungary and besieged Buda. In the following year Süleymân replied by leading a large army into Hungary and advancing to the fortress of Güns, some sixty miles from Vienna, where he hoped to force Charles V to fight a pitched battle. At this moment Charles' admiral, Andrea Doria, took Coron in the Morea from the Ottomans. Realizing that he now had to open a second front in the Mediterranean, the sultan placed all Ottoman naval forces under the command of the famous Turkish corsair and conqueror of Algiers, Hayreddîn Barbarossa, appointing him *kapudan-i deryâ*—grand admiral—with orders to cooperate with the French. Since 1531 the French had been trying to persuade the sultan to attack Italy and now they sought a formal alliance. In 1536 this alliance was concluded. The sultan was ready to grant the French, as a friendly nation, freedom of trade within the empire. The ambassadors concluded orally the political and military details of the alliance and both parties kept them secret. Francis' Ottoman alliance provided his rival with abundant material for propaganda in the western Christian world. French insistence convinced Süleymân that he could bring the war to a successful conclusion only by attacking Charles V in Italy. The French were to invade northern Italy and the Ottomans the south. In 1537 Süleymân brought his army to Valona in Albania and besieged Venetian ports in Albania and the island of Corfu, where a French fleet assisted the Ottomans. In the following year, however, the French made peace with Charles. Francis had wished to profit from the Ottoman pressure by taking Milan, and when the emperor broke his promise he reverted to his 'secret' policy of alliance with the Ottomans.

In the Mediterranean Charles captured Tunis in 1535, but in 1538 Barbarossa defeated a crusader fleet under the command of Andrea Doria at Préveza, leaving him undisputed master of the Mediterranean.

When Francis again approached the sultan in 1540 he told Charles' ambassadors, come to arrange a peace treaty, that he was unable to conclude a peace unless Charles returned French territory. There was close cooperation between the Ottomans and the French between 1541 and 1544, when France realized that peaceful negotiations would not procure Milan.

In 1541 Zapolya died, and Ferdinanad again invaded Hungary. Süleymân once again came to Hungary with his army, this time bringing the country under direct Ottoman rule as an Ottoman province under a beylerbeyi.[14] He sent Zapolya's widow and infant son to Transylvania, which was then an Ottoman vassal state. Since 1526 Ferdinand had possessed a thin strip of Hungarian territory in the west and north, to which the Ottomans, as heirs to the Hungarian throne, now laid claim. In 1543 Süleymân again marched into Hungary with the intention of conquering the area, and at the same time sent a fleet of 110 galleys, under the command of Barbarossa, to assist Francis. The Franco-Ottoman fleet besieged Nice and the Ottoman fleet wintered in the French port of Toulon. In return, a small French artillery unit joined the Ottoman army in Hungary. This cooperation, however, was not particularly effective. With the worsening of relations with Iran Süleymân wanted peace on his western front. As in 1533, he concluded an armistice with Ferdinand, which included Charles. According to this treaty, signed on 1 August 1547, and to which Süleymân made France a party, Ferdinand was to keep the part of Hungary already in his possession in return for a yearly tribute of thirty thousand ducats.

Three years later war with the Habsburgs broke out again when Ferdinand tried to gain control of Transylvania. The Ottomans repulsed him, and in 1552 established the new *beylerbeyilik* of Temesvár in southern Transylvania.

When the new king, Henry II, came to the throne in France he realized the need of maintaining the Ottoman alliance in the struggle against Charles V. The French alliance was the cornerstone of Ottoman policy in Europe. The Ottomans also found a natural ally in the Schmalkalden League of German Protestant princes fighting Charles V. At the instigation of the French, Süleymân approached the Lutheran princes, urging in a letter that they continue to cooperate with France against the pope and emperor. He assured them that if the Ottoman armies entered Europe he would grant the princes amnesty. Recent research has shown that Ottoman pressure between 1521 and 1555 forced the Habsburgs to grant concessions to the Protestants and was a factor in the final official recognition of Protestantism. In his letter to the Protestants, Sulëymân intimated that he considered the Protestants close to the Muslims, since they too had destroyed idols and risen against the Pope. Support and protection of the Lutherans and Calvinists against Catholicism would be a keystone of Ottoman policy in Europe. Ottoman policy was thus intended to main-

---

[14]A governor of a Turkish province.—ED.

tain the political disunity in Europe, weaken the Habsburgs and prevent a united crusade. Hungary, under Ottoman protection, was to become a stronghold of Calvinism, to the extent that Europe began to speak of 'Calvino-turcismus'. In the second half of the sixteenth century the French Calvinist party maintained that the Ottoman alliance should be used against Catholic Spain, and the St. Bartholomew's Day Massacre of the Calvinists infuriated the Ottoman government.

It should be added that at first Luther and his adherents followed a passive course, maintaining that the Ottoman threat was a punishment from God, but when the Turkish peril began to endanger Germany the Lutherans did not hesitate to support Ferdinand with military and financial aid; in return they always obtained concessions for Lutheranism. Ottoman intervention was thus an important factor not only in the rise of national monarchies, such as in France, but also in the rise of Protestantism in Europe.

Charles V, following the example of the Venetians, entered into diplomatic relations with the Safavids of Iran, forcing Süleymân to avoid a conflict with the Safavids, in order not to have to fight simultaneously in the east and west. . . .

When the Ottomans renewed the war in central Europe, the Persians counterattacked, and in 1548 Süleymân, for the second time, marched against Iran. This war lasted intermittently for seven years. By the Treaty of Amasya, signed on 29 May 1555, Baghdad was left to the Ottomans.

These Ottoman enterprises resulted, in the mid-sixteenth century, in a new system of alliances between the states occupying an area stretching from the Atlantic, through central Asia, to the Indian Ocean. In this way the European system of balance of power was greatly enlarged. . . . In an inscription dating from 1538 on the citadel of Bender;[15] Süleymân the Magnificent gave expression to his world-embracing power:

> I am God's slave and sultan of this world. By the grace of God I am head of Muhammad's community. God's might and Muhammad's miracles are my companions. I am Süleymân, in whose name the *hutbe*[16] is read in Mecca and Medina. In Baghdad I am the shah, in Byzantine realms the Caesar, and in Egypt the sultan; who sends his fleets to the seas of Europe, the Maghrib[17] and India. I am the sultan who took the crown and throne of Hungary and granted them to a humble slave.

---

[15]A Turkish fortress in Moldavia.—Ed.

[16]The sermon following the Friday prayer in which the sultan's name was mentioned.—Ed.

[17]An Arabic term for North Africa, from Egypt to the Atlantic.—Ed.

The voivoda Petru[18] raised his head in revolt, but my horse's hoofs ground him into the dust, and I conquered the land of Moldavia.

But in his final years international conditions became unfavourable to the Ottomans and Süleymân's attempt at world-wide domination met its first decisive failures.

The Peace of Cateau-Cambrésis in 1559 established Spanish hegemony in Europe, and as France was drawn into civil war she ceased to be the Ottomans' main ally in European politics. The withdrawal from Malta in 1565 and Süleymân's last Hungarian campaign in 1566 marked the beginning of a halt in the Ottoman advance into central Europe and the Mediterranean.

Review and Study Questions

1. From these selections, what sort of picture do you derive of Suleiman?

2. In the face of the overwhelming superiority of the Turks, how do you account for Suleiman's failure to conquer Europe?

3. Why were the Christian forces so disastrously defeated at the battle of Mohács?

4. Why did Suleiman fail in his siege of Vienna?

5. What role did Suleiman play in European diplomacy?

Suggestions for Further Reading

There are no Turkish sources for Suleiman available in English. See two bibliographical articles by Bernard Lewis, "The Ottoman Archives," *Journal of the Royal Asiatic Society* (1951), 139–55, and "The Ottoman Archives," *Report on Current Research* (Washington, 1956), 17–25. Halil Inalcik, *The Ottoman Empire: The Classical Age 1300–1600,* tr. Norman Itzkowitz and Colin Imber (New York and Washington: Praeger, 1973), excerpted for this chapter, is the only narrative history in English based on Turkish sources. Of some value, however, are the relevant chapters in L. S. Stavrianos, *The Balkans since 1453* (New York: Rinehart, 1958), the standard work on the subject. Also useful is Peter F. Sugar, *Southeastern Europe under Ottoman Rule, 1354–1804* (Seattle and London: University of Washington Press, 1977),

---

[18]The last independent ruler of Moldavia, more commonly known as the pretender Jacob Basilicus.—ED.

although it is organized topically and geographically and is of limited value as a historical work. A classic work of the same sort is A. H. Lybyer, *The Government of the Ottoman Empire in the Time of Suleiman the Magnificent* (Cambridge: Harvard University Press, 1913). Norman Itzkowitz, *Ottoman Empire and Islamic Tradition* (New York: Knopf, 1972) is a useful brief general survey of Ottoman history and culture. A useful and interesting article is Merle Severy, "The World of Suleyman the Magnificent," *National Geographic Magazine*, 172, No. 5 (November 1987), 552–601. Another interesting source, excerpted in this chapter, is C. T. Forster and F. H. B. Daniell, *The Life and Letters of Ghiselin de Busbecq* (Geneva: Slatkine Reprints, 1971 [1881]); it contains an account on Suleiman by a Western diplomat.

Of the biographies of Suleiman, the best, even though it is a generation old, is still Roger B. Merriman, *Suleiman the Magnificent 1520– 1566* (New York: Cooper Square, 1966 [1944]), excerpted for this chapter. Of considerable value is a popular work by Antony Bridge, *Suleiman the Magnificent, Scourge of Heaven* (New York: Franklin Watts, 1983), mainly because it focuses on the role of Suleiman in Europe; unfortunately, it has no critical apparatus and only a perfunctory bibliography. Less valuable are the relevant chapters in Noel Barber, *The Lords of the Golden Horn: From Suleiman the Magnificent to Kamal Ataturk* (London: Macmillan, 1973). This work is simplistic and journalistic, emphasizing the most sensational episodes in Turkish domestic history.

Because of this chapter's emphasis on Suleiman's European ambitions, the standard histories of Europe in the Age of the Reformation are of some value. Two of the best are Harold J. Grimm, *The Reformation Era*, 2nd ed. (New York: Macmillan, 1973) and A. G. Dickens, *Reformation and Society in Sixteenth-Century Europe* (New York: Harcourt, Brace, 1966). Two topical works are also recommended: Sir Charles Oman, *A History of the Art of War in the Sixteenth Century* (London: Methuen, 1937) and S. A. Fischer-Galati, *Ottoman Imperialism and German Protestantism 1521–1555* (Cambridge: Harvard University Press, 1959).

ELIZABETH I, THE ARMADA, AND "THE BLACK LEGEND"

1533   Born
1558   Succeeded to the throne
1587   Execution of Mary Stuart
1588   Defeat of Spanish Armada
1603   Died

"She had a sharp tongue, a vile temper, almost no feminine delicacy, and little or no feminine modesty. Of personal loyalty and affection she seems to have commanded little or none."[1] The woman thus so unflatteringly described was Elizabeth I, Queen of England; the describer, Conyers Read, the most eminent American scholar of Tudor England. And yet Read goes on to point out, as he did in a dozen other works, that Elizabeth was "Good Queen Bess" to the great bulk of her subjects and that she has held an unrivaled place in the affections of the English since the end of the sixteenth century. Most other modern Elizabethan scholars would agree. They would also agree that despite their own learned assessments of the importance of one aspect or another of Elizabeth's reign—her management of the economy, her relations with Parliament, her domestic religious settlement—the most enduring of all Elizabethan traditions is that of Elizabeth and her England pitted against the Spain of Philip II, culminating in the dramatic English victory over the Spanish Armada in the late summer of the year 1588.

This hardy tradition has its origin in the Armada fight itself and in the events surrounding it. English hostility to Spain was growing for a number of reasons: sympathy for the beleaguered French Huguenots and the Protestants of Holland locked in their own desperate struggle with Philip; the undeclared sea war with Spain that English privateers

---

[1]Conyers Read, "Good Queen Bess," *American Historical Review*, 31 (1926), 649.

and pirates had already been carrying on for a generation; as well as the gnawing fear of a domestic fifth column of Spanish spies and English Catholics ready to betray their country for the sake of their religion. Holinshed's famous *Chronicle,* for example, quotes a speech given by one "Maister Iames Dalton" in the year 1586 having to do with the designs of certain captive traitors and Spanish sympathizers, one of whom "vomited these prophane words out of his vncircumcised mouth; that it was lawfull for anie of worship in England, to authorise the vilest wretch that is, to séeke the death of hir highnese whose prosperous estate the italish préest and Spanish prince doo so maligne." Dalton goes on to decry "an inuasion long since pretended" and the popish threats "that would burn hir bones, and the bones of all such as loued hir, either alive or dead [and] that this was to de doone, when they held the sterne of gouernement; which shall be, when errant traitors are good subjects, and ranke knaues honest men."[2]

In the years immediately following the Armada, such sentiments were even more strongly voiced. Sir Walter Raleigh in his spirited account of "The Last Fight of the Revenge," written in 1591, spoke of "how irreligiously [the Spanish] cover their greedy and ambitious pretences with that veil of piety," and how they "more greedily thirst after English blood than after the lives of any other people of Europe, for the many overthrows and dishonours they have received at our hands, whose weakness we have discovered to the world, and whose forces at home, abroad, in Europe, in India, by sea and land, we have even with handfuls of men and ships over thrown and dishonoured."[3]

Thus, by the end of the sixteenth century, the major elements of what modern Hispanic scholars have come to call "The Black Legend" were substantially formed: Spain was England's implacable enemy, cruel in victory, craven in defeat; Spaniards were treacherous and cowardly, made more so by their "popery"; and, though outmanned and out-gunned, English ships could either defeat Spanish ships or, if not, at least show how "beardless boys" could go to heroic death. The center of the legend was the Armada, which, "more than any other event, implanted anti-Hispanism in the English consciousness."[4] And Queen Elizabeth became the exemplar of the virtues of her nation and the symbol of its hostility to Spain.

---

[2]*Holinshed's Chronicle* (London, 1808; rpt. New York: AMS Press, 1965), IV, 920.

[3]Sir Walter Raleigh, *Selected Prose and Poetry,* ed. Agnes M. C. Latham (London: University of London–Athlone Press, 1965), pp. 85, 87.

[4]William S. Maltby, *The Black Legend in England: The Development of Anti-Spanish Sentiment, 1558–1660* (Durham, N.C.: Duke University Press, 1971), p. 84.

The Legendary Elizabeth

SIR FRANCIS BACON

Elizabeth's "Gloriana" image was a bit tarnished during the last years of her reign by grievances that had finally begun to surface, by the residue of unfulfilled hopes and unredeemed promises, and by a general restlessness after almost half a century of her rule. But the succession of her Stuart cousin James I shortly restored Elizabeth's luster. The Elizabethan Age and Elizabeth herself assumed heroic stature when compared with James I, "who feared his own shadow and manifested such unkingly habits as drivelling at the mouth, picking his nose, and closeting himself with pretty young men."[5] Yet it was not his personal habits, no matter how offensive, not even his penchant for playing at "kingcraft" or the muddle he made of the religious settlement that most alienated James's English subjects; it was his resolution to abandon the tradition of hostility to Spain, indeed to court a Spanish-Catholic alliance.

Sir Francis Bacon (1561–1626) was a functionary of James's court and one of the leading men of affairs in the new reign. But he had also been a figure of Elizabeth's court and a member of Parliament during the Armada. Though he had not advanced under Elizabeth as grandly as he thought his merits deserved, still, looking back to her reign, even the cold and analytical Bacon could not help being moved. In the summer of 1608, the year following his appointment by James as Solicitor General, Bacon wrote in Latin a memorial to Elizabeth that he titled "On the Fortunate Memory of Elizabeth Queen of England." He circulated the piece privately to a few friends but provided that it be published only after his death. Bacon was not only a stupendous genius but also a good judge of his own advantage.

"On the Fortunate Memory of Elizabeth Queen of England" is of considerable interest because it is the mature reflection of one who had been close to the center of events. The memorial is equally important because it shows a renewed interest in "the heroic Elizabeth" in the light of her unheroic successor and the new foreign and religious policies he was already considering. Bacon was writing a memorial not only to Elizabeth but to an age of giants now sadly past.

---

[5]Lacey Baldwin Smith, *The Elizabethan World* (Boston: Houghton Mifflin, 1967), pp. 204–5.

I account . . . as no small part of Elizabeth's felicity the period and compass of her administration; not only for its length, but as falling within that portion of her life which was fittest for the control of affairs and the handling of the reins of government. She was twenty-five years old (the age at which guardianship ceases) when she began to reign, and she continued reigning until her seventieth year; so that she never experienced either the disadvantages and subjection to other men's wills incident to a ward, nor the inconveniences of a lingering and impotent old age. . . .

Nor must it be forgotten withal among what kind of people she reigned; for had she been called to rule over Palmyrenes or in an unwarlike and effeminate country like Asia, the wonder would have been less; a womanish people might well enough be governed by a woman; but that in England, a nation particularly fierce and warlike, all things could be swayed and controlled at the beck of a woman, is a matter for the highest admiration.

Observe too that this same humour of her people, ever eager for war and impatient of peace, did not prevent her from cultivating and maintaining peace during the whole time of her reign. And this her desire of peace, together with the success of it, I count among her greatest praises; as a thing happy for her times, becoming to her sex, and salutary for her conscience. . . .

And this peace I regard as more especially flourishing from two circumstances that attended it, and which though they have nothing to do with the merit of peace, add much to the glory of it. The one, that the calamities of her neighbours were as fires to make it more conspicuous and illustrious; the other that the benefits of peace were not unaccompanied with honour of war,—the reputation of England for arms and military prowess being by many noble deeds, not only maintained by her, but increased. For the aids sent to the Low Countries, to France, and to Scotland; the naval expeditions to both the Indies, some of which sailed all round the globe; the fleets despatched to Portugal and to harass the coasts of Spain; the many defeats and overthrows of the rebels in Ireland;—all these had the effect of keeping both the warlike virtues of our nation in full vigour and its fame and honour in full lustre.

Which glory had likewise, this merit attached,—that while neighbour kings on the one side owed the preservation of their kingdoms to her timely succours; suppliant peoples on the other, given up by ill-advised princes to the cruelty of their ministers, to the fury of the populace, and to every kind of spoliation and devastation, received relief in their misery; by means of which they stand to this day.

Nor were her counsels less beneficent and salutary than her succours; witness her remonstrances so frequently addressed to the

King of Spain that he would moderate his anger against his subjects in the Low Countries, and admit them to return to their allegiance under conditions not intolerable; and her continual warnings and earnest solicitations addressed to the kings of France that they would observe their edicts of pacification. That her counsel was in both cases unsuccessful, I do not deny. The common fate of Europe did not suffer it to succeed in the first; for so the ambition of Spain, being released as it were from prison, would have been free to spend itself (as things then were) upon the ruin of the kingdoms and commonwealths of Christendom. The blood of so many innocent persons, slaughtered with their wives and children at their hearths and in their beds by the vilest rabble, like so many brute beasts animated, armed, and set on by public authority, forbade it in the other; that innocent blood demanding in just revenge that the kingdom which had been guilty of so atrocious a crime should expiate it by mutual slaughters and massacres. But however that might be, she was not the less true to her own part, in performing the office of an ally both wise and benevolent.

Upon another account also this peace so cultivated and maintained by Elizabeth is a matter of admiration; namely, that it proceeded not from any inclination of the times to peace, but from her own prudence and good management. For in a kingdom laboring with intestine faction on account of religion, and standing as a shield and stronghold of defence against the then formidable and overbearing ambition of Spain, matter for war was nowise wanting; it was she who by her forces and her counsels combined kept it under; as was proved by an event the most memorable in respect of felicity of all the actions of our time. For when the Spanish fleet, got up with such travail and ferment, waited upon with the terror and expectation of all Europe, inspired with such confidence of victory, came ploughing into our channels, it never took so much as a cockboat at sea, never fired so much as a cottage on the land, never even touched the shore; but was first beaten in a battle and then dispersed and wasted in a miserable flight with many shipwrecks; while on the ground and territories of England peace remained undisturbed and unshaken.

Nor was she less fortunate in escaping the treacherous attempts of conspirators than in defeating and repelling the forces of the enemy. For not a few conspiracies aimed at her life were in the happiest manner both detected and defeated; and yet was not her life made thereby more alarmed or anxious; there was no increase in the number of her guards; no keeping within her palace and seldom going abroad; but still secure and confident, and thinking more of the escape than of the danger, she held her wonted course, and made no change in her way of life.

Worthy of remark too is the nature of the times in which she flourished. For there are some times so barbarous and ignorant that it is as easy a matter to govern men as to drive a flock of sheep. But the lot of this Queen fell upon times highly instructed and cultivated, in which it is not possible to be eminent and excellent without the greatest gifts of mind and a singular composition of virtue. . . .

With regard to her moderation in religion there may seem to be a difficulty, on account of the severity of the laws made against popish subjects. But on this point I have some things to advance which I myself carefully observed and know to be true.

Her intention undoubtedly was, on the one hand not to force consciences, but on the other not to let the state, under pretence of conscience and religion, be brought in danger. Upon this ground she concluded at the first that, in a people courageous and warlike and prompt to pass from strife of minds to strife of hands, the free allowance and toleration by public authority of two religions would be certain destruction. Some of the more turbulent and factious bishops also she did, in the newness of her reign when all things were subject to suspicion—but not without legal warrant—restrain and keep in free custody. The rest, both clergy and laity, far from troubling them with any severe inquisition, she sheltered by a gracious connivency. This was the condition of affairs at first. Nor even when provoked by the excommunication pronounced against her by Pius Quintus (an act sufficient not only to have roused indignation but to have furnished ground and matter for a new course of proceeding), did she depart almost at all from this clemency, but persevered in the course which was agreeable to her own nature. For being both wise and of a high spirit, she was little moved with the sound of such terrors; knowing she could depend upon the loyalty and love of her own people, and upon the small power the popish party within the realm had to do harm, as long as they were not seconded by a foreign enemy. About the twenty-third year of her reign, however, the case was changed. And this distinction of time is not artificially devised to make things fit, but expressed and engraved in public acts.

For up to that year there was no penalty of a grievous kind imposed by previous laws upon popish subjects. But just then the ambitious and vast design of Spain for the subjugation of the kingdom came gradually to light. . . .

. . . It is true, and proved by the confession of many witnesses, that from the year I have mentioned to the thirtieth of Elizabeth['s reign] (when the design of Spain and the Pope was put in execution by that memorable armada of land and sea forces) almost all the priests who were sent over to this country were charged among the other offices belonging to their function, to insinuate that matters could not long stay as they were, that a new aspect and turn of things would be seen shortly, and that the state of England was cared for both by the Pope and the Catholic princes, if the English would but be true to themselves. . . .

. . . This so great a tempest of dangers made it a kind of necessity for Elizabeth to put some severer constraint upon that party of her subjects which was estranged from her and by these means poisoned beyond recovery, and was at the same time growing rich by reason of their immunity from public offices and burdens. And as the mischief increased, the origin of it being traced to the seminary priests, who were bred in foreign parts, and supported by the purses and charities of foreign princes, professed enemies of this kingdom, and whose time had been passed in places where the very name of Elizabeth was never heard except as that of a heretic excommunicated and accursed, and who (if not themselves stained with treason) were the acknowledged intimates of those that were directly engaged in such crimes, and had by their own arts and poisons depraved and soured with a new leaven of malignity the whole lump of Catholics, which had before been more sweet and harmless; there was no remedy for it but that men of this class should be prohibited upon pain of death from coming into the kingdom at all; which at last, in the twenty-seventh year of her reign, was done. Nor did the event itself which followed not long after, when so great a tempest assailed and fell with all its fury upon the kingdom, tend in any degree to mitigate the envy and hatred of these men; but rather increased it, as if they had utterly cast off all feeling for their country, which they were ready to betray to a foreign servitude. . . .

The "New" Elizabeth

JAMES ANTHONY FROUDE

James Anthony Froude (1818–1894), for all the criticism he received—his Oxford rival E. A. Freeman called him "the vilest brute that ever wrote a book"[6]—was surely one of the most influential historians "that ever wrote a book." The book on which both his reputation and his influence most firmly rest is his massive, twelve-volume *History of England from the Fall of Wolsey to the Defeat of the*

---

[6]Quoted in F. Smith Fussner, *Tudor History and Historians* (New York: Basic Books, 1970), p. 55.

Spanish Armada. Froude began work on it about 1850, and it was published in two-volume installments roughly every other year between 1856 and 1870 to a rising chorus of popular acclaim. Ignoring the factual inaccuracies that bothered Froude's fellow scholars, the public was delighted by his preference for advocacy rather than objectivity. The people tended to agree with Froude that history proclaimed, or should proclaim, "the laws of right and wrong." Moreover, they agreed that right resided in the Church of England and wrong, more often than not, in the Church of Rome. If proof was needed for their prejudices—or his—it was abundantly available in the profusion of facts that crowded Froude's *History* and gave it an unequalled sense of authenticity. For Froude was one of the first modern British historians to go extensively to the original sources for his research; he was aided by the fact that only in his lifetime was the great mass of English public documents of the Tudor Age at last being systematically edited and published.

Froude considered the Tudor Age to be the pivot of all English history. The topical limits he set to his own great *History* display his thesis. The fall of Wolsey and Henry VIII's break with Rome marked the start of the English Reformation; the defeat of the Spanish Armada marked the triumph of English Protestantism and the beginning of England's supremacy in the modern world. Like his lifelong friend Carlyle, Froude was more impressed with people than with large economic or social forces. Heroic people accomplish heroic deeds. Henry VIII was Froude's hero, standing stalwart and unblinking at the beginning of his narrative. At the other end stood the most heroic deed in English history, the defeat of the Armada. Yet careful research revealed that Elizabeth, Henry's daughter, was—at least by Froude's standards—considerably less than heroic. Where Henry had been defiant, Elizabeth preferred to negotiate. Where Henry had carried the fight to the enemy, Elizabeth was suspicious of fighting and more than reluctant to throw her resources into the great national effort against Spain. Even when the fight was inevitable, she was stingy of her support and vacillating in her resolve. Worst of all, Froude found her, at the most charitable, to be a guarded and circumstantial Protestant, perhaps even a crypto-Catholic. If Henry VIII was Froude's hero, Elizabeth was his burden. In order to reconcile his low opinion of Elizabeth with the importance he attached to the Armada, Froude made the triumph over the Armada a victory "in spite of" Elizabeth, the product of the patient policy of her great Protestant advisers and the selfless heroism of her seamen.

It may be charged that Froude, more than most historians, took his conclusions to his sources and then found them there. But this failing is surely not unique with him. Even his severest critics today admit that Froude's *History* is "one of the great masterpieces of English historical literature,"[7] that it is "a classic"[8] for its period, and that "more than any other nineteenth-century English historian James Anthony Froude set the nineteenth-century version of Tudor history."[9] An indispensable part of that version was Froude's equivocal image of the "new" Elizabeth.

We turn now to the summation of Froude's account of Elizabeth and the Armada, from the conclusion of his *History.*

It had been my intention to continue this history to the close of Elizabeth's life. The years which followed the defeat of the Armada were rich in events of profound national importance. They were years of splendour and triumph. The flag of England became supreme on the seas; English commerce penetrated to the farthest corners of the Old World, and English colonies rooted themselves on the shores of the New. The national intellect, strung by the excitement of sixty years, took shape in a literature which is an eternal possession of mankind, while the incipient struggles of the two parties in the Anglican Church prepared the way for the conflicts of the coming century, and the second act of Reformation. But I have presumed too far already on the forbearance of my readers in the length to which I have run, and these subjects, intensely interesting as they are, lie beyond the purpose of the present work. My object, as I defined it at the outset, was to describe the transition from the Catholic England with which the century opened, the England of a dominant Church and monasteries and pilgrimages, into the England of progressive intelligence; and the question whether the nation was to pass a second time through the farce of a reconciliation with Rome, was answered once and for ever by the cannon of Sir Francis Drake. The action before Gravelines of the 30th of July, 1588, decided the largest problems ever submitted in the history of mankind to the arbitrement of force. Beyond and beside the immediate fate of England, it decided that Philip's revolted Provinces should never be reannexed to the Spanish Crown. It broke the back of Spain, sealed the fate of the Duke of Guise,[10] and though it could not prevent the civil war, it assured the ultimate succession of the

---

[7]Conyers Read, *Bibliography of British History: Tudor Period, 1485–1603*, 2nd ed. (Oxford: Clarendon Press, 1959), p. 30.

[8]*Ibid.*

[9]Fussner, p. 55.

[10]The leader of the radical Catholic League in the French Wars of Religion.—ED.

King of Navarre.[11] In its remoter consequences it determined the fate of the Reformation in Germany; for had Philip been victorious the League must have been immediately triumphant; the power of France would have been on the side of Spain and the Jesuits, and the thirty years' war would either have never been begun, or would have been brought to a swift conclusion. It furnished James of Scotland with conclusive reasons for remaining a Protestant, and for eschewing for ever the forbidden fruit of Popery; and thus it secured his tranquil accession to the throne of England when Elizabeth passed away. Finally, it was the sermon which completed the conversion of the English nation, and transformed the Catholics into Anglicans. . . .

. . . The coming of the Armada was an appeal on behalf of the Pope to the ordeal of battle and the defeat of Spain with its appalling features, the letting loose of the power of the tempests—the special weapons of the Almighty—to finish the work which Drake had but half completed, was accepted as a recorded judgment of heaven. The magnitude of the catastrophe took possession of the nation's imagination. . . . Had the Spanish invasion succeeded, however, had it succeeded even partially in crushing Holland and giving France to the League and the Duke of Guise, England might not have recovered from the blow, and it might have fared with Teutonic Europe as it fared with France on the revocation of the Edict of Nantes. Either Protestantism would have been trampled out altogether, or expelled from Europe to find a home in a new continent; and the Church, insolent with another century or two of power, would have been left to encounter the inevitable ultimate revolution which is now its terror, with no reformed Christianity surviving to hold the balance between atheism and superstition.

The starved and ragged English seamen, so ill furnished by their sovereign that they were obliged to take from their enemies the means of fighting them, decided otherwise; they and the winds and the waves, which are said ever to be on the side of the brave. In their victory they conquered not the Spaniards only, but the weakness of their Queen. Either she had been incredulous before that Philip would indeed invade her, or she had underrated the power of her people: or she discerned that the destruction of the Spanish fleet had created at last an irreparable breach with the Catholic governments. At any rate there was no more unwholesome hankering after compromise, no more unqueenly avarice or reluctance to spend her treasure

---

[11]The sometime leader of the French Protestant Huguenots who became King Henry IV in 1594.—ED.

in the cause of freedom. The strength and resources of England were flung heartily into the war, and all the men and all the money it could spare was given freely to the United Provinces and the King of Navarre. The struggle lasted into the coming century. Elizabeth never saw peace with Spain again. But the nation throve with its gathering glory. The war on the part of England was aggressive thenceforward. One more great attempt was made by Philip in Ireland, but only to fail miserably, and the shores of England were never seriously threatened again. Portugal was invaded, and Cadiz burnt, Spanish commerce made the prey of privateers, and the proud galleons chased from off the ocean. In the Low Countries the tide of reconquest had reached its flood, and thenceforward ebbed slowly back, while in France the English and the Huguenots fought side by side against the League and Philip. . . .

[Yet] for Protestantism Elizabeth had never concealed her dislike and contempt. She hated to acknowledge any fellowship in religion either with Scots, Dutch, or Huguenots. She represented herself to foreign Ambassadors as a Catholic in everything, except in allegiance to the Papacy. Even for the Church of England, of which she was the supreme governor, she affected no particular respect. She left the Catholics in her household so unrestrained that they absented themselves at pleasure from the Royal Chapel, without a question being asked. She allowed the country gentlemen all possible latitude in their own houses. The danger in which she had lived for so many years, the severe measures to which she was driven against the seminary priests, and the consciousness that the Protestants were the only subjects she had on whose loyalty she could rely, had prevented her hitherto from systematically repressing the Puritan irregularities; but the power to persecute had been wanting rather than the inclination. The Bishops with whom she had filled the sees at her accession were chosen necessarily from the party who had suffered under her sister. They were Calvinists or Lutherans, with no special reverence for the office which they had undertaken; and she treated them in return with studied contempt. She called them Doctors, as the highest title to which she considered them to have any real right; if they disputed her pleasure she threatened to unfrock them; if they showed themselves officious in punishing Catholics, she brought them up with a sharp reprimand; and if their Protestantism was conspicuously earnest, they were deposed and imprisoned. . . .

To permit the collapse of the Bishops, however, would be to abandon the Anglican position. Presbytery as such was detestable to Elizabeth. She recognised no authority in any man as derived from a source distinct from herself, and she adhered resolutely to her own purpose. So long as her own crown was unsafe she did not venture on any general persecution of her Puritan subjects; but she checked all their efforts to make a change in the ecclesiastical system. She found a man after her own heart for the see of Canterbury in Whitgift; she filled the other sees as they fell vacant with men of a similar stamp, and she prepared to coerce their refractory "brethren in Christ" into obedience if ever the opportunity came.

On the reconciliation of the Catholic gentry, which followed on the destruction of the Spanish fleet, Elizabeth found herself in a position analogous to that of Henry IV of France. She was the sovereign of a nation with a divided creed, the two parties, notwithstanding, being at last for the most part loyal to herself.

Both she and Henry held at the bottom intrinsically the same views. They believed generally in certain elementary truths lying at the base of all religions, and the difference in the outward expressions of those truths, and the passionate animosities which those differences engendered, were only not contemptible to them from the practical mischief which they produced. On what terms Catholics and Protestants could be induced to live together peaceably was the political problem of the age. Neither of the two sovereigns shared the profound horror of falsehood, which was at the heart of the Protestant movement. They had the statesman's temperament, to which all specific religions are equally fictions of the imagination. . . .

To return to Elizabeth.

In fighting out her long quarrel with Spain and building her Church system out of the broken masonry of Popery, her concluding years passed away. The great men who had upheld the throne in the days of her peril dropped one by one into the grave. Walsingham died soon after the defeat of the Armada, ruined in fortune, and weary of his ungrateful service. Hunsdon, Knollys, Burghley, Drake, followed at brief intervals, and their mistress was left by herself, standing as it seemed on the pinnacle of earthly glory, yet in all the loneliness of greatness, and unable to enjoy the honours which Burghley's policy had won for her. The first place among the Protestant powers, which had been so often offered her and so often refused, had been forced upon her in spite of herself. "She was Head of the Name," but it gave her no pleasure. She was the last of her race. No Tudor would sit again on the English throne. . . . She was without the intellectual emotions which give human character its consistency and power. One moral quality she possessed in an eminent degree: she was supremely brave. For thirty years she was perpetually a mark for assassination, and her spirits were never affected, and she was never frightened into cruelty. She had a proper contempt also for idle luxury and indulgence. She lived simply, worked hard, and ruled her household with rigid economy. But her vanity was as insatiable as it was commonplace. No flattery was too tawdry to find a welcome with her, and as she had no repugnance to false words in others, she was equally liberal of them herself. Her entire nature was saturated with artifice. Except when speaking some round untruth Elizabeth never could be simple. Her letters and her speeches were as fantastic as her dress, and her meaning as involved as her policy. She was unnatural even in her prayers, and she carried her affectations into the presence of the Almighty. . . .

Vain as she was of her own sagacity, she never modified a course recommended to her by Burghley without injury both to the realm and to herself. She never chose an opposite course without plunging into embarrassments, from which his skill and Walsingham's were barely able to extricate her. The great results of her reign were the fruits of a policy which was not her own, and which she starved and mutilated when energy and completeness were needed. . . .

But this, like all other questions connected with the Virgin Queen, should be rather studied in her actions than in the opinion of the historian who relates them. Actions and words are carved upon eternity. Opinions are but forms of cloud created by the prevailing currents of the moral air. Princes, who are credited on the wrong side with the evils which happen in their reigns, have a right in equity to the honour of the good. The greatest achievement in English history, the "breaking the bonds of Rome," and the establishment of spiritual independence, was completed without bloodshed under Elizabeth's auspices, and Elizabeth may have the glory of the work. Many problems growing out of it were left unsettled. Some were disposed of on the scaffold at Whitehall, some in the revolution of 1688; some yet survive to test the courage and the ingenuity of modern politicians.

Elizabeth and the "Invincible" Armada

GARRETT MATTINGLY

Twentieth-century Elizabethan scholarship has largely forsaken the "standard" view of Elizabeth that, more than anyone else, Froude helped to frame. Froude's Elizabeth is both too simple and too doctrinaire: Elizabeth was neither. There have been literally hundreds of special studies and monographs on various aspects of Elizabeth's reign and even a number of biographies. But despite this profusion of writing, there is not yet a comprehensive general interpretation of her for our time or an entirely satisfactory biography.

The same cannot be said, however, of the Armada, for that great and popular adventure found its definitive twentieth-century interpretation in the work of Garrett Mattingly, professor of history at Columbia University until his death in 1962. In addition to the sources that Froude had used to such advantage, Mattingly had access to even more and better British sources, for the process of editing and publishing the public documents of the Tudor Age had continued, and new archives and collections had been opened. French and Netherlandish archives were available to him, as well as collections in Italy and Spain. Thus Mattingly had the advantage of a rounded collection of materials that earlier scholars, whether English or Spanish, had not had. And he had the disposition to write a balanced account, free of the special pleading and the special point of view that were ultimately Froude's greatest flaws.

The following excerpt is taken not from Mattingly's slim and elegant masterpiece, *The Armada,*[12] but from a carefully abbreviated account that he prepared for the Folger Shakespeare Library monograph series, entitled *The "Invincible" Armada and Elizabethan England.* It was his last work.

Not surprisingly, the work deals primarily with the Armada rather than with Elizabeth. But many elements of a contemporary view of Elizabeth—even though that view has not entirely coalesced—can be discovered. Mattingly admires Elizabeth's grasp of foreign policy, which reached beyond a simplistic hostility to Spain. He admires her courage to resist the opinions of her naval advisers that the war should be carried to Spanish waters, opinions that she seemed to be almost alone in opposing. The queen's courage was the greater when we realize, as Mattingly points out, that she was already past "the peak of her popularity and prestige." Finally, Mattingly admires the tenacity that enabled Elizabeth to maintain the peace, no matter how tenuously, for thirty years and that led her into war only when it could be fought on her terms. The victory over the Armada was indeed Elizabeth's victory, and, in the words of Froude, she may have the glory of it.

Probably no event in England's military history, not even the battles of Trafalgar and Waterloo, not even the battle of Hastings, has been so much written about, celebrated, and commented upon as the repulse of the Spanish Armada by English naval forces after nine days of dubious battle from the Eddystone to Gravelines in the summer of

---

[12](Boston: Houghton Mifflin, 1959).

1588. The repulse foiled decisively, as it turned out, the Spanish plan to invade England with the Duke of Parma's army of the Netherlands, covered and supported by a Spanish fleet, and reinforced by the troop transports and supply ships it convoyed. At first the significance of the repulse was by no means clear. As it became clearer, the chroniclers of both combatants tended to magnify, oversimplify, and distort the event. English writers, pamphleteers, and historians hailed the victory, first as a sign of God's favor to the champions of the Protestant cause, later as evidence of the manifest destiny of an imperial people. . . .

. . . By now, through the efforts of two generations of historians, Spanish and English, most of the mistakes about the Armada campaign and the Anglo-Spanish naval war have been corrected and a more balanced emphasis restored. So far, however, no general account of the correction has been drawn up. Let us attempt one here.

We shall have to begin with the long period of uneasy peace, cold war, and "war underhand," undeclared and peripheral, before the actual outbreak of major hostilities. In general, historians both English and Spanish have tended to assume that since war was coming anyway the sooner it came the better, and that any policy that postponed its coming was feeble, shortsighted, and mistaken. Most English historians have been certain that Elizabeth should have unleashed her sea dogs against the Spanish colossus long before she did and have blamed or excused her for feminine weakness, gullibility at the hands of smooth Spanish diplomats, and miserly reluctance to spend money. The chorus of blame begins in the correspondence of the leading Puritans of her own day. They were always bewailing to one another the Queen's vacillation, her stubborn refusal to subsidize Protestant leaders on the Continent as liberally as they would have liked to be subsidized, her obstinate belief that peace with the armies of Antichrist could still be preserved. The chorus of blame swelled through the centuries until it culminated in the thundering voice of James Anthony Froude, who could as little conceal his boundless, uncritical admiration for the male vigor of Henry VIII, who led England into one vainglorious, financially ruinous war after another, as he could his scorn for the feminine weakness of Henry's daughter Elizabeth, who preferred to save money and stay out of trouble. Since Froude, the chorus of blame has subsided somewhat, but its echoes are still distinctly audible. . . .

. . . Elizabeth . . . and her peace party had reasons more cogent (if any reasons can be more cogent) than prudence and economy. No ruler of this century was more sensitive to the economic interests of his subjects. She knew the importance of an outlet in the Netherlands— Antwerp for choice—for the vent of English cloth, on which, after agriculture, the prosperity of her realm depended. If there was a tradition of more than a hundred years of alliance with Spain, the tradition of alliance with Flanders, with "waterish Burgundy," was as old as any coherent English foreign policy at all. In Flanders, Zeeland, and Holland were the ports not only through which English goods could most cheaply and safely reach the Continent, but from which an invasion of England could be launched most quickly and easily. And on the frontier of Flanders lay France, divided for the moment by religious civil wars, but in area, population, productivity, and centralized power easily the greatest state in Europe. Somebody had to guard the Netherlands from France—if not Spain, then England.

Elizabeth preferred to have the Spanish bear the burden. . . .

There was still one tie between Elizabeth and Philip stronger than profitable trade, old alliances, or strategic necessities. That was the life of Mary Queen of Scots. For nearly twenty years Mary Stuart had been part guest, part prisoner of her cousin. Since she was a devout Catholic and the next in succession to the English throne, she had always been the center of plots by English Catholics. . . . But with each plot the outcry for Mary's life grew stronger, and at last Elizabeth could no longer resist the clamor. When in February, 1587, the ax fell, the die was cast. As soon as Philip heard the news and had taken his characteristic time to ponder the consequences, he began to put the creaky machinery of his painfully devised plans for the invasion of England into high gear.

His plans were further delayed by Drake's brilliant raid down the Spanish coast. On the whole that raid has been duly appreciated and well described, but perhaps for the sake of dramatic narrative the emphasis on its importance has been somewhat distorted. . . .

The real damage Drake did the Spaniards was afterward, by his operations off Cape St. Vincent. His mere presence there, though he found no one to fight with, kept the Spanish fleet from assembling. But more, he swept up along the coast a swarm of little coasting vessels, most of them laden with hoops and barrel staves ready to be made into casks for the food and drink of the invasion fleet. Without tight casks made of seasoned wood, provisions spoiled and wine and water leaked away. Drake burned the seasoned barrel staves. They were almost all the fleet at Lisbon was expecting, far more than it could ever collect again. This was the secret, mortal wound. Drake knew exactly what he was doing, but most of his biographers seem not to have appreciated it. . . .

After a description of the Spanish preparations for the Armada, Mattingly continues.

If Spanish historians have been too severe with their admiral and not critical enough of his sovereign, English historians have usually made the opposite mistake. From October, 1587, on, the English commanders by sea, Drake and Hawkins and finally even Lord Howard of Effingham, the Lord Admiral, had clamored to be let loose on the coast of Spain. If the smell of booty to be won by the sack of undefended Spanish towns had anything to do with their eagerness, they did not say so to the Queen. What they proposed was that they blockade the Spanish coast, fight the Spanish when they came out, perhaps prevent their sortie, or even destroy them in port. On the whole, English naval historians have warmly approved their plan and condemned the Queen for squelching it. Perhaps they were thinking of Nelson's ships, or Collingwood's. Elizabethan ships had not the same sea-keeping qualities. If they had taken station off Lisbon in November, by April they would have been battered and strained, sails and spars and rigging depleted, crews decimated or worse by ship's fever and scurvy, and provisions exhausted. Even if none of them had foundered, and such foundering was not unlikely, the English fleet would have been in no condition to face an enemy for weeks, perhaps for months. And the cost in pounds, shillings, and pence would have been staggering. Elizabeth, who had kept a wary eye on naval accounts for forty years, knew this. What she probably did not know was that had the fleets met off the Spanish coast and the English adopted the same tactics they later used off the Eddystone, as they surely would have done, they would have fired every shot in their lockers before they had done the Spanish any appreciable harm, and would have been obliged to scuttle home in search of more munitions, while the Spanish could have marched grandly into the Channel. Partly by prudence and partly by luck, Elizabeth's preference that the battle, if there had to be one, should be fought in home waters was a major contribution to English victory. . . .

. . . About the strength and composition of the two fleets there is actually very little doubt. The Armada sailed from Lisbon with 130 ships. . . . Opposing this force, English lists show 197 ships. Actually, not all of these saw action; some of them, though not so many nor such large ships as in the Spanish fleet, were mere supply ships, practically noncombatants, and a good many, a slightly higher percentage than in the Armada, were under a hundred tons, incapable of carrying guns heavier than a six-pounder and useful mainly for scouting and dispatch work. The first line of the English fleet was twenty-one Queen's galleons of two hundred tons and upward, roughly comparable in size and numbers with the ten galleons of

Portugal and ten galleons of the Indian Guard which made up the Spanish first line, but tougher, harder hitting, and, on the whole, bigger.

The myth of the little English ships and the huge Spanish ones has long since been refuted by naval historians, without, of course, being in the least dispelled. Taking the official tonnage lists of the two first lines, the biggest ship in either fleet is English, and the rest pair off in what seems like rough equality. . . . We do know that in comparison with their English adversaries the Spanish were seriously undergunned. . . . In such guns, especially the culverin type, firing round shot of from four to eighteen pounds for three thousand yards or more, the English were superior by at least three to one. . . .

There follows a detailed description of the battle, the stiff Spanish discipline, the long-range gun battles that did little but deplete shot and powder supplies, and the crucial failure of Parma to "come out" with his barge-loads of soldiers to board the waiting fleet. They were blockaded by the Dutch in the tidal waters, safe from the deep-water Spanish fleet. Then came the English attack on the Armada mounted with fire ships and fire power and finally the famous storm in the channel that permitted the Armada to "escape" to the north and to its ultimate destruction, sailing around the British Isles in a desperate and futile attempt to return home.

When, on the thirtieth anniversary of her reign, the Queen went in state to St. Paul's, where the captured Spanish banners had been hung up, the kneeling, cheering throngs hailed her as the victorious champion of her kingdom and their faith. The next few years were probably those of Elizabeth's greatest popularity, at least around London, and this was almost certainly due to her having come forward at last as the open champion of the Protestant cause, to her gallant conduct in the months of danger, and to the victory, by divine intervention almost everyone believed, which crowned her efforts. It is probable, too, that the victory gave a lift to English morale. It may be that a good many Englishmen, like a good many other Europeans, though not like Elizabeth's sea dogs, had doubted that the Spanish could ever be beaten. Now they knew that they could. The thoughtful and the well-informed understood, however, that England had not won a war, only the first battle in a war in which there might be many more battles. England was braced for the struggle.

Review and Study Questions

1. What were the main features of Bacon's characterization of Queen Elizabeth?
2. What were the main features of Froude's characterization of Queen Elizabeth?
3. What were the main features of Mattingly's characterization of Queen Elizabeth?

Suggestions for Further Reading

To a considerable extent, the central problem of Elizabethan scholarship has been to disentangle the historical Elizabeth from the Elizabeth of legend. This chapter is really about an aspect of that process, for the defeat of the Spanish Armada was a powerful force in creating the Elizabeth legend. The historical Elizabeth still tends to elude scholars, but of all the books on her, the best modern work is still probably Sir John E. Neale, *Queen Elizabeth I* (London: J. Cape, 1961), reprinted a dozen times since its publication in 1934. Of the newer books on Elizabeth, the best by far is Lacey Baldwin Smith, *Elizabeth Tudor: Portrait of a Queen* (Boston: Little, Brown, 1975). But students may prefer Elizabeth Jenkins, *Elizabeth the Great* (New York: Coward, McCann and Geoghegan, 1958), a lively, personal-psychological biography, or the attractive, heavily illustrated Neville Williams, *The Life and Times of Elizabeth I* (New York: Doubleday, 1972). Two additional competent and straightforward biographies are also recommended: Joel Hurstfield, *Elizabeth I and the Unity of England,* "Teach Yourself History Library" (New York: Macmillan, 1960), and Paul Johnson, *Elizabeth I: A Biography* (New York: Holt, Rinehart and Winston, 1974). Jasper Ridley, *Elizabeth I: The Shrewdness of Virtue* (New York: Viking, 1988) is a readable, if somewhat superficial, biography, not too flattering to the queen. Students may find interesting Carolly Erickson, *The First Elizabeth* (New York: Summit Books, 1983), a general biography that has a tinge of contemporary feminism. Especially recommended is Alison Plowden, *Elizabeth Regina: The Age of Triumph, 1588–1603* (New York: Times Books, 1980), the culminating work in a series of books on Elizabeth, this one dealing precisely with the period of her life emphasized in this chapter.

Among the great monuments in modern Tudor scholarship are the studies of two of the men around Elizabeth by Conyers Read, *Mr. Secretary Walsingham and the Policy of Queen Elizabeth,* 3 vols. (Hamden, Conn.: Archon Books, 1967 [1925]), and *Mr. Secretary Cecil and Queen Elizabeth* (New York: Knopf, 1955) and its sequel *Lord Burghley and*

Queen Elizabeth (New York: Knopf, 1960); these books are detailed and complex. Students may prefer the lighter and briefer Neville Williams, *All the Queen's Men: Elizabeth I and Her Courtiers* (New York: Macmillan, 1972). Two works on Elizabeth and her age are especially recommended: A. L. Rowse, *The England of Elizabeth: The Structure of Society* (New York: Macmillan, 1950), the first of two volumes on the Elizabethan Age, the massive and lively work of a controversial and dynamic British scholar, and Lacey Baldwin Smith, *The Elizabethan World* (Boston: Houghton Mifflin, 1967). On the broader topic of Tudor England, the basic work is G. R. Elton, *England under the Tudors,* rev. ed. (London: Methuen, 1974); but students should see also A. J. Slavin, *The Precarious Balance: English Government and Society, 1450–1640* (New York: Knopf, 1973), an important revisionist study of the internal structure of Tudor England.

The standard work on the Armada is Garrett Mattingly, *The Armada* (Boston: Houghton Mifflin, 1959), eminently readable and exciting. Felipe Fernandez-Armesto, *The Spanish Armada: The Experience of the War in 1588* (Oxford and New York: Oxford University Press, 1988) is an up-to-date work that supplements Mattingly. For more detailed diplomatic history background, the best work is probably R. B. Wernham, *Before the Armada: The Emergence of the English Nation, 1485–1588* (New York: Harcourt, Brace and World, 1966), and for a closer look at the technical-naval aspects of the Armada, Michael A. Lewis, *The Spanish Armada* (New York: Crowell, 1960). An excellent revisionist account of the Armada is David A. Howarth, *The Voyage of the Armada, The Spanish Story* (New York: Viking, 1981). There is a recent definitive biography of Don Alonso Perez de Guzman, by Peter Pierson, *Commander of the Armada: The Seventh Duke of Medina Sidonia* (New Haven: Yale University Press, 1989). For an account of the growth of the English anti-Spanish sentiment, see William S. Maltby, *The Black Legend in England: The Development of Anti-Spanish Sentiment, 1558–1660* (Durham, N.C.: Duke University Press, 1971). For Mary Queen of Scots, the diplomatic linchpin in the whole background of the Armada, see the large and thoroughly readable biography by Antonia Fraser, *Mary, Queen of Scots* (New York: Delacorte Press, 1969), and Alison Plowden, *Danger to Elizabeth: The Catholics under Elizabeth I* (New York: Stein and Day, 1973), a work on a related topic.

AKBAR:
THE GREAT MOGHUL

1542   Born
1556   Succeeded to the throne
1562   Began personal rule
1575   Conquest of Bengal
1579   Infallibility Decree
1586   Conquest of Kashmir
1591   Conquest of Sind
1601   Conquest of the Deccan
1605   Died

Jalal-ud-din Muhammad Akbar was only a boy when, in January of the year 1556, his weak and incompetent father Humayun died in an accidental fall. As one chronicler put it, "He stumbled out of life as he had stumbled through it." This was not to be the case with Akbar, whose name means "great": he was destined to be the greatest of all the Moghul emperors.

At his succession Akbar was only thirteen—strong-willed, impulsive, and untrained. He had rejected all efforts to educate him. Earlier, after the court astrologers had laboriously fixed the most propitious day for beginning the boy's education, they found that he "had attired himself for sport and had disappeared." He never returned to school, and he remained illiterate, the only Moghul emperor to do so. Abul Fazl, his dutiful biographer, speaks delicately of this failing and tries to put a good face on it, pointing out "that this lord of lofty wisdom and special pupil of God should not be implicated and commingled with ordinary human learning . . . that the knowledge of this king of knowers was of the nature of a gift, and not of an acquirement."[1]

At his father's death, Akbar could claim to rule only the Punjab, on the Indian northwest frontier, and the area around Delhi. His fledgling state was consolidated and extended by the able and faithful regent his father had appointed, Bayram Khan. But by 1562 Akbar

---

[1]Abul Fazl, *Akbar-nama,* tr. H. Beveridge (Calcutta: Asiatic Society Bibliotheca Indica, 1907–1939), I, 519.

had put Bayram Khan aside, and his personal reign began. His chief problem was the jealous independence of the Hindu Rajput princes immediately to the east in the region of Rajasthan. When one of these princes, the Raja of Jaipur, needing a military alliance, offered Akbar his daughter in marriage, Akbar accepted—but only on condition that the *raja* accept his suzerainty. The *raja* agreed. This formula Akbar then proceeded to apply with the other Rajput princes. They were permitted to continue to hold their territories provided they acknowledged Akbar as emperor, paid tribute, supplied troops for him when required, and concluded marriage alliances with him. Further, they and their sons were brought into the emperor's military service, enriched and honored, some becoming generals and provincial governors. But Akbar could be as ruthless as he was accommodating. The state of Mewar refused to acknowledge his supremacy. He personally laid siege to its principal fortress, Chitor, and when it fell in 1568 he massacred all thirty thousand of its defenders. This stern example brought nearly all the remaining Rajput princes into alliance with him.

After conquering the province of Gujarat to the southwest, with its port of Surat, which dominated the trade in Indian goods to the west and the Muslim pilgrim traffic to Mecca, and thus consolidating his power in northwest India, Akbar turned eastward to the rich and ancient region of Bengal. Bengal was held by another Muslim-Afghan ruler. Akbar forced him to recognize his suzerainty in 1575, and when, in the following year, he rebelled and was defeated and killed, Akbar annexed Bengal to the Moghul Empire. In 1586 Kashmir to the north was conquered and in 1591 Sind to the southwest. Between 1596 and 1601 his forces gradually penetrated the great southern plateau of the Deccan. By 1601 Akbar ruled virtually the entire subcontinent.

In Praise of Akbar: Akbar-nama

ABUL FAZL

Akbar had proved himself a mighty conqueror, but in the course of his conquests he had also proved himself a brilliant and innovative ruler by virtue of his religious and administrative reforms. He recognized that his dynasty could not be secure unless it somehow reconciled the vast Hindu majority of the people to Muslim rule, and that his own rule could not be secure unless it recognized the claims and ambitions of the native Hindu princes. We have already noted his policy of conciliation toward the Rajput princes. This in itself was not entirely new. Earlier Muslim rulers had found it necessary to enlist Hindu support. But the Hindus had always been subordinates rather than partners. The ruling force was foreign and alien. It was the genius of Akbar to grant true equality to his Hindu subjects and to confer genuine respect on their institutions. "The essential pillar of this policy was the settlement with the Rajput chiefs and the policy of partnership which sprang from it."[2] They accepted the authority of the Moghul Empire, and in exchange they were left in control of their lands as Moghul agents. To preserve their dignity, they were allowed to beat their drums in the streets of the capital—a sign of royalty—and to enter the Hall of Public Audience fully armed. They were taken into the imperial service as genuine equals. No office or honor was closed to them—some were even among Akbar's most trusted confidential advisers. His policy of intermarriage of his dynasty with Hindu ruling houses was a final recognition of equality.

But Akbar aimed to reconcile himself not only with the Hindu ruling houses but with the Hindu community as a whole. To this end he implemented a series of administrative reforms that marked the entire course of his reign. More important, he granted religious toleration, not only to Hinduism but to other religions, including Judaism and Christianity—nearly unheard of in Muslim lands—and intimately associated himself with these diverse religions.

For an account of these policies we turn to the massive *Akbarnama: The History of Akbar,* written by Abul Fazl. Abu al-Fazl ibn

---

[2]Percival Spear, *India: A Modern History,* new and rev. ed. (Ann Arbor: University of Michigan Press, 1972), p. 132.

49

Mubarak (1551–1602) was not only a contemporary of Akbar; he was a close personal friend and, along with his brother the poet Faizi and his father Shaikh Mubarak, a minister of the court. Fazl was Akbar's official court historian, and the emperor not only received Fazl's completed work but had each successive chapter read to him while he corrected and commented on them. This alone would have tended to give a laudatory cast to the work. But the work is more than simply laudatory: its most obvious quality is its outrageously exaggerated flattery. Yet Fazl does not falsify events; he simply presents them in a totally partisan manner. To Fazl's credit, however, he truly believed what he wrote. He was an unabashed advocate of divine right monarchy and an equally unabashed admirer of Akbar, who was, to him, the ideal monarch. He was also, fully as much as Akbar, a freethinker in religion and philosophy and hence an enthusiast for his king's policy of toleration. But with all its faults and limitations, the *Akbar-nama* "must be treated as the foundation for a history of Akbar's reign."[3] The work was written in the ornate Persian court language, and some of that quality comes through even in the translation. It is organized, in chronicle fashion, on a year-by-year basis. Our excerpt begins with the year 1562.

One of the glorious boons of his Majesty the Shāhinshāh[4] which shone forth in this auspicious year was the abolition of enslavement. The victorious troops which came into the wide territories of India used in their tyranny to make prisoners of the wives and children and other relatives of the people of India, and used to enjoy them or sell them. His Majesty the Shāhinshāh, out of his thorough recognition of and worship of God, and from his abundant foresight and right thinking gave orders that no soldier of the victorious armies should in any part of his dominions act in this manner. . . . It was for excellent reasons that His Majesty gave his attention to this subject, although the binding, killing or striking the haughty and the chastising the stiff-necked are part of the struggle for empire—and this is a point about which both sound jurists and innovators are agreed—yet it is outside of the canons of justice to regard the chastisement of women and innocent children as the chastisement of the contumacious. If the husbands have taken the path of insolence, how is it the fault of the wives, and if the fathers have chosen the road of opposition what fault have the children committed? . . .

---

[3]V. A. Smith, *Akbar the Great Mugal 1542–1605* (Delhi et al.: Chand, 1966), p. 338.

[4]This is a title borrowed from Persian court usage meaning "King of Kings," i.e., Emperor.—ED.

As the purposes of the Sh̲āhin̲sh̲āh were entirely right and just, the blissful result ensued that the wild and rebellious inhabitants of portions of India placed the ring of devotion in the ear of obedience, and became the materials of world-empire. Both was religion set in order, for its essence is the distribution of justice, and things temporal were regulated, for their perfection lies in the obedience of mankind. . . .

One of the occurrences [of the year 1563] was that the joyous heart, of H. M.[5] the Sh̲āhin̲sh̲āh turned towards hunting, and he went to the neighbourhood of Mathura with a select party. The hunting was successful. One day that tiger-hunter hunted seven tigers. Five were levelled with the dust by arrow and bullet, and one that repository of courage caught alive and so was the subject of a thousand wonderings. The other was caught by the united efforts of a number of bahadurs. In the same hunt he joined worship with pleasure and became distributor of justice. It was brought to his notice that for a long time it was the custom in India for the rulers to take sums from the people who came to sacred spots to worship, proportionate to their rank and wealth. This (worship) was called Karma.[6] The Sh̲āhin̲sh̲āh in his wisdom and tolerance remitted all these taxes. . . . He looked upon such grasping of property as blameable and issued orders forbidding the levy thereof throughout his dominions. . . .

One of the great gifts which H. M. the Sh̲āhin̲sh̲āh made at the beginning of this year [1564] was the remission of the *Jizya* throughout India.[7] Who can estimate the amount thereof? As the far-seeing glance of the Sh̲āhin̲sh̲āh looked to the administration of the world, he paid great attention to the issuing of this edict, which might be regarded as the foundation of the arrangement of mankind. In spite of the disapproval of statesmen, and of the great revenue, and of much chatter on the part of the ignorant, this sublime decree was issued. By this grand gift, thousands of leading-reins and lassoes were made for the stiff-necked ones of the age. . . .

His (Abkar's) keen eye is the astrolabe of the substantive sun—his truth-discerning heart is the celestial observatory of Attributes—he is of noble lineage, of joyous countenance—of right disposition—of open brow—of well-proportioned frame—of magnanimous nature—of lofty genius—of pure purpose—of enduring faith—of perfect

---

[5]This abbreviation, used throughout in the translation, stands for "His Majesty."—ED.

[6]"Fate" or "destiny" in Hindu religious thought.—ED.

[7]This was a yearly tax on all non-Muslim subjects of the Empire—ED.

wisdom—begirt with varied talents—of wide capacity—of high honour—of splendid courage—of right judgment—of choice counsel—
of generosity unfeigned—of boundless forgiveness, abundant in
graciousness—at peace with all-compendium of dominion—of plente-
ous sincerity—multiple of single-minded warriors—abounding in
wealth—accumulator of the world's rarities—of pure heart—un-
spotted by the world—leader of the spiritual realm—of enduring alert-
ness! How has he been gathered together into one place? Or how doth
a single body upbear him on the shoulders of genius?

At this time[8] when the capital (Fatḥpūr Sikrī) was illuminated by
his glorious advent, H. M. ordered that a house of worship
('Ibādatkhāna) should be built in order to the adornment of the
spiritual kingdom, and that it should have four verandahs (aiwān).
Though the Divine bounty always has an open door and searches
for the fit person, and the inquirer, yet as the lord of the universe,
from his general benevolence, conducts his measures according to
the rules of the superficial, he chose the eve of Friday,[9] which bears
on its face the colouring (*ghāza*) of the announcement of auspicious-
ness, for the out-pouring (ifāzat). A general proclamation was issued
that, on that night of illumination, all orders and sects of mankind—
those who searched after spiritual and physical truth, and those of
the common public who sought for an awakening, and the inquirers
of every sect—should assemble in the precincts of the holy edifice,
and bring forward their spiritual experiences, and their degrees of
knowledge of the truth in various and contradictory forms in the
bridal chamber of manifestation. . . .

At this time, when the centre of the Caliphate (Fatḥpūr Sīkrī) was
glorified by H. M.'s advent, the former institutions were renewed,
and the temple of Divine knowledge was on Thursday nights illuminated by the light of the holy mind. On 20 Mihr, Divine month, 3
October 1578, and in that house of worship, the lamp of the privy
chamber of detachment was kindled in the banqueting-hall of social
life. The coin of the hivers of wisdom in colleges and cells was
brought to the test. The clear wine was separated from the lees, and
good coin from the adulterated. The wide capacity and the toleration
of the Shadow of God were unveiled. Ṣūfī,[10] philosopher, orator,

---

[8]The order for the building of the 'Ibādatkhāna was given in February–March,
1575.

[9]Thursday evening. The Muslim holy day was Friday, but it began with sunset the
previous day.—ED.

[10]Sufi, a modified, mystical form of Islam that attracted millions of former Hindus
and Buddhists to the Muslim faith.—ED.

jurist, Sunnī,[11] Shīa,[12] Brahman,[13] Jatī,[14] Sīūrā,[15] Cārbāk,[16] Naza-rene,[17] Jew, Ṣābī (Sabīan),[18] Zoroastrian, and others enjoyed exquisite pleasure by beholding the calmness of the assembly, the sitting of the world-lord in the lofty pulpit (*mimbar*), and the adornment of the pleasant abode of impartiality. The treasures of secrets were opened out without fear of hostile seekers after battle. The just and truth-perceiving ones of each sect emerged from haughtiness and conceit, and began their search anew. They displayed profundity and medita-tion, and gathered eternal bliss on the divan of greatness. The con-ceited and quarrelsome from evilness of disposition and shortness of thought descended into the mire of presumption and sought their profit in loss. Being guided by ignorant companions, and from the predominance of a somnolent fortune, they went into disgrace. The conferences were excellently arranged by the acuteness and keen quest of truth of the world's Khedive.[19] . . . The Shāhinshāh's court became the home of the inquirers of the seven climes, and the assem-blage of the wise of every religion and sect. . . .

In Criticism of Akbar:
Muntakhabu-T-Tawarikh

AL-BADAONI

Another contemporary historian of Akbar was al-Badaoni (1540–1615), whose great work, *Muntakhabu-T-Tawarikh, Abstract of Histories,* is an account, in three large volumes, of the family of Akbar, the reign of Akbar himself, and of the leading intellectuals of the age. It was not an

---

[11]Sunni, the majority sect of Islam.—ED.

[12]Shia, a minority sect of Islam.—ED.

[13]Brahman, i.e., Hindu.—ED.

[14]Jati, a sect of the Jain religion.—ED.

[15]Siura, another term for the Jains.—ED.

[16]Carbak, an outlawed Hindu sect.—ED.

[17]Nazarene is the term Fazl usually uses for Christians.—ED.

[18]Sabi, native Indians of a sect converted centuries earlier and sometimes called the Christians of St. John.—ED.

[19]A Turkish term for "ruler."—ED.

official history but a private work, even a secret one, which might have been lost had it not been discovered among Badaoni's papers after his death. It is as different as possible from Fazl's work. It was motivated by the author's devout, even bigoted commitment to the orthodox, conservative Sunni sect of Islam. He was convinced that Akbar had hopelessly damaged Muslim orthodoxy by his policy of religious toleration. He included in his denunciation his fellow historian Abul Fazl who, in his view, had not only abetted the emperor's apostasy but had prevented him (Badaoni) from receiving preferment at the hands of the emperor. Nevertheless, it is the opinion of the greatest modern biographer of Akbar that this "hostile criticism of Akbar . . . is of the highest value as a check on the turgid panegyric composed by the latitudinarian Abul Fazl. It gives information about the development of Akbar's opinions on religion which is not to be found in the other Persian histories."[20]

The excerpt begins with Badaoni's account of Akbar's Ibadat-khanah, the center for the discussion of religions.

. . . the Emperor came to Fathpūr. There he used to spend much time in the *'Ibādat-khānah* in the company of learned men and Shaikhs. And especially on Friday nights, when he would sit up there the whole night continually occupied in discussing questions of Religion, whether fundamental or collateral. The learned men used to draw the sword of the tongue on the battle-field of mutual contradiction and opposition, and the antagonism of the sects reached such a pitch that they would call one another fools and heretics. The controversies used to pass beyond the differences of Sunnī, and Shī'ah, of Hanīfī and Shāf'i,[21] of lawyer and divine, and they would attack the very bases of belief.

. . . Then the Mullās became divided into two parties, and one party took one side and one the other, and became very Jews and Egyptians for hatred of each other. And persons of novel and whimsical opinions, in accordance with their pernicious ideas, and vain doubts, coming out of ambush decked the false in the garb of the true, and wrong in the dress of right, and cast the Emperor, who was possessed of an excellent disposition, and was an earnest searcher after truth, but very ignorant and a mere tyro, and used to the company of infidels and base persons, into perplexity, till doubt was heaped upon doubt, and he lost all definite aim, and the straight wall of the clear Law, and of firm Religion was broken down, so that after five or six years not a trace of Islām was left in him: and every thing was turned topsy turvy. . . .

---

[20]V. A. Smith, *Akbar the Great Mogul*, p. 339.

[21]Two of the four schools of Islamic jurisprudence.—ED.

Crowds of learned men from all nations, and sages of various religions and sects came to the Court, and were honoured with private conversations. After enquiries and investigations, which were their only business and occupation day and night, they would talk about profound points of science, the subtleties of revelation, the curiosities of history, and the wonders of tradition, subjects of which large volumes could give only an abstract and summary: and in accordance with the saying:—"Three things are dangerous, Avarice satisfied: desire indulged: and a man's being pleased with himself." Everything that pleased him, he picked and chose from any one except a Moslem, and anything that was against his disposition, and ran counter to his wishes he thought fit to reject and cast aside. From childhood to manhood, and from manhood to his declining years the Emperor had combined in himself various phases from various religions and opposite sectarian beliefs, and by a peculiar acquisitiveness and a talent for selection, by no means common, had made his own all that can be seen and read in books. Thus a faith of a materialistic character became painted on the mirror of his mind and the storehouse of his imagination, and from the general impression this conviction took form, like an engraving upon a stone, that there are wise men to be found and ready at hand in all religions, and men of asceticism, and recipients of revelation and workers of miracles among all nations and that the Truth is an inhabitant of every place: and that consequently how could it be right to consider it as confined to one religion or creed, and that, one which had only recently made its appearance and had not as yet endured a thousand years! And why assert one thing and deny another, and claim preeminence for that which is not essentially pre-eminent?

He became especially firmly convinced of the doctrine of the transmigration of souls, and he much approved of the saying:—*"There is no religion in which the doctrine of Transmigration has not a firm hold."* And insincere flatterers composed treatises in order to establish indisputable arguments in favour of this thesis. And having instituted research into doctrines of the sects of the Hindū unbelievers, of whom there are an endless and innumerable host, and who possess numbers of sacred books, and yet do not belong to the *Ahl-i-Kitāb*,[22] he took so much pleasure in such discussions, that not a day passed but a new fruit of this loathsome tree ripened into existence. . . .

Learned monks also from Europe, who are called *Pādre*, and have an infallible head, called *Pāpā*, who is able to change religious ordinances as he may deem advisable for the moment, and to whose

---

[22]Literally "people of the book," referring to Jews and Christians, who worship the same God as Muslims and whose scriptures contain divine truth.—Ed.

authority kings must submit, brought the Gospel, and advanced proofs for the Trinity. His Majesty firmly believed in the truth of the Christian religion, and wishing to spread the doctrines of Jesus, ordered Prince Murād to take a few lessons in Christianity under good auspices, and charged Abu-l-Fazl to translate the Gospel. . . .

Fire-worshippers also came from Nousārī in Gujrāt, proclaimed the religion of Zardusht[23] as the true one, and declared reverence to fire to be superior to every other kind of worship. They also attracted the Emperor's regard, and taught him the peculiar terms, the ordinances, the rites and ceremonies of the Kaiānians.[24] At last he ordered that the sacred fire should be made over to the charge of Abu-l-Fazl, and that after the manner of the kings of Persia, in whose temples blazed perpetual fires, he should take care it was never extinguished night or day, for that it is one of the signs of God, and one light from His lights. . . .

Every precept which was enjoined by the doctors of other religions he treated as manifest and decisive, in contradistinction to this Religion of ours, all the doctrines of which he set down to be senseless, and of modern origin, and the founders of it as nothing but poor Arabs, a set of scoundrels and highway-robbers, and the people of Islām as accursed. But in the course of time the truth of this verse in its hidden meaning developed itself: "Fain would they put out the light of God with their mouths! but, though the Infidels abhor it, God will perfect his light." By degrees the affair was carried to such a pitch that proofs were no longer considered necessary for abolishing the precepts of Islām. . . .

I have made bold to chronicle these events, a course very far removed from that of prudence and circumspection. But God (He is glorious and honoured!) is my witness, and sufficient is God as a witness, that my inducement to write this has been nothing but sorrow for the faith, and heart-burning for the deceased Religion of Islām, which 'Anqā-like turning its face to the Qāf of exile, and withdrawing the shadow of its wings from the dwellers in the dust of this lower world, thenceforth became a nonentity, and still is so. And to God I look for refuge from reproach, and hatred, and envy, and religious persecution. . . .

And in these days, when reproach began to spread upon the doctrines of Islām, and all questions relating thereto, and ever so many wretches of Hindūs and Hindūizing Musalmāns brought unmitigated reviling against the Prophet, and the villainously irreligious Ulamā[25]

---

[23]Persian Zoroastrianism.—Ed.

[24]An old Persian dynasty.—Ed.

[25]The Islamic learned community.—Ed.

in their works pronounced the Emperor to be without sin, and contenting themselves with mentioning the unity of God, they next wrote down the various titles of the Emperor, and had not the courage to mention the name of the Prophet (God be gracious to him and his family, and give them peace in defiance of the liars!) this matter became the cause of general disgrace, and the seeds of depravity and disturbance began to lift their heads in the empire. Besides this base and low men of the higher and lower classes, having accepted the collar of spiritual obedience upon their necks, professed themselves his disciples. They became disciples through the motives of hope and fear, and the word of truth could not proceed out of their mouths. . . .

At this time a document made its appearance,[26] which bore the signatures and seals of Makhdūm-ul-mulk, of Shaikh 'Abd-un-nabī *çadr-uç-çudūr,* of Qāzī Jalāl-ud-dīn of Multān, *qāzī-l-quzāt,* of Çadr Jahān the *muftī* of the empire, of Shaikh Mubārak the deepest writer of the age, and of Ghāzi Khān of Badakhshān, who stood unrivalled in the transcendental sciences. The subject-matter of the document was the setting of the absolute superiority of the *Imām-i-'ādil* over the *Mujtahid* and the investigation of the grounds of this superiority. . . . I shall copy the document *verbatim:*—

"Petition.

Whereas Hindūstān is now become the centre of security and peace, and the land of justice and beneficence, a large number of people, especially learned men and lawyers, have immigrated and chosen this country for their home. Now we, the principal 'Ulamā, who are not only well-versed in the several departments of the Law and in the principles of jurisprudence, and well acquainted with the edicts which rest on reason or testimony, but are also known for our piety and honest intentions, have duly considered the deep meaning, *first,* of the verse of the Qur'ān: "Obey God, and obey the prophet, and those who have authority among you," and, *secondly,* of the genuine Tradition: "Surely the man who is dearest to God on the day of judgment is the *Imām-i-'ādil;* whosoever obeys the Amīr, obeys Thee; and whosoever rebels against him, rebels against Thee," and, *thirdly,* of several other proofs based on reasoning or testimony; and we have agreed that the rank of *Sultān-i-'ādil,*[27] is higher in the eyes of God than the rank of a *Mujtahid.*[28] Further we declare that the king of Islām, Amīr of the Faithful, shadow of God in the world, *Abu-l-Fath Jalāl-ud-dīn Muhammad Akbar*

---

[26] The so-called Infallibility Decree.—Ed.

[27] Just ruler.—Ed.

[28] Authority on points of law.—Ed.

Padshāh Ghāzī (whose kingdom God perpetuate!) is a most just, a most wise, and a most God-fearing king. Should therefore in future a religious question come up, regarding which the opinions of the Mujtahids are at variance, and His Majesty in his penetrating understanding and clear wisdom be inclined to adopt, for the benefit of the nation, and as a political expedient, any of the conflicting opinions, which exist on that point, and issue a decree to that effect, we do hereby agree that such a decree shall be binding on us and on the whole nation.

Further, we declare that, should His Majesty think fit to issue a new order, we and the nation shall likewise be bound by it, provided always that such order be not only in accordance with some verse of the Qur'ān, but also of real benefit to the nation; and further, that any opposition on the part of his subjects to such an order passed by His Majesty shall involve damnation in the world to come, and loss of property and religious privileges in this.

This document has been written with honest intentions, for the glory of God, and the propagation of Islām, and is signed by us, the principal 'Ulamā and lawyers, in the month of Rajab of the year nine hundred and eighty-seven (987) [1579–80]."

The draft of this document, when presented to the Emperor, was in the handwriting of Shaikh Mubārak. The others had signed it against their will, but the Shaikh had added at the bottom that he most willingly signed his name; for this was a matter to which for several years he had been anxiously looking forward.

No sooner had His Majesty obtained this legal document, than the road of deciding any religious question was open; the superiority of the intellect of the Imām was established, and opposition was rendered impossible. All orders regarding things which our law allows or disallows were abolished, and the superiority of the intellect of the Imām became law. They called Islām a travesty.

A Modern Assessment of Akbar

BAMBER GASCOIGNE

Every modern writer on the Moghul Empire has had to deal with Akbar's administrative and religious reforms, and most find them the well-spring of his greatness as an emperor. One of the best of the modern commentators is the British journalist and historical popularizer Bamber Gascoigne. His work *The Great Moghuls* is one of the most reliable treatments of the complex history of Moghul India, solidly based on the sources—including Fazl and Badaoni—and on the best current specialists' research.

At the age of twenty-three Abul Fazl arrived at Fatehpur Sikri to enter Akbar's service—in the very same year, 1574, as another equally brilliant young man, Badauni. From early in his childhood Abul Fazl had known Badauni, eleven years his senior, because Badauni had studied at Agra under Abul Fazl's father, Shaikh Mubarak. Each now immediately caught Akbar's eye; each seemed destined for a most promising career; and they were to become, between them, the two most important historians of the period. But their paths rapidly diverged and the vast difference between their two careers and their two books symbolizes neatly the gulf which opened in the second half of Akbar's reign and which made these seem years of calamity to the more orthodox Muslims among Akbar's subjects, many of whom came to believe that the emperor had become a Hindu. Badauni was a strict Sunni, whereas Abul Fazl was a freethinker, as were his elder brother, Faizi, and his father, Shaikh Mubarak. The appointment of the three members of this talented family to positions at court was an ominous reversal for the rigidly orthodox and until now very powerful members of the *ulama*, or religious hierarchy.

Shaikh Mubarak and his two sons rapidly became the most influential group at Akbar's court, largely because their eclecticism chimed so well with his. The shaikh himself took the leading place among the palace divines. His elder son, Faizi, became the poet laureate. And Abul Fazl launched with a will into the many tasks which would bring him ever closer into the emperor's trust. The more affairs at Fatehpur Sikri went the elegant and carefree way of Abul Fazl and Faizi, the more Badauni and his like felt excluded. Badauni claims to have upbraided Abul Fazl one day for his notorious heresies and to have been enraged by the cool reply 'I wish to wander for a few days in the vale of infidelity for sport' though the story does less than justice to the political seriousness underlying Abul Fazl's wish to broaden the regime's religious basis. With poignant irony the two rival intellectuals were each as young men given the rank of twenty horse and were made to share the same task—supervising the branding of horses for muster. Abul Fazl knuckled down to it, and in Badauni's words, 'by his intelligence and time-serving qualities' managed to raise himself from here to the highest positions in the realm, 'while I from my inexperience and simplicity could not manage to continue in the service'. Badauni

soon sank to the official level of a mere translator. Akbar, with characteristic lack of concern for Badauni's bigotry, gave him the four-year
task of translating into Persian the Hindi classic the *Mahabharata*,
which he predictably found nothing but 'puerile absurdities of which
the eighteen thousand creations may well be amazed . . . but such is my
fate, to be employed on such works'. Badauni hardly appears in Abul
Fazl's book, but the latter looms large in Badauni's as the 'man that set
the world in flames' and as being 'officious and time-serving, openly
faithless, continually studying the emperor's whims, a flatterer beyond
all bounds'. The two men's books make together a perfect pair of
commentaries on the reign. Badauni's, crotchety, bigoted, ruthlessly
honest with himself as well as with others, is much the more readable
and in modern terms is far better written. It was compiled in secret and
only discovered in 1615 after both Akbar and Badauni were dead.
Abul Fazl's, in which a mere list of Akbar's good qualities can run to
several pages, was commissioned by the emperor and was read aloud to
him as each stage was completed—and no doubt again and again
subsequently. Yet it carries one along by the sheer confident profusion
of its flowery Persian metaphors and can also be surprisingly vivid, as
when a holy man has 'for thirty years in an unnoticed corner been
gathering happiness on an old mat'. The difference between the two
histories is that between a brilliant diary and the most magnificent of
ornamental scrolls.

Akbar's own bent for religious speculation was encouraged not only
by Shaikh Mubarak's family but also by wider currents of opinion in
India at the time. Within Islam there had long been a tradition of
free-thinking mysticism, known as Sufism, which was opposed to the
rigid distinctions of orthodoxy, and in the past century this had been
joined in India by similar stirrings within Hinduism, in particular the
Bhakti movement and the beginnings of the Sikh religion, both of
which included a rejection of the caste system and a belief in a personal God. By 1575 Akbar's interest in comparative religion had become so strong that he built a special *ibadat-khana* or 'house of worship' in which to hold religious discussions. The building, which no
longer exists, was an extension of a deserted hermit's cell. It was
situated behind the mosque at Fatehpur Sikri and Akbar would go
there after prayers in the mosque on Thursday evenings—the Muslim day is calculated as beginning at dusk, rather than midnight, so
Thursday evening was for Akbar and his mullahs the evening of the
holy day, Friday.

His intention, as in his *diwan-i-khas*, was to sit in the middle and digest
the arguments from all sides. He was deeply shocked—and sufficiently
inexperienced in academic matters to be surprised—when the learned
divines whom he invited to participate immediately fell out over who

should sit where, but this was finally settled by separating the rival groups to the four sides of the building. The discussions went on long into the night; much perfume was wafted on the air; and Akbar had a pile of money in front of him, as he always did on any comparable occasion, with which he hoped to reward the most persuasive and elegant contributions. But here too he was disappointed. Badauni records that in no time the learned doctors were calling each other 'fools and heretics', and the arguments soon went beyond subtle sectarian differences and threatened to undermine the very foundations of belief, until the participants 'became very Jews and Egyptians for hatred of each other'. The foundations of Akbar's belief, perhaps already shaky, were certainly further disturbed by these performances; such furious differences of opinion within the Muslim community, to whom the discussions were at this stage restricted, seemed to him to cast doubts on Islam itself and his next step was to throw the debate open to learned men from other religions. Eventually he included Hindus, Jains, Zoroastrians, Jews and even a small group who came to play a prominent and most interesting part in the court life at Fatehpur Sikri, three Jesuit fathers from the Portuguese colony at Goa. . . . They were Rudolf Aquaviva, an Italian aristocrat whose uncle became General of the Society of Jesus; Antony Monserrate, a Spaniard who later left a very full account of his experiences in the land of the Moghul; and Francis Henriquez, a Persian convert from Islam who was expected to act as interpreter. . . .

Akbar always treated the 'Nazarene sages', as Abul Fazl called them, with the greatest courtesy; he liked them to sit near him, and would often draw them aside for private conversation; he sent them food from the royal table; when Monserrate was ill he visited him, and he had even gone to the trouble to learn a special Portuguese greeting for the occasion; and he could sometimes be seen walking in public places with his arm around Father Aquaviva. On religious matters he was just as cooperative; he was prepared to kiss their sacred books and holy images; he came to see the crib which they had built for their first Christmas at Fatehpur Sikri, and when he entered their little chapel he took off his turban; he appointed Abul Fazl to teach them Persian and allowed Monserrate to become tutor to his son Murad, then about eleven, even tolerating 'In the name of God and of Jesus Christ, the true Prophet and Son of God' at the head of each of the prince's exercises; he allowed the fathers to preach, to make conversions and to hold a large public funeral for a Portuguese who died at court, processing through the streets with crucifix and candles; he even took in good part the Jesuits' chiding him for his surplus of wives.

It is not surprising that the missionaries felt encouraged, but they were soon to be disappointed. They had mistaken Akbar's fascination with all religions for an inclination to join theirs. It seems that Christianity appealed to him at least as much as any other religion—though he was distressed, among other things, that Christ should have allowed himself the indignity of being crucified and felt that once up there he should have used his special powers to get down—and it has sometimes been suggested that Akbar was consciously hoping to find in Christianity a religion with which he could solve his empire's communal hostilities by imposing it from the top on Muslims and Hindus alike, precisely, in fact, as the Jesuits themselves intended. But he was too shrewd a politician to imagine that he could solemnly decree a new religion for India, and it is likely that his interest in Christianity derived almost entirely from his personal love of speculation. It is typical that when he did finally decide on his own religion it should turn out to be so generalized, its main distinguishing feature being a vague nimbus of divinity around his own person, and that he should have made so little effort to spread it beyond his own circle of friends. The announcement in 1582 of this new religion, known as the *din-i-Ilahi* or 'religion of God', finally showed the fathers that their efforts had failed. They returned to Goa but at Akbar's request other missions followed them, and on several more occasions Christian hopes were raised high only to be dashed again. . . .

If the Jesuits were wrong in believing that Akbar was moving towards Christianity, the Muslims were certainly right in their conviction that he was drifting away from orthodox Islam. That he was doing so was as much as anything a matter of policy. The principle of a medieval Islamic state gave very great powers to the mullahs, since it was believed that the correct way of doing everything could be found in the Koran or in one or two long established commentaries on it. The ruler must therefore abide by the book and the book was best interpreted by those who had devoted their lives to religion. . . .

Akbar used the undignified squabbles between the Muslim divines in the *ibadat-khana* as an opportunity to limit the power of the priesthood. In 1579 appeared the famous *mahzar* or so-called decree of infallibility, in which it was stated that if there was disagreement among the learned about the meaning of any part of the Koran, it would in future be Akbar who had the deciding say on which of the contending interpretations should be accepted; and further that if he chose to take any step for the good of the state, it should be accepted by all unless it could be shown to be against the Koran. The decree was sound Islamic theory in so far as it placed the book above all, but it did represent a fairly startling upheaval, at least in concept, in the relationship between the *ulama* or body of learned men and the temporal power. . . . The decree of infallibility was signed by several divines but only one of them, Abul Fazl's father Shaikh Mubarak, put his name to it with enthusiasm, as a note below his signature testified. Having probably been largely Mubarak's idea, the decree marked a definite advance in the power at court of the shaikh and his two sons, and was a serious blow to the orthodox—particularly when coupled with other indications about this time of the direction which Akbar's thoughts were taking. In 1579 he put an end to the custom of sending vast sums of money each year to Mecca and Medina for distribution to the poor; in 1580 he gave up his annual pilgrimage to Ajmer; in 1584 he rejected the Muslim system of dating events from the Hegira, or flight of the prophet from Mecca to Medina, and replaced it with a new chronology beginning with his own accession (Abul Fazl explains that Akbar found it 'of ominous significance' to date things from the Hegira, presumably because of the mention of flight); finally he had had the effrontery to begin preaching and reciting the *khutba*[29] himself in the mosque, although on the very first occasion he had to stop halfway, when he began trembling in what appears to have been another of his quasi-mystical seizures. Together with the decree of infallibility, this personal performance in the mosque was perhaps the most offensive of all to the orthodox. It implied that Akbar was conferring on himself the status of a learned divine. Their next shock was when he seemed to take the process one stage further and present himself simply as divine.

The *din-i-Ilahi,* Akbar's new religion based on a vague and mystical liberalism, was at the very best unspecific about how far Akbar straddled the dividing line between mortal and divine. The new chronology dating from his accession was known as the Divine Era. And considerable outrage was caused when he decided to stamp on his coins the potentially ambiguous phrase *Allahu akbar;* the ambiguity derives from the fact that *akbar* means great as well as being the emperor's name so that the words could mean either 'God is great' or 'Akbar is God'. This has seemed to various modern historians the most blatant assumption of divinity, but it need not have been so. When a shaikh accused Akbar of having intended the second meaning he replied indignantly that it had not even occurred to him. His claim sounds far-fetched; and the fact that he had taken the unusual step of removing his own name and titles from his coins, in order to substitute this phrase, suggests that he was not unaware that it included his name as well as God's . . . and it seems likely that Akbar was amused by the ambiguity rather than taking it as a serious statement of his own identity.

---

[29]A prescribed sermon read at Friday noon prayers in the mosque, acknowledging the authority of the reigning prince.—ED.

In all these steps Akbar was energetically supported if not actually led by Shaikh Mubarak and his sons. Abul Fazl's biography of Akbar is liberally sprinkled with epithets suggesting his divinity, and he attributes to the emperor several miracles, including even the making of rain. The emphasis throughout Abul Fazl's writing is on religious toleration—he was a man who practised what he preached, having a Hindu, a Kashmiri and a Persian wife—and within the space of one paragraph he calls the Muslims of Kashmir 'narrow-minded conservatives of blind tradition' but praises the Hindu priests of the same province for not loosening 'the tongue of calumny against those not of their faith'. His stated aim in studying and describing the culture and philosophy of the Hindus was so that 'hostility towards them might abate, and the temporal sword be stayed awhile from the shedding of blood'.

Akbar's progression away from orthodox Islam towards his own vague religion was no doubt part of a conscious effort to seem to represent all his people—the Rajputs, for example, saw their rajas much like Abul Fazl's image of Akbar, both human and divine—and it fitted in with a general policy which included his adoption of Hindu and Parsee festivals and his increasing abstinence from meat in the manner of Hindus. But it also fulfilled a personal need. He was drawn to mysticism, fond of lonely contemplation, eager for any clue to the truth, and if that truth should touch him with divinity there were always precedents within the family; Humayun had indulged in a mystical identification of himself with light, and through light with God; Timur, more conventionally, used to refer to himself as the 'shadow of Allah on earth'. Akbar's religious attitudes seem to have been a happy blend of personal inclination and state policy.

Review and Study Questions

1. How does Abul Fazl manifest his outrageous partisanship in the *Akbar-nama*?

2. How do the two contemporary accounts of Akbar's religious toleration differ from each other?

3. What was the source of al-Badaoni's hostility to Akbar's religious toleration?

4. Why were Abul Fazl and al-Badaoni such bitter enemies? How did this affect their appraisals of Akbar?

5. Given the background of Akbar, could he really be an "infallible" judge of religious and intellectual matters?

Suggestions for Further Reading

The works of Fazl, excerpted for this chapter from Abu-l-Fazl, *The Akbar-nama,* tr. H. Beveridge, 3 vols. (Delhi: Rare Books, 1972) and Badaoni, excerpted for this chapter from Abul-l-Qadir ibn-l-Muluk Shah, Al-Badaoni, *Muntakhabu-T-Tawarikh,* tr. and ed. W. H. Lowe, rev. ed. 3 vols. (Patna, India: Academica Asiatica, 1973), are the only two complete contemporary histories of Akbar's reign, although several partial accounts exist. These can best be sampled in H. M. Elliot and John Dowson, eds., *The History of India, As Told by Its Own Historians,* 2d ed. (Calcutta: Susil Guypta, Ltd., 1955), 8 vols. The interesting account by the Jesuit Father Antony Monserrate is, unfortunately, still in its original Latin, but is summarized with substantial parts translated in Sir. E. D. Maclagan, "The Jesuit Missions to the Emperor Akbar," *Journal of the Asiatic Society of Bengal,* 65, part i (1896), 38–113. Though not a connected history, another large three-volume work by Abul Fazl, *Ain-i Akbari,* tr. H. Blochmann and H. S. Jarrett (Calcutta: Asiatic Society of Bengal, 1873–94), presents a detailed account of Akbar's administrative system.

The best modern biography of Akbar is still Vincent A. Smith, *Akbar the Great Mogul, 1542–1605,* 2nd rev. ed. (Delhi et al.: S. Chand and Co., 1966). A much larger and more detailed work is the learned Ashirbadi Lal Srivastava, *Akbar the Great,* vol. I, *Political History, 1542–1645 A.D.,* vol. II, *Evolution of Administration, 1556–1645 A.D.* (Agra, Delhi, Jaipur: Shiva Lal Agarwala, 1962). There are two old and rather brief biographies of Akbar in English, neither of them critical or based on primary sources: G. B. Malleson, *Akbar and the Rise of the Mughal Empire,* "Rulers of India" (Oxford: Clarendon Press, 1894) and Lawrence Binyon, *Akbar* (Edinburgh: Peter Davies, Ltd., 1932). The chapter on Akbar in Sri Ram Sharma, *The Religious Policy of the Mughal Emperors,* 3rd rev. ed. (New York: Asia Publishing House, 1972) is a very reliable and substantial account.

There are a number of works on the Moghul Empire or on late medieval India, including the Moghul period. The most detailed are two works by A. L. Srivastava, *History of India, 1000–1707* (Jaipur, Agra, Indore: Shiva Lal Agarwala and Co., 1964) and *The Mughal Empire (1526–1803 A.D.),* 7th rev. ed. (Agra: Shiva Lal Agarwala and Co., 1970). Two less satisfactory and older books are Stanley Lane-Poole, *Mediaeval India under Mohammedan Rule (A.D. 712–1764),* 2 vols. (London: Ernest Benn, 1903) with many revised editions; and S. M. Edwardes and H. L. O. Garrett, *Mughal Rule in India* (Delhi et al.: Chand [1900]). The best and most up-to-date history of the Moghuls is Bamber Gascoigne, *The Great Moghuls* (New York et al.: Harper & Row, 1971), excerpted for this chapter.

There are a great many general histories of India that devote chapters or sections to Akbar. Among the most useful are Stanley Wolpert, *A New History of India* (New York: Oxford University Press, 1977); Percival Spear, *India: A Modern History,* new ed. rev. (Ann Arbor: University of Michigan Press, 1972); Francis Watson, *A Concise History of India* (New York: Scribner, 1975); and finally, an old standard work by Vincent A. Smith, in a third edition edited by Percival Spear, with the section containing the Moghuls revised by J. B. Harrison: *The Oxford History of India* (Oxford: Clarendon Press, 1967).

The Tokugawa Art Museum, Nagoya

TOKUGAWA IEYASU SHOGUN: "THE OLD BADGER"

1543	Born
1560	Restored to his family lands
1567	Assumed the family name of Tokugawa
1590	Succeeded to Edo (Tokyo)
1600	Won battle of Sekigahara
1603	Appointed shogun
1605	Abdicated in favor of his son Hidetada
1616	Died

The Shogun Tokugawa Ieyasu was a mass of contradictions. Short, squat, and ugly, he was given the enshrinement name, after his death, of "The Light of the East, the Ultimate Made Manifest." A devoted family man, intent upon founding a dynasty, he ordered the suicide of his eldest son and heir on suspicion of sedition, and thus put his dynasty at risk. An unlettered man, he became the great patron of Confucian scholarship in Japan. He relentlessly pursued his last rival, the pretender Hideyori, the son of his old friend and lord, and forced him to commit suicide; yet his self-proclaimed motto was "Requite malice with kindness." A samurai warrior who had devoted his life to battle, he was a devout Buddhist and founded a reign of peace in Japan that would last for more than 250 years.

Ieyasu was born in 1543, the son of a samurai and minor daimyo (feudal landholder) in eastern Japan. Such men had dominated the political life of Japan since the end of the cultivated Heian age in the twelfth century. From time to time a measure of order had been imposed by the appointment of a shogun by the emperor, who was himself strictly a ceremonial and religious figure. The shogun was the military ruler of the nation, the head of the *bakufu,* the military or "tent" government. But there were long periods when no one held the shogunate and when military chaos prevailed. It was in such a period that Ieyasu grew up.

By his warrior skills Ieyasu gained advancement in the service of superior feudal lords, becoming such a lord himself. By the age of forty he had not only been able to secure great military power but had persuaded the emperor to grant him the family name of Tokugawa, thus linking him to the ancient and illustrious warrior family of Minamoto, the family of past shoguns. In 1582 he offered his services to the leading feudal lord of Japan, Hideyoshi. He quickly became Hideyoshi's most dependable vassal and was rewarded with enormous land holdings centered upon the village of Edo—the future Tokyo. He fortified the site and consolidated his position as master of eastern Japan. In the power struggle following the death of Hideyoshi, Tokugawa defeated all his rivals in a great pitched battle at Sekigahara, northeast of Kyoto, to become the undisputed master of Japan.

By 1603 he was able to demand that the imperial court appoint him shogun. On February 12, a delegation from the Emperor Gayozei called upon Tokugawa with his appointment as shogun and a host of other supporting titles, each contained in a lacquered box. As each box was opened and the appointment letter removed, the box was filled with gold dust and returned. Within a month Tokugawa had taken up residence in a new castle he had ordered built for himself at Kyoto—Nijo Castle. A new shogunal dynasty had begun. Two years later he abdicated in favor of his son Hidetada, thus assuring the succession of the Tokugawa family.

Both as shogun and as retired shogun, Tokugawa retained control of foreign affairs. He was mainly concerned with trade. This came to involve him in a complex set of relations not only with Japan's traditional trading partner, China, but with agents of the European maritime states, intent upon trade with Japan but intent also upon extending their religious beliefs—whether Catholic or Protestant. Tokugawa welcomed the trade and the new technology that came with it, but he grew increasingly suspicious of western religious motives and the meddling of missionaries in what he regarded as the internal affairs of Japan. By 1614 he had prohibited all western missionary activity—the beginning of the process of closing Japan to the West that would last until the nineteenth century.

By the time of his death in 1616 Tokugawa had fathered sixteen children by an assortment of consorts and concubines—five daughters, who were well and strategically married, and eleven sons, six of them still living when Tokugawa died. The dynasty was secure.

The Legacy

TOKUGAWA IEYASU

Tokugawa was undeniably one of the greatest military figures in his nation's history. But increasingly, especially after becoming shogun, he tried to avoid military engagements and military solutions to political problems. He had concluded that they were not only costly but disruptive; he much preferred conciliation. And he spent the last dozen years of his life creating a system of government that would make peace and order the rule of Japanese life. To a remarkable degree he succeeded. The government he perfected lasted almost totally unchanged for two centuries, the longest period of such peace and order in Japan's history.

In the course of his reign Tokugawa issued many orders, edicts, and codes of conduct to regulate all levels of society, including the imperial court and the court aristocrats, the daimyo, even the religious shrines and temples. One of the most important and interesting of these edicts is the *Buke Hyaku Kajo*, the "Legacy of Ieyasu." It was written near the end of Tokugawa's life and is a set of instructions to his successors in the shogunate, embodying his views on how the government should be carried on by them. It exists in a number of editions, including a complete critical edition in the *Transactions of the Japan Society of London*, which takes account of the later revisions of the work. The edition excerpted below is the one edited and translated by A. L. Sadler in his *The Maker of Modern Japan: The Life of Tokugawa Ieyasu*, which is the standard English biography of the great shogun. It consists of those parts of the text that can be incontestably attributed to Tokugawa.

The instructions take the form, typical of the age of Tokugawa, of a series of maxims in the Chinese manner, presented in a random, seemingly casual order. Despite the apparent lack of order, the document contains recurring themes. There are continual references to the standard Chinese works on governance, especially the Confucian works; the document itself was written in Chinese. It places strong emphasis on benevolence and compassion as principles of governance as well as of personal conduct. There are reminders of the structure of vassalage Tokugawa had created—with House Retainers, Family Vassals, and Outside Lords—and of how he manipulated that structure. There are cautions against the overt use of military power, and the sort of exhortations to craft and patience that caused Tokugawa to be known

71

as "the Old Badger" to his contemporaries. It is filled with specific advice to future shoguns based on Tokugawa's own experience, and often contains personal reminiscences.

The duty of the lord of a province is to give peace and security to the people, and does not consist in shedding lustre on his ancestors, and working for the prosperity of his descendants. The supreme excellence of T'ang of the Yin dynasty and Wu of the Chou dynasty lay in making this their first principle.[1] There must be no slighting of the Imperial Dignity or confusing the order of Heaven and Earth, Lord and Subject.

The civil and military principles both proceed from Benevolence. However many books and plans there may be the principle is the same. Know therefore that herein lies the way of ruling and administering the Empire. . . .

If the lord is not filled with compassion for his people and the people are not mindful of the care of their lord, even though the government is not a bad one, yet rebellions will naturally follow. But if the lords love Benevolence, then there will be no enemies in the Empire.

If Benevolence abides in the Empire there is no distinction between domestic and foreign or noble and commoner, for the sun and moon shine on the clean and unclean alike. The Sage established the law on this principle, and according to it there are fixed and immutable rules applying to the degree of intimacy, rank, the three allegiances, and the eight rules. If one man is supreme in the Empire then all warriors are his retainers, but he does not make retainers of the whole people. There is the distinction of Outside Families and our own Family, Outside Lords (Tozama) and House Retainers (Hatamoto). Outside houses are those that are temporarily powerful. Family vassals or Fudai are those bound to us by lineage and history, whose ancestors did loyal service to our house as is clear to all by their records. Since their fidelity and affection exceeds that of the Outside houses, these others must not be displeased at this preference, resting as it does on such a basis.

In employing men and recognizing ability, if the Fudai are overlooked and the Tozama elevated there will be inward rage and outward regret, and loyal retainers will naturally be lost. One thing is

---

[1]T'ang of Yin and Wu of Chou were the founders of these two Chinese dynasties.—ED.

quite certain, men are not all saints and sages. This fact it is well to bear very much in mind.

All feudatories, whether Fudai or Tozama, are to have their fiefs changed after a certain number of years, for if they stay long in one place and get used to their positions these lords will lose their fidelity and become covetous and self-willed, and eventually oppress their subjects. This changing of fiefs shall be according to the conduct of these lords.

If there be no direct heir to the Shogunate, then the question of succession must be settled by a conference of the veteran houses of Ii, Honda, Sakai, Sakakibara, and others, after careful consideration.

Should anyone break the laws I have laid down, even if he be a son or heir, he shall not succeed. The Chief Senator (Tairo) and Senators (Roshin) shall then hold a consultation and shall choose a suitable person from among the branch families of our house (Kamon) and make him head of the family.

The right use of a sword is that it should subdue the barbarians while lying gleaming in its scabbard. If it leaves its sheath it cannot be said to be used rightly. Similarly the right use of military power is that it should conquer the enemy while concealed in the breast. To take the field with an army is to be found wanting in the real knowledge of it. Those who hold the office of Shogun are to be particularly clear on this point. . . .

If your defences are according to my instructions traitors will not be able to spy them out. But even so, if another family plans to overthrow this Empire the attempt will only be made when those who uphold it are given up to drink and dissipation. It is inevitable that those who are incapacitated by these things should be deprived of office and commit suicide.

In ordinary matters, if one does not disobey these instructions of mine, even if he is far from being a sage, he will commit no great fault.

From my youth I have not valued silver or gold or treasures. Virtue only I have treasured. And now I have thus attained this office. If we always consider without ceasing the golden words that declare that it is by learning that emolument comes, we can always attain our purpose. . . .

When the Empire is at peace do not forget the possibility of war, and take counsel with the Fudai vassals that the military arts be not allowed to deteriorate. And be temperate in your habits.

The sword is the soul of the warrior. If any forget or lose it he will not be excused. . . .

The descendants of those retainers who were loyal to our ancestors, except they become traitors to our house, must never have their fiefs confiscated, even if their conduct is not good.

Authority to subdue the whole Empire was granted by Imperial Edict to the Shogun, and he was appointed Lord High Constable (Sotsui-Hoshi). The orders that the Shogun issues to the country are its law. Nevertheless every province and district has its particular customs, and it is difficult, for example, to enforce the customs of the Eastern Provinces in the Western, or those of the North in the South, so that these customs must be left as of old and not interfered with. . . .

In accordance with ancient precedent, a Court of Judgment is to be established, and there, in the light of these articles I have drawn up and without regarding the high or repressing the low, justice is to be done openly to all.

Now the officials who administer justice in this court are the pillars of the government of the country. Their character shall be carefully considered, and they shall be chosen and appointed after consultation with the veteran councillors. This will be no easy task. . . .

Nagasaki in Hizen is the port at which foreign shipping arrives. It shall be administered by one of the most trusted retainers chosen from the fudai vassals. The great lords of the neighbouring territories shall also be instructed to furnish guards, that our military might may be demonstrated to all countries. It is strictly forbidden that any of these ships shall enter any other port but Nagasaki.

The entertainment tendered to foreigners who come to pay their respects shall be as heretofore. It shall not be rough or scanty. It shall brilliantly reveal the Imperial Benevolence and Divine Might. . . .

Confucianism and Shinto and Buddhism are different systems, but are no more than direction in the way of virtue and punishment of evil. According to this view, their sects may be adopted and their principles followed. They must not be hindered, but disputes among them must be strictly prohibited. It is evident from past history that such have been a misfortune to the Empire. . . .

Since one person differs from another in disposition, when men are appointed to offices this should be tested, and their tendencies observed and their ability estimated, so that the office may be well filled. A saw cannot do the work of a gimlet, and a hammer cannot take the place of a knife, and men are just like this. There is a use for both sharp and blunt at the right time, and if this is not well apprehended the relation of lord and vassal will become disturbed. This article is to be considered carefully.

Lords of provinces both great and small and lords of fiefs and officials both in and outside Edo shall hold official stipend, and rank only if they conduct themselves properly. If he offend, the greatest feudatory or official, even if he be a relation of our house (Kamon), shall be punished. So in their persons shall they the better guard the Shogun's office. . . .

I was born of the family of Matsudaira of the province of Mikawa, of the lineage of Seiwa Genji, but on account of the enmity of a neighbouring province I had for long to suffer hardships among the common people. But now, I am happy to say, encompassed by the grace of Providence I have restored the ancestral lines of Serata, Nitta, and Tokugawa, and from henceforth the successive generations of my family are to use these four names. This is in accordance with the saying (of Confucius): Pay all respect to your parents, and follow the customs of your ancestors. . . .

The distinction between wife and concubine is on the principle of lord and vassal. The Emperor has twelve consorts, the great lords may have eight, high officials five, and ordinary samurai two. Below these are the common people. Thus have the ancient sages specified in the *Li Chi*,[2] and it has always been the rule. But fools ignorant of this treat their wife with less respect than a favourite concubine, and so confuse the great principle. This has always been the cause of the fall of castles and the ruin of countries. Is it not well to be warned? And know too that those who give way to these inclinations are no loyal samurai.

The business of a husband is to protect the family outside, while that of the wife is to look after it at home. That is the order of the world. Should the wife, on the contrary, be the one to guard the house the husband loses his function, and it is a sure sign that the house will be destroyed. It is the disorder of the crowing hen. All samurai should beware of it. Its existence will assist you to judge people.

When I was young I desired nothing but to subdue hostile provinces and take vengeance on the enemies of my father's house. But since I discovered the teaching of Yuyo[3] that helping the people and thus tranquillizing the country is the Law of Nature, I have undeviatingly followed it until now. Let my descendants continue my policy. If they reject it they are no posterity of mine. For be very certain that the people are the foundation of the country.

The Supreme Sovereign of the Empire looks on the people as children under his protecting care, and my family to which the administration of his realm is committed should exhibit this attitude even more. This is what is called Benevolence. Benevolence includes the

---

[2] The *Li Chi* was the Book of Ceremonies.—ED.

[3] Yuyo: this reference is obscure.—ED.

Five Relationships, and the distinction of superior and inferior. In accordance with it I make a difference in intimacy between the Fudai and the Tozama Daimyos. That is government according to the natural way of the world. It is not favouritism or prejudice or self-interest. It must not be polluted either by tongue or pen. And as to the degree of this intimacy with retainers, whether deep or the reverse, you must know how to maintain a deep reserve.

Since I have held this office of Shogun I have drawn up these many statutes, both amplifying and curtailing the ancient regulations of the Minamoto house. But with a view to transmitting and not to creating, for they are no new laws decreed at my will. Thus I have drawn them up in this form as an exemplar. They may not always hit the mark exactly, but they will not be far out. In all things administration is not so much a matter of detail as of understanding past history. I have no time to add more.

Tokugawa's Practical Revolution

GEORGE SANSOM

The earlier Western histories of Japan tended to take the view that the closing of the country to Western influences that took place early in the Tokugawa period resulted in a deadening stagnation from which Japan was rescued only by forceful European intervention in the mid-nineteenth century. Contemporary interpretation has, however, largely revised this Eurocentric judgment. The age of Tokugawa is now seen as one of significant growth in Japan's institutional structures. The dynamic of this period was provided by the conversion of the daimyo into regional rulers and by the creation of a new national hegemony under the Tokugawa shogunate.

One of the leading figures in this contemporary view of the Tokugawa period is the British scholar George Sansom, who has produced "by far the outstanding writing on pre-twentieth-century Japan."[4] His earlier works dealt essentially with cultural history; but then he turned to the long-delayed task of providing an up-to-date

---

[4]John Whitney Hall, *Japanese History: New Dimensions of Approach and Understanding* (Washington, D.C.: Service Center for Teachers of History, The American Historical Association, 1961), pp. 10–11.

political history of Japan. The second volume of this work is *A History of Japan, 1334–1615*, which is excerpted below.

Sansom stresses the practical, revolutionary nature of the reforms instituted by Tokugawa that were essentially responsible for the ensuing long period of peace and order.

Ieyasu died on the first of June, 1616, in his seventy-fifth year. Although he had devoted much of his time since the death of Hideyoshi to urgent military problems and had fought two vital campaigns to ensure his supremacy, he had by no means neglected questions of civil government during the last fifteen years of his life. Indeed, in 1605, only two years after his appointment as Shōgun, he resigned the office in favour of his son Hidetada in order to be free to pay full attention to the political structure which was to sustain the power of the house of Tokugawa. His resignation and the succession of Hidetada were also intended to give public notice that the office was to be hereditary in the Tokugawa family. Himself a triumphant warrior, Ieyasu was determined that his family should hold what he had won, and that there should be an end to civil war. It was his purpose to devise a system which would hold in check the ambitions of the most powerful barons, who, though they had submitted to him after Sekigahara, were of uncertain loyalty. . . .

The basis of Ieyasu's civil policy was to distribute fiefs in such a way that his most trusted vassals occupied domains from which they could keep watch and ward upon barons whose allegiance was doubtful. The dependable vassals were known as Fudai, or hereditary lieges of the house of Tokugawa, in contrast to the Tozama, the "Outside Lords," with whom Ieyasu had no hereditary tie. Most of the Fudai daimyos held fiefs of about 50,000 koku[5] or less, with the exception of Matsudaira Tadayoshi (Ieyasu's fifth son) at Kiyosu, who had 500,000 koku, and Ii Naomasa at Hikone with 100,000. They were all placed at strategic points from Kyoto eastward along the Tōkaidō and the Nakasendō to Yedo.

In the Tozama, powerful lords who had been neutral or had adhered to Ieyasu after Sekigahara, he had little trust. He treated them with formal respect, but they were carefully watched and given little opportunity to plan combinations against the Bakufu. They were frequently called upon to perform tasks that put them to great expense, as for example when they were given the unwelcome privilege

---

[5]The *koku* was a measure of rice, about five bushels.—ED.

of building or repairing citadels, supposedly in the interest of the nation. . . .

Ieyasu took all possible steps to thwart alliances and agreements among the Tozama, imposing limits on the size of their castles and on the capacity of the transport craft used by the barons in coastal provinces. Where possible he reduced their freedom of movement by appointing Fudai vassals to neighbouring fiefs. . . .

Although Ieyasu paid unremitting attention to civil affairs, he made no attempt to organize a coherent system of government. He dealt with problems as they arose, and his methods had a military flavour. He was determined to secure obedience, and it was his method to give direct orders rather than to govern by legislation. He did, it is true, issue a code to guide the behaviour of the military class, but not until the end of his career. It was a collection of rules known as Buke Sho-Hatto, or Ordinances for the Military Houses. . . .

The issuing of this document was little more than a formality or a matter of record, since Ieyasu had already achieved his purpose of subjecting the Tozama by the methods just described, and by increasingly harsh treatment as his earlier forms of pressure succeeded. But even more effective than direct coercion was the great addition to his own strength that resulted from his economic enterprises. He was immensely wealthy, as the Christian missionaries frequently reported in their letters home. After Sekigahara he had vastly enlarged the scope of Tokugawa property rights by taking into his direct jurisdiction the cities of Yedo, Kyoto, Ōsaka, Nagasaki, Yamada, and Nara. . . .

After the establishment of a mint at Fushimi in 1601 he profited by the minting of gold and silver coinage for circulation throughout the country. But perhaps his greatest interest was in foreign trade, which he desired to promote not only as a source of revenue for himself but also on grounds of national policy. The foreign trade of Japan had for too long been in the hands of the Portuguese.

After the invasion of Korea official relations between Japan and China had come to an end, but imports from China were still essential to the Japanese economy or, to put it more correctly, to the economy of the ruling class, who could not dispense with the silks and other luxuries to which they had become accustomed during the period of licensed trade. Fortunately for them the Portuguese, who were allowed to trade with China, could meet Japanese needs by the regular supply of Chinese goods carried in their trading vessels from Macao to Japan. . . .

This favourable treatment of foreigners lasted through the year 1611, when suddenly the Tokugawa government reversed its policy and began to prohibit the preaching and practice of the Christian faith. The reasons for this change are still the subject of controversy, but they were clearly political rather than religious. Ieyasu was determined to get rid of all missionaries, and on January 27, 1614, he issued an edict suppressing Christianity in Japan. The churches in Kyoto were destroyed and the missionaries taken into custody. Some Japanese Christians of high rank were arrested and sent into exile, among them being the "Christian daimyo" Takayama Ukon, who died in Manila a year later. A few poor Japanese believers were punished for refusing to abjure their faith, and some were imprisoned; but the edict was really directed not against the common people but against members of the military class, because their Christian beliefs were thought to be inconsistent with loyalty to their overlords. During Ieyasu's lifetime no foreign missionary was put to death, though many flouted his decree. . . .

The business of national government was conducted by Ieyasu on the same general lines as the regulation of a fief by a powerful daimyo. He gave orders to his subordinates, who carried them out to the best of their ability. It was characteristic of the early stage of the Tokugawa Bakufu that there was no clear division of functions, for although Ieyasu depended upon his trusted vassals, the Fudai, to carry out his plans, he also depended upon various people of lower standing who happened to come to his notice. He made use of monks and Confucian scholars to draft the Buke Sho-Hatto, and he was in close touch with prominent merchants and other men who had special knowledge or experience. They were usually gifted persons, and they took the place of regular functionaries. . . . From 1615 for two hundred and fifty years Japan was at peace under the rule of the Tokugawa Shōguns.

A More Cautious View

EDWIN O. REISCHAUER

A scholar of Japanese history of equal standing with Sansom is Edwin O. Reischauer. Born in Japan of American missionary parents, Reischauer studied both in the West and in Japan and is a long-time Harvard professor. In the course of World War II he served as a Senior Research Analyst for the War Department and in the Department of State, and from 1961 to 1966 he was ambassador to Japan. For more than forty years he has been the leading interpreter of

Japan for American readers, and his many books represent "the most up-to-date interpretations of the causative forces in Japanese history, and provide the best balanced view of the interaction of political, social, and economic factors."[6]

Reischauer's narrative and analysis of the founding of the Tokugawa shogunate does not differ radically from Sansom's. But in interpretive terms he does return to a cautiously modified form of the earlier "stagnation" interpretation. He views the extremely conservative nature of the Tokugawa shogunate as responsible for holding back normal social and economic progress and keeping Japan frozen in an antiquated political and social order.

The political vacuum created by the death of Hideyoshi was soon filled by his foremost vassal, Tokugawa Ieyasu, who had been Hideyoshi's deputy in eastern Japan, where he had built himself a castle headquarters at the small village of Edo, the future Tokyo. In 1600, Ieyasu decisively defeated a coalition of rivals, and fifteen years later he destroyed the remnants of Hideyoshi's family when he captured the great Osaka castle, as much by trickery as by the huge forces he had mustered for the siege. Ieyasu, warned by the fate of the heirs of Nobunaga and Hideyoshi, was obsessed with the idea of building a political system strong enough to survive his death. Political stability became his primary goal, and it was equally sought by his successors. In this they were eminently successful. During the first half of the seventeenth century they created a political system which was to endure almost unchanged for two and a half centuries. In fact, they established a state of absolute peace, internal and external, that has never been matched over a comparable period of time by any other nation. Unfortunately, they secured peace and stability by a series of rigid controls over society, by ruthless suppression of many of the most creative tendencies in the Japan of that day, by isolating Japan from the rest of the world, and by preserving in unchanging form many feudal institutions and attitudes of the late sixteenth century, which became increasingly anachronistic during the next two centuries. In short, the Tokugawa system was extremely conservative even by the standards of early seventeenth-century Japanese society and became increasingly more so as time passed. . . .

The Tokugawa, in their search for stability, froze the political system as it had evolved by the late sixteenth century. They left the bulk of the country divided among a large number of autonomous daimyo, and sought merely to control these daimyo through preponderant military

---

[6]Hall, *Japanese History*, p. 11.

power and a system of careful supervision. . . . The shoguns reserved for themselves a personal domain of about 7 million *koku* (out of a total estimated national yield of 26 million), and also controlled directly all major cities, ports, and mines.

The country was in a sense divided into two halves: the Tokugawa group and the outsiders. On the one side was the shogun, the "related" (*shimpan*) daimyo, who were branches of the Tokugawa family, and the "hereditary" (*fudai*) daimyo, who had been vassals of Ieyasu even before his victory in 1600. These together provided both the military defense and the administration of the Tokugawa shogunate. On the other side were the "outer" (*tozama*) daimyo. These were the survivors of the allies, neutrals, and enemies of Ieyasu in the great battle of 1600 who had recognized him as their overlord only after his victory. . . .

The holdings of the shogun and daimyo were not scattered haphazardly about Japan. Almost all the central part of the country, including the Kanto Plain in the east and the old capital district in the west, was held by the Tokugawa group. This central area was not only the strategic heart of the country, but contained most of the larger plains, the bulk of the urban population, and was the economically most advanced region. . . .

The outer daimyo, some of whom nursed old hostilities toward the Tokugawa, were relegated largely to the northern and western peripheries of the nation, in north and west Honshu and the islands of Shikoku and Kyushu, where they were sometimes interlarded with related or hereditary daimyo assigned to keep watch over them.

While the daimyo were all in theory autonomous, the Tokugawa actually worked out a careful system of checks and controls to prevent any of them or any combination of them from becoming a military challenge to the shogunate. The bulk of Japan's fighting men remained divided among the daimyo, but the size of their respective forces and the extent of their fortifications were strictly controlled by Edo. Intermarriage and other contracts between the daimyo families were carefully supervised. Though the daimyo domains paid no taxes to the central government, the Tokugawa called on them freely for construction work at Edo or other national services, and so kept them from amassing excessive wealth. The Edo government also developed a category of officials known as *metsuke*, who acted on the one hand as censors in ferreting out cases of maladministration by Tokugawa officials, and on the other hand as secret police spying on all men or groups who could be a menace to Tokugawa rule. The Edo shogunate thus has the dubious distinction of being one of the first governments in the world to develop an extensive and efficient secret police system and to make of it a major organ of state.

The most important measure taken by Edo to ensure its control over the daimyo was the development of a system of hostages and service at the shogunal court. Under the name of *sankin kotai* ("alternating in attendance"), most daimyo spent every other year in Edo, but kept their wives and children permanently there as hostages. A close watch was kept at important barriers on the highways leading into Edo for women leaving and firearms entering the city, since the departure of hostages or the smuggling in of weapons might have foreshadowed a revolt. Naturally, each daimyo had to maintain a large establishment in Edo, and sometimes several in the case of the bigger domains. These were serious economic drains on daimyo resources and an enrichment of the shogun's capital city. The annual comings and goings of the daimyo to Edo, accompanied by long trains of retainers, also constituted a great expense, but at the same time these daimyo processions, particularly on the Tokaido road from Kyoto to Edo, provided one of the more spectacular aspects of life during the Tokugawa period.

To perpetuate their rule, the Tokugawa needed not only to control the daimyo but to guarantee their own solidarity and ensure that the stupidity or ineptness of some future shogun would not destroy the regime. While they left the age-old fiction of imperial rule undisturbed, contenting themselves with the status of shogun, that is, the "generalissimo" of the emperor's military forces, they in fact established close surveillance and strict control over the imperial court, while giving it fairly generous economic treatment as the ultimate source of their own legitimacy. Aware that the deaths of Nobunaga and Hideyoshi had led almost at once to the downfall of their families, Ieyasu passed on the title of shogun to one of his less gifted but more stable sons in 1605, with the result that his own death in 1616 produced no political repercussions. He and his early successors also developed a complicated but strong central administration, quite capable of ruling the land with or without the shoguns, most of whom proved to be little more than figureheads. . . .

Two things should be noted about this governmental system. It was highly bureaucratic, despite its feudal social background. Eligibility for positions was determined primarily by hereditary status, but within this limitation, actual appointments, particularly to the higher posts, depended largely on talent. When Japan had in theory adopted the Chinese bureaucratic form of government in the seventh and eighth centuries, no true bureaucracy had developed. Now, even though the outward forms of government remained feudal, a true bureaucracy started to emerge, and with the passing of the years developed the typical strengths and weaknesses of that form of government. The other point worth mentioning is the strong tendency toward collective responsibility rather than personalized leadership. The figureheads remained individuals, but actual leadership was assumed by councils or officials working in pairs. Japan's genius for anonymous, bureaucratic, group leadership had already become well established. . . .

As early as 1608 Ieyasu appointed a prominent Confucian philosopher to be "attendant scholar" at his court. From this small beginning grew a strong school of Confucianism at Edo that taught the orthodox interpretation as it had been formulated in China in the twelfth century by Chu Hsi (Shushi in Japanese). Soon groups of thinkers, representing various other schools of Confucianism, grew up in opposition to the orthodox school. One of the results of this scholarly interest in Confucianism in Tokugawa Japan was the development within the samurai class of a body of trained scholars and thinkers who, as statesmen, contributed to the efficient administration of the government and, as philosophers and teachers, helped keep Japan intellectually alive despite the oppressive limitations of the political and social system.

The long period of interest in Confucianism also served to imbue the people as a whole with many of the high ethical and moral standards of the Chinese, particularly their ideal of selfless and just public service and their passion for education. Buddhism remained the dominant religion of the masses and enjoyed official patronage, but Confucianism became the strongest intellectual and ethical force in Japan. . . .

Perhaps the most drastic measures taken by the Edo government to ensure political stability were in the field of foreign relations, which, with the coming of Europeans to East Asian waters, assumed a new significance for the Japanese. The first Europeans to reach Japan were Portuguese mariners who landed on an island off the southern tip of Kyushu around 1543. Trade relations sprang up between the Portuguese and the feudal lords of western Kyushu. The Japanese showed immediate interest in the firearms of the Europeans and their use spread rapidly throughout Japan, greatly changing the nature of warfare.

Contacts with the Portuguese took on a new aspect when St. Francis Xavier, the famous Jesuit missionary, introduced Christianity to Japan during a two-year stay from 1549 to 1551. He and the Jesuits who followed him met with considerable success in their proselytizing. . . .

Hideyoshi and the Tokugawa who followed him had no particular objections to Christianity on religious grounds, but they looked upon it with deep suspicion as a political menace to their rule. The Christians, as a sizable group of Japanese owing some sort of allegiance to a remote European "ruler," the pope, were in their eyes a group which could not be trusted and might prove a threat to the reestablished unity of Japan. . . . In 1609 the Dutch established a trading post at Hirado, an island off the northwest coast of Kyushu, and the English, too, set up a trading post there in 1613. At about the same time Ieyasu reverted to Hideyoshi's policy of persecution, and his successor in 1617 reinstated the extreme measure of executing missionaries and native believers. In the next few years all the missionaries were either killed or forced to leave Japan, and thousands of Japanese Christians either apostatized or suffered the death of martyrs. A common practice of the time was to order people suspected of being Christians to tread upon a cross or some other sacred symbol, and to kill those who refused to comply. . . .

Despite this policy of extreme national isolation, the Tokugawa were wise enough not to cut off all contact with other nations. They preserved Nagasaki as a window looking out on the rest of the world. Chinese merchants were allowed to visit and trade there under careful supervision, and the Dutch trading post at Hirado was moved to a small island in Nagasaki harbor, where the Dutch merchants were kept in virtual year-round imprisonment. The measures the early Tokugawa took to ensure the continuance of their regime were indeed drastic. They stifled the normal social and economic development of the country and so isolated Japan from the rest of the world that she began to drop far behind Europe in scientific and industrial achievements. Even Japan's population stopped growing after about 1700 and remained relatively static at about 30 million people during the remaining century and a half of Tokugawa rule.

It must be admitted, however, that the Tokugawa were supremely successful in establishing the political stability they sought. Between the middle of the seventeenth century and the middle of the nineteenth, no revolution, disturbance, or incident in any way threatened their rule. . . .

The long peace of the Tokugawa era was, of course, in many ways a blessing. At the same time, the Tokugawa held back the wheels of normal social and economic progress and fixed on the nation an antiquated political and social order. They preserved in Japan a feudal structure and mentality far longer than these could have lasted in a freer society or one more open to pressures from abroad. What had been essentially a conservative political and social system when founded in the early seventeenth century was preserved almost intact until the middle of the nineteenth century. Then a Japan still intellectually and socially bound by this antiquated system was suddenly confronted again by the Europeans, who during the intervening two centuries had made tremendous strides forward in almost all fields of human endeavor.

Review and Study Questions

1. What are the leading principles of government you can derive from the "Legacy of Ieyasu"?

2. What is your assessment of Tokugawa as a ruler?

3. What were the relations of Tokugawa's Japan with the European nations? How did these relations affect Japan?

4. How does Reischauer's interpretation of Tokugawa differ from Sansom's?

Suggestions for Further Reading

An extremely useful annotated bibliographic guide is John Whitney Hall, *Japanese History: New Dimensions of Approach and Understanding* (Washington, D.C.: Service Center for Teachers of History, The American Historical Association, 1961). The sources for the Tokugawa period—as for all the earlier periods of Japanese history—are a problem. The period is very well documented but the documents are all in Japan and untranslated. A few exist in selections, like *Sources of the Japanese Tradition,* ed. Ryusaka Tsunoda, Wm. T. de Bary, and Donald Keene (New York: Columbia University Press, 1958), or *Sources of Japanese History,* ed. David John Lu, vol. I (New York et al.: McGraw-Hill Book Co., 1974); fewer still exist as insertions or appendices in narrative works, like "The Legacy of Tokugawa Ieyasu," in A. L. Sadler, *The Maker of Modern Japan: The Life of Tokugawa Ieyasu* (London: Allen and Unwin, 1977 [1937]), excerpted for this chapter.

The standard biography of Tokugawa is A. L. Sadler, *The Maker of Modern Japan,* just cited. But there is a recent, excellent biography by Conrad Totman, *Tokugawa Ieyasu: Shogun* (San Francisco: Heian International, Inc., 1983). Totman is one of a very few current western authorities on the Tokugawa period, and students are also referred to his excellent survey, *Japan before Perry: A Short History* (Berkeley: University of California Press, 1987), which stresses the Tokugawa period. A similar work is George Sansom, *A History of Japan, 1334–1615* (Stanford: Stanford University Press, 1961), excerpted for this chapter. An older standard work is still useful—the massive James Murdoch and Isoh Yamagata, *A History of Japan,* vol. II, *During the Century of Early Foreign Intercourse (1542–1651)* (London: Kegan Paul, Trench, Trubner and Co., 1925); as is the topically organized Jonathan Norton Leonard, *Early Japan* in the "Great Ages of Man" series (New York: Time–Life, 1968).

There are a number of very good books on specialized topics in the

Tokugawa period: Conrad D. Totman, *Politics in the Tokugawa Bakufu 1600–1843* (Cambridge: Harvard University Press, 1967); Harold Bolitho, *Treasures among Men: The Fudai Daimyo in Tokugawa Japan* (New Haven and London: Yale University Press, 1974); Herschel Webb, *The Japanese Imperial Institution in the Tokugawa Period* (New York and London: Columbia University Press, 1968); *Studies in the Institutional History of Early Modern Japan*, ed. John W. Hall and Marius B. Jansen (Princeton: Princeton University Press, 1968); and Herman Ooms, *Tokugawa Ideology: Early Constructs, 1570–1680* (Princeton: Princeton University Press, 1985).

Among the best general works in which Tokugawa and the Tokugawa period are treated is Edwin O. Reischauer, *Japan: The Story of a Nation*, 2nd ed. (New York: Knopf, 1974), excerpted for this chapter. There is a third edition (1981) of this book in which the treatment of this period is somewhat abbreviated. Also recommended is another of Reischauer's books, co-authored with Albert M. Craig, *Japan: Tradition and Transformation* (Boston: Houghton Mifflin, 1978) and G. B. Sansom, *Japan: A Short Cultural History*, rev. ed. (New York: Appleton-Century-Crofts, 1962); John Whitney Hall, *Japan from Prehistory to Modern Times* (New York: Delacorte Press, 1970); and Mikiso Hane, *Modern Japan: A Historical Survey* (Boulder and London: Westview Press, 1986).

GALILEO GALILEI

THE CRIME
OF GALILEO

1564	Born
1592	Became professor of mathematics, University of Padua
1610	Invented Galilean telescope
1632	Published *A Dialogue Concerning the Two Chief World Systems*
1633	Condemned by Inquisition
1642	Died

In the opening years of the seventeenth century, Galileo Galilei was one of the most famous people in the world. Since 1592 he had been professor of mathematics at the great University of Padua, and in 1610 became "first philosopher and mathematician" to the grand duke of Tuscany, Cosimo dei Medici, who had been his tutorial student. He was the familiar of princes, wealthy patricians, high officials of the church, and other scientists and mathematicians all over Europe. He was the principal advocate in Italy for the new natural philosophy, the usual name for the scientific interests that were beginning to become a passion with scientists and laymen alike.

In 1609 Galileo had heard about the development of a primitive perspective instrument by some Dutch spectacle makers that made distant objects appear larger and nearer. He built such an instrument himself and promptly improved its magnification so dramatically that it could be used for practical astronomical observation. He had invented the Galilean telescope. He observed the surface of the moon, the phases of Venus, the moons of Jupiter, the first hint of Saturn's rings, the phenomenon of sunspots, and that the Milky Way was actually a collection of enormously distant stars. In the following year, he published these observations in a little pamphlet volume entitled *Sidereus nuncius* [The Starry Messenger]. It was an instant sensation.

Even more exciting to Galileo than his astronomical discoveries was the support they clearly gave to the Copernican theory of the universe—that the sun and not the earth was its center and that the planets, including the earth, rotated around the sun, "the lamp that illumines the whole universe." Galileo had long believed in the validity of the rational and mathematical arguments that Copernicus had put forward in 1543 in his *De revolutionibus orbium coelestium.* Galileo had corresponded with his great German contemporary, the astronomer Johannes Kepler, also a dedicated Copernican, and had been free in letters to friends and colleagues in his espousal of the Copernican theory. He eagerly entered into a number of controversies with conservative academics who refused to accept the truth or consequences of his astronomical observations. In a dispute over the nature of sunspots in 1612, Galileo, in defending his own views on these phenomena, publicly and in print unequivocally endorsed the Copernican theory.

But by this time the Copernican theory was running into serious trouble, and so was Galileo. The Copernican theory was not simply a theory that one was free or not to accept—at least not in Catholic countries. For the church had long since accepted the older Ptolemaic model of the earth-centered universe, and it had become an integral part of the official Catholic ideology. Thus the whole issue of Copernicanism became not merely an astronomical and mathematical proposition; it was a religious issue, and a dangerous one. The new Catholic attitude of the early seventeenth century was that of the Counter Reformation church, the revived and militant church prepared more than ever to defend its ancient truths. There was little disposition to accommodate radical new views that stood in opposition to established doctrine, and even less disposition to tolerate those who held such radical views. Moreover, from 1613 to 1615, in a series of published letters—actually treatises—Galileo had tried to defend the new sciences generally and the Copernican theory specifically in arguments that were as much theological as they were scientific. He was a loyal son of the church, and he wanted passionately to prevent its making a tragic error in this entire matter of the new theory of the universe.

But it became increasingly clear that the church was moving the other way, Galileo went himself to Rome early in 1615 to defend Copernicanism. He was courteously enough received by great churchmen, some of whom listened to him patiently and a few of whom supported his views. But then, on February 25, 1616, after a careful examination by a committee of theologians, the doctrine of Copernicus was formally condemned by the Congregation of the Index, summoned by Pope Paul V himself. It would have been condemned out of hand as heretical except for Galileo's friend, Cardinal Bellarmine, who intervened to have it declared simply "erroneous in the faith." But what about Galileo? He was not only a vocal and celebrated advocate of the now condemned theory, but he had already been denounced to the Inquisition by a number of his enemies. At the pope's own order he was summoned, on the day following the decree, to appear before Cardinal Bellarmine, the chief theologian of the church, and told that he must neither "hold nor defend" the theory of Copernicus.

Galileo returned to Florence heartbroken. He kept silent on the issue for the next seven years and devoted himself to noncontroversial work. Then in 1623 Maffeo Barberini, his longtime friend and supporter, was elected Pope Urban VIII. Galileo hastened to Rome, confident that he could secure the revocation of the decree of 1616 and gain permission to write the great book he had long planned, "*On the System or Constitution of the World,* an immense design, full of philosophy, astronomy, and geometry."[1] He was wrong on both counts. The pope refused to reverse the condemnation of the Copernican theory. Moreover, failing totally to understand what Galileo really wanted, he would permit him to write about the constitution of the world only if he would write about both the Copernican system and the Ptolemaic and if he did not presume to choose between them.

Galileo agreed, and in 1632 he published his *Dialogue Concerning the Two Chief World Systems—Ptolemaic and Copernican.*

---

[1]From a letter to Belisario Vinta quoted in Galileo Galilei, *Dialogue on the Great World Systems,* ed. Giorgio de Santillana (Chicago: University of Chicago Press, 1953), Historical Introduction, p. xi.

The Two Chief World Systems

GALILEO GALILEI

The idea of a great, far-ranging work on the nature of the universe as seen in Copernican terms had long obsessed Galileo. He had mentioned it in 1597 in a letter to Kepler. In 1610, in the *Starry Messenger*, he had referred to it as a forthcoming book. And references to it continued to crop up in his writings. But that was all changed by the pope's injunction of 1624. He would have to write a quite different book. He struggled with it, delayed by illness and family responsibilities. It was finally completed in January 1630, and he began the task of getting it licensed by the church to be printed. Rome delayed for almost two years and finally, under pressure from the Florentine ambassador, granted the imprimatur, with some trifling revisions to the title page. Florentine church authorities had already given their approval. The book, published in Florence on February 21, 1632, took the form of a dialogue with three participants. Filippo Salviati, a Florentine nobleman, friend, and supporter of Galileo, was represented as the advocate for Copernicanism. An imaginary character, Simplicio, was the defender of the Ptolemaic-Aristotelian traditional arguments. And the Venetian patrician Giovanni Sagredo, uncommitted to either view, was the audience to whom the other two addressed themselves. It was set in Sagredo's palace in Venice and ran through four days of conversation.

The book was an immediate success despite its large size, its abstruse subject, and its formidable mathematics. Within five months every copy was sold. In large part it was successful because it was controversial. In clear and unmistakable violation of the ban of the church, Galileo defended the Copernican theory—and boldly said as much in his preface. In the dialogue itself, the arguments of Simplicio for the Ptolemaic view are systematically and enthusiastically demolished. At the very end of the dialogue, there is a weak and perfunctory admission by both disputants that no one can "limit and restrict the Divine power or wisdom to some particular fancy of his own" or really "discover the work of His hands." It was no more than the merest lip service to the demand that the pope had made of Galileo.

Here is Galileo's preface.

Several years ago there was published in Rome a salutary edict which, in order to obviate the dangerous tendencies of our present age, imposed a seasonable silence upon the Pythagorean opinion that the earth moves.[2] There were those who impudently asserted that this decree had its origin not in judicious inquiry, but in passion none too well informed. Complaints were to be heard that advisers who were totally unskilled at astronomical observations ought not to clip the wings of reflective intellects by means of rash prohibitions.

Upon hearing such carping insolence, my zeal could not be contained. Being thoroughly informed about that prudent determination, I decided to appear openly in the theater of the world as a witness of the sober truth. I was at that time in Rome; I was not only received by the most eminent prelates of that Court, but had their applause; indeed, this decree was not published without some previous notice of it having been given to me. Therefore I propose in the present work to show to foreign nations that as much is understood of this matter in Italy, and particularly in Rome, as transalpine diligence can ever have imagined. Collecting all the reflections that properly concern the Copernican system, I shall make it known that everything was brought before the attention of the Roman censorship, and that there proceed from this clime not only dogmas for the welfare of the soul, but ingenious discoveries for the delight of the mind as well.

To this end I have taken the Copernican side in the discourse, proceeding as with a pure mathematical hypothesis and striving by every artifice to represent it as superior to supposing the earth motionless—not, indeed, absolutely, but as against the arguments of some professed Peripatetics.[3] These men indeed deserve not even that name, for they do not walk about; they are content to adore the shadows, philosophizing not with due circumspection but merely from having memorized a few ill-understood principles. . . .

In the course of the third day, we find the most outspoken defense of Copernicus. Salviati is speaking:

. . . I have often seen Jupiter and Venus together, twenty-five or thirty degrees from the sun, the sky being very dark. Venus would

---

[2]It was believed by Galileo, as earlier by Copernicus, that the ancient Greek heliocentric theory—probably actually first enunciated by Aristarchus—was one of the teachings of Pythagoras.—ED.

[3]The usual name for Aristotelians which is to say, in this context, defenders of the Ptolemaic theory. The term literally means "those who walk about."—ED.

appear eight or even ten times as large as Jupiter when looked at with the naked eye. But seen afterward through a telescope, Jupiter's disc would be seen to be actually four or more times as large as Venus. Yet the liveliness of Venus's brilliance was incomparably greater than the pale light of Jupiter, which comes about only because Jupiter is very distant from the sun and from us, while Venus is close to us and to the sun.

These things having been explained, it will not be difficult to understand how it might be that Mars, when in opposition to the sun and therefore seven or more times as close to the earth as when it is near conjunction, looks to us scarcely four or five times as large in the former state as in the latter. Nothing but irradiation is the cause of this. For if we deprive it of the adventitious rays we shall find it enlarged in exactly the proper ratio. And to remove its head of hair from it, the telescope is the unique and supreme means. Enlarging its disc nine hundred or a thousand times, it causes this to be seen bare and bounded like that of the moon, and in the two positions varying in exactly the proper proportion.

Next in Venus, which at its evening conjunction when it is beneath the sun ought to look almost forty times as large as in its morning conjunction, and is seen as not even doubled, it happens in addition to the effects of irradiation that it is sickle-shaped, and its horns, besides being very thin, receive the sun's light obliquely and therefore very weakly. So that because it is small and feeble, it makes its irradiations less ample and lively than when it shows itself to us with its entire hemisphere lighted. But the telescope plainly shows us its horns to be as bounded and distinct as those of the moon, and they are seen to belong to a very large circle, in a ratio almost forty times as great as the same disc when it is beyond the sun, toward the end of its morning appearances.

SAGR. O Nicholas Copernicus, what a pleasure it would have been for you to see this part of your system confirmed by so clear an experiment!

SALV. Yes, but how much less would his sublime intellect be celebrated among the learned! For as I said before, we may see that with reason as his guide he resolutely continued to affirm what sensible experience seemed to contradict. I cannot get over my amazement that he was constantly willing to persist in saying that Venus might go around the sun and be more than six times as far from us at one time as at another, and still look always equal, when it should have appeared forty times larger.

SAGR. I believe then that in Jupiter, Saturn, and Mercury one ought also to see differences of size corresponding exactly to their varying distances.

SALV. In the two outer planets I have observed this with precision in almost every one of the past twenty-two years. In Mercury no observations of importance can be made, since it does not allow itself to be seen except at its maximum angles with the sun, in which the inequalities of its distances from the earth are imperceptible. Hence such differences are unobservable, and so are its changes of shape, which must certainly take place as in Venus. But when we do see it, it would necessarily show itself to us in the shape of a semicircle, just as Venus does at its maximum angles, though its disc is so small and its brilliance so lively that the power of the telescope is not sufficient to strip off its hair so that it may appear completely shorn.

It remains for us to remove what would seem to be a great objection to the motion of the earth. This is that though all the planets turn about the sun, the earth alone is not solitary like the others but goes together in the company of the moon and the whole elemental sphere around the sun in one year, while at the same time the moon moves around the earth every month. Here one must once more exclaim over and exalt the admirable perspicacity of Copernicus, and simultaneously regret his misfortune at not being alive in our day. For now Jupiter removes this apparent anomaly of the earth and moon moving conjointly. We see Jupiter, like another earth, going around the sun in twelve years accompanied not by one but by four moons, together with everything that may be contained within the orbits of its four satellites.

SAGR. And what is the reason for your calling the four Jovian planets "moons"?

SALV. That is what they would appear to be to anyone who saw them from Jupiter. For they are dark in themselves, and receive their light from the sun; this is obvious from their being eclipsed when they enter into the cone of Jupiter's shadow. And since only that hemisphere of theirs is illuminated which faces the sun, they always look entirely illuminated to us who are outside their orbits and closer to the sun; but to anyone on Jupiter they would look completely lighted only when they were at the highest points of their circles. In the lowest part—that is, when between Jupiter and the sun—they would appear horned from Jupiter. In a word, they would make for Jovians the same changes of shape which the moon makes for us Terrestrials.

Now you can see how admirably these three notes harmonize with the Copernican system, when at first they seemed so discordant with it. From this, Simplicio will be much better able to see with what great probability one may conclude that not the earth, but the sun, is the center of rotation of the planets. And since this amounts to placing the earth among the world bodies which indubitably move about the sun (above Mercury and Venus but beneath Saturn, Jupiter, and

Mars), why will it not likewise be probable, or perhaps even necessary, to admit that it also goes around? . . .[4]

SIMP. But what anomalies are there in the Ptolemaic arrangement which are not matched by greater ones in the Copernican?

SALV. The illnesses are in Ptolemy, and the cures for them in Copernicus. First of all, do not all philosophical schools hold it to be a great impropriety for a body having a natural circular movement to move irregularly with respect to its own center and regularly around another point?[5] Yet Ptolemy's structure is composed of such uneven movements, while in the Copernican system each movement is equable around its own center. With Ptolemy it is necessary to assign to the celestial bodies contrary movements, and make everything move from east to west and at the same time from west to east, whereas with Copernicus all celestial revolutions are in one direction, from west to east. And what are we to say of the apparent movement of a planet, so uneven that it not only goes fast at one time and slow at another, but sometimes stops entirely and even goes backward a long way after doing so? To save these appearances, Ptolemy introduces vast epicycles, adapting them one by one to each planet, with certain rules about incongruous motions—all of which can be done away with by one very simple motion of the earth. Do you not think it extremely absurd, Simplicio, that in Ptolemy's construction where all planets are assigned their own orbits, one above another, it should be necessary to say that Mars, placed above the sun's sphere, often falls so far that it breaks through the sun's orb, descends below this and gets closer to the earth than the body of the sun is, and then a little later soars immeasurably above it? Yet these and other anomalies are cured by a single and simple annual movement of the earth. . . .

At the end of the discourse of the fourth day, there occurs the weak disclaimer of both systems. Salviati is speaking again:

To you, Sagredo, though during my arguments you have shown yourself satisfied with some of my ideas and have approved them highly, I say that I take this to have arisen partly from their novelty rather than

---

[4] The Copernican theory not only described the earth's planetary movement but its rotation. The Ptolemaic, of course, held that neither kind of motion existed.—ED.

[5] Galileo was apparently unaware of his friend Kepler's theory about the elliptical orbits of the planets. But even if he did know about it, he never accepted the notion himself.—ED.

from their certainty, and even more from your courteous wish to afford me by your assent that pleasure which one naturally feels at the approbation and praise of what is one's own. And as you have obligated me to you by your urbanity, so Simplicio has pleased me by his ingenuity. Indeed, I have become very fond of him for his constancy in sustaining so forcibly and so undauntedly the doctrines of his master. And I thank you, Sagredo, for your most courteous motivation, just as I ask pardon of Simplicio if I have offended him sometimes with my too heated and opinionated speech. Be sure that in this I have not been moved by any ulterior purpose, but only by that of giving you every opportunity to introduce lofty thoughts, that I might be better informed.

SIMP. You need not make any excuses; they are superfluous, and especially so to me, who, being accustomed to public debates, have heard disputants countless times not merely grow angry and get excited at each other, but even break out into insulting speech and sometimes come very close to blows.

As to the discourses we have held, and especially this last one concerning the reasons for the ebbing and flowing of the ocean, I am really not entirely convinced,[6] but from such feeble ideas of the matter as I have formed, I admit that your thoughts seem to me more ingenious than many others I have heard. I do not therefore consider them true and conclusive; indeed, keeping always before my mind's eye a most solid doctrine that I once heard from a most eminent and learned person, and before which one must fall silent, I know that if asked whether God in His infinite power and wisdom could have conferred upon the watery element its observed reciprocating motion using some other means than moving its containing vessels, both of you would reply that He could have, and that He would have known how to do this in many ways which are unthinkable to our minds. From this I forthwith conclude that, this being so, it would be excessive boldness for anyone to limit and restrict the Divine power and wisdom to some particular fancy of his own.

SALV. An admirable and angelic doctrine, and well in accord with another one, also Divine, which, while it grants to us the right to argue about the constitution of the universe (perhaps in order that the working of the human mind shall not be curtailed or made lazy) adds that we cannot discover the work of His hands. Let us, then, exercise these activities permitted to us and ordained by God, that we

---

[6]Much of the argument of the day had been devoted to Galileo's theory that the ocean tides were related to the rotation of the earth—a mistaken notion.—ED.

may recognize and thereby so much the more admire His greatness, however much less fit we may find ourselves to penetrate the profound depths of His infinite wisdom.

The Crime of Galileo

GIORGIO DE SANTILLANA

The pope was furious. He had every reason to believe he had been betrayed by Galileo's *Dialogue*. Galileo's enemies were clamoring for his condemnation. The process of an inquiry by the Inquisition was begun, and in less than a year Galileo was summoned to Rome to stand trial. In June 1633 he was judged to have held and taught the Copernican theory, against the teachings of the church. This was the crime of Galileo. He was ordered to recant and did so. The normal sentence of life imprisonment was commuted to house arrest by the pope, and Galileo was permitted to return to his estate near Florence where he lived and worked for the remaining eight years of his life.

His "crime" remains the center of the Galileo biography. Why did he do it? It was not an unwitting or accidental transgression. It was a clear and willful act of defiance. Was he courting martyrdom? Nothing in his behavior before or during his trial suggests it. One can only conclude that the vindication of his ideas was an important enough issue for the risk involved. And what risk did he take? He had obviously violated the spirit of the pope's instructions about the *Dialogue,* but his book had been licensed by the pope's own censors in Rome and Galileo could claim that he had legally abided by the pope's instructions—no matter how badly.

But there was another set of instructions, going back to the original condemnation of Copernicanism in 1616 and Galileo's interview with Cardinal Bellarmine. What had he been told or not told by the cardinal? It is clear that when the judgment of the Inquisition was finally made, Galileo was surprised and outraged at the severity of the sentence. Why? Because he had reason to believe he had stayed within the letter of the church's law on the matter. Two documents had turned up in the course of the trial, both having to do with the crucial interview with Bellarmine. One was in the Inquisition's file and was an official minute by its commissary general stating that he had been present at the interview and had personally warned Galileo not to hold or teach the theory of Copernicus "in any way whatsoever." Galileo claimed to know nothing about such a warning. And he, in turn, produced a certified copy of Cardinal Bellarmine's considerably milder charge to him. If the one document was a surprise to Galileo, the other was a surprise to the court. Bellarmine's certificate had not become a part of the record. Given this ambiguity, Galileo had reason to expect leniency, indeed, may have been promised leniency if he would simply recant. But the case had become as much a trial for the church as for Galileo, and he had to be made an example. Hence the severity of his sentence.

By most accounts, the crux of Galileo's trial and the charges against him was that now remote interview with Cardinal Bellarmine seventeen years before, and the conflicting documents. Many scholars have speculated about this matter. We excerpt opinions by two of the leading modern Galileo scholars. The first is that of Giorgio de Santillana from his book *The Crime of Galileo*.

What can be the conclusion concerning that famous injunction of 1616? It is, and will remain to the end, the kingpin of the case. With it, from the legal aspect, the trial stands or falls. It came to our notice how everything connected with it was being surrounded all along with a screen of vague, reticent, or misleading language so as to protect it from indiscreet curiosity.

Some curiosity is therefore in order. We are going to review the evidence, starting from the two critical documents. . . . One of them is the injunction; the other is Bellarmine's certificate.

"Friday, the twenty-sixth [of February]. At the palace, the usual residence of the Lord Cardinal Bellarmino, the said Galileo, having been summoned and being present before the said Lord Cardinal, was, in presence of the Most Reverend Michelangelo Segizi of Lodi, O.P., Commissary-General of the Holy Office, by the said Cardinal, warned of the error of the aforesaid opinion and admonished to abandon it; and immediately thereafter, before me and before witnesses, the Lord Cardinal being still present, the said Galileo was by the said Commissary commanded and enjoined, in the name of His Holiness the Pope and the whole Congregation of the Holy Office, to relinquish altogether said opinion that the Sun is the center of the world and immovable and that the Earth moves; nor further to hold, teach, or defend it in any way whatsoever, verbally or in writing; otherwise proceedings would be taken against him in the Holy Office; which injunction the said Galileo acquiesced in and promised to obey. Done at Rome, in the place aforesaid, in the presence of R. Bandino Nores and Agostino Mongardo, members of the household of said Cardinal, witnesses."

"We, Roberto Cardinal Bellarmino, having heard that it is calumniously reported that Signor Galileo Galilei has in our hand abjured and has also been punished with salutary penance, and being requested to state the truth as to this, declare that the said Signor Galileo has not adjured, either in our hand, or the hand of any other person here in Rome, or anywhere else, so far as we know, any opinion or doctrine held by him; neither has any salutary penance been imposed on him; but that only the declaration made by the Holy Father and published by the Sacred Congregation of the Index has been notified to him, wherein it is set forth that the doctrine attributed to Copernicus, that the Earth moves around the Sun and that the Sun is stationary in the center of the world and does not move from east to west, is contrary to the Holy Scriptures and therefore cannot be defended or held. In witness whereof we have written and subscribed these presents with our hand this twenty-sixth day of May, 1616."

. . . The first document looks gravely irregular both as to form and as to its place in the file; [and] the instructions of the Congregation to Bellarmine, as well as Bellarmine's subsequent report on what he had done that day, agree with his certificate and *not* with the injunction; and . . . there was in fact no allowable ground for an injunction as things stood.

We have seen further that in his most carefully considered piece of writing, the Preface to the *Dialogue,* Galileo deliberately mentions the famous audience as a signal distinction. He is actually calling the authorities to witness against the rumors that had been spread of a secret recantation. This would have been to provoke them foolishly if he had not been quite assured that things stood, in fact, so.

The natural supposition is that the record was hastily fabricated in 1632 when the authorities were trying to get a case against Galileo. . . .

Thus the matter stood for decades; it seemed suspended pending new evidence. This came eventually, not from any document, but from new physical means of analysis. In 1927 Laemmel, with the cooperation of the Vatican authorities, submitted the doubtful page first to soft X-rays and then to the much more rigorous test of the Hanau ultraviolet lamp. The result left no doubt on one point at least: the pages had never been tampered with. . . . The text is in exactly the same hand as other neighboring and certainly genuine documents; hence, it was written at or about the same time. To this we can add a clinching argument: the contemporary pagination shows that the original, if there ever was one, never got into the file; and therefore the decision to replace it with a falsification must have been taken then and there.

Still, there is something that remains hard to explain. The operation is curiously botched. The lack of an original alone might be construed as a mishap, for an inserted double sheet may drop out, but the wrong substitute job in the wrong place is painfully lasting evidence. A regular judge would have had to throw out the injunction on that evidence alone; even the judges of 1633 did not dare rely too much on it.

Should one see here plain cynical disregard for regularity? We would doubt it very much. Regularity was a fetish with the administration, and any such detectable irregularity always entailed a risk for its author. It would almost look as though the thing had been done by someone not in full control of events and having to make shift with what he had. Even so, from a Commissary-General able to arrange things at his will, one might expect more resourceful solutions. . . .

So there might remain a point of doubt. Let us check our conclusions as they stand by assuming the opposite to be true, namely, that things happened as written and that Galileo really stands guilty of violating his instructions. We would then have to say that the protocol was accidentally lost as soon as made out: that the official doing the pagination never noticed its absence; that someone noticed it soon afterward; and that it was deemed sufficient to insert a transcription which can only have been done from memory, for, if the original had been available somewhere, it would have been put back into place. It does not sound very convincing.

Thus we are led back perforce to our version, and the question why the operation was carried out so and not otherwise turns out to be simply a statement of the Commissary's best judgment, based upon what he thought could be done and could not be done. The straight fact that emerges is that it was not held to be quite essential to have the protocol—or, rather, that, following Bellarmine's audience, it was deemed better to have no protocol at all rather than an authentic version of that audience. And so we may be led to conclude that the Commissary simply decided to do without one. Regularity has its limits. But, it would seem, falsification has too.

We know that there had been a strong tension in 1616 between the higher authorities who had decided on diplomacy and the Dominicans, bent at that time on repression. Vatican quarters several times hinted to Guicciardini that "the monks" were relentless. We may then reconstruct as follows: The Commissary, as he watched the scene (we know he was present), was disgusted with the easy way in which Galileo was let off, and he decided to omit the protocol, although his instructions were clear, and the witnesses already designated, obviously by the Cardinal himself. On going back to his office, he told his assistant to arrange a more helpful minute of the proceedings. "And," he may have added, "make it stiff, just in case. What they don't know doesn't hurt them; when trouble arises, it is we who have to take it on." Or it may be, of course, that the assistant, Father Tinti, did the job on his own initiative. But it seems very unlikely. This theory would have the merit of explaining naturally why the protocol was omitted from the pagination as well as accounting for the other facts in the case.

To look at that silent sheet now, after three centuries, gives one a strange feeling, as though it were trying to tell us something. The first part, which reproduces the papal decree, is dealt out with well-practiced smoothness. As soon as it comes to the injunction, the lines get closer, and the writing becomes less legible, as though the writer were unconsciously trying to duck.

The falsification as such is, then, beyond doubt—truly by modern standards, an exceedingly modest one. Father Segizi would never have dared forge a protocol. He had done a little something, the least he could do, in order to provide a toehold for prosecution if that were needed. . . .

Going back to Galileo, we can see that the course of events agrees with our previous conclusion. For not only, as we have shown, did Galileo feel completely confident that the officials were mistaken when the matter was finally revealed to him (and that would have been rather the time for him to grovel) but those very officials demonstrated, by their manner of handling the procedure of injunction when it was really necessary (viz., in order to summon Galileo to Rome), the elaborate context of rules in which such an act is framed. Here was a man who had patently fooled them, who was now subtly evading and challenging them; and yet a whole contraption had to be worked out in order to have something that would serve for an injunction without a previous refusal to motivate it. . . .

In the light of these later events it appears all the more incongruous that in 1616, when all was still clear, the Commissary should have sprung forward brandishing his threat *incontinenti,* as soon as Bellarmine had considerately informed Galileo that his theory had been found wrong, without even giving him the time to declare his acquiescence to the new ruling.

These problems really all reflect to the credit of the institution. In fear of its own absolute and unlimited powers, it had framed for itself such a rigid set of rules that, when the need came for cutting corners, it could not do so by merely stretching the interpretation. As a result, certain officials, who held the view that when a job has to be done it has to be done, did not shrink from altering the records without the acquiescence of their superiors. . . .

To maintain that Bellarmine himself was a party to the deceit ought to be out of the question. The operation seems to begin and end in the office of the Commissary-General of the time, Father Michelangelo Segizi, among those implacable Dominicans to whom Guicciardini alludes, "fired with holy zeal" [and] convinced that mathematicians are a tool of the Devil, who thought it an excellent precaution against the Adversary to put in this pretended registration. No one need be deceived by it if he did not want to, they thought; and, meanwhile, here was a trap to snare the Evil One in case of need. As it happened, it was Pope Urban and the Congregation who were to be snared in it. . . .

It might still be asked, finally: Why did Galileo in person never pronounce himself explicitly on the subject? He was the man to know. Well, we do have a fairly explicit statement from him—as explicit as he could make it without contempt of court. . . . He told the judges that he would not recite the formula of abjuration, even at the risk of dire penalties, *if it contained anything implying that he had ever deceived his censors and specifically in the matter of extorting a license.* And in fact it does not, although the sentence was built upon this specific accusation, and hence a penitential admission was in order. But, if he does *not* admit that he did "artfully and cunningly" refrain from telling about the injunction, then Galileo is saying as clearly as he can, in the face of the authorities, that the injunction never existed. And this ought to answer the question.

A Historical Speculation

STILLMAN DRAKE

Giorgio de Santillana argues in the foregoing passage that the injunction forbidding Galileo "to hold, teach, or defend . . . in any way whatsoever, verbally or in writing" the theory of Copernicus was a forgery, done by or at the bidding of Father Michelangelo Segizi, the commissary general of the Inquisition.

In the following excerpt, Stillman Drake, the principal translator of Galileo's writings and an acknowledged authority on Galileo, maintains that the disputed document is not a forgery. Rather, he sees it as a case of bureaucratic inertia, a notation routinely made, duly filed, and forgotten for seventeen years. He makes his case in what he calls "a historical speculation," a reconstruction of what must have happened in the background of "one of the most dramatic trials in history."

Two theories have long prevailed concerning the events of February 26, 1616, when Galileo was called before Cardinal Bellarmine and admonished to abandon the Copernican theory. Either theory has strong points in its favor and equally strong objections. One theory places Galileo in a good light and the Church in a bad one; the other reverses this. Competent scholars for nearly a century—that is, since all the known documents have been opened to examination and publication—have taken one side or the other, or have scrupulously withheld judgment. No real third alternative, to the best of my knowledge, has been put forth. . . .

. . . Everything seems to hinge upon the reliability of one crucial document, the copy of a supposed minute of the proceedings, bound into the official records used by the Inquisition at Galileo's trial in 1633. Advocates of the theory, which places Galileo in a good light, led in recent years by Professor Santillana, regard this document as a fabrication, a spurious account that includes events which never took place. This entails certain difficulties, for the minute has precisely the same authority as most of the documents which must be accepted in order to reconstruct the events. But this apparent disadvantage is not fatal, since the adversaries of this view labor under similar difficulties. In accepting the minute at its face value, they in turn are constrained to give a labored explanation of the existence or meaning of two or three documents of unquestioned authenticity. . . .

The two received theories appear to be poles apart, especially when considered in terms of the fundamental question whether the minute itself is true or false. Any third alternative may seem preposterous. Yet I shall advance the thesis that another theory is tenable; furthermore, that in the light of this theory, neither of the two prevalent interpretations is far from the truth, nor are they so far apart as they have previously seemed to be. . . .

In the winter of 1615–1616, Galileo debated often and publicly at Rome on the topic of the earth's motion. In these debates he succeeded in demolishing the position of his opponents, even if he did not win many converts to his own views. It was an inevitable consequence of his position that certain statements in the Bible would have to be reinterpreted. Now, freedom to interpret the Bible was a sore point with Catholic authorities at the time; this was one of the particular issues between them and the founders of various Protestant sects. Hence Galileo's plea that the Church continue to tolerate the teachings of Copernicus was one that could not be readily granted.

Though personally unsympathetic with the intellectuals of his time, Pope Paul V was cautious about alienating this influential group. Accordingly he consulted Cardinal Bellarmine, who was not only the leading theologian at Rome but was also an able administrator. As theologian, Bellarmine remarked that so long as astronomers took the idea of the earth's motion only hypothetically, there was no overt contradiction of the Bible; as administrator, he maintained that it was always a poor idea for the Church to take an official position on any matter where decision could be postponed or avoided. The Pope replied that he was aware of all this, but that Galileo was making an infernal nuisance of himself and had forced matters to a point where some official action had to be taken. In that event, answered Bellarmine, it would be necessary to stop all theological discussions of the earth's motion and to correct or suppress any books containing theological arguments in its favor. The proper procedure would be to submit the question to a duly constituted committee of theologians and to base official action on their ruling, the nature of which was easily predictable. Galileo, he was certain, would obey such an edict as a good Catholic; and since he alone was the present source of difficulty, the problem would be solved without the actual prohibition of Copernicanism. To make sure of this, however, he would undertake to test Galileo's obedience privately before the edict was published, and if there were any doubt about his cooperation, stronger measures could be applied. In view of the strong support Galileo enjoyed politically, intellectually, and in Church circles, it would be good to avoid the appearance of any personal or vindictive action in the matter.

Satisfied with Bellarmine's advice, the Pope appointed a council which duly reported its findings against the doctrine of the motion of the earth and stability of the sun. On the twenty-fifth of February, 1616, the Pope specifically instructed Bellarmine to call Galileo before him and admonished him to abandon these views as contrary to Scripture. If he refused, then the Commissary General of the Inquisition was to command him in the presence of a notary and witnesses to desist from such teachings, lest he be imprisoned. It is perfectly clear from the wording of this order that two separate actions were contemplated, the second to ensue only if the first failed; and it is equally clear that the presence of a notary and witnesses would be entirely out of place at the first action, which was to be informal and friendly in character.

Seghizzi, the Commissary General, was present when the Pope gave these instructions. He belonged to the Dominican order, which traditionally had charge of the Inquisition. He did not particularly like or trust the Jesuits, who had usurped the role of the Dominicans as leaders in Catholic education, and he was especially distrustful of the relatively liberal views of Bellarmine. Accordingly he decided to be personally present at Bellarmine's interview with Galileo, in order to make sure that if Galileo did object, Bellarmine would not reason with him and win him over rather than subject him to official action by the Inquisition. Thus on the morning of the twenty-sixth, shortly after Bellarmine had dispatched two of his familiars (special officers of arrest attached to the household of each Cardinal Inquisitor) to fetch Galileo, Seghizzi with a notary and some Dominican fathers paid a visit to Bellarmine's residence.

The visit was unusual, and Bellarmine quickly guessed its true purpose, which was personally offensive to him. At his age, and in his high position, he did not need any lesser officials present to see that he carried out his assignment properly. Still, there was no tactful way to get rid of them, and he could scarcely order them out of his house. Before long, the arrival of the officers with Galileo was announced. Bellarmine rose and went to the door of the audience chamber to greet Galileo, hat in hand, as was his custom with every guest of whatever condition. Indignant at Seghizzi's abuse of his hospitality and determined to render it pointless, he said in low tones to Galileo as they turned to enter, "His Holiness expects your precise obedience to what I am about to tell you." Then they returned together to the Cardinal's chair, and after seating himself, Bellarmine benignly announced to Galileo the decision of the council and admonished him to obey it.

Meanwhile, Seghizzi was thinking rapidly. He was no fool, and he guessed easily enough that Bellarmine had warned Galileo to voice no objection. Thus he had not only been outwitted, but by the very act of coming uninvited he had cut off any chance, however slight, that Galileo might be recalcitrant and that Bellarmine would turn him over to the Inquisition. Time was running out. There was only one way to save the day. When the Cardinal had finished his admonition, the Commissary was ready. Without allowing Galileo time for any reply, he proceeded to deliver his own stringent precept not to hold, defend or teach Copernicanism in any way, orally or in writing, lest Galileo suffer imprisonment. The latter, forewarned, simply replied that as a good son of the Holy Church he would obey, perhaps adding that he was relieved to know that the matter had at last been settled by superhuman authority, and thanking the Cardinal for his having given him advance notice of the edict that would soon be published.

The notary, sublimely ignorant of the Pope's instructions, was faithfully recording these events, and had written that the Commissary "immediately and without holding back" had delivered his precept on the heels of the Cardinal's admonition. Bellarmine was astonished and exasperated at this further affront to his dignity and clear disobedience of the Pope's orders by the Commissary. But he knew precisely what to do. Taking Galileo by the arm and ushering him to the door, he said that he was pleased by his submission to the Church, and that at another time he wished to speak further with him, but that he had important business to discuss with the others and could not detain him longer that day. If Seghizzi tried to interrupt, the Cardinal quelled him with a glance. When Galileo was safely out of doors, he returned and asked the Commissary to confer with him privately.

Seghizzi may have begun the conference by angrily remonstrating against Galileo's having been permitted to leave without signing the notary's account of the interview. Bellarmine replied that it would have done little good for Galileo to sign this, since he himself had not the slightest intention of putting his name to a wholly illegal proceeding in direct violation of the Pope's orders. Seghizzi would do well to destroy this minute, he said. If the Pope were ever told precisely what had happened, he would be much incensed. . . .

Bellarmine gave his report to the Pope and the Cardinals of the Inquisition on March third precisely as if his own admonition were all that had been given to Galileo. Seghizzi, who was present, said not a word. The Pope then gave instructions for publication of the edict. . . .

In 1632, when the *Dialogue* was finally published and sent to Rome, the principal persons involved in the proceedings of 1616 were all dead except Galileo. The cardinals and officers of the Inquisition in 1633 had no reason whatever to doubt the authenticity of the copied minute as a faithful account of the instructions given to Galileo in 1616. Thus the rage of Pope Urban VIII, who had been Galileo's friend, is not hard to understand. It appeared to him that Galileo had persuaded him to permit publication of an "impartial" discussion of the Ptolemaic and Copernican theories, while concealing from him a specific injunction never to teach the latter theory in any way. On the other hand, Galileo was not aware of any misdeed, for he had faithfully followed Bellarmine's instruction to remember only his admonition, treating all else as if it had never happened. Nor did Galileo suspect that the official records belied this instruction, for Bellarmine had been a Cardinal of the Inquisition and presumably had had authority to guard the record consistent with his own affidavit.

Thus was the ground laid for one of the most dramatic trials in history. At its outset, both sides were acting in good faith. When Galileo was interrogated about the events of 1616, he gave precisely the account that Bellarmine had told him to give, and he produced a copy of Bellarmine's certificate in support of this, adding that he could produce the original if required. Considering that none of the inquisitors could possibly have suspected the existence of such a document, it must indeed have created a sensation in the mind of the new

Commissary, Maculano. However, he calmly entered it in the record and proceeded with his examination. Galileo frankly admitted that some Dominican fathers were present on the occasion of the interview, but said he did not remember that any of them spoke to him. . . .

Maculano now pursued the question by asking whether, if he should read to Galileo what had actually been said at the time, Galileo would recall it. Galileo stood his ground resolutely, saying that he had frankly stated his recollection, and that he did not know that such a reading would alter his memory. Maculano then read to him the additional phrase "or teach in any way," and asked him if he remembered who had said this to him. Galileo reiterated that he did not recall anything having been said to him except by Cardinal Bellarmine. But for the first time, he now realized what the records must contain, and it was already too late for him to admit that anyone else had spoken to him. . . . Nor could Galileo's judges admit that he had been accused on the basis of a defective document in their own records.

Nevertheless, these men were judges and jurors of a strict tribunal, and they could not ignore the evidential value of Galileo's document. It is true that on April seventeenth, a committee of experts had found that Galileo had at least defended Copernicanism in the *Dialogue*, so that if the inquisitors were to drop the charge that he had been enjoined not to teach it in any way, he could still be found guilty of defending it. But no one wanted to drop the original charge at the cost of impugning the official records. . . .

It is apparent. . . that the trial was resumed only after Galileo had been induced to "cop a plea"; that is, had been promised a light sentence if he would cooperate by confessing to some lesser crime than that with which he was originally charged. It was a fair deal for both sides. Galileo could not hope to get off scot-free, and the inquisitors, with any kind of confession from him, could ignore the preponderance of the weight of Galileo's evidence over theirs on the crucial charge. Galileo's confession was duly handed in on April thirtieth. He said in effect that vanity had induced him to produce arguments of his own in favor of Copernicus without providing equally strong answers, but he insisted that there had been no wrong intention on his part. His defense, presented ten days later, explained the circumstances under which he had secured the affidavit from Bellarmine and stated that ". . . the two phrases in addition to 'hold' and 'defend,' which are 'teach' and 'in any way,' which I hear are contained in the command given to me and recorded, came to me as entirely new and [previously] unheard, and I do not think I should be doubted if in the course of fourteen or sixteen years they were lost to my memory. . . ."

At the end of April, the intention had been to make Galileo's punishment very light: probably a short term of imprisonment and some conventional religious penances. . . . But by the time the Cardinals of the Inquisition met again to pass sentence, at least one among them must have doubted the wisdom of letting him off lightly. . . . The only solution was to keep Galileo under physical arrest, while making the conditions of his detention easy for him. So long as he remained in the custody of the Inquisition, he would not dare breathe a word against that institution or in favor of Copernicanism, for the penalty against "relapsed heretics" was death.

Review and Study Questions

1. To what extent (and why) did Galileo violate his instructions from the pope in presenting the two world systems?

2. What do you think really happened during Galileo's interview with Cardinal Bellarmine?

3. Why was Galileo so conspicuously singled out by the church for persecution on so abstruse a subject as celestial mechanics?

4. Is there any justification for the position of the church in this matter? Discuss.

5. Can Galileo be judged culpable at all in these proceedings? Discuss.

Suggestions for Further Reading

There are two standard modern editions of Galileo's *Dialogue,* the one excerpted for this chapter, Galileo Galilei, *Dialogue Concerning the Two Chief World Systems—Ptolemaic and Copernican,* tr. and ed. Stillman Drake, foreword by Albert Einstein, 2nd ed. (Berkeley and Los Angeles: University of California Press, 1967), which is an entirely new translation and edition; and Galileo Galilei, *Dialogue on the Great World Systems,* in the Salusbury translation, rev. and ed. Giorgio de Santillana (Chicago: University of Chicago Press, 1953), which is a revised and annotated edition of the translation by the Englishman Thomas Salusbury in 1661. An anthology of Galileo's earlier writings, leading up to the *Dialogue,* is *Discoveries and Opinions of Galileo,* tr. and ed. Stillman Drake (New York: Doubleday, 1957). There are also two modern editions of Galileo's last major publication, *The Two New Sciences,* a treatise on mechanics and motion also written in dialogue form, which most authorities consider his most important scientific work. One is based on the definitive Italian national edition of 1913 by Antonio Favoro, *Dialogues concerning Two New Sciences,* tr. Henry

Crew and Alfonso de Salvio (Evanston: Northwestern University Press, 1950); the other is a totally new edition and translation, Galileo Galilei, *Two New Sciences*, tr. and ed. Stillman Drake (Madison: University of Wisconsin Press, 1974). And there are recent editions of two of Galileo's earlier writings, both edited by Stillman Drake: *Cause, Experiment, and Science: A Galilean Dialogue Incorporating a New English Translation of Galileo's "Bodies That Stay Atop Water and Move in It"* (Chicago: University of Chicago Press, 1981) and *Telescopes, Tides, and Tactics: A Galilean Dialogue About the "Starry Messenger" and Systems of the World* (Chicago: University of Chicago Press, 1983). Most of the documents relative to Galileo's trial are either excerpted or reproduced in Karl von Gebler, *Galileo Galilei and the Roman Curia*, tr. Mrs. George Sturge (London: C. K. Paul, 1879; rpt. 1977).

Few figures have been so much revised and reappraised as Galileo. There are three works (among many) that have collected reflective essays on him: *Homage to Galileo*, Papers presented at the Galileo Quadricentennial, University of Rochester, October 8 and 9, 1964, ed. Morton F. Kaplon (Cambridge: M.I.T. Press, 1965); *Galileo Reappraised*, ed. Carlo L. Golino (Berkeley and Los Angeles; University of California Press, 1966); and *Galileo, Man of Science*, ed. Ernan McMullin (New York and London: Basic Books, 1967).

The best treatment of Galileo as a scientist is Stillman Drake, *Galileo at Work: His Scientific Biography* (Chicago and London: University of Chicago Press, 1978). There is also a detailed critique of his *Dialogue on the Two World Systems*, William R. Shea, *Galileo's Intellectual Revolution* (London: Macmillan, 1972). The best biography is probably still Giorgio de Santillana, *The Crime of Galileo* (Chicago: University of Chicago Press, 1955). But the best brief biography is surely Stillman Drake, *Galileo* "Past Masters Series" (New York: Hill and Wang, 1981). The slightly more general work by Ludovico Geymonat, *Galileo Galilei: A biography and inquiry into his philosophy of science*, tr. and ed. Stillman Drake (New York, Toronto, and London: McGraw-Hill, 1965), is also recommended. Pietro Redondi, *Galileo Heretic*, tr. Raymond Rosenthal (Princeton, N.J.: Princeton University Press, 1987) is a brilliant and exciting revisionist account of Galileo's "crime." Students may be interested in a book by the brilliant and provocative popularizer Arthur Koestler, *The Sleep Walkers: A history of man's changing vision of the universe* (New York: Macmillan, 1968 [1959]), which ends with an account and assessment of the work of Galileo and Newton.

CLIVE OF INDIA: THE GREATEST NABOB

1725	Born
1743	First voyage to India
1756	Appointed governor general
1757	Victory at the battle of Plassey
1762	Created First Baron Clive of Plassey
1764–67	Governor General of the East India Company in India a second time
1772–73	Vindicated by Parliamentary inquiry
1774	Died

In 1743, when Robert Clive went to India, the British had already been there almost a century and a half in the form of the British East India Company, one of the world's greatest trading corporations. The company's headquarters were located at Madras on the southern Bengali coast; it remained essentially a trading operation and sought and exercised little political power. Its interests were almost completely mercantile—the trade in spices, gems, precious metals, cotton and silk, and later tea. The profits were enormous and almost untrammeled because the company enjoyed extraterritorial status and paid only a token subsidy to the Mogul empire. In addition, its factors and agents shared in those profits, being permitted to carry on personal trading ventures. When these men returned to England with their wealth they were called Nabobs.[1] Robert Clive was to become the greatest Nabob.

Clive was the son of a lawyer and impoverished small landowner who sent him to India to make the fortune with the East India Company that he could not hope to make in England. Once in India Clive volunteered for the military service and was commissioned an ensign. He immediately took part in the desultory fighting between the French and the English, a reflection of the hostilities of these two

---

[1] A corruption of the Indian title for Viceroy to the Mogul, *Nawab.*—ED.

113

powers in the tangled wars and alliances of Europe. Clive proved a very successful soldier, earning the name *Sabrit Jang* ("steady in war"). He was also a very successful trader and became a wealthy man.

Following a three-year interval in England Clive, now a colonel in the Royal Army, came again to Madras, where the directors of the East India Company appointed him their governor general. In 1756 there was an upsurge in military activity. The Nawab of Bengal, in alliance with the French, took the city of Calcutta, and Clive was given the command for its relief. He regained Calcutta and pushed on to engage the Nawab and the French at the battle of Plassey on June 23, 1757. Though by no means a major battle it was a decisive victory for Clive and the company, both of whom profited greatly as a result. The company gained a virtual monopoly of the trade of Bengal, and Clive saw a vast increase in his already substantial fortune.

In 1760, Clive returned to England, where he was hailed as a military hero, a "Heaven-born General." He was shortly given a peerage as First Baron Clive of Plassey and knighted.

Robert Clive: His Own Story

ROBERT CLIVE

On the eve of his return to India and his second term as Governor General in 1764, Clive addressed to the directors of the East India Company a detailed report on his accomplishments leading up to the Battle of Plassey, on the growth of his personal fortune, and his assessment of the status of the company. The following excerpt is taken from that report.

The last Election of the India Directors drew many unjust attacks on my character; and it is probable, I may be censured by some, for having suffered such reports as were spread against me during the contest to have remained so long unanswered; but knowing, that even the authors of them could not themselves believe them and conscious to myself, that every part of my conduct, in the great share I had in the management of the Company's affairs, would bear the most rigid scrutiny, and the more known be the more approved; I held them in too much contempt to merit any answer. But as I find the unjust attack on my character has been followed by an attack on my fortune, and insinuations thrown out to justify these proceedings, very injurious to my honour, I reluctantly submit to vindicate myself, and must rely upon the candour of the Proprietors, not to impute it to ostentatious vanity, if in speaking of myself I do aver, that I founded all my actions in their service on honourable motives. . . .

I was appointed, by the gentlemen of Fort St. George, commander in chief of the troops sent for the recovery of the Company's settlements in Bengal, on board the fleet commanded by Admiral Watson. On our arrival in the Ganges, we found the unhappy remains of a once flourishing colony on board a few merchants ships in that river. We landed, drove the enemy from Fort William, and put the Company's Governor and Council in possession. The Nabob then came down with an army of sixty or seventy thousand men, and a heavy train of artillery, flushed by his late successes against the English. The King's and Company's forces, consisting of a battalion of 450 men, a battalion of Seapoys,[2] and a body of sailors from the squadron, at-

---

[2]A general term used by the English for native Indian troops.—ED.

tacked the Nabob in his camp, and defeated him. We then made a treaty with him, by which he engaged to restore all the effects he had taken. In consequence of which, the Governor and Council recovered in goods and money to a large amount.

War being declared against France, we took Chandernagore; and having convincing proofs, that the Nabob's firm intention was to extirpate the English, as soon as the troops and squadron left the river, we entered into an alliance with Meer Jaffier Ally Cawn, a general officer in Nabob's service, and near relation to the Nabob; and accordingly a treaty was concluded between us, the chief object of which was, on the part of our ally, a full satisfaction to the Company and all the inhabitants, for the losses they had sustained by the capture of Fort William, and other factories which the Nabob had plundered, with grants of lands and privileges; and, on the Company's part, to place and support him in the government of the three provinces of Bengal, Bahar, and Orixa. . . .

The Nabob then, agreeable to the known and usual custom of eastern princes, made presents, both to those of his own court, and to such of the English, who by their rank and abilities had been instrumental in the happy success of so hazardous an enterprize, suitable to the rank and dignity of a great Prince. I was one amongst the many who benefited by his favour. I never sought to conceal it, but declared publicly, in my letters to the secret committee of the India Directors, that the Nabob's generosity had made my fortune easy, and that the Company's welfare was now my only motive for staying in India. What injustice was this to the Company? They could expect no more than what was stipulated in the treaty. Or what injunction was I under to refuse a present from him who had the power to make me one, as the reward of honourable services? I know of none. I had surely myself a particular claim, by having devoted myself to the Company's military service, and neglected all commercial advantages. What reason then can be given, or what pretence would the company have to expect, that I, after having risqued my life so often in their service, should deny myself the only honourable opportunity that ever offered of acquiring a fortune, without prejudice to them, who, it is evident, would not have had more for my having had less. When the Company had acquired a million and an half sterling, and a revenue of near 100,000 £ per annum, from the success of their forces under my command; when ample restoration had been made to those whole fortunes suffered by the calamity of Calcutta; and when individuals had, in consequence of that success, acquired large estates; what would the world have said, had I come home, and rested upon the generosity of the present Court of Directors? . . .

Soon after the battle Plassey, the Nabob, of his own free motion, without the least hint or application from me, sent a petition to the court of Dehli, that I might be created an Omrah, or Lord of the Empire. In the beginning of the year 1758, the Nabob received and delivered me the patent (with other honours accompanying it); by which I was created an Omrah of the command of 5000 foot, and the rank of 6000 horse.

According to the custom of the country, the Soubah assigns a Jaghire, or estate, within his own provinces, to support the dignity of the new created Omrah; but at the time I received the patent of creation, I knew of no such intention in the Nabob, whose friendship for me gave way to other views. . . . Bound by treaty and interest, it behoved us to secure the attachment and dependency of the Nabob. We immediately took the field, and relieved him, for the present, from the inconveniencies he laboured under from his own forces, who over-awed by our presence, desisted from their demands. Being joined by 8000 horse and foot, under the command of his son the young Nabob, we marched four hundred miles in twenty-three days, and forced the enemy to raise the siege of Patna, the capital of the province of Bahar, and pursued them two hundred miles further. . . . In the mean time, the Nabob's army had again surrounded him, and were become more outrageous than ever; and he was upon the point of being put to death, when the news of our success dispersed them, and they became as submissive and fawning, as they were being daring and insolent.

Services rendered at such a crisis, convinced him at last of the value of such sincere allies. On my return from the north he came to meet me, and after many obliging expressions, that I had saved his life, and made him a second time Soubah. . . .

I shall now proceed to lay before the Proprietors the measures taken by my adversaries, subsequent to the election, and the reasons they assign to support them.

But I shall first take notice, that by the services rendered to the Nabob, the Company not only recovered the misfortunes sustained from the late Nabob, with the possessions I have already mentioned, but also acquired, and had delivered into their hands, the absolute power over the three provinces of Bengal, Bahar, and Orixa, whose ordinary annual revenues produce three millions and a half sterling; insomuch that they were enabled to set up and establish in the Soubahship any person, they thought fit. . . .

This power the Company, soon after I left Bengal, exercised, and in 1761 they entered into a treaty with Mahomed Coffin Cawn, son-in-law to Meer Jaffier, for that purpose. . . . By this treaty the Company acquired a much larger district of country, than they before enjoyed under the treaty with Meer Jaffier, together with a larger estate and interest in those lands, than they had in those before granted; for the annual amount of the lands last acquired were near 600,000 £ and instead of reserving to the government the usual rents of homage which those lands were subject to, both the lands and those rents were granted to the Company. . . .

I have before acknowledged, that my fortune arose from the grateful bounty of the Nabob for my services to him; and altho' I shall ever think of my services to the Company with pleasure, yet the Company cannot say I owe them any thing in point of gratitude. . . .

My adversaries cannot therefore say I acquired my fortune out of the property of the Company, or in diminution of that of my country, or any of my fellow-subjects: on the contrary, it is well known, that had it not been for the successes we were blessed with, this kingdom would never have had the benefit of one farthing of the money which had been brought into it, in consequence of those successes. This being the case, one might have expected, after so many years service to the Company, and under the circumstances I have described, they would at least have permitted me to have had the quiet enjoyment of that fortune I had so obtained. . . .

I have before taken notice, that his Majesty's arms, and those of the Company, by the revolution brought about whilst I was the Commander in Chief, acquired the great power and influence the Company enjoyed in Bengal, when I left that country; and that that power after I came away, was made use of to depose the Prince who sat on the throne whilst I was there, and, to establish Mahomed Coffin Cawn in his stead. It is under these circumstances, that the Directors make use of the 2d reason. Now to give that reason its utmost latitude, it can amount to no more than an admission from the Company, that I had once a good right to require from them the payment of my Jaghire: but that this right is now defeated by a subsequent act, entirely effected by their own agents abroad. The weight and justice of this argument I leave to your considerations. . . .

Monsieur Dupleix, the commander in chief of the French forces in India, obtained a title of honour, inferior to mine, and had several Jaghires granted him by the Nabob of the Decan in Lands, ceded to the French Company, which he enjoyed for several years after he returned to Europe, and indeed until the lands, upon which the Jaghires were granted, were taken from the French. And Monsieur Dupleix considered his title of honour as an advantage to the French in those parts. . . .

I shall end this memorial with some observations on the Company's affairs, at the time the loss of their possessions in Bengal happened, and the regaining those possessions, with all their present great advantages.

When the news of the misfortunes in Bengal first reached Madrass, the whole town was flung into a consternation, equal to that of the Court of Directors, when the first advices of it were brought to England. I leave it to Mr. Payne, who was then at the head of the Direction, to describe what he and others suffered from their apprehensions for the Company. Indeed it is the general opinion, that nothing but the sudden advice of the recovery of that valuable settlement, which followed so close upon the news of its loss, could have prevented the Company's sinking under such a misfortune.

It was the unanimous opinion of the Governor and Council of Madrass, that the Company could not exist without their possessions in Bengal. . . . These considerations, and a thorough persuasion that the Company must fall, if Bengal was not recovered, induced the Governor and Council of Madrass, to send such a force as might answer that purpose: I was the person fixed upon to execute their designs and as the force sent was more than could be spared consistent with the safety of the Company's possessions on the coast of Coromandel, at that critical time (being just at the eve of a war with France) they invested me with a power, independant of the Governor and Council of Fort William, that when the Company were reinstated in their possessions, they might be able to recall such part of the forces under my command, as might be thought consistent with the Company's interest in other parts of India.

As soon as the sufferers of Bengal were restored to their habitations, by the re-taking of Calcutta, and to peace, by the defeating of Surajah Dowla, they called upon me to give up that independant power, which the Governor and Council of Madrass had thought necessary to intrust me with, which demand I could not comply with, without being guilty of a breach of trust. . . .

Let the Proprietors paint to themselves what I must have suffered, under such a complication of distressed circumstances; and let the Directors remember, that under all these disadvantages, I took upon me to march, and the English arms alone gained the battle of Plassey. It is true, the Directors, in their first flow of gratitude, conferred upon me an honour, I believe, never paid to any other before, or since, by addressing a letter of thanks to me alone, signed by the whole court; and that I might be convinced of the sincerity of their sentiments, they sent no less than six or eight of them, which I have in my possession. But as length of time, and circumstances, seem to have produced another way of thinking in these gentlemen, I hope the Proprietors will excuse me, if I assert, for the last time, that by the great acquisitions of wealth obtained by this event, and by the large sums of money paid into their cash, for bills, the Company were enabled to supply every exigence, and answer the demands of every settlement in India, during the whole course of the war. To Madrass alone, was sent upwards of 300,000 £ which must inevitably have fallen, without such assistance; and with that place, all India. The Company who used to send to India several hundred thousand pounds a year, in bullion, were relieved from that difficulty; which, at such a juncture, they never could have surmounted; and from February 1758, the time they received the advice of our success, to this day, they have sent very little to the coast, and still less to Bengal; so that this alone has been a saving to the nation of some millions sterling. The lands ceded to the Company by Coffin Cawn, and all the advantages gained by the deposition of Meer Jaffier, must appear as much a consequence of the battle of Plassey, as the advantages which were gained immediately after that victory: the whole amounting to 700,000 £ a year, may, at 10 years purchase, be valued at 7 millions sterling; the restitution made to the sufferers of Calcutta, and what was given by Meer Jaffier to the navy, army, and others, may be reckoned at 2,000,000 £ fortunes acquired since, at a moderate computation, 1,500,000 £ the Company themselves likewise received from Surajah Dowla and Meer Jaffier 1,500,000 £ upon the whole, a clear gain to the nation of twelve millions sterling.

I shall conclude this subject with appealing to the Court of Directors, for the truth of these facts, and call upon them to declare whether they think without the battle of Plassey, and its consequences, the East-India Company would have been at this time existing? As great numbers of the Proprietors may be unacquainted with these transactions, I hope they will excuse the necessity I have been under, of laying the whole before them, which I submit to their consideration, justice, and candour.

Clive and Imperialism

THOMAS BABINGTON MACAULAY

During the course of Clive's second term as governor general from 1764 to 1767 he laid the foundation for the takeover of the East India Company territories by the British government and the consequent creation of British India. The company had already extended its control over Bengal and several other northern states. But it had also extended the corrupt practices that had already created so many Nabobs, including Clive. Despite the advantages these practices had provided him, Clive immediately moved against them. He cut swollen allowances, limited the size of gifts that could be accepted from native princes, regulated private trading, and disciplined the military officers who were threatening mutiny. He also secured the approval of the Mogul to all the territorial gains the company had made, thus casting a veil of legality over that process.

The accomplishments of Clive were the subject of a thoughtful essay by the British historian Thomas Babington Macaulay a generation after Clive's death. In this essay, as in his other works, Macaulay celebrates the virtues of British imperialism, of which India was the crown jewel. He paints Clive as the major figure in the acquisition of British India. But he also deals with the propriety—or impropriety—of his building his immense fortune in the course of his service to the company and the state.

The entire history of British India is an illustration of the great truth, that it is not prudent to oppose perfidy to perfidy, and that the most efficient weapon with which men can encounter falsehood is truth. During a long course of years, the English rulers of India, surrounded by allies and enemies whom no engagement could bind, have generally acted with sincerity and uprightness; and the event has proved that sincerity and uprightness are wisdom. English valor and English intelligence have done less to extend and to preserve our Oriental empire than English veracity. All that we could have gained by imitating the doublings, the evasions, the fictions, the perjuries which have been employed against us, is as nothing when compared with what we have gained by being the one power in India on whose word reliance can be placed. No oath which superstition can devise, no hostage however precious, inspires a hundredth part of the confidence which is produced by the "yea, yea," and "nay, nay," of a British envoy. No fastness, however strong by art or nature, gives to its inmates a security like that enjoyed by the chief who, passing through the territories of powerful and deadly enemies, is armed with the British guarantee. . . . A hostile monarch may promise mountains of gold to our sepoys, on condition that they will desert the standard of the Company. The Company promises only a moderate pension after a long service. But every sepoy knows that the promise of the Company will be kept: he knows that if he lives a hundred years his rice and salt are as secure as the salary of the Governor General; and he knows that there is not another state in India which would not, in spite of the most solemn vows, leave him to die of hunger in a ditch as soon as he had ceased to be useful. The greatest advantage which a government can possess is to be the one trustworthy government in the midst of governments which nobody can trust. This advantage we enjoy in Asia. . . .

The shower of wealth now fell copiously on the Company and its servants. A sum of eight hundred thousand pounds sterling, in coined silver, was sent down the river from Moorshedabad to Fort William. . . . Trade revived; and the signs of affluence appeared in every English house. As to Clive, there was no limit to his acquisitions but his own moderation. The treasury of Bengal was thrown open to him. . . . [He] walked between heaps of gold and silver, crowned with rubies and diamonds, and was at liberty to help himself. He accepted between two and three hundred thousand pounds . . . but we cannot acquit him of having done what, if not in itself evil, was yet of evil example. Nothing is more clear than that a general ought to be the servant of his own government, and of no other. It follows that whatever rewards he receives for his services ought to be given either by his own government, or with the full knowledge and approbation of his own government. This rule ought to be strictly maintained even with respect to the merest bauble, with respect to a cross, a medal, or a yard of colored ribbon. But how can any government be well served, if those who command its forces are at liberty, without its permission, without its privity, to accept princely fortunes from its allies? It is idle to say that there was then no Act of Parliament prohibiting the practice of taking presents from Asiatic sovereigns. It is not on the Act which was passed at a later period for the purpose of preventing any such taking of presents, but on grounds which were valid before that Act was passed, on grounds of common law and common sense, that we arraign the conduct of Clive. . . .

At the same time, it must be admitted that, in Clive's case, there were many extenuating circumstances. He considered himself as the general, not of the Crown, but of the Company. The Company had, by implication at least, authorized its agents to enrich themselves by means of the liberality of the native princes, and by other means still more objectionable. It was hardly to be expected that the servant should entertain stricter notions of his duty than were entertained by his masters. Though Clive did not distinctly acquaint his employers with what had taken place, and request their sanction, he did not, on the other hand, by studied concealment, show that he was conscious of having done wrong. On the contrary, he avowed with the greatest openness that the Nabob's bounty had raised him to affluence. Lastly, though we think that he ought not in such a way to have taken anything, we must admit that he deserves praise for having taken so little. He accepted twenty lacs of rupees. It would have cost him only a word to make the twenty forty. It was a very easy exercise of virtue to declaim in England against Clive's rapacity; but not one in a hundred of his accusers would have shown so much self-command in the treasury of Moorshedabad. . . . It was clear that Clive had been guilty of some acts which it is impossible to vindicate without attacking the authority of all the most sacred laws which regulate the intercourse of individuals and of states. But it was equally clear that he had displayed great talents, and even great virtues; that he had rendered eminent services both to his country and to the people of India. . . .

Clive committed great faults; and we have not attempted to disguise them. But his faults, when weighed against his merits, and viewed in connection with his temptations, do not appear to us to deprive him of his right to an honorable place in the estimation of posterity.

From his first visit to India dates the renown of the English arms in the East. Till he appeared, his country-men were despised as mere peddlers, while the French were revered as a people formed for victory and command. His courage and capacity dissolved the charm.

Clive's Parliamentary Hearing

MARK BENCE-JONES

In 1762 following a terrible famine in India the shares of the East India Company fell so drastically that it faced bankruptcy and thousands of English shareholders faced ruin. As a result Parliament launched an inquiry into the policies of the company and of Lord Clive. Clive, who was now a member of Parliament, defended himself in a series of detailed and eloquent speeches that carried his case and gained his vindication. The following excerpt from his most recent biography picks up the narrative at the end of the hearing.

Having made his celebrated plea, 'leave me my honour, take away my fortune', he bowed and walked out, with tears in his eyes, followed by loud and repeated cries of 'Hear, hear!' Entering his carriage, he drove back home, not knowing whether he had 'a sixpence to call his own in the morning'. . . . As soon as Clive had gone, Burgoyne[3] proposed his resolution. He had toned it down. It no longer accused Clive of obtaining his £234,000 illegally; but it still said that in doing so, he had 'abused the powers with which he was entrusted, to the evil example of the servants of the public'. He was seconded by Meredith, who leant over backwards to praise Clive's earlier achievements. And then Hans Stanley, a junior member of the Government, and Rose Fuller, a distinguished Parliamentarian described as 'an old, honest, independent veteran of integrity', proposed that Burgoyne's resolution should be cut in half, so as to separate the bare statement that Clive had received the £234,000 from the passage about his having abused his powers and given a bad example.

There followed a long and heated debate on this amendment. . . . Burke himself, and other members of the Rockingham group, now rallied to Clive's defence, the most significant voice among them being that of Admiral Sir Charles Saunders, who, 'with rough naval indignation', declared that Clive was being treated like Sir Walter Ralegh. The Admiral spoke as a 'Rockingham', but he also spoke for the ordinary, decent men in the House, the country squires, the soldiers and sailors. These men regarded Clive as the hero of Arcot and were determined to stand by him, however little brief they may have had for the other Nabobs. They also stood for the proverbial English fair play, which now came to Clive's rescue, just as the English sympathy for the under-dog, another facet of the same national virtue, had brought the liberals on to the side of his enemies.

When the 'King's Friends' from the Government followed the 'Rockinghams' into the Clive camp, the issue was a foregone conclusion. Stanley's amendment was carried by 155 votes to 95, Lord North voting with the minority. The first, and harmless, part of Burgoyne's resolution was then passed; the severed tail containing the sting was rejected without a division. Wedderburn then took the initiative and moved 'that Robert, Lord Clive, did, at the same time, render great and meritorious services to this country', which was carried almost unanimously. 'Lord Clive has thus come out of the fiery trial much brighter than he went into it,' wrote Burke on the day after the debate. 'His gains are now recorded, and not only condemned, but actually approved by Parliament. His reputation, too, for ability, stands higher than ever.'[4]

---

[3] The parliamentarian who had carried the debate against Clive.—Ed.

[4] The remainder of the bill was passed almost without debate, that part which initiated the takeover of British India from the East India Company in favor of the crown.—Ed.

Because Clive died by his own hand within two years of being attacked in Parliament, it has been generally assumed that he never recovered from the ordeal, and that for the last few months of his life he was sunk in melancholy. This is a myth, originally put about by his enemies, to imply that he suffered remorse for his alleged misdeeds, and then used by the historians of a later age to show that his persecutors drove him to suicide. It was easy to believe that the depression, from which he had suffered at intervals since his youth, should now have overwhelmed him; although this depression was pathological, and seems to have occurred more as a reaction to success than as a result of adversity.

He is only once recorded as having suffered from depression during his last months. These months may well have been happier than any other time since his return from India. He was coming to terms with ill-health: 'I am so well acquainted with my own constitution at present that I think I may venture to say that with care and attention I may make the rest of my days tolerably easy,' he wrote in April 1774. . . .

Summer turned into a wet autumn. Clive stood too long by the river at Oakly supervising an improvement and caught a bad cold. On November 5, he left for Bath, full of catarrh, and when he arrived there he was too ill even to drink the waters. After a fortnight he was worse, but insisted on going to London. . . . The journey to London was a nightmare; he was unable to eat or even to swallow. By the time they reached Berkeley Square on the night of November 20, he was once again tormented by his old abdominal complaint. He kept pointing to his belly and groaning, as he suffered acute spasms of pain. The next day was as bad; he tried to make up his mind whether to return immediately to Bath or to stay in London; he took every medicine he could think of, including larger doses of opium than his physician, Dr. John Fothergill, considered safe.

On November 22, he appears to have been better; he decided to return to Bath, and ordered his carriage for the afternoon. In the late morning, he joined Margaret, Strachey and Jane for a game of whist. He had taken a purge, and at about noon was obliged to retire to the water-closet. There, it would seem that his pain returned with all its violence; and in a paroxysm of agony, he thrust his penknife into his throat.

Clive's family tried to conceal the fact of his suicide, with the result that his death has remained something of a mystery down to the present day. The newspapers put out contrary reports: some said he had died of an apoplectic fit, others that he had taken an overdose of opium against his doctor's orders. That he died of an overdose was the general belief in the first few days following his death. But even then, there were rumours of suicide. By the middle of December it was generally believed that he had cut his throat. Had this belief been false, Clive's family would surely have contradicted it. Instead, when Strachey wrote to Francis on January 3, telling him of Clive's death, he was suspiciously silent as to the circumstances. At the same time, Sykes, who would have been as close to the circle of Clive's intimates as any outsider, and who would have wished to present Clive in the best possible light, told Hastings that he had without doubt cut his throat. Then there is the account in Malcolm's biography, written with the help and approval of Ned, which implies suicide while not stating as much in so many words.

Most conclusive of all is the eye-witness account given by Jane Strachey to her son some time before her own death in 1824.[5] Her memory may have played her false as regards the details, but she certainly would not have distorted the central fact to Clive's detriment. . . .

Clive's ambitions for India were less clear-cut than those for his family and himself. As a Company man, who declared categorically against 'carrying our arms beyond Bengal', he might not wholly have welcomed the prospect of a British India stretching from Cape Comorin to the Khyber, from Burma to the Arabian Sea, and of the granddaughter of George III reigning in place of the Mogul, which was the state of affairs little more than a century after he obtained the *Diwani*.[6] Yet before he died he had grown convinced that the gentlemen of Leadenhall Street could never be equal to ruling an empire such as he had won; and having repeatedly expressed the fear that his empire would be lost through ineptitude, he would surely have rejoiced in the knowledge that the men who came after him would, on the contrary, enlarge it many times over.

But for the labours of these men, of Warren Hastings, Wellesley and Dalhousie, of Elphinstone, the Metcalfes and the Lawrences, Clive's empire would not have endured. Whether that empire would have existed at all had it not been for Clive is another question. There were plenty of soldiers like Coote or Munro who were just as good at winning battles as he was, possibly better. And there was a much greater statesman and administrator in Hastings. But to conjure up an empire in eighteenth-century India, where autocrats meant more than committees, it required that the mystique of the victorious general and the ability to rule should be combined in one man, as they were in Clive. In addition, it required a much rarer quality, which Clive also had, in common with many of the great men of history,

---

[5]One of Clive's daughters.—ED.

[6]The headquarters of the East India Company.—ED.

notably Churchill: that almost superhuman power and energy to get things done, and to inspire others to give of their best. Clive might well have been the only Englishman in the India of his time who had this power to the extent necessary for bringing an empire into being, and tiding it over the first few perilous years.

Review and Study Questions

1. What was the significance of the Battle of Plassey?
2. How did Clive acquire his fortune?
3. How do you evaluate Macaulay's assessment of how Clive acquired his fortune?
4. What were the circumstances of Clive's death?

Suggestions for Further Reading

Clive's own writings are sparse. He was not a reflective man and never essayed any extended account of his accomplishments in India beyond the letter to the directors of the East India Company, excerpted in this chapter, and the somewhat more extended remarks in his parliamentary defense of 1772. Those remarks may be found in their entirety in *Parliamentary Debates* for 1772, starting at p. 327. His papers are still available only in manuscript collections with the exception of the letter to the company directors, also excerpted in this chapter. His correspondence has not been collected. Some excerpts from his correspondence and from other family papers are available in one of his earlier biographies, Sir John Malcolm, *The Life of Robert, Lord Clive: Collected from the Family Papers communicated by the Earl of Powis*, 3 vols. (London: John Murray, 1836).

From the Malcolm biography on through the nineteenth century the British biographies of Clive tend to be dominated by the enthusiasm for imperialism. The Macaulay essay, excerpted for this chapter, is one of the better examples. The early twentieth century biographies tend to be somewhat uncritical and bland, such as G. W. Forest, *The Life of Lord Clive*, 2 vols. (Westminster: A. Constable, 1903) or R. J. Minney, *Clive of India* (London: Jarrolds, 1931). There are a couple of conspicuous exceptions: One of the best studies of Clive is A. M. Davies, *Clive of Plassey* (New York: Scribner's Sons, 1939), as is H. H. Dodwell, *Dupleix and Clive, The Beginnings of Empire* (London: Methuen, 1920). See also Dodwell's relevant chapters in *The Cambridge History of India*, vol. V *British India*, 3rd ed. (Delhi et al.: S. Chand and

Co., 1968). The best of the more recent biographies is Mark Bence-Jones, *Clive of India* (London: Constable, 1974), excerpted for this chapter.

There are a number of important studies of aspects of Clive's career. His service in Parliament is treated in the standard Sir Lewis Namier and John Brooke, *The History of Parliament, The House of Commons 1754–1790* (New York: Oxford University Press, 1964). His victory at Plassey, its context, and consequences are the subject of Michael Edwardes, *The Battle of Plassey and the Conquest of Bengal* (London: Batsford, 1963), the best treatment of the topic. On the British East India Company, with which Clive was so closely associated throughout his career, the best book is Lucy S. Sutherland, *The East India Company in Eighteenth Century Politics* (Oxford: Oxford University Press, 1952), a work of detailed research still unequaled.

On the larger subject of colonialism and British rule in India the earlier British works tend to be imperialistic as the Indian works tend to be nationalistic. An exception to this latter group is R. C. Majumdar et al., *An Advanced History of India* (New York: St. Martin's Press, Inc., 1967), especially Part III, Bk. I. Among the best English works on Indian colonialsim are Sir Penderel Moon, *The British Conquest and Dominion of India* (London: Duckworth, 1989), Michael Edwardes, *British India 1772–1947, A Survey of the nature and effects of alien rule* (New York: Taplinger, 1968), and Sir Percival Griffiths, *The British Impact on India* (New York: Archon, 1965).

Among the general histories of India two excellent works are Percival Spear, *The Oxford History of Modern India* (Oxford: Clarendon Press, 1965) and Stanley Wolpert, *A New History of India*, 3rd ed. (Oxford and New York: Oxford University Press, 1989).

CATHERINE THE GREAT: EMPRESS OF ALL THE RUSSIAS

1729	Born
1744	Betrothed to Grand Duke Peter of Russia
1762	Succession of Peter as Peter III, his deposition, and Catherine's succession as empress
1767	Constitutional commission
1768–74	War with Turkey
1792–95	Partition of Poland
1796	Died

Catherine the Great of Russia was not a Russian at all. She was a German princess of the small and obscure house of Anhalt-Zerbst, born in 1729 and christened Sophie Friederike Auguste. When she was only fourteen, Catherine was selected by the Russian Empress Elisabeth, the daughter and successor of Peter the Great, to be the wife of the Russian heir apparent, Elisabeth's nephew the Grand Duke Peter. The marriage took place the following year.

Peter was as fully German as Catherine; in fact, they were cousins. His father, the Duke of Holstein-Gottorp, had also been a minor German prince, and Peter never lost his fondness for things German. His interests—including his political interests—as well as his tastes were German. Indeed, he despised everything Russian. Even after his accession to the Russian throne, Peter's ideal was Frederick the Great of Prussia.

Catherine, on the other hand, had readily given up her German name, at the insistence of the Empress Elisabeth, and had taken the Russian name Yekaterina—Catherine. She gave up her Lutheran religion just as readily and received instruction in the traditional Russian Orthodox faith. And she plunged into the task of learning the Russian language, as well as everything she could about Russian history and government.

The early years of Catherine's marriage were a nightmare. Peter hated her, lived apart from her, and openly flaunted his mistresses. He was crude and violent, drunken, and probably impotent. Their son Paul, born in 1754, may well have been fathered by one of the lovers Catherine had begun to take, albeit somewhat more discreetly than her husband.

On the death of the Empress Elisabeth in January 1762, Peter succeeded to the Russian throne as Peter III. His abuse of Catherine continued, and he began planning to set her aside in favor of his current mistress. But this behavior was overshadowed by Peter's abuse of his nation. Abandoning himself entirely to his German tastes and interests, he demanded that Russian icons be removed from the churches and that Russian priests adopt the dress of Lutheran pastors. His admiration for Frederick the Great led him to attempt a series of unpopular reforms of the military based on Prussian practices. He also withdrew Russia from the Seven Years' War, in which Russia had been allied with Austria and France against Prussia, and forged a new alliance with the Prussian king. These events and the widespread antipathy to Peter III brought about a military coup against him.

In St. Petersburg, the rebellious regiments appealed to Catherine. It was clearly no coincidence that among the leaders of the coup were Grigory Orlov, Catherine's lover, and his brothers. She promptly set herself at the head of the rebellious troops and, with their support, had herself proclaimed empress. Peter was deposed and murdered. He had reigned for only six months.

Catherine's Own Story

THE MEMOIRS OF CATHERINE THE GREAT

All her life Catherine was a compulsive writer, and much of what she wrote was about herself, her plans, her ambitions and aspirations, and her views of history and politics. She also wrote abundant letters to her family, her ministers, her friends, her favorites, and her lovers. This mass of material contains, among other things, the elements of an autobiography, including several accounts of the events leading up to Catherine's accession to the Russian throne. All the accounts break off at this point.

The following excerpt is taken from two sources. One was written shortly after the events described; the other, from a letter to one of her former lovers, Count Poniatowski, was also written within weeks of her accession. Together they form a vigorous, fast-moving narrative of her succession and of the rebellion that brought an end to the reign of her hated husband Peter III. Although it was widely believed that Catherine had some complicity not only in the rebellion but in the death of her husband as well, perhaps even ordering his murder, her account clearly states that Peter died of natural causes.

The account begins with the death of the Empress Elisabeth.

The death of the Empress Elisabeth plunged all Russians into deep mourning, especially all good patriots, because they saw in her successor a ruler of violent character and narrow intellect, who hated and despised the Russians, did not know his country, was incompetent to do hard work, avaricious and wasteful, and gave himself up wholly to his desires and to those who slavishly flattered him.

After he was master, he left his business to two or three favorites and gave himself up to every kind of extravagance. First he took from the clergy their possessions in land, and introduced a thousand useless innovations, for the most part in the army. He despised the laws, and to put it briefly, justice was for him who offered the most. Dissatisfaction spread everywhere and the poor opinion they had of him made them finally misinterpret the little good that he did. His more or less considered plans were: to start a war with Denmark on account of Schleswig, to change the religion, to divorce his wife and marry his mistress, and to ally himself with the king of Prussia, whom he called his master and to whom he insisted he had sworn the oath of allegiance. He wished to surrender to him a part of his troops. Scarcely any of his plans did he keep secret.

After the death of the Empress, his aunt, various proposals were made secretly to Empress Catherine. But she never wished to listen to them, hoping always that time and circumstances would somehow alter her unhappy situation, all the more as she knew for certain that they could not attack her position or her person without great danger. The nation was completely devoted to her and saw in her their only hope. Various groups had been formed to put a stop to the suffering of their Fatherland. Each of these groups separately turned to her; the one knew nothing of the other.

She listened to them and did not take from them all hope, but always bade them wait, because she believed that things would not come to the worst and because she believed that every change of that kind was a misfortune. She regarded her duties and her reputation as a strong barrier against ambition. Even the danger that she ran was a new luster whose worth she recognized. Peter III was a permanent patch on a very beautiful face.

Catherine's attitude toward the nation has always been irreproachable. She has never wanted, wished, or desired anything but the success of this nation, and her whole life will be employed for the sole purpose of furthering the welfare and happiness of the Russian people.

Having reached the opinion, however, that things were growing worse, Catherine let the different groups know that the time had come for them to combine and consider ways and means. An insult which her husband offered her in public gave an excellent excuse.[1] So it was agreed that after his return from the country he should be arrested in his apartment and declared incompetent to reign. His mind was really no longer just right and certainly he did not have in the whole kingdom a worse enemy than himself. Not all were of the same opinion. Some wished that it should happen in favor of his son; others, in favor of his wife.

Three days before the arrival of the time set, Lieutenant Passek, one of the principals in the plot, was arrested in consequence of the imprudent talk of a soldier. Three brothers Orlov, the eldest of whom was a captain of artillery, began to act at once. The Hetman[2] and the

---

[1]At a public banquet celebrating his peace with Prussia, Peter shouted abusively at Catherine, "Silly woman!"—Ed.

[2]The leader of the Cossacks.—Ed.

Privy Counsellor Panin thought it was too early. But the former sent of their own accord to the second brother with a coach to Peterhof to fetch the Empress.

Alexei Orlov appeared at six o'clock in the morning on June 28 (Old Style), and awakened her from her sleep. When she heard that Passek was arrested and that for the sake of her own safety there was no more time to lose, she arose and drove to the city. She was received on her arrival by the elder Orlov and Prince Bariatinsky and conducted to the barracks of the Izmailovsky Regiment, where on her arrival only twelve men were present and a petty officer and everything seemed quiet. The soldiers knew all about it but remained in their rooms; but when they came they hailed her as Autocrat and Empress.

The joy of the soldiers and the people was indescribable. She was conducted from here to the Semyonovsky Regiment; the people came to meet her dancing and shouting for joy. Thus escorted, she repaired to the Kazan Cathedral, where the Horse Guard made their appearance in transports of joy. The grenadiers of the Preobrashensky Regiment also came. The people asked pardon because they were the last to arrive; their officers had wished to hold them back, otherwise they would certainly have been the first. After them came the artillery and Villebois, Master of Ordnance. Amid the shouts of numberless people the Empress reached the Winter Palace, where the Synod, the Senate, and all the high dignitaries were assembled. The manifesto and the oath were drawn up and everyone recognized her as sovereign. . . . Count Vorontsov, the Chancellor, came as envoy from the deposed Emperor to reproach the Empress for her flight and ask her for her reasons. She told him to enter, and when he had very earnestly presented the purpose of his mission, she told him she would let him know her answer. He went, and in another room he was generally advised to take the new oath of allegiance. He said that to relieve his conscience he would like to write a letter and make a report on the success of his mission; then he would take the oath. This was permitted him.

After him came Prince Troubetsky and Field Marshal Shuvalov. They had been sent to hold back the first two regiments of which they were the chiefs and to kill the Empress. They cast themselves at her feet and informed her of their mission. Thereupon they went away to take the oath.

When all this had been dispatched, the Grand Duke and several divisions which were to guard the city were left in the care of the senate. The Empress, however, in the uniform of the guards (she had had herself appointed a Colonel of the Guards) departed on horseback at the head of the regiments. They marched the whole night and towards morning arrived at a small monastery two versts[3] from Peterhof. Hither the Vice-Chancellor, Prince Golitsin, brought a letter from the deposed Emperor to the Empress. A little later General Izmailov came with a similar commission.

The following circumstance gave the occasion for this. On the 28th, the Emperor was to come from Oranienbaum where he was staying to Peterhof for dinner. When he learned that the Empress had driven away from there he was disturbed and sent several persons to the city. Since however all the streets leading thither were guarded at the order of the Empress, none of them came back. He knew that there were two regiments about thirty versts from the city and had sent for them to come to his defense. But these regiments had attached themselves to the Empress. . . .

The following day he wrote . . . two letters. . . . In the first he requested that he might be allowed to return to Holstein with his mistress and his favorites; in the second he offered to renounce the throne and begged only for his life. He had about 1,500 armed men, Holstein troops, more than a hundred cannon, and several Russian divisions with him. The Empress sent General Izmailov back with a letter, in which she demanded this resignation. Peter III quietly wrote this document and then came with General Izmailov, his mistress, and his favorite Gudovich to Peterhof. To protect him from being torn to pieces by the soldiers, he was given a reliable guard with four officers under the command of Alexei Orlov.

While preparations were being made for his departure to Ropsha, a very pleasant but quite unfortified country palace, the soldiers began to grumble. They said that for three hours they had not seen the Empress. Prince Troubetsky was frankly trying to make peace between the monarch and her husband. It must be made clear to her that she must resist; she would certainly be betrayed and hurl herself and all those with her to destruction. When Catherine heard of this talk she went to Prince Troubetsky and bade him enter his carriage and drive to the city, while she would make the round of the troops on foot.

As soon as the soldiers saw her, the shouts of joy and jubilation began again; Peter III was sent to his destination.

With the arrival of nightfall the Empress was advised to return to the city, because for two days she had not slept and had scarcely eaten anything. But the troops begged her not to leave them, and she agreed with pleasure when she saw their great enthusiasm for her. Half-way there, they rested for three hours, and towards 10 o'clock in

---

[3]A *verst* is about two-thirds of a mile.—ED.

the morning of June 30th (Old Style), 1762, the Empress, at the head of the troops and the artillery and amid the indescribable jubilation of the multitude, rode into Petersburg. A more beautiful sight can not be imagined. Her court went ahead and the troops had oak-leaves in their hats and caps. They had stamped under their feet all the new articles of clothing they had received from Peter III.[4]

Thus she arrived in triumph at the Summer Palace, where all the people of rank and importance were assembled to wait for her. The Grand Duke came to meet her in the middle of the court. When the Empress caught sight of him, she dismounted and kissed him.

The applause was endless. They went to church, where a Te Deum was sung to the thunder of cannon. The exultation of the people went on the whole day but no kind of disorder occurred.

The Empress had gone to bed and had scarcely fallen asleep, when Lieutenant Passek came to awaken her and bade her to get up. For the fatigue, the long wakefulness, and the wine had helped to make hotter heads than usual, and loyalty to her had aroused in the Izmailovsky Regiment fears for her safety. Without a moment's delay the people had set forth to defend her. When they were told that there was nothing to fear and that she was asleep, they declared that in this matter they could and would only believe their own eyes.

So the Empress arose at two o'clock in the morning, and came out to them. When the soldiers saw her they raised a shout of joy. But in a serious tone she bade them go to bed and allow her to sleep. They should have confidence in her officers, and she urged them strongly to obey them. This they promised, while they begged her pardon and reproached each other because they had been persuaded to waken her in this way. They went home quite peacefully, often looking back to see her as long as it was possible. (Incidentally, in Petersburg there is scarcely any night in summer.)

For the two following days the jubilee held on the entire day, but there were no excesses and no disorders. This is certainly remarkable with such great excitement. . . .

Then I sent the deposed Emperor, under the command of Alexei Orlov with four officers and a division of peaceful chosen people, to a remote and very pleasant place called Ropsha, 25 versts from Petersburg, while decent and suitable quarters were fitted up in Schluesselburg, and so had time to provide relays of horses for him.

But the good God arranged it otherwise! The anxiety had caused him to have a diarrhœa, which lasted for three days and still continued on the fourth. On this day he drank immoderately, for he had

---

[4]These were their hated Prussian-style uniforms.—ED.

everything he wanted except his freedom. (He had incidentally asked for his mistress, his dog, his negro, and his violin; but in order to avoid a scandal and prevent increasing the excitement of his guards I had only sent him the last three.) He was attacked by a hæmorrhoidal colic and fever phantasies. For two days he was in this condition; this was followed by great weakness and in spite of all that medical aid could do he breathed his last, after he had asked for a Lutheran pastor.

I feared the officers might have poisoned him. Therefore I had the body dissected; but it was completely proved that not the least trace of poison existed. His stomach was quite healthy, but an inflammation of the intestines and a fit of apoplexy had carried him off. His heart was unusually small and quite shrunken. . . .

Catherine in Her Own Time

PRINCE M. M. SHCHERBATOV

Although Catherine did not belong to the lineage of Peter the Great, she was, in most respects, the heir to his policies and ambitions and is rightly called Catherine the Great. Her reign, which was to last for thirty-four years, began with the coup that deposed her husband. The enemies he had made, most notably the military and the more liberal elements of the aristocracy, supported Catherine. She could not afford the risk of foreign hostility, so she sought friendly relations not only with Russia's traditional allies, France and Austria, but with Prussia as well. She also had to deal with a nearly empty treasury. To do this she completed the secularization of the enormous properties of the church, a move wholly in line with the reforms of Peter the Great. Although she was personally opposed to serfdom, she reorganized and strengthened that hateful system as a concession to the nobility, whose support for her was essential.

She hoped to frame a liberal constitution for her country, and in 1767 she convened a commission to that end, wrote a *Nakaz* (an instruction) to the commission, and prepared a draft of the constitution she favored and a proposal for a law code. She had drawn her constitutional principles from contemporary English and French liberal philosophers, many of whom she corresponded with, including Voltaire, d'Alembert, and Diderot; Diderot even came to Russia to visit with the empress. She enjoyed a great reputation in the circles of the European intelligentsia. But at home her liberal political schemes failed completely.

In foreign affairs she turned to a war with Turkey in 1768 that lasted until 1774 and brought Russia the territories of the Khanate of Crimea and domination of the entire northern shore of the Black Sea. In 1792 Catherine intervened in the affairs of Poland and annexed most of the Ukraine, while Prussia annexed most of western Poland. In response to an uprising led by the Polish patriot Tadeusz Kosciuszko in 1794, Catherine and her allies Prussia and Austria annexed the rest of Poland, and that nation disappeared from the map of Europe.

In addition to adding immense territories to Russia, Catherine fostered urbanism, trade, and communication, and the Russian economy burgeoned in her reign. In her private life, she continued to have a string of lovers—more than twenty in all—but only one of them, Grigory Potemkin, enjoyed any measure of political influence and that because of his abilities rather than because of his status as the empress's favorite. She was and remained an autocrat, and she could no more than her contemporaries Frederick the Great of Prussia or Joseph II of Austria conceive of government except in terms of absolutism.

Catherine the Great was admired abroad and loved at home, but not by all her subjects. While she had brought an end to open opposition, many, especially of the conservative old nobility, continued to deplore her, if not to oppose her. One of these was Prince M. M. Shcherbatov. Shcherbatov belonged to one of the oldest and proudest families of the Russian traditional nobility, and throughout his life he was preoccupied with the status and condition of this class. He was also a scholar and historian and a minor functionary of the government under Catherine. His appraisal of her is contained in his tract *On the Corruption of Morals in Russia,* a work of his old age and a summation of his reflections on the direction of Russian history in his age. It was not published until the end of the nineteenth century.

A woman not born of the blood of our sovereigns, who deposed her husband by an armed insurrection, she received, in return for so virtuous a deed, the crown and sceptre of Russia, together with the title of "Devout Sovereign," in the words of the prayer recited in church on behalf of our monarchs.

It cannot be said that she is unqualified to rule so great an Empire, if indeed a woman can support this yoke, and if human qualities alone are sufficient for this supreme office. She is endowed with considerable beauty, clever, affable, magnanimous and compassionate on principle. She loves glory, and is assiduous in her pursuit of it. She is prudent, enterprising, and quite well-read. However, her moral outlook is based on the modern philosophers, that is to say, it is not fixed on the firm rock of God's Law; and hence, being based on arbitrary worldly principles, it is liable to change with them.

In addition, her faults are as follows: she is licentious; and trusts herself entirely to her favourites; she is full of ostentation in all things, infinitely selfish, and incapable of forcing herself to attend to any matters which may bore her. She takes everything on herself and takes no care to see it carried out, and finally she is so capricious, that she rarely keeps the same system of government even for a month.

For all that, once on the throne, she refrained from taking cruel vengeance on those who had previously vexed her. She had with her her favourite, Grigory Grigor'evich Orlov, who had helped her to accede to the throne. He was a man who had grown up in alehouses and houses of ill-repute. He had no education, and had hitherto led the life of a young reprobate, though he was kind and good-hearted.

This was the man who reached the highest step which it is possible for a subject to attain. . . .

The Empress herself, selfish woman that she is, wishes, it seems, to increase the power of vice, not only by her own example, but by her actual encouragement of it. Fond of glory and ostentation, she loves flattery and servility. . . .

Flattery having reached such a peak at Court among men employed in affairs of state, people have begun to flatter in other ways. If anyone builds a house with money partly given by her or that he has stolen, he invites her to the housewarming, where he writes the following words in illuminations: "A Gift to You from Your Subjects"; or else he inscribes on the house: "By the Generosity of Catherine the Great," forgetting to add: "But to the Ruination of Russia." Or else, festivals are given in her honour, gardens are built, with impromptu spectacles and decorations, everywhere showing flattery and servility.

To add to the corruption of women's morals and of all decency, she has set other women the example of the possession of a long and frequent succession of lovers, each equally honoured and enriched, thus advertising the cause of their ascendancy. Seeing a shrine erected to this vice in the heart of the Empress, women scarcely think it a vice in themselves to copy her; rather, I suppose, each thinks it a virtue in herself that she has not yet had so many lovers!

Although she is in her declining years, although grey hair now covers her head and time has marked her brow with the indelible signs of age, yet her licentiousness still does not diminish. She now realizes that her lovers cannot find in her the attractions of youth, and that neither rewards, nor power, nor gain can replace for them the effect which youthfulness can produce on a lover.

Trying to conceal the ravages of time, she has abandoned her former simplicity in dress, and though in her youth she disliked cloth-of-gold, and criticized the Empress Elisabeth Petrovna for leaving a wardrobe large enough to clothe a whole army, she herself has started to show a passion of her own for inventing suitable dresses and rich adornments for them, and has thus given rise to the same luxury, not only in women but also in men.

I remember, when I entered the Court in 1768 there was only one coat in the whole Court that was embroidered in gold—a red cloth coat, belonging to Vasily Il'ich Bibikov. In April 1769, the Empress was angry with Count Ivan Grigor'evich Chernyshov for arriving at Czarskoe Selo on her birthday in an embroidered coat; but in 1777 when I retired from Court, everyone wore clothes of cloth-of-gold with embroidery even on ordinary days, and were now almost ashamed to have embroidery only on the edge of their garments. . . .

Generally speaking, women are more prone to despotism than men; and as far as she is concerned, it can justly be averred that she is in this particular a woman among women. Nothing can irritate her more than that when making some report to her, men quote the Laws in opposition to her will. Immediately the retort flies from her lips: "Can I then not do this irrespective of the laws?"

But she has found no one with the courage to answer that she can indeed, but only as a despot, and to the detriment of her glory and the nation's confidence. . . .

The whole reign of this monarch has been marked by events relating to her love of glory. The many institutions founded by her apparently exist for the good of the nation. In fact they are simply symbols of her love of glory, for if she really had the nation's interest at heart, she would, after founding them, have also paid attention to their progress. But she has been content simply with their establishment and with the assurance that she will be eternally revered by posterity as their founder; she has cared nothing for their progress, and though she sees their abuses she has not put a stop to them. . . .

The wars that have been started attest to this still more. Poniatowski[5] was raised to the Polish throne out of favouritism; it was wished to provide him with an autocratic form of government, contrary to the

---

[5]A Polish émigré nobleman and one of Catherine's lovers whom she did indeed install as king of Poland in 1764.—ED.

Polish liberties. The protection of the Dissidents was undertaken; and instead of striving to invite these victims of religious persecution to join their co-religionists in Russia, and thereby to weaken Poland and strengthen Russia, occasion was given for a war with Turkey, fortunate in its events, but costing Russia more than any previous war. The Fleet was sent to Greece and under God's protection won a victory; but the only motive behind this expedition was love of glory. Poland has been partitioned, thereby strengthening the houses of Austria and Brandenburg, and losing Russia her powerful influence over Poland. The Crimea has been acquired, or rather, stolen, a country which, because of its difference of climate, has proved a graveyard for Russians. . . .

My conscience assures me that all my descriptions, however black they may be, are unbiased; truth alone and the corruption into which all my fellow-subjects have fallen and from which my country groans, have compelled me to commit them to paper. And so, from a fair description of the morals of the Empress, it is quite possible to see the disposition of her heart and soul.

True friendship has never resided in her heart, and she is ready to betray her best friend and servant in order to please her lover. She has no maternal instincts for her son, and her rule with everyone is to cajole a man beyond measure and respect him as long as he is needed, and then in her own phrase "to throw away a squeezed-out lemon." . . .

Having painted this sad picture, I do not think I need to state whether she has faith in God's Law, for if she had, then God's Law itself might improve her heart and set her steps on the path of truth. But no: carried away by her indiscriminate reading of modern writers, she thinks nothing of the Christian religion, though she pretends to be quite devout.

A Modern Appraisal
of Catherine the Great

ISABEL DE MADARIAGA

From Shcherbatov's sour and critical contemporary appraisal of the empress as well as from Catherine's own carefully shaped and self-serving account of the beginning of her reign, we pass to a more balanced, modern account. It is taken from the best recent biography of her, *Catherine the Great: A Short History* by Isabel de Madariaga. Madariaga rejects the traditional view that Catherine was a hypocrite for such things as her policies on serfdom and her abandonment of liberal politics in favor of absolutism or that she was slavishly beholden to the nobility. Instead, she argues that Catherine's reign is best understood in terms of the goals and limits of an eighteenth-century reformer, not a revolutionary like Peter I.

Catherine ruled Russia from 1762 to 1796. "In an absolute monarchy, everything depends on the disposition and character of the Sovereign," the British Envoy to Russia, Sir James Harris, observed in 1778. The ruler sets the tone in every field far more than in a limited monarchy, as Great Britain was at the time, or in a democracy, as the United Kingdom is today. Peace or war, prosperity or poverty, a free and easy intellectual and social life, or a society isolated from outside influences and dragooned into conformity, all this depended to a great extent on the character of the individual ruler.

The personality of Catherine thus merits some attention. Inevitably it changed a good deal over the thirty-four years of her reign. Yet some features of her character remained present throughout. She was to begin with a woman of an optimistic and cheerful temperament, looking on the bright side of things, not easily depressed or downhearted. This shows clearly in her letters to Potemkin, who, on the contrary, was subject to formidable bouts of despondency, for instance at the beginning of the second Turkish war in 1787, when after the loss of his precious fleet in a storm on the Black Sea he was prepared to throw up his command and evacuate the Crimea. Catherine wrote letters to him full of encouragement, urging him to believe that a bold spirit would overcome failures, advising him about his indigestion, which she was sure contributed to his depression. "Goodbye, my friend," she concluded one letter in 1788, "neither time, nor distance, nor anyone on earth will change my thoughts of you and about you."

It was this same positive temper which enabled her to steer her way through the shoals at the Russian court while she was still grand duchess and gave her the courage to embark on the *coup d'état* which brought her to the throne. Its success should not conceal from one how dangerous failure might have been. Imprisonment in a convent would have been the mildest penalty she might have had to suffer. Throughout her life Catherine showed very strong and steady nerves at moments of crisis: during the early plots against her; during the Pugachev

Revolt,[6] when she had to be dissuaded by her ministers from going herself to Kazan to restore morale after the sacking of the city by Pugachev. But her health did not remain unaffected by these crises and she suffered from frequent headaches and digestive disorders.

By the standards of her time Catherine was a well-read woman of considerable breadth of interest and intellectual curiosity. She was interested in politics, history, education, literature, linguistics, architecture, painting. In her literary as in her legislative production she was pragmatic in her approach, pedantic in her execution, and eclectic as regards her sources. She seemed to feel that if the law described down to the last detail precisely how its provisions were to be implemented, better results would be achieved. In the Russian context, no doubt she was right to think that the careful drafting of laws would prevent misinterpretation. In her Instruction of 1767, she had quoted Montesquieu's dictum that you cannot change customs by means of laws but only by means of other customs; but her faith in the power of law to change conduct survived and shows through in her major legislative innovations.

A hard-working woman, Catherine rose early, lit her fire, made her black coffee and settled down at her desk to indulge in her "scribbling." A blank sheet of paper made her fingers itch to start writing. After a few hours devoted to her literary or political activities, she would see her secretaries and ministers, withdraw to perform her toilette in private and only appear in her dressing room for her hair to be dressed. She did not go in for the elaborate court ritual of the *lever* and the *coucher* (receptions on getting up and going to bed) still practised at the French court. In private Catherine dressed simply in a loose silk gown, but on state occasions she was richly dressed and wore splendid jewels. Dinner was usually at 2 p.m. and, since the Empress was not interested in food, it was notoriously bad. Catherine was also very abstemious, and did not drink even wine unless her Scottish physician, Dr. Rogerson, prescribed it.

The afternoon was devoted to reading or working, or seeing specially invited guests, such as Diderot or Grimm. The Empress would then play for a while with her grandchildren, and adjourn to spend the evening at the theatre or at her private parties in the Hermitage. These were completely informal. It was forbidden to rise when the Empress stood up, and those who had the right to attend talked, gambled, played paper games or went in for theatricals until about 10

---

[6]An uprising led by a former Cossack officer, Yemelyan Pugachev, which broke out during the first Turkish war and lasted until 1775, the most serious rebellion in Russian imperial history.—ED.

p.m. when the Empress, who never took any supper, withdrew attended by her current favourite, and the guests dispersed in search of a well-provided table and a better cook than Catherine's.

All those who ever attended the court bear witness to the grace and dignity with which Catherine conducted herself, to the ease and charm of her manners. Claude Carloman de Rulhière, who was attached to the French Embassy in St. Petersburg at the time of Catherine's *coup d'état,* described her appearance in 1762:

> She has a noble and agreeable figure; her gait is majestic, her person and deportment is full of graces. Her air is that of a sovereign. All her features proclaim a superior character. . . . Her brow is broad and open, her nose almost aquiline. . . . Her hair is chestnut coloured and very beautiful, her eyebrows brown, her eyes brown [they were in fact blue] and very beautiful, acquiring a bluish tint in certain lights; her complexion is dazzling. Pride is the principal feature of her physiognomy. The pleasantness and kindness of her expression are, to the eye of a keen observer, rather the consequence of a great desire to please. . . .

The desire to impress, not only by her physical presence but by her intellectual qualities, is noted by many observers of Catherine, beginning with the adventurer Count Casanova, and it explains the well-merited reputation she had for vanity. . . . The Chevalier de Corberon, who was not admitted to Catherine's small court circle and was therefore somewhat jaundiced, regarded Catherine as a "comédienne," always acting a part.

Whether she was acting a part or not, Catherine throughout her life showed her ability to get on with people in all ranks of life. Her servants adored her and remained with her for years; her secretaries were well treated, and the diary kept by A.V. Khrapovitsky, himself a poet and writer, who was her private secretary in the years 1782 to 1793 and also helped her with her literary works, illustrates her kindness, her consideration for his health and welfare. She was always well received by the common people on her various travels throughout Russia, and it was the aristocracy, not the people, who cold-shouldered her in Moscow. Of course personal access to the palace and to the presence of the Empress was much easier in those days than it is today to the presence of kings, presidents and ministers, for she did not have to be protected against terrorists, journalists or photographers. Catherine drove about the streets of St. Petersburg in an open sledge at night, with just a few attendants, in perfect security. The public—decently dressed—was admitted to the imperial parks, and wherever she travelled Catherine gave receptions to which the local nobility and townspeople were invited. The French Ambassador, Ségur, describes how after one such lengthy reception the Empress emerged with her cheeks coloured bright pink with rouge from having kissed so many of the painted faces of the merchants' ladies.

Life was also made easier for her ministers by her commonsensical and unpretentious approach to work. Ministers did not have to stand in her presence like Disraeli or Gladstone before Queen Victoria. The letters and notes she wrote asking for advice, and the letters she received with advice, reflect a genuine partnership in the search for a solution to a particular legislative or administrative problem. Where her correspondence over a particular legislative project can be followed, as with Count Sievers over the Statute of Local Administration of 1775, it is clear that her advisers and ministers had no hesitation in countering her ideas and expressing their own. The minutes of the meetings of the Council of State frequently reflect the vigorous debate which took place. On the other hand Catherine could also write stinging rebukes to officials who failed her.

Within the mental climate of her time and of her position as ruler, Catherine also showed more originality than any previous ruler of Russia and than most rulers at the time in Europe, except perhaps the Grand Duke Leopold of Tuscany, in her thoughts about changing the nature and the structure of Russian central government by altering the relationship of the central power and the corporate forces in Russian society, forces to which she had herself given legal form. It is here that the influence of William Blackstone's *Commentaries on the Laws of England* (in a French translation) is so noteworthy. Catherine made over 700 pages of notes from Blackstone and wrote various drafts at different times of the changes in the constitutional structure she proposed to introduce.

In a manner typical of her industrious nature, she hoped to begin to draw up her final plans in the course of her journey to the Crimea in 1787, and ordered her secretary to collect all her notes on Blackstone to take with her, as well as a copy of her Instruction, which she wished to compare with her notes on Blackstone. Familiar with her plans and never at a loss for a compliment, Khrapovitsky exclaimed that one day Russians would treasure her work as the English treasured their Magna Carta. Throughout her journey Catherine continued to work on her plans for constitutional reform. From what one can tell of her intentions, she viewed her project as a means of consolidating absolute government in Russia by making it more responsive to the various estates and more efficient. The most novel feature she drew from her reading of Blackstone was her plan for a high court, which seemed to have some of the legislative features of the British Parliament and some of its judicial elements. The separate chambers into which the proposed High Court was to be divided would have appointed councillors, but also assessors, elected by the local nobles, townspeople and state peasants.

Though Catherine never completed even a draft law, these papers show that as late as 1787 she could still contemplate fundamental reform, which associated elected representatives of the free estates with the machinery of central government in a way which was not even to be thought of again until the reign of Alexander II (1856–81). It is not possible to tell what inspired her to think such institutions necessary or advisable in Russia. Did something remain of her lengthy conversations with Diderot in 1774, who had urged her to keep the Legislative Commission in being and who had warned her, "All arbitrary government is bad, even the arbitrary government of a good, strong, just and wise master. . . . He deprives the nation of the right to deliberate, to wish, or not to wish to oppose, to oppose even that which is good. In a society of men, the right of opposition seems to me a natural right, inalienable and sacred." The best of despots "is a good shepherd who reduces his subjects to the condition of animals; he makes them lose the sense of liberty. . . ."

It is unfortunately also not possible to tell on the evidence available at present whether Catherine abandoned her projects because of the outbreak of war with Turkey in 1787, or because she was feeling old and discouraged, or because of her dismay at the use made of their power by elected "representatives" of the people in the French Revolution. . . .

It was Catherine's private life which really exercised the gossip-mongers of the time (and later). By twentieth-century standards there was nothing abnormal about it until her breach with Grigory Orlov in 1772—he had been her lover for twelve years and was the father of her son, A. Bobrinskoy, never legitimized, but known to be hers, and recognized as his brother by Paul I. (The rumour that she had five daughters by Orlov is quite unsubstantiated.) During their liaison Orlov seems to have conducted himself in such a way as not to arouse violent hostility. He was brave, lazy, good-natured, neither very intelligent nor very cultured. He played a prominent part in court functions and festivities. But he was a liberal-minded man and he should be remembered for two initiatives: he invited the Genevese philosopher Rousseau, who quarrelled with everybody, to settle in Russia (presumably with Catherine's consent);[7] and he sponsored a number of projects on his estates to find an alternative to serfdom for the establishment of peasants on the land, also with Catherine's knowledge and approval.

---

[7]Rousseau, unlike Diderot, did not avail himself of this invitation.—ED.

Catherine was induced to dismiss Orlov in 1772 because of his un-faithfulness, and she chose a new lover, whom she did not love and who was given no governmental post, simply because she could not live alone. Something of her emotional life at this time is known, for she described it in moving terms in a letter to Grigory Potemkin with whom the great love affair of her life began in December 1773. Potemkin was already a lieutenant-general in the army, and had distinguished him-self in the war against the Turks. He was probably thirty-four years old—ten years younger than Catherine and a bold, enterprising, imagi-native, moody, arrogant, witty and intelligent man. He ceased to be Catherine's lover in 1776, but he kept his official positions to the sur-prise of many at court, who expected him to be dismissed when Cather-ine took a new lover, P. V. Zavadovsky. But he remained the most powerful figure at court, and continued as Catherine's principal ad-viser and confidant. It is possible that he was her husband—there were rumours that a religious ceremony had taken place—at any rate she trusted him absolutely. His role at her side can be compared to that of Leicester beside Elizabeth I of England. A woman ruler, however able, needs someone very reliable indeed to command her armies, someone who will not turn against her (as Essex did against Elizabeth). Cather-ine found her helpmate in Potemkin, who continued to dominate the scene at her side until his death in 1791. . . .

But the favourites who followed Zavadovsky (who was dismissed in 1778) did nothing to increase Catherine's reputation. She needed their companionship both as lovers and as partners in her intellectual and cultural activities, but only two of them, A. D. Lanskoy (1780–4) and A. Dmitriyev Mamonov (1786–9), seem to have been reasonably well educated and capable of providing Catherine the woman with the affection and friendship she craved for. . . .

Later, A. Dmitriyev Mamonov betrayed Catherine's affection in a different way, by falling in love with one of her maids of honour. Deeply hurt, Catherine dismissed him and arranged his marriage. As the Empress grew older, her favourites became younger, and though they were not given prominent political positions, their closeness to Catherine meant that they were the channel by which private and even corrupt influence could be brought to bear. Catherine was now beginning to feel her age. She had grown very stout, though accord-ing to the French painter, Mme Vigée Lebrun, she remained very charming, with her white hair framing a noble face, and beautiful, very white hands. . . .

The great Russian historian N. M. Karamzin, though critical par-ticularly of the corruption and neglect of the public interest in the last years of Catherine II, nevertheless wrote in a memorandum he drew up for Alexander I in 1811 that "should we compare all the known epochs of Russian history, virtually all would agree that Catherine's epoch was the happiest for Russian citizens; virtually all would prefer to have lived then than at any other time." . . .

It is essential to realize how little opposition there was to the form of government, absolutism, in Russia. The bulk of the population accepted the legitimacy of the regime however much some people might disagree with some policies. Government operated largely as a partnership between the nobility, the townspeople and the Crown, and the political class in a largely illiterate and materially still very primitive country was minute. Individuals might criticize specific policies, but the Russian political system provided no channels for groups to form with common programmes. There were only small patronage and clientele circles around specific magnates. This explains the importance of the favourites and of high-ranking ministers like Prince A. A. Vyazemsky or Alexander Vorontsov. They all became rich (or richer) and Catherine's favourites were given high rank. Nobles anxious for promotion gravitated towards one or other of the magnates as long as their favour lasted. . . .

On the other hand the rising of the assigned peasants in the Urals in 1763–4 and the rising led by Pugachev in 1773–4 are clear indications of popular dissatisfaction with specific government policies among Cossacks, state peasants, industrial serfs and privately owned serfs. But the discontented did not normally coalesce into one single, massive opposition; they usually formed single-issue groups among the peasantry, anxious to escape from the tyranny of a particular landowner. Moreover the dissatisfaction felt by the peasants was part of a widespread, formless hatred of and revolt against the modern state, which taxed them, called them up to serve in the army (or, worse, the navy), instead of leaving them in peaceful occupation of all the land, without any officials, officers or landowners intervening between them and a benevolent tsar.

There is one aspect of the opposition to Catherine which has so far been much less well documented. The example which the Empress so glaringly provided of total disregard for the rules of domestic morality—acceptable at that time in a man, totally unforgivable in a woman—turned many of the Church hierarchy, such as Metropolitan Platon of Moscow, and of the more straitlaced nobles, of which there were many, and the Moscow freemasons against her. Catherine's private life was contrasted with the apparent domestic happiness of Paul (he was more discreet). She was accused of corrupting young people and family life by her example, and the Russian court, particularly in its later years, rivalled French society, or the grand Whig society of England, in its dissoluteness, though high standards of decorum were always maintained in public.

Lower down the social scale, there was considerable opposition to Catherine's secularization of Church lands, to the widespread closure of monasteries and convents, and the concentration of monks and nuns in a smaller number of larger establishments. Local minor nobles and townspeople appealed to be allowed to keep open at their own expense small convents which they had often endowed in the past and which acted as refuges for their wives and sisters—requests which were sometimes granted. Unofficially, women's groups in provincial towns set up self-supporting "women's communities," in which women could live a disciplined and religious life, and undertake good works without being officially rated as nuns. What one might call the conservative opposition to Catherine's "enlightenment policies" needs further study.

It is still too early to make a considered judgment on the impact of Catherine's reign in Russia, and to interpret her policies with any certainty. . . .

The traditional view for a long time has been that Catherine was so badly in need of noble support to keep the throne that she deliberately increased the power of the nobles over their serfs, and governed in such a way as to consolidate noble domination and exploitation of the human and material resources of the country. This theory is still found in some modern histories of her policies, but it no longer commands general agreement. In the light of the work that has been done mainly by British and American historians it is now more possible to see both what the Empress tried to achieve and what obstacles faced her. By temperament, as well as because she was aware that she had no legitimate claim to the throne, Catherine wished to prove herself a reformer, in the spirit of German cameralism as modified by the enlightenment. Her policies were presented to the Russian (and to the European) public clothed in the language of the enlightenment. But there was a considerable discrepancy between her aims and her achievements. It is this discrepancy between the rhetoric in which she expressed her aims and hopes and the actual performance of the institutions she created which has left her open to the charge of hypocrisy. But she was no hypocrite. She believed in her reforms, but she had to use the human tools to hand, and there is no doubt that, while she found many great administrators, most of the officials on whom she had to rely did not live up to her expectations. Was she informed of these inadequacies? Did she turn a blind eye? We cannot tell at this stage. What remains true however is that Catherine was the first ruler of Russia to conceive of drawing up legislation setting out the corporate rights of the nobles and the townspeople, and the civil rights of the free population of the country. The nobility, the townspeople and the free peasants were given a legal framework within which these rights could be pressed. She was also the first ruler ever to establish special courts to which the state peasants had access and in which they could and did sue merchants and nobles. During her reign the individual—other than the serf or the soldier—was allowed more space, more responsibility, more security, more dignity. For a while an increasingly diversified Russian society escaped from the overwhelming pressure of the militarization imposed on it by Peter I and restored by Paul I.

Catherine did not increase the power of the nobles over the serfs, nor did she turn large numbers of Russian state peasants into private serfs. She did not, as we know, free the serfs, or even attempt to regulate relations between serfs and landowners by law. Her hold on the throne was not strong enough to enable her to put through a policy which would have been opposed by the whole of the Russian political elite, both the nobility and the townspeople. She did not have the power of coercion necessary to enforce a policy which would have to be put through by the very people who benefited from the *status quo*. But that should not be the sole criterion by which she is judged.

Catherine was not a revolutionary like Peter I, who forced his policies on a reluctant society without counting the human cost. She paid attention to public opinion; as she said to Diderot, "what I despair of overthrowing I undermine." Her absolute authority rested, as she well knew, on her sensitivity to the possible.

Review and Study Questions

1. How did Catherine succeed to the throne of Russia?
2. What were Catherine's weaknesses and strengths as a ruler? Discuss.
3. What are the main features of Prince Shcherbatov's characterization of the Empress Catherine? Discuss what may have accounted for his views.
4. In what respects do you consider Catherine an eighteenth-century reformer, as Isabel de Madariaga argues she was?

Suggestions for Further Reading

There are a substantial number of Catherine the Great's own writings. These include two collections of letters: *The Correspondence of Catherine the Great When Grand-Duchess, with Sir Charles Hanbury-Williams and Letters from Count Poniatowski*, ed. and tr. the Earl of

Ilchester and Mrs. Longford-Brooke (London: Thornton Butter-worth, 1928), and *Voltaire and Catherine the Great: Selected Correspondence,* ed. and tr. A. Lentin (Cambridge, Mass.: Oriental Research Partners, 1974). Catherine's published works also include two editions of her memoirs: *The Memoirs of Catherine the Great,* ed. Dominique Maroger (London: Hamish Hamilton, 1955), and *The Memoirs of Catherine the Great,* tr. Katherine Anthony (New York: Knopf, 1927), excerpted for this chapter. Two related collections of sources are *Memoirs of Catherine II and the Court of St. Petersburg, during Her Reign and That of Paul I, by One of Her Courtiers* (Paris: Grolier Society, c. 1930) and a series of documents, *Russia under Catherine the Great,* 2 vols. (Newtonville, Mass.: Oriental Research Partners, 1977–1978).

There are dozens of biographies of Catherine, many of them by professional biographers and popular writers who tend to fall back on the malicious gossip and salacious rumor of Catherine's own time. A few of them, however, can be recommended; the best is probably Henri Troyat, *Catherine the Great,* tr. Joan Pinkham (New York: Dutton, 1980), by a distinguished French literary man and experienced biographer of several notable Russian figures. Ian Grey, *Catherine the Great: Autocrat and Empress of All Russia* (London: Hodder and Stoughton, 1961) and Vincent Cronin, *Catherine: Empress of All the Russias* (New York: William Morrow, 1978) are both competent professional biographies. Zoé Oldenbourg, *Catherine the Great,* tr. Anne Carter (New York: Random House, 1965), is an appealing book by a great historical novelist, dealing mainly with Catherine's early years; it is sympathetic, extremely readable, but not entirely reliable. Much to be preferred is J. T. Alexander, *Catherine the Great—Life and Legend* (London: Oxford University Press, 1989), a recent work on the young Catherine by a competent professional Russian historian. The best modern biographer of Catherine is Isabel de Madariaga, *Catherine the Great: A Short History* (New Haven: Yale University Press, 1990), excerpted for this chapter. J. T. Alexander, *Autocratic Politics in a National Crisis: The Imperial Government and Pugachev's Revolt* (Bloomington, Ind.: Indiana University Press, 1969) is a detailed study of Pugachev's rebellion. Another special study, of the serfdom problem, is J. Blum, *Lord and Peasant in Russia from the Ninth to the Nineteenth Century* (Princeton, N.J.: Princeton University Press, 1961). Still another special study is Marc Raeff, *The Origins of the Russian Intelligentsia: The Eighteenth-Century Nobility* (New York: Harcourt Brace and World, 1966). Another, dealing with economic history, is A. Kahan, *The Plow, the Hammer and the Knout: An Economic History of Eighteenth-Century Russia* (Chicago: University of Chicago Press, 1985).

On "the world of Catherine the Great," two international conference proceedings are useful: *Russia and the West in the Eighteenth Century*, ed. A. G. Cross (Newtonville, Mass.: Oriental Research Partners, 1983) and *Russia and the World of the Eighteenth Century*, ed. R. P. Bartlett, A. G. Cross, and Karen Rasmussen (Columbus, Ohio: Slavica Publishers, 1988). Also of this type is Miriam Kochan, *Life in Russia under Catherine the Great* (London: Batsford and Putnam, 1969), a small book dealing with such topics as the nobility, serfs, industry and trade, and enlightened despotism, by a popular writer on Russian history; it makes no claim to distinguished scholarship. A really distinguished book of this sort is Isabel de Madariaga, *Russia in the Age of Catherine the Great* (New Haven: Yale University Press, 1981).

For larger-scale historical background, two among many general Russian histories that can be recommended are Michael T. Florinsky, *Russia: A Short History*, 2nd ed. (London: Macmillan, 1969) and Nicholas V. Riasanovsky, *A History of Russia*, 2nd ed. (New York: Oxford University Press, 1984).

NAPOLEON: CHILD OR BETRAYER OF THE REVOLUTION?

Was Napoleon a child of the French Revolution? Napoleon himself felt that he was. And in one sense at least, the assertion is undeniably true. The Revolution had broken the caste system of the old military order, just as it had broken the social order of the Old Regime generally. In the struggling revolutionary republic, threatened with invasion and armed reprisal from every side, any man who showed the ability and the willingness to serve could advance in the military— even such an apparently unpromising officer as the young Napoleon Bonaparte, with his heavy Italian accent, his mediocre record as a military cadet and a junior officer, and his consuming interest in the politics of his native Corsica, which seemed to preclude any involvement in the great events that had been shaking France since 1789.

But Napoleon was not indifferent to those events. As early as 1791, he had become a member of the Jacobin Club in his garrison town of Valence, in the south of France, and was an outspoken advocate of Jacobin radicalism. His political views, rather than any proven military ability, secured for him his first important commission as com-

155

mander of artillery at the siege of Toulon against the royalists and the British. Napoleon was successful, and he caught the eye of the military commissioner Augustin Robespierre, who praised the young officer in a letter to his brother Maximilien, then at the zenith of his political career in Paris. Napoleon was appointed commandant of artillery in the army of Italy. But Robespierre and his faction soon fell from power, and Napoleon, deprived of his command, was arrested. After a brief imprisonment, he departed for Paris to try to rescue his fortunes.

In 1795 the National Convention, its tenure running out, submitted to referendum the so-called Constitution of the Year III,[1] with its accompanying decree that two-thirds of the convention's members must be returned to the new legislative assembly. The royalists, enraged at this attempt to ensure continued radical domination of the government, rose in revolt. Someone remembered that the young radical Napoleon was in Paris, and he was given effective command of the defense of the convention. As the rebels marched on 13 Vendémiaire, Year IV (October 5, 1795), Napoleon had already positioned his artillery and coolly ordered it to fire. The famous "whiff of grapeshot" carried the day—though there is no record that Napoleon used the phrase—and friends and enemies alike began to call him "Général Vendémiaire." He was now a force to be reckoned with in the politics of the Revolution.

When the new government was formed, headed by a Directory, Napoleon was its military adviser. Within a year, he was given command of the army of Italy. The Italian campaign was at that time verging on failure, but Napoleon turned it around. He gained the loyalty of his troops—largely by authorizing them to live off the land they conquered in lieu of the pay their republic had failed to provide—and he won battles. Within less than a year, Napoleon was the master of Italy. Far exceeding his authority, he set up a series of Italian republics and forced the Austrians out of Italy entirely. Then Napoleon returned to Paris once more to engineer the Treaty of Campo Formio with the defeated Austrians. Although the Directory was far from pleased, Napoleon was fast becoming a popular hero.

Britain, with its formidable sea power and its wealth and industry, was clearly France's most dangerous enemy, and the Directory had formulated a plan for an invasion of England from across the channel. Napoleon was placed in command of the operation. After a cur-

---

[1]The early leaders of the Revolution had proclaimed a new calendar dating from the overthrow of the Old Regime. Napoleon would later return France to the common usage.—Ed.

sory inspection, he rejected the plan, arguing instead for a strike at the British lifeline to India—a campaign in Egypt. Napoleon was able to overcome the Directory but not the British sea power and the squadrons of Lord Nelson. The Egyptian campaign was a disaster. But rather than admit defeat, Napoleon returned to France and proclaimed a victory when in fact there was none. The French people believed him.

In 1799 Napoleon, with Abbé Sieyès, an ambitious member of the Directory, engineered a coup d'état. The coup, which took place on 18–19 Brumaire, Year VIII (November 9–10, 1799), was successful, and the Directory was replaced by a Consulate of three men, one of them Napoleon. Within a matter of weeks, a new "Constitution of the Year VIII" was proclaimed, making Napoleon First Consul and the government of France a military dictatorship. It is true that the constitution was overwhelmingly approved by plebiscite, after the fact. It is true that under its authority Napoleon launched far-reaching reforms, moving the nation in the direction of order and stability. But it is also true that the French nation had succumbed to the myth of Napoleon, a myth that was ultimately founded upon his military invincibility and—at least in Napoleon's mind—upon continued military victories.

In 1802 Europe might well have had peace. Even Britain had agreed to the Treaty of Amiens. For achieving this diplomatic coup, Napoleon was granted lifetime tenure as First Consul, but even this did not satisfy his ambition. Napoleon demanded an empire and he got it: on May 18, 1804, he was proclaimed Emperor of the French. In the years that followed, Napoleon compiled an incredible list of military victories: he defeated the Austrians at Ulm and the Austrians and Russians at Austerlitz in the winter of 1805, the Prussians at Jena and Auerstädt in the fall of 1806, and the Russians alone at Eylau and Friedland in the spring and summer of 1807. By this time, Napoleon had redrawn the map of western Europe, and his own relations sat on half a dozen thrones. His plan was to organize the Continent against the stubborn British; to this end, he signed an agreement with the new Russian emperor, Alexander I, dividing Europe between them.

In 1810 Napoleon, standing at the apex of his power, decided to disregard his agreement with Alexander and invade Russia. It was a disastrous miscalculation, and it proved to be the crucial turning point in Napoleon's career. Out of the almost half a million men who had massed on the banks of the Neman in the summer of 1812, fewer than ten thousand remained after the winter's march back from Moscow. The myth of Napoleon was shattered, and the powers of Europe rose up against him. Not only had he defeated and humiliated them, but he had brought them the Revolution. Even if he had subverted the Revolution in France, he had, nevertheless, exported its principles along with his conquests. To the Old Regime of Europe, this was Napoleon's greatest insult, the ultimate betrayal that they could not forgive. But it was also perhaps Napoleon's most enduring claim to having been one of the makers of World history, for, whatever his motives, Napoleon introduced the Age of Revolution that persisted on the Continent, in one guise or another, through most of the nineteenth century and that fundamentally changed the nature of European government and society.

Napoleon was forced to abdicate and was exiled to the Mediterranean island of Elba. But even as the victors were gathering to undo his work and the Bourbons were returning to France, Napoleon escaped from Elba. This was the beginning of his Hundred Days. As Napoleon, with an escort of grenadiers, approached Grenoble, he met the first battalion sent to intercept him. His secretary, the Marquis de Las Cases, described the scene:

> The commanding officer refused even to parley. The Emperor without hesitation, advanced alone, and one hundred of his grenadiers marched at some distance from him, with their arms reversed. The sight of Napoleon, his costume, and in particular his grey military great coat, produced a magical effect on the soldiers, and they stood motionless. Napoleon went straight up to a veteran whose arm was covered with *chevrons*, and very unceremoniously seizing him by the whisker, asked him whether he would have the heart to kill his Emperor. The soldier, his eyes moistened with tears immediately thrust the ramrod into his musket, to show that it was not loaded, and exclaimed, "See, I could not have done thee any harm: all the others are the same." Cries of *Vive l'Empereur!* resounded on every side. Napoleon ordered the battalion to make half a turn to the right, and all marched on to Paris.[2]

With every mile resistance melted, and cries of *Vive l'Empereur!* swelled up from the throngs that lined the roads and from garrison troops and militia. Napoleon had returned and France was his. Even after the catastrophe at Waterloo, an officer lying in the mud with a shattered thigh cried out, "He has ruined us—he has destroyed France and himself—yet I love him still."[3]

But what of the Revolution? The old veteran on the road to Grenoble and the wounded officer on the field of Waterloo wept for their

---

[2]The Count de Las Cases, *Memoirs of the Life, Exile, and Conversations of the Emperor Napoleon,* new ed. (New York: Eckler, 1900), III, 295.

[3]Louis Antoine Fauvelet de Bourrienne, *Memoirs of Napoleon Bonaparte,* ed. R. W. Phipps (New York: Scribner's, 1891), IV, 204.

emperor, not for the lost cause of the Revolution. Thousands unquestionably shared their views. But many thousands more were convinced that, despite the terrible cost of Napoleon's search for glory, he had carried the Revolution to its proper, even to its inevitable conclusion. Napoleon himself wrote:

> I purified a revolution, in spite of hostile factions. I combined all the scattered benefits that could be preserved; but I was obliged to protect them with a nervous arm against the attacks of all parties; and in this situation it may be truly said that the public interest, *the State, was myself.*[4]

The wheel had come full circle. Napoleon "the child of the Revolution" echoed the words often ascribed to Louis XIV: "I am the state."

---

[4]Las Cases, *Memoirs,* III, 255–56.

Napoleon's Memoirs

THE COUNT DE LAS CASES

When, after Waterloo, Napoleon was sent into exile again, this time to the tiny, distant island of St. Helena in the south Atlantic, he was only forty-five years old, apparently in the prime of life. Might he not escape once more, even against all odds? Might he not be called back by one or another of the victorious allies, already beginning to quarrel among themselves? Might not France even summon its emperor again? Napoleon was planning for any eventuality, as carefully and methodically as he might plan a military campaign.

Napoleon had, of course, some limited contact with the Bonapartists in France, but this was restricted by the tight control over the island. He was able to carry on some correspondence, though much of it consisted of complaints to the British government about the conditions of his exile. But mainly Napoleon devoted himself to his memoirs, which he dictated to his secretary, the Marquis de Las Cases. Las Cases carefully transcribed the material, and then Napoleon read and corrected it himself.

Memoirs of the Life, Exile, and Conversations of the Emperor Napoleon is a vast and complicated work—four volumes in its final published form. In addition to Napoleon's own recollections of events, discourses, and opinions, it contains comments, reflections, and interpolations by Las Cases. It details Napoleon's bitter, petty, continuing controversy with the authorities on the island whose task it was to maintain his captivity. But primarily the book is Napoleon's own apologia, the justification for his policies and his career, directed to his own French people, to the allies, and to the tribunal of history. To Napoleon, the book was his final weapon.

It is in this work, more than in any other place, that we see the precise terms in which Napoleon considered himself the child, the inheritor, the "purifier" of the Revolution.

"The French Revolution was not produced by the jarring interests of two families disputing the possession of the throne; it was a general rising of the mass of the nation against the privileged classes." . . . The principal object of the Revolution was to destroy all privileges;

to abolish signorial jurisdictions, justice being an inseparable attribute of sovereign authority; to suppress feudal rights as being a remnant of the old slavery of the people; to subject alike all citizens and all property to the burdens of the state. In short, the Revolution proclaimed equality of rights. A citizen might attain any public employment, according to his talent and the chances of fortune. The kingdom was composed of provinces which had been united to the Crown at various periods: they had no natural limits, and were differently divided, unequal in extent and in population. They possessed many laws of their own, civil as well as criminal: they were more or less privileged, and very unequally taxed, both with respect to the amount and the nature of the contributions, which rendered it necessary to detach them from each other by lines of custom-houses. France was not a state, but a combination of several states, connected together without amalgamation. The whole had been determined by chance and by the events of past ages. The Revolution, guided by the principle of equality, both with respect to the citizens and the different portions of the territory, destroyed all these small nations: there was no longer a Brittany, a Normandy, a Burgundy, a Champagne, a Provence, or a Lorraine; but the whole formed a France. A division of homogeneous territory, prescribed by local circumstances, confounded the limits of all the provinces. They possessed the same judicial and administrative organization, the same civil and criminal laws, and the same system of taxation. The dreams of the upright men of all ages were realized. The opposition which the Court, the Clergy, and the Nobility, raised against the Revolution and the war with foreign powers, produced the law of emigration and the sequestration of emigrant property, which subsequently it was found necessary to sell, in order to provide for the charges of the war. A great portion of the French nobility enrolled themselves under the banner of the princes of the Bourbon family, and formed an army which marched in conjunction with the Austrian, Prussian, and English forces. Gentlemen who had been brought up in the enjoyment of competency served as private soldiers; numbers were cut off by fatigue and the sword; others perished of want in foreign countries; and the wars of La Vendée and of the Chouans, and the revolutionary tribunals, swept away thousands. Three-fourths of the French nobility were thus destroyed; and all posts, civil, judicial, or military, were filled by citizens who had risen from the common mass of the people. The change produced in persons and property by the events of the Revolution, was not less remarkable than that which was effected by the principles of the Revolution. A new church was created; the dioceses of Vienne, Narbonne, Féjus, Sisteron, Rheims, &c., were superseded by sixty new dioceses, the boundaries of which were circumscribed, in Concordat,[5] by new Bulls applicable to the present state of the French territory. The suppression of religious orders, the sale of convents and of all ecclesiastical property, were sanctioned, and the clergy were pensioned by the State. Everything that was the result of the events which had occurred since the time of Clovis, ceased to exist. All these changes were so advantageous to the people that they were effected with the utmost facility, and, in 1800, there no longer remained any recollection of the old privileges and sovereigns of the provinces, the old parliaments and bailiwicks, or the old dioceses; and to trace back the origin of all that existed, it was sufficient to refer to the new law by which it had been established. One-half of the land had changed its proprietors; the peasantry and the citizens were enriched. The advancement of agriculture and manufactures exceeded the most sanguine hopes. France presented the imposing spectacle of upwards of thirty millions of inhabitants, circumscribed within their natural limits, and composing only a single class of citizens, governed by one law, one rule, and one order. All these changes were conformable with the welfare and rights of the nation, and with the justice and intelligence of the age.

The five members of the Directory were divided. Enemies to the Republic crept into the councils; and thus men, hostile to the rights of the people, became connected with the government. This state of things kept the country in a ferment; and the great interests which the French people had acquired by the Revolution were incessantly compromised. One unanimous voice, issuing from the plains of France and from her cities and her camps, demanded the preservation of all the principles of the Republic, or the establishment of an hereditary system of government, which would place the principles and interests of the Revolution beyond the reach of factions and the influence of foreigners. By the constitution of the year VIII the First Consul of the Republic became Consul for ten years, and the nation afterwards prolonged his magistracy for life: the people subsequently raised him to the throne, which it rendered hereditary in his family. The principles of the sovereignty of the people, of liberty and equality, of the destruction of the feudal system, of the irrevocability of the sale of national domains, and the freedom of religious worship, were now established. The government of France, under the fourth dynasty, was founded on the same principles as the Republic. It was a moderate and constitutional monarchy. There was as much differ-

---

[5]The agreement (1801) between Napoleon and Pope Pius VII that restored Catholicism to France, though largely on Napoleon's terms.—ED.

ence between the government of France under the fourth dynasty and the third, as between the latter and the Republic. The fourth dynasty succeeded the Republic, or, more properly speaking, it was merely a modification of it.

No Prince ever ascended a throne with rights more legitimate than those of Napoleon. The crown was not presented to him by a few Bishops and Nobles; but he was raised to the Imperial throne by the unanimous consent of the citizens, three times solemnly confirmed.[6] Pope Pius VII, the head of the Catholic religion, the religion of the majority of the French people, crossed the Alps to anoint the Emperor with his own hands, in the presence of the Bishops of France, the Cardinals of the Romish Church, and the Deputies from all the districts of the Empire.[7] The sovereigns of Europe eagerly acknowledged Napoleon: all beheld with pleasure the modification of the Republic, which placed France on a footing of harmony with the rest of Europe, and which at once confirmed the constitution and the happiness of that great nation. Ambassadors from Austria, Russia, Prussia, Spain, Portugal, Turkey, and America, in fine, from all the powers of Europe, came to congratulate the Emperor. England alone sent no ambassador: she had violated the treaty of Amiens, and had consequently again declared war against France. . . .

The English declaration of war (1803) precipitated the imperial phase of Napoleon's career, during which, in victory after victory, he defeated the great powers of Europe. He hoped to complete his plans for Europe and for himself in the attack upon Russia. Here he reflects upon those plans and upon the Russian war.

. . . "That war should have been the most popular of any in modern times. It was a war of good sense and true interests; a war for the repose and security of all; it was purely pacific and preservative; entirely European and continental. Its success would have established a balance of power and would have introduced new combinations, by which the dangers of the present time would have been succeeded by future tranquillity. In this case, ambition

---

[6]A reference to the successive plebiscites that Napoleon used to gain approval of his modifications in the government. The last sanctioned his assumption of the imperial title.—ED.

[7]Though the pope was present, Napoleon placed the crown on his own head, as depicted in the famous painting of the occasion by the court painter Jacques-Louis David.—ED.

had no share in my views. In raising Poland,[8] which was the keystone of the whole arch, I would have permitted a King of Prussia, an Archduke of Austria, or any other to occupy the throne. I had no wish to obtain any new acquisition; and I reserved for myself only the glory of doing good, and the blessings of posterity. Yet this undertaking failed, and proved my ruin, though I never acted more disinterestedly, and never better merited success. As if popular opinion had been seized with contagion, in a moment, a general outcry, a general sentiment, arose against me. I was proclaimed the destroyer of kings—I, who had created them! I was denounced as the subverter of the rights of nations—I, who was about to risk all to secure them! And people and kings, those irreconcileable enemies, leagued together and conspired against me! All the acts of my past life were now forgotten. I said, truly, that popular favour would return to me with victory; but victory escaped me, and I was ruined. . . ."

The ruin brought upon him by the Russian war was purely fortuitous, claims Napoleon, and in no way can obscure his true accomplishments.

"I closed the gulf of anarchy and cleared the chaos. I purified the Revolution, dignified Nations and established Kings. I excited every kind of emulation, rewarded every kind of merit, and extended the limits of glory! This is at least something! And on what point can I be assailed on which an historian could not defend me? Can it be for my intentions? But even here I can find absolution. Can it be for my despotism? It may be demonstrated that the Dictatorship was absolutely necessary. Will it be said that I restrained liberty? It can be proved that licentiousness, anarchy, and the greatest irregularities, still haunted the threshold of freedom. Shall I be accused of having been too fond of war? It can be shown that I always received the first attack. Will it be said that I aimed at universal monarchy? It can be proved that this was merely the result of fortuitous circumstances, and that our enemies themselves led me step by step to this determination. Lastly, shall I be blamed for my ambition? This passion I must doubtless be allowed to have possessed, and that in no small degree; but at the same time, my ambition was of the highest

---

[8]His creation of an independent Poland was an indignity Russia would not endure. It was over this matter that the Russian campaign actually began.—ED.

and noblest kind that ever, perhaps, existed—that of establishing and of consecrating the empire of reason, and the full exercise and complete enjoyment of all the human faculties! And here the historian will probably feel compelled to regret that such ambition should not have been fulfilled and gratified!" Then after a few moments of silent reflection: "This," said the Emperor, "is my whole history in a few words."

On Politics, Literature, and National Character

MADAME DE STAËL

There were many who, like one hostile critic, regarded Napoleon simply as "the Corsican ogre." But there were other, more thoughtful critics who, though they condemned Napoleon, tried to understand why they did so. One of these was Anne-Louise-Germaine, Madame de Staël (1766–1817). She was the daughter of the Swiss banker Jacques Necker, who, as Minister of Finance to Louis XVI, had tried without much success—and without much imagination—to rescue France from fiscal chaos on the eve of the Revolution. Madame de Staël had grown up in the highest circles of the French aristocracy and the court, marrying the Swedish ambassador to France, Eric Magnus de Staël-Holstein, in 1786. She lived through the Revolution and knew most of its leading figures, as she did Napoleon and the men of the counterrevolution.

But Madame de Staël was more than simply a fashionable aristocrat. She was one of the last great luminaries of the Age of Enlightenment and one of the most important European writers of her time. She was also one of Napoleon's most perceptive and persistent critics. Though Madame de Staël was a passionate champion of liberty and an outspoken French patriot, she was no friend of the Revolution. But then, she observed, neither was Napoleon! He was, in her view, nothing less than its most sinister subverter. Napoleon tried first to moderate her views, then to persuade her of his good intentions, but he failed altogether to understand the basis of her hostility. Finally, he sent her into exile, and from Switzerland, Germany, Russia, and England she continued to observe and to write about the unfolding of the events she had foreseen. We turn now to *Madame de Staël: On Politics, Literature, and National*

Character, and her account of the rise and fall of Napoleon, so different in every way from his own.

The Directory was not inclined to peace, not because it wished to extend French rule beyond the Rhine and the Alps but because it believed war useful for the propagation of the republican system. Its plan was to surround France with a belt of republics. . . .

General Bonaparte was certainly less serious and less sincere than the Directory in the love of republican ideas, but he was much more shrewd in estimating a situation. He sensed that peace would become popular in France because passions were subsiding and people were weary of sacrifices; so he signed the Treaty of Campo Formio with Austria.

General Bonaparte distinguished himself as much by his character and mind as by his victories, and the imagination of the French was beginning to attach itself to him strongly. A tone of moderation and nobility prevailed in his style, which contrasted with the revolutionary gruffness of the civil leaders of France. The warrior spoke like a magistrate, while the magistrates expressed themselves with martial violence. . . .

It was with this feeling, at least, that I saw him for the first time in Paris. I could find no words of reply when he came to me to tell me that he had sought my father at Coppet and that he regretted having passed through Switzerland without having seen him. But when I was somewhat recovered from the confusion of admiration, a very strong sense of fear followed. Bonaparte at that time had no power; he was even believed to be somewhat threatened by the jealous suspicions of the Directory. So the fear he inspired was caused only by the extraordinary effect of his person upon nearly all who approached him. I had seen men worthy of respect, and I had seen fierce men: there was nothing in the impression Bonaparte produced upon me that recalled either the former or the latter. I very quickly saw, in the various occasions I had to meet him during his stay in Paris, that his character could not be defined by the words we ordinarily use; he was neither good, nor fierce, nor gentle, nor cruel, like others we know. Such a being, having no equals, could neither feel nor arouse any sympathy: he was more than a human being or less than one. His appearance, his mind, and his speech were foreign in nature—an added advantage for subjugating the French.

Far from being reassured by seeing Bonaparte more often, I was made increasingly apprehensive. I had a vague feeling that no emotions of the heart could influence him. He considers a human being a fact or a thing, not a fellow man. He does not hate nor does he love. For him, there is nothing but himself; all others are ciphers.

Every time I heard him speak I was struck by his superiority: yet it had no resemblance to that of men educated and cultivated by study or by social intercourse, such as may be found in England or France. But his speech showed a feeling for the situation, like the hunter's for his prey. . . .

General Bonaparte, at this same time, the end of 1797, sounded public opinion regarding the Directors; he realized that they were not liked but that republican sentiment made it as yet impossible for a general to take the place of civilian officials. The Directory proposed to him the assault upon England. He went to examine the coasts, and, quickly seeing that this expedition was senseless, returned resolved to attempt the conquest of Egypt.

Bonaparte has always sought to seize the imagination of men and, in this respect, he knows well how one must govern when one is not born to the throne. An invasion of Africa, the war carried to an almost fabulous country like Egypt, must make an impression upon every mind. . . .

But in his climb to power, Napoleon depended not only upon his growing military reputation.

The most potent magic that Bonaparte used to establish his power was the terror the mere name of Jacobinism inspired, though anyone capable of reflection knew perfectly well that this scourge could not reappear in France. People readily pretend to fear defeated parties in order to justify harsh measures. Everyone who wants to promote the establishment of despotism forcefully reminds us of the terrible crimes of demagogy. It is a very simple technique. So Bonaparte paralyzed every form of resistance to his will by the words: *Do you want me to hand you over to the Jacobins?* And France bowed down before him, no man bold enough to reply to him: *We shall be able to fight the Jacobins and you.* In short, even then he was not liked, only preferred. He almost always presented himself in competition with another cause for alarm, in order to make his power acceptable as a lesser evil. . . .

We cannot watch too attentively for the first symptoms of tyranny; when it has grown to a certain point, there is no more time to stop it. One man sweeps along the will of many individuals of whom the majority, taken separately, wish to be free but who nevertheless surrender because people fear each other and do not dare to speak their thoughts freely. . . .

General Bonaparte decreed a constitution in which there were no safeguards. Besides, he took great care to leave in existence the laws announced during the Revolution, in order to select from this detestable arsenal the weapon that suited him. The special commissions, deportations, exiles, the bondage of the press—these steps unfortunately taken in the name of liberty—were very useful to tyranny. To adopt them, he sometimes advanced reasons of state, sometimes the need of the times, sometimes the acts of his opponents, sometimes the need to maintain tranquillity. Such is the artillery of phrases that supports absolute power, for "emergencies" never end, and the more one seeks to repress by illegal measures the more one creates disaffected people who justify new injustices. The establishment of the rule of law is always put off till tomorrow. This is a vicious circle from which one cannot break out, for the public spirit that is awaited in order to permit liberty can come only from liberty itself. . . .

It was particularly advantageous to Bonaparte's power that he had to manage only a mass. All individual existence was annihilated by ten years of disorder, and nothing sways people like military success; it takes great power of reason to combat this tendency instead of profiting from it. No one in France could consider his position secure. Men of all classes, ruined or enriched, banished or rewarded, found themselves one by one equally, so to speak, in the hands of power. Bonaparte, who always moved between two opposed interests, took very good care not to put an end to these anxieties by fixed laws that might let everyone know his rights. To one man he returned his property, while another he stripped of his forever. The First Consul reserved to himself the power of determining, under any pretext, the fate of everything and everyone.

Those Frenchmen who sought to resist the ever-increasing power of the First Consul had to invoke liberty to struggle against him successfully. But at this word the aristocrats and the enemies of the Revolution cried "Jacobinism," thus supporting the tyranny for which they later sought to blame their adversaries. . . .

I sensed more quickly than others—and I pride myself on it— Bonaparte's tyrannical character and intentions. The true friends of liberty are in this respect guided by an instinct that does not deceive them. But my position, at the outset of the Consulate, was made more painful by the fact that respectable society in France thought it saw in Bonaparte the man who had saved them from anarchy or Jacobinism. They therefore vigorously condemned the spirit of opposition I displayed toward him. . . .

Madame de Staël's opposition led to her exile. But even in exile she continued to comment upon Napoleon and upon the rise and finally the decline of his military and political fortunes. In 1813, following the Russian disaster, the allies invaded France, heading for Paris.

From the moment the Allies passed the Rhine and entered France it seemed to me that the prayers of the friends of France must undergo a complete change. I was then in London, and one of the English Cabinet Ministers asked me what I wished for. I ventured to reply that my desire was to see Bonaparte victorious and slain. The English had enough greatness of soul to make it unnecessary for me to conceal this French sentiment from them. Yet I was to learn, in the midst of the transports of joy with which the city of the conquerors reverberated, that Paris was in the power of the Allies. At that moment I felt there was no longer a France: I believed Burke's prediction realized and that where France had existed we should see only an abyss. The Emperor Alexander, the Allies, and the constitutional principles adopted through the wisdom of Louis XVIII banished this gloomy presentiment.

There was, nevertheless, something of grandeur in Napoleon's farewell to his troops and to their eagles, so long victorious. His last campaign had been long and skillful: in short, the fatal magic that bound France's military glory to him was not yet destroyed. Thus the conference at Paris must be blamed for having made his return possible. . . .

Many people like to argue that Bonaparte would still be emperor if he had not attempted the expeditions against Spain or Russia. This opinion pleases the supporters of despotism, who insist that so fine a government could not be overthrown by the very nature of things but only by an accident. I have already said, what observation of France will confirm, that Bonaparte needed war to establish and maintain absolute power. A great nation would not have supported the dull and degrading burden of despotism if military glory had not ceaselessly moved or exalted the public spirit. . . .

I shall never forget the moment when I learned, from one of my friends the morning of March 6, 1815, that Bonaparte had landed on the French coast. I had the misfortune to foresee at once the consequences of that event—as they have since taken place—and I thought the earth was about to open under me. I said, "There will be no liberty if Bonaparte wins and no national independence if he loses." Events, it seems to me, have borne out this sad prediction only too well. . . .

. . . Enlightened men could see in Bonaparte nothing but a despot, but by a rather fatal conjunction of circumstances this despot was presented to the nation as the defender of its rights. All the benefits achieved by the Revolution, which France will never willingly give up, were threatened by the endless rashness of the party that wants to repeat the conquest of Frenchmen, as if they were still Gauls. And that part of the nation that most feared the return of the Old Regime thought they saw in Bonaparte a way to save themselves from it. The most fatal association that could overwhelm the friends of liberty was that a despot should join their ranks—should, so to speak, place himself at their head—and that the enemies of every liberal idea should have a pretext for confusing popular violence with the evils of despotism and thus make tyranny appear to be the result of liberty itself. . . . If it was criminal to recall Bonaparte, it was silly to try to disguise such a man as a constitutional monarch. . . .

Whether Napoleon lives or perishes, whether or not he reappears on the continent of Europe, only one reason moves me to speak of him: the ardent wish that the friends of liberty in France completely separate their cause from his and beware of confusing the principles of the Revolution with those of the Imperial *régime.* I believe I have shown that there is no counter-revolution so fatal to liberty as the one he made.

A Modern Napoleon

GEORGES LEFEBVRE

Napoleon has been the most enduringly fascinating figure in modern history, the subject of literally thousands of books—more than 200,000 by some estimates. Recent opinion has tended to divide along precisely the lines that appeared in Napoleon's own time—as suggested in the first two selections of this chapter—either "for" or "against" him, to borrow from the title of a famous book on the Napoleonic tradition.[9] The following selection is from *Napoleon: From 18 Brumaire to Tilsit 1799–1807,* by the distinguished French historian Georges Lefebvre, considered by many competent critics to have been the best modern scholar of the Napoleonic age. But Lefebvre was also a great authority on the French Revolution, and so we turn to him for his view on the relationship of Napoleon to the Revolution and his answer to the question of whether Napoleon

---

[9]Pieter Geyl, *Napoleon: For and Against,* tr. Olive Renier (New Haven: Yale University Press, 1949).

was its child or its betrayer. It is the opinion of Lefebvre that the Revolution had betrayed itself long before Napoleon became its conscious heir; that only in the most elementary sense of its giving him the opportunity to rise to power could Napoleon be considered its offspring; that—as Madame de Staël argued—Napoleon was always the same, from the beginning to the end of his career, an autocrat; and that he did not purify the Revolution but rather manipulated it.

That the French Revolution turned to dictatorship was no accident; it was driven there by inner necessity, and not for the first time either. Nor was it an accident that the Revolution led to the dictatorship of a general. But it so happened that this general was Napoleon Bonaparte, a man whose temperament, even more than his genius, was unable to adapt to peace and moderation. Thus it was an unforeseeable contingency which tilted the scale in favour of "la guerre éternelle."

For a long time the republicans had wanted to strengthen the central authority. One need only look at the constitutions they gave to the vassal states: in Holland, the members of the Directory controlled the treasury; in Switzerland, they appointed government officials; in Rome, they appointed judges as well. In the Helvetic and Roman Republics every department already possessed a "prefect." All this is not to mention the Cisalpine Republic, which was Bonaparte's personal fief. . . . The coup d'état of 18 Fructidor had provided the occasion sought by Sieyès, Talleyrand, and Bonaparte, but they let the opportunity slip. In Year VII, however, they hoped to bring about a new one. Without realizing it, the republicans were giving way to a tendency which, ever since the start of the civil and foreign wars, was pushing the Revolution in the direction of a permanent and all-powerful executive, that is to say toward dictatorship. It was this social revolution that drove the dispossessed nobility far beyond insurrection. Subsidized by enemy gold, it exploited the wartime hardships—that inexhaustible source of discontent—and particularly the monetary and economic crisis, thereby intending to turn the people against the government. The French did not want a return to the Old Regime, but they suffered and they held their leaders responsible for it. At every election the counter-revolution hoped to regain power. It was awareness of this danger that led the Mountain[10] in 1793 to declare the Convention in permanent session until the peace. The Thermidorians

---

[10]The popular name given to the radical faction in the Convention.—ED.

had intended to restore elective government, but they immediately returned to Jacobin expediency by passing the Decree of the Two-Thirds. Next, the Directory, overwhelmed by the elections of 1797, re-established the dictatorship on 18 Fructidor. Yet as long as the Constitution of Year III continued to exist, this dictatorship, put to the test each year, required a host of violent measures and could never be brought into working order. So it was still necessary to revive the principle of 1793 and invest it with permanence until such time as peace, settled once and for all, would persuade the counter-revolution to accept the new order. It was in this respect that Napoleon's dictatorship became so much a part of the history of the French Revolution. No matter what he may have said or done, neither he nor his enemies were ever able to break this bond, and this was a fact which the European aristocracy understood perfectly well.

In 1799, as in 1793, the Jacobins wished to establish a democratic dictatorship by relying on the Sans-culottes[11] to push it through the councils. Taking advantage of the crisis preceding the victory at Zurich, they succeeded in forcing the passage of several revolutionary measures: a compulsory loan, the abolition of exemptions from military service, the law of hostages, a repeal of assignments on public revenues which had been granted to bankers and government contractors, withholdings on the rente and on salaries, and finally, requisitions. These measures constituted a direct attack on bourgeois interests and brought that class to action. Thus it was symbolic that assignments on public revenues were restored the very night of 19 Brumaire. The Idéologues who gathered around Madame de Condorcet at Auteuil or in the salon of Madame de Staël wanted neither a democratic dictatorship nor even a democracy. . . . Madame de Staël expressed their desire: to devise a representative system of government which would assure power to the moneyed and talented "notables." Sieyès, who had become a Director, took his inspiration from the Decree of the Two-Thirds. Together with his friends he wanted to select the membership of the newly constituted bodies which would then expand themselves by co-optation, leaving to the nation only the role of electing candidates. Furthermore, those already in office saw in this plan the chance to keep themselves in power.

The people having been eliminated as an obstacle to the dictatorship of the bourgeoisie, only the army remained. The Directory had already sought its help on 18 Fructidor, Year V, and had managed to keep the upper hand, despite serious incursions. Now, however, the

---

[11]Another popular name for the urban proletariat, especially of Paris, who tended to support Jacobin radicalism.—Ed.

situation was very different in that steadfast republicans, not royalists, were to be driven out. Only a popular general could have carried it through, and Bonaparte's sudden return destined that it should be he. The will of the nation which was invoked to justify 18 Brumaire played no part in the event. The nation rejoiced at the news that Bonaparte was in France because it recognized an able general; but the Republic had conquered without him, and Masséna's victory[12] had bolstered the reputation of the Directory. Consequently, the responsibility for 18 Brumaire lies on that segment of the republican bourgeoisie called the Brumairians, whose leading light was Sieyès. They had no intention of giving in to Bonaparte, and they chose him only as an instrument of their policy. That they propelled him to power without imposing any conditions, without even first delimiting the fundamental character of the new regime, betrays their incredible mediocrity. Bonaparte did not repudiate the notables, for he too was not a democrat, and their collaboration alone enabled him to rule. But on the evening of 19 Brumaire, after they had hurriedly slapped together the structure of the Provisional Consulate, they should not have harboured any more illusions. The army had followed Bonaparte, and him alone. He was complete master. Regardless of what he and his apologists may have said, his rule was from its origins an absolute military dictatorship. It was Bonaparte alone who would decide the questions on which the fate of France and Europe hinged.

What sort of a man was he? His personality evolved in so singular a manner that it defies portrayal. He appeared first as a studious officer full of dreams, garrisoned at Valence and Auxonne. As a youthful general, on the eve of the battle of Castiglione, he could still hold a council of war. But in the final years as Emperor, he was stupefied with his own omnipotence and was infatuated with his own omniscience. And yet distinctive traits appear throughout his entire career: power could do no more than accentuate some and attenuate others.

Short-legged and small in stature, muscular, ruddy, and still gaunt at the age of thirty, he was physically hardy and fit. His sensitivity and steadiness were admirable, his reflexes quick as lightning, and his capacity for work unlimited. He could fall asleep at will. But we also find the reverse: cold humid weather brought on oppression, coughing spells, dysuria; when crossed he unleashed frightful outbursts of temper; overexertion, despite prolonged hot baths, despite extreme sobriety, despite the moderate yet constant use of coffee and tobacco,

---

[12]At Zurich over the Russians.—Ed.

occasionally produced brief collapses, even tears. His mind was one of the most perfect that has ever been: his unflagging attention tirelessly swept in facts and ideas which his memory registered and classified; his imagination played with them freely, and being in a permanent state of concealed tension, it never wearied of inventing political and strategic motifs which manifested themselves in unexpected flashes of intuition like those experienced by poets and mathematicians. This would happen especially at night during a sudden awakening, and he himself referred to it as "the moral spark" and "the after midnight presence of the spirit." This spiritual fervour shone through his glittering eyes and illuminated the face, still "sulphuric" at his rise, of the "sleek-haired Corsican." This is what made him unsociable, and not, as Hippolyte Taine would have us think, some kind of brutality, the consequence of a slightly tarnished *condottiere* being let loose upon the world in all his savagery. He rendered a fair account of himself when he said, "I consider myself a good man at heart," and indeed he showed generosity, and even kindness to those who were close to him. But between ordinary mortals, who hurried through their tasks in order to abandon themselves to leisure or diversion, and Napoleon Bonaparte, who was the soul of effort and concentration, there could exist no common ground nor true community. Ambition—that irresistible impulse to act and to dominate—sprang from his physical and mental state of being. . . .

Ever since his military school days at Brienne, when he was still a poor and taunted foreigner, timid yet bursting with passion, Napoleon drew strength from pride in himself and contempt for others. Destined to become an officer, his instinct to command without having to discuss could not have been better served. Although he might on occasion have sought information or opinion, he alone was master and judge. Bonaparte's natural propensity for dictatorship suited the normal practice of his profession. In Italy and in Egypt he introduced dictatorship into the government. In France he wanted to put himself forward as a civilian, but the military stamp was indelibly there. He consulted often, but he could never tolerate free opposition. More precisely, when faced with a group of men accustomed to discussion, he would lose his composure. This explains his intense hatred of the Idéologues. The confused and undisciplined, yet formidable masses inspired in him as much fear as contempt. Regardless of costumes and titles, Bonaparte took power as a general, and as such he exercised it. . . .

. . . Having entered into a life of action, he still remained a thinker. This warrior was never happier than in the silence of his own study, surrounded by papers and documents. In time he became more practical, and he would boast that he had repudiated "ideology." Nevertheless, he was still a typical man of the eighteenth century, a rationalist, a philosophe. Far from relying on intuition, he placed his trust in reason, in knowledge, and in methodical effort. . . .

He seemed to be dedicated to a policy of realism in every way, and he was, in fact, a realist in execution down to the slightest detail. . . . And yet he was a realist in execution only. There lived in him an alter-ego which contained certain features of the hero. It seems to have been born during his days at the military academy out of a need to dominate a world in which he felt himself despised. Above all he longed to equal the semi-legendary heroes of Plutarch and Corneille. His greatest ambition was glory. "I live only for posterity," he exclaimed, "death is nothing, but to live defeated and without glory is to die every day." His eyes were fixed on the world's great leaders: Alexander, who conquered the East and dreamed of conquering the world; Caesar, Augustus, Charlemagne—the creators and the restorer of the Roman Empire whose very names were synonymous with the idea of a universal civilization. From these he did not deduce a precise formulation to be used as a rule, a measure, or a condition of political conduct. They were for him examples, which stimulated his imagination and lent an unutterable charm to action. . . . That is why it is idle to seek for limits to Napoleon's policy, or for a final goal at which he would have stopped: there simply was none. . . .

That a mind so capable of grasping reality in certain respects should escape it in others . . . can only be due to Napoleon's origins as much as to his nature. When he first came to France, he considered himself a foreigner. Until the time when he was expelled from Corsica by his compatriots in 1791, his attitude had been one of hostility to the French people. Assuredly he became sufficiently imbued with their culture and spirit to adopt their nationality; otherwise he could never have become their leader. But he lacked the time to identify himself with the French nation and to adopt its national tradition to the point where he would consider its interests as a limitation upon his own actions. Something of the uprooted person remained in him; something of the *déclassé* as well. He was neither entirely a gentleman nor entirely common. He served both the king and the Revolution without attaching himself to either. This was one of the reasons for his success, since he could so easily place himself above parties and announce himself as the restorer of national unity. Yet neither in the Old Regime nor in the new did he find principles which might have served as a norm or a limit. . . .

What about moral limits? In spiritual life he had nothing in common with other men. Even though he knew their passions well and deftly turned them to his own ends, he cared only for those that would reduce men to dependence. He belittled every feeling that elevated men to acts of sacrifice—religious faith, patriotism, love of freedom—because he saw in them obstacles to his own schemes. Not that he was impervious to these sentiments, at least not in his youth, for they readily led to heroic deeds; but fate led him in a different direction and walled him up within himself. In the splendid and terrible isolation of the will to power, measure carries no meaning.

Review and Study Questions

1. In what ways did Napoleon view himself as the child of the French Revolution?

2. Why did Napoleon, in the end, fail in his imperial military plans?

3. Why was Madame de Staël so bitterly critical of Napoleon?

4. How does Georges Lefebvre interpret Napoleon's relationship to the Revolution?

5. In your view, was Napoleon a child or a betrayer of the Revolution?

Suggestions for Further Reading

Napoleon is linked inescapably with both the French Revolution that created him and with the nineteenth-century age of revolution that he created. Thus, the first category of books to be recommended for Napoleon and his age are those that treat this large topic. The best general work is probably Erich J. Hobsbawm, *The Age of Revolution: Europe 1789–1848* (Cleveland: World, 1962); it is a book of ideas rather than a factual survey, and the author is interested in the continuing social and cultural trends of the revolutionary age, in which he includes the topic of England and its industrial revolution. Of the same sort is Norman Hampson, *The First European Revolution, 1776–1850* (New York: Harcourt, Brace and World, 1969), a brief, attractive survey and analysis that plays down the role of Napoleon in favor of the continuity of the idea of revolution. Donald Sutherland, *France 1789–1815: Revolution and Counterrevolution* (New York: Oxford University Press, 1986) is a revisionist social history emphasizing the importance of classes and ideologies across the whole French nation. George Rudé, *Revolutionary Europe, 1783–1815* (New York: Harper & Row, 1966) is a good summary, while somewhat more comprehensive is Franklin L. Ford, *Europe, 1780–1830* (London: Longman, 1970); both are excellent, straightforward accounts.

The outstanding modern work on the French Revolution itself is Georges Lefebvre, *The French Revolution*, 2 vols., vol. 1, tr. Elizabeth M. Evanson (New York: Columbia University Press, 1962), vol. 2, tr. John Hall Stewart and James Friguglietti (New York: Columbia University Press, 1964), along with Lefebvre's brilliant analytical work, *The Coming of the French Revolution, 1789*, tr. R. R. Palmer (Princeton, N.J.: Princeton University Press, 1947). R. R. Palmer, *The World of the French Revolution* (New York: Harper & Row, 1969) is a highly interpretive, brief, readable, analytical survey, while M. J. Sydenham, *The French Revolution* (New York: Putnam, 1965) is a brief, largely political history. Alfred Cobban, *The Social Interpretation of the French Revolution* (Cambridge: Cambridge University Press, 1964) is a major critical work, revising much of the sociological theorizing about classes that had marked a generation of revolutionary studies. Cobban argues that the land-owning class eventually triumphed in revolutionary France and that in the course of the French Revolution the shift from title to property as the basis for social status was finally made. Norman Hampson, *A Social History of the French Revolution* (Toronto: Toronto University Press, 1963) is a briefer and more balanced treatment of the same themes. Two recent revisionist histories of the French Revolution can also be recommended: Simon Schama, *Citizens: A Chronicle of the French Revolution* (New York: Knopf, 1989), which stresses the brutality of the revolution, and J. F. Bosher, *The French Revolution* (New York: Norton, 1988), which stresses the background forces of the revolution.

Georges Lefebvre is the most important authority on Napoleon, as he is on the Revolution. See his *Napoleon*, 2 vols., vol. 1 *Napoleon from 18 Brumaire to Tilsit, 1799–1807*, tr. H. F. Stockhold, vol. 2 *Napoleon from Tilsit to Waterloo, 1807–1815*, tr. J. E. Anderson (New York: Columbia University Press, 1969); the first volume is excerpted in this chapter. J. C. Herold, *The Age of Napoleon* (New York: Harper & Row, 1963) is not only a lush and beautiful book but an interpretive study; Herold is not an admirer of Napoleon and considers him at the best an ungrateful child of the Revolution. On the other hand, Robert B. Holtman, *The Napoleonic Revolution* (Philadelphia: Lippincott, 1967), sees Napoleon as a dramatic and important innovator in a score of fields, thus preserving the best gains of the Revolution. Felix M. Markham, *Napoleon and the Awakening of Europe*, "Teach Yourself History Library" (New York: Macmillan, 1954), and his *Napoleon I: Emperor of the French* (New York: New American Library, 1964) are good short biographies. Several special studies are also recommended. For military history see the good, comprehensive, straightforward account in David G. Chandler, *The Campaigns of Napoleon* (New York: Macmillan, 1966) and Owen Connelly, *Blundering to Glory: Napoleon's Military Cam-*

paigns (Wilmington, Del.: Scholarly Resources, 1987), a brilliant study of Napoleon as a strategic improviser. For specific studies of two crucial campaigns, see Christopher L. Hibbert, *Waterloo: Napoleon's Last Campaign* (New York: New American Library, 1967) and Richard K. Riehn, *1812: Napoleon's Russian Campaign* (New York: McGraw-Hill, 1990). A related work is the dramatic and exciting Edith Saunders, *The Hundred Days* (New York: Norton, 1964). The best book on Napoleon's army is John R. Elting, *Swords around a Throne: Napoleon's Grande Armée* (London: Free Press, 1988). Geoffrey Ellis, *The Napoleonic Empire* (Atlantic Highlands, N.J.: Humanities Press International, 1991) is an attractive, brief survey of the main institutions of Napoleon's imperial state.

Two books by R. F. Delderfield deal with the last years of Napoleon's military career: *The Retreat from Moscow* (New York: Atheneum, 1967) and *Imperial Sunset: The Fall of Napoleon, 1813–14* (Philadelphia: Chilton, 1968). An extremely interesting work on a subtopic of Napoleon is J. Christopher Herold, *Bonaparte in Egypt* (New York: Harper & Row, 1962). Pieter Geyl, *Napoleon: For and Against,* tr. Olive Renier (New Haven: Yale University Press, 1949), is a famous book of Napoleonic historiography. Finally, highly recommended is the luminous biography by J. Christopher Herold, *Mistress to an Age: A Life of Madame de Staël* (Indianapolis, Ind.: Bobbs-Merrill, 1958).

SIMÓN BOLÍVAR:
EL LIBERTADOR

1783   Born
1799   Traveled in Europe
1810   Joined the revolution in Venezuela
1813   Assumed the political dictatorship of
       Venezuela
1819   Victory at battle of Boyacá
1822   Victory at battle of Pichincha
1824   Victory at battle of Ayacucho
1826   Convened a general American con-
       gress in Panama
1826   Failed attempt on his life
1830   Died

By the early nineteenth century most of Latin America had been under Spanish rule for almost 300 years. And it was, from the beginning, a colonial rule of the most repressive sort. In the words of Bolívar himself,

> We have been harrassed by a conduct which has not only deprived us of our rights but has kept us in a sort of permanent infancy with regard to public affairs. . . . So negative was our existence that I can find nothing comparable in any other civilized society.[1]

But even in this unlikely environment the stirrings of revolutionary reaction had begun. Napoleon's invasion of Spain had upset Spanish authority in the New World. In the spring of 1810 a junta rose against the Spanish governor of Venezuela and expelled him. A year later Venezuela declared its independence.

Simón Bolívar had already joined the revolution. He was the son of a wealthy, aristocratic Spanish-Creole family in Venezuela who had been educated in Spain. Bolívar had traveled widely in Spain and in France, where he became acquainted with the liberal political and

---

[1]From "The Jamaican Letter," as excerpted in *The Liberator, Simón Bolívar, Man and Image*, ed. David Bushnell (New York: Knopf, 1970), p. 13.

social works of Enlightenment writers. When he returned to Venezuela he entered the army of the new republic and soon emerged as the champion of strong government for the new republics of Hispanic America. Throughout the next year Bolívar defeated the Spaniards in six pitched battles and regained control of the capital. He entered Caracas on August 6, 1813, was given the title of *El Libertador,* and assumed the office of dictator.

In the following year he was defeated by the Spanish, who recaptured Caracas. Bolívar fled to Jamaica. In his exile there he wrote his most important political statement, "The Letter from Jamaica," in which he laid out his scheme for the reconstitution of Latin America. Bolívar proposed a series of constitutional republics, each with an hereditary upper house, an elected lower house, and a president elected for life.

In the meantime, in 1815, Spain had sent a massive expeditionary force to deal with its rebellious colonies, and Bolívar had returned to Venezuela to lead the opposition. He repeatedly defeated Spanish armies and began the organization of civil governments in Venezuela, Colombia, Ecuador, Bolivia, and Peru. By 1825 Bolívar had reached the apex of his career. His authority extended from the Caribbean to the Argentine border. He had achieved a series of treaties of alliance among Colombia, Peru, Mexico, Central America, and the United Provinces of Río de la Plata.

But the nascent nationalism of the new republics rebelled against Bolívar's centralist ideas and, civil war broke out again. Bolívar was able to quell the rebellion but not the desire for independence. He assumed dictatorial powers in 1828. This led to an abortive attempt on his life and the resumption of civil war. Bolívar realized that his continued stay in office presented a danger to the very states whose independence he had created. On May 8, 1830, he left Bogatá, planning to depart for Europe. Illness forced him to abandon his plans and, toward the end of 1830, the liberator of South America died in the house of a Spanish admirer in Santa Maria. In his final illness, he said in despair that with all his accomplishments he had only "plowed the sea."

Memoirs of Simón Bolívar

GENERAL H. L. V. DUCOUDRAY HOLSTEIN

These memoirs were not actually written by Bolívar. It is true that Bolívar was a prolific writer; a lifetime of high public office and military command left a large residue of official papers and correspondence. Some bits of autobiographical matter have been preserved, but, on the whole, Bolívar was much too busy—and too modest—to undertake his memoirs. Rather, this document was written by General H. L. V. Ducoudray Holstein, a friend, colleague, and associate and one of the many foreign officers attracted to Bolívar's cause. He had served as Bolívar's chief of staff and, as the general observed in his preface, "he lived in such intimacy" with Bolívar, "that he slept on various occasions in the same room with him" (p. 7). Thus, the accounts he gives are accurate in their particulars. The narrative excerpted here runs to his first liberation of Caracas in 1813.

Simon Bolivar was born in the city of Caracas, July 24th, 1783, and is the second son of Don Juan Vicente Bolivar y Ponte, a militia colonel in the plains of Aragua; his mother, Dona Maria Concepcion Palacios y Sojo; and both were natives of Caracas, and were Mantuanos.[2] They died; the first in 1786, the latter in 1789.

Young Bolivar was sent to Spain at the age of 14, in compliance with the customs of the wealthy Americans of those times, who usually spent in one year in Europe, the amount of several years income at home; seeking offices and military decorations, that were often put up to the highest bidder, under the administration of Manual Godoy, Prince of the Peace. The young Americans were likewise accustomed to go to Spain, to complete their education, and to pursue their studies in the profession of law, physic, or theology; for, according to the laws of the times, no American was

---

[2]Los Mantuanos, or los familias Mantuanas, were, in Caracas, a kind of nobility, and this is the distinctive title there of rich families of birth. In New Greneda, the opulent families of high birth, were never called Mantuanas; this distinction existed alone in Caracas.—Ed.

admitted to the bar, and allowed to practise in his profession in the Universities of old Spain, nor could he exercise his profession at home. Without a diploma from a University in Spain, no American could, at least in New Greneda, have the honor of being a Capuchin Friar! But as the object of young Simon was, to see the world, and not in any manner to study seriously, he paid little attention to any pursuit, other than that of pleasure, and of satisfying his desire to witness the different scenes of life. He, however, devoted some time to the study of Jurisprudence.

He was at this period lieutenant in the corps of militia in the plains of Aragua, of which his father had been commander. He had an elder brother, who died in 1815, and two sisters, who enjoyed an annual income of from 40 to 50,000 dollars, the produce of several considerable estates, and particularly of an extensive *Hato*, on which were raised large herds of cattle. These estates were at no great distance from the city of Caracas; and at one or other of them, Bolivar and his family usually resided. San Mateo, was, however, the place he always preferred. It was the largest of his possessions, where between 1000 and 1500 slaves were regularly kept, before the revolution. His residence in the valley of Aragua, not far from the lake of Valencia, was beautiful and striking.

From Spain Bolivar passed into France, and resided at Paris, where he remained a number of years, enjoying at an early period, all the pleasures of life, which, by a rich young man, with bad examples constantly before him, can, there, easily be found. I have remarked that whenever Bolivar spoke to me of the Palais Royal, he could not restrain himself from boasting of its delights. It was on such occasions, that all his soul was electrified; his physiognomy became animated, and he spoke and acted with such ardor as showed how fond he was of that enchanting abode, so dangerous to youth.

His residence in Paris, and especially at the Palais Royal, has done him great injury. He is pale, and of a yellowish colour, meagre, weak and enervated.[3]. . .

Bolivar returned in 1802 to Madrid, where he married one of the daughters of Don Bernardo del Toro, uncle of the present Marquis of this name. His father in law, who was born in Caracas, resided in Madrid. Bolivar was but 19 years of age, and his lady 16. They returned in 1809, to Caracas, and lived in a retired manner on their estates. Shortly after, his lady was taken ill and died, without leaving any offspring.

---

[3]He was actually suffering from tuberculosis, from which he finally died.—ED.

Bolivar acquired, in the course of his travels, that usage of the world, that courtesy and ease of manners, for which he is so remarkable, and which have so prepossessing an influence upon those who associate with him.

In the year 1823, Mr. Ackerman published in London, a very interesting monthly periodical in the Spanish language, under the title of "El Mensagero." It is entirely devoted to the affairs of the new Spanish republics. It contains, among other articles, *Biographical Sketch of Gen. Bolivar,* in which the author asserts that the young Bolivar, during his residence in Paris, gave himself up to all the possible amusements of young men of his age: "Still," said the author, "he was assiduous to obtain the dear object he has had always in view, as the accomplishment of all his wishes, and his ambition, namely, *that of making with eagerness, all possible acquaintances which might have been useful to him for the emancipation of his country!*"

I must beg leave to assert, that shortly before the revolution of the 19th April, 1810, at Caracas, the names of Gen. Miranda, Don Manual Gual, the Corregidor T. M. Espana, Narino, Fea, and others, appeared on the list of those who declared their intention to liberate their country from the Spanish yoke. On the memorable day of the 19th April, when the Capt. Gen. Emparan was deposed, and his functions performed by a patriotic Junta, the chiefs of this revolution were the Alcade [Mayor] Don Martin Tobar, Don Francisco Salias, Carlos Manchado, Mariano Montilla, Joseph Felix Ribas, and others; but the name of Simon Bolivar is not among them; he was at his ease, on one of his estates, in the valley of Aragua, and refused to take any part in it, although his cousin, Joseph Felix Ribas, labored to engage him as an active associate. Shortly after, the Junta gave him his option of a civil or military post, under the new patriotic government. Their offer was refused, and the pressing solicitations of his friends and relations were of no avail. Finally, he accepted the appointment of a commission to London, with the grade of Colonel in the militia. M. Luis Mendez y Lopez, who, during several years, was the agent of Venezuela at London, was at this time, his colleague in the mission.

If Bolivar, as stated in Mr. Ackerman's Magazine, had from his youth formed the idea of liberating his country, he would have seized this opportunity of joining the chiefs of the revolution, and would have accepted a post under the government of the Junta, and the Congress: He did neither, although the members of these two bodies in 1810 and 11, offered him any post that might suit his views. On his return from London, he retired to his estate, without taking any part in public affairs.

Mr. Ackerman's Magazine says, secondly, that Bolivar, *from* the time of the earthquake,[4] came to join Miranda, who had then his head quarters at Vittoria, and that he was a colonel in the army. This is a mistake. Bolivar was named *eight months before* the earthquake, governor of the fortress of Porto Cabello; but he came not to join Miranda at Vittoria. After his secret departure from that fortress, and his leaving his garrison in the night, he dared not appear before Miranda; because he justly feared that he should be tried before a Court Martial, for having secretly in the night, together with some of his officers, and without leave or orders, left the strongest place in Venezuela, which Miranda had confided to his care. He sent Thomas Montilla, one of the officers who embarked with him, to Vittoria, with the news of this event, and with his excuses to Gen. Miranda; the particulars of which I mean to give in their proper place. Bolivar was then Lieutenant Colonel in Miranda's staff. . . .

All that can be said, with truth and impartiality, of Gen. Bolivar's patriotism, is, that it began with his being at the head of the army and the government; or, to speak more plainly; Gen. Bolivar began from 1813, to be a zealous and ardent patriot, because from January 7 that year, until the present day (July 1828) he has not ceased to have, either, the three powers, legislative, executive and judiciary, united in himself, or to have, together with the executive power, the direction of all civil and military operations: the congress of Colombia and Peru, having been entirely submissive to the wishes of its President, Liberator or Protector, as will be shown more particularly in the course of this Biography.

When the patriotic Junta assembled at Caracas, its members, among whom Bolivar had various friends, were anxious to see him taking an active part in their government; and proposals were made to him to choose a civil or a military office, with the assurance that his choice should be complied with, but in vain. He declined every office, under the pretext of the state of his health. At last the Junta proposed to him a mission to London, with the rank of colonel in the militia, and in company, with his friend Louis Lopez y Mendez. This offer he accepted; and they both departed for London in June, 1810.

Bolívar had returned from England and at last assumed an active role in the revolution, taking up a military command.

General Bolivar entered the western provinces of Venezuela. He was joined by many thousands of his countrymen, who driven to despair

---

[4]This earthquake, which occurred in 1812, devastated the city of Caracas.—ED.

by the cruelties of the Spaniards, had no choice but to fight, or perish. He divided his forces into two strong corps, gave the command of one to his major general Ribas, and put himself at the head of the other. Both proceeded by forced marches, through different roads to Caracas, crossing the department of Truxillo and the province of Barinas. The Spaniards were beaten easily at Niquitao, Betioque, Barquisimeto and Barinas. At the last place, governor Tiscar, like general Cagigal, thought all was lost, and deserted his troops. He fled to St. Tomas de la Angostura, in the province of Guayana, where, like the other, he found himself in safety.

As soon as general Monteverde was apprised of the rapid progress of the patriots, he rallied his best troops at Lostaguanes, where general Ribas attacked him soon afterwards. The attack had but just commenced, when the greatest part of his cavalry, composed of natives, passed over to the patriots and soon decided the victory in their favor. Monteverde lost some hundreds of his men, and was obliged to shut himself up with the remainder, in the fortress of Porto Cabello.

General Bolivar advanced rapidly upon Caracas, and found very little or no resistance on the part of the enemy, who had concentrated his forces against the column of general Ribas. As soon as governor Fierro heard of the approach of general Bolivar, he hastily assembled a great council of war, in which it was concluded to send deputies to Bolivar, proposing a capitulation. This was made and signed at Vittoria, about a year after the famous capitulation between general Miranda and Monteverde. By this treaty Bolivar promised that no one should be persecuted for his political opinions, and that every one should be at liberty to retire with his property from Venezuela, and go whithersoever he pleased.

While the deputies were assembled at Vittoria, governor Fierro, seized, like Cagigal and Tiscar, by panic and terror, decamped in the night time, secretly, and so hastily that he left, as was afterwards ascertained, a very large amount of silver money. He left also more than 1500 Spaniards, at the discretion of the enemy. He embarked at Laguira, and arrived in safety at the little island of Curacao. The flight of their governor, of which the inhabitants and the garrison were not informed, until day break the next morning, left the city in the greatest trouble, for he left not a single order. The Spanish party being dissolved, every one was left to provide for his own safety. Its principal chiefs, Monteverde, Cagigal, Fierro and Tiscar, acting in conformity, each to his own will, had all placed themselves in safety indeed, but without the least union or vigor: Monteverde remained in Porto Cabello without sending forth any order; Cagigal remained with Tiscar, at Angostura; and Fierro in the island of Curacao.

It was therefore an easy task for Bolivar to enter the capital of his native land, and to take possession of the greatest part of Venezuela. His entry into Caracas, (August 4th, 1813,) was brilliant and glorious. The friends of liberty, who had suffered so severely, surrounded him from every corner of the country, and welcomed his arrival with many signs of joy and festivity. The enthusiasm was universal, reaching every class and sex of the inhabitants of Caracas. The fair sex came to crown their liberator. They spread the ground with many flowers, branches of laurel and olive, on his passage through the streets of the capital. The shouts of thousands were mingled with the noise of artillery, bells, and music, and the crowd was immense. The prisons were opened, and the unfortunate victims of liberty came forth with pale and emaciated faces, like spectres from their graves. But notwithstanding this appalling sight, the people indulged not their sentiments and feelings of vengeance against the authors of such cruel deeds. They committed no disorder. No European Spaniard, Isleno, friar or priest, was dragged from his hiding place, nor even sought for; all were happy, and thought only of rejoicing.

The entry of Gen. Bolivar into Caracas, was certainly the most gratifying event of his whole military career. And notwithstanding his enterprise and his victories were greatly facilitated by the astonishing pusilanimity of his enemies, he deserves great praise for his perseverance, and for the conception of such an undertaking, in which he sacrificed a considerable part of his fortune, to furnish his troops with the means of following him.

A Patriotic Appraisal

FELIPE LARRAZÁBAL

Felipe Larrazábal was a distinguished nineteenth-century Venezuelan writer and an enormous admirer of Bolívar. His *Life of Bolivar,* from which the following excerpt is taken, appeared in 1865. It was the first documented, full-scale biographical study of Bolívar. It went through numerous editions and for many years it was the standard work. Though it was not an altogether bad work of scholarship, it was marred by the themes of ultra-patriotism, heroic virtue, and providentialism that became standard features of the Latin American Bolivarian literature and remain so even today.

In those times of obscurantism and oppression, God took from the treasures of his goodness a soul that He endowed with intelligence, justice, strength, and gentleness. "Go," He said, "carry light to the mansion of night; to make just and happy those who ignore justice and do not know liberty."

That soul was Bolívar's; this is the charge that Providence entrusted to him.

A noble and lofty spirit, humane, just, liberal, Bolívar in the virtues and talents of his person was one of the most gifted men the world has known; so perfect and unique, that in his goodness he was like Titus, in his good luck and successes Trajan, in his civility Marcus Aurelius, in his valor Caesar, in his wisdom and eloquence Augustus. Of great and very notable memory, unaffected and sociable with his friends, cultured and moderate in his pleasures, he knew how to join the gracefulness of the pen with the bravery of the sword. In danger he showed himself courageous, in toils strong, in adversity constant, in resolution ardent and of insurmountable integrity. Like Charlemagne, and better than Charlemagne, he had the skill to do great things with ease and difficult things quickly. Who ever conceived such vast plans? Who carried them out more smoothly? A sure and lively glance, a rapid intuition of things and of the moment, a prodigious spontaneity for improvising gigantic plans, the science of war reduced to a calculation of minutes, immense vigor of conception, and a fertile, creative, inexhaustible spirit . . . behold Bolívar. Victory in him was always inspiration. Skilled in war, unequaled in counsel, he was neither made proud by triumphs, nor broken by reverses, nor tempted by covetousness (the mortal poison of reason and truth), nor overcome by fatigue, nor stirred up by ambition. Light and perpetual honor of South America, and principally of Caracas his native land, the name of Bolívar will persist as long as the world endures!

If a large part of fortune is for a man to come in his epoch (for eminent individuals often depend on the times), we must confess that Bolívar came in the proper day. From the time he appeared on the grandiose scene of the South American revolution, he excited expectation and symbolized determination. Prompt in thinking as in doing, he combined, as if once again in Caesar, the favors of nature and the splendors of art.

A great excellence, of an intense singularity, that excites the admiration and moves and captivates the will! . . .

If there has been a man in whom the passion to command would be excusable; if there was one in whose breast ambition, asleep or in suspense, could powerfully awaken, it was BOLIVAR! . . . To have opened the way for himself across the ruins of a powerful empire and to increase in virtue and in fortune until he touched the limit of greatness and of human glory; to liberate Venezuela, New Granada, and Ecuador, beginning his bold undertaking with 250 men; to pursue the Spaniards to beyond the Desaguadero in [Upper] Peru and conquer their armies in Junín and Ayacucho; these are exploits worthy of immortality, which, inspiring admiration, might also give pretexts for the burning love of power. More than 40,000 soldiers of Spain, directed by excellent leaders, backed by fortified places and ports and by the moral strength of 300 years of domination, occupied and defended these very rich and vast possessions. Bolívar with his talent and his constancy brought an army out of nothing and tore them away *forever!* . . . The peoples greeted him with the tender title of "Liberator," and millions of men entrusted him with their existence, their repose and liberty. Well then, that genius without rival, who knew how to conquer all obstacles and crown himself with laurels; that man who could boast of his work and grow dizzy with his own omnipotence had no ambition; he never used his good fortune to increase his riches, nor did he allow his spirit to be perverted with the poison of vanity or of presumption. In all the periods of glory and prosperity for the republic, he renounced supreme command. Twenty years he served Colombia in the capacity of soldier and magistrate, and in that long period of time he reconquered the fatherland, freed three republics, conjured away many civil wars, and four times returned his omnipotence to the people, gathering together *spontaneously* four constituent congresses. BOLIVAR, then, destroyed the deceits of his enemies and overcame their black accusations with the ingenousness of his conduct. Emulation has been unable to stain him and malice has been blinded by the brilliance of truth.

On a certain occasion, in Lima (1825), the Liberator was receiving the visit of his friends; and the conversation became more and more interesting with the recollection of the victories that from Carabobo to Ayacucho had given independence to South America. "I hope that history will take account of my name," Bolívar said, "because, in the end, it is something to have humbled the Lion of Castile from Caracas and the Caribbean Sea to the Andes of Peru. . . ." Those who were present, all enthusiasts for the Liberator, vied in admiring his dazzling career and finally fell to discussing the "necessity of Bolívar's remaining in command." Various were the reasons adduced to support this opinion, which the Liberator attacked saying that his aspiration had not been command, but to contribute to the freedom of America, whose grievous and cruel sacrifices could not be tolerated with indifference and calm.

When the party was ended, the Liberator entered his private room and wrote a most beautiful letter to his sister María Antonia, in Caracas. Abandoned to the intimacy of fraternal trust and speaking to her with his soul on his lips, he said, *"Next year I shall go there without fail, to live in retirement and in the delights of domestic quiet. Now America is free and I have no more to do. I loathe command, and the agitation of public life is detestable to me, now that the cause that put the sword in my hands has disappeared. In Caracas, in Anauco or any other point I shall live content."*

What words! What simple and sublime style! Now America is free and I have no more to do! . . . It resembles what Moses said: "And God finished His work and rested.". . .

A Modern Bolívar

J. B. TREND

The following excerpt is taken from *Bolivar and the Independence of Spanish America* by the British historian J. B. Trend. The part of the narrative excerpted deals with the last few years of Bolívar's life and the foiled attempt to assassinate him. In this section the author presents his view that Bolívar was not only the liberator of Spanish America but, in a real sense, its dictator. It is in this regard a thoroughly revisionist work, as far as possible distant from such adulatory books as Larrazábal's *Life of Bolívar.*

Bolívar had never had any great illusions on the possibility of applying democratic principles whole-heartedly in South America; and some of his biographers have considered that, once in supreme command, he took little trouble to conceal his impatience with doubting liberals. The first thing was to restore order; and he did not hesitate to sacrifice personal liberties in order to do so. To stamp out anarchy, he employed all the forces of reaction; and the chief forces which could serve his purpose, in a country where all political tradition had been lost in the wars of independence, were just those forces which were most damaging to his political ideals: the army and the church. The army was represented by ambitious generals who were hoping to carve provinces for themselves out of the remains of the Colombian Union; there was not one of sufficient stature to dream of succeeding Bolívar. Sucre might have done so, but he was murdered not long before Bolívar's own death. There remained the clergy, supported by the religiosity of the rich and the fanaticism of the poor; and these, Bolívar resolved to exploit. His decrees show him bent on suppressing liberalism, which all dictators have invariably regarded as the fountainhead of anarchy; and he increased the army to something like four times its original size. With the church on his side, and the army—and his own personal influence, which was still considerable—Bolívar thought that the Colombian Union might still be saved.

Bolívar's dictatorship was at once acknowledged by Páez.[5] The astute *llanero* saw that the independence of Venezuela was now assured; it was already a state within a state, and he meant to keep a free hand in the country which he already ruled. Bolívar realized this; yet he was always conciliatory, and his letters to Páez are written in the friendliest terms.

In Colombia, Bolívar's enemies took to conspiracy, though Páez would not let them cross the border and conspire on Venezuelan soil. "Behead Bolívar," one of their wits remarked, "cut off his feet, and you are left with *oliva*, the symbol of peace and tranquillity." Their aim, as one of the survivors described it, 25 years afterwards, was to capture Bolívar and his ministers and put Santander[6] at the head of the government. Santander was certainly privy to the plot. There was talk of assassination; but an attempt on Bolívar, when riding with two friends near Bogotá, was frustrated by Santander himself. That was on the 21st September [1826]; the next attempt was fixed for the 28th. But on the 25th one of the conspirators was arrested, and the others determined to act that same night before he could give anything away under cross-examination.

Bolívar had been warned, but he thought that the usual guard at the Presidential Palace—the old Palacio de San Carlos—was enough. O'Leary was away; all the other aides, except one, were on sick leave. The Liberator, too, was feeling ill and depressed. The faithful who saw eye to eye with him were few. His presence still aroused enthusiasm and devotion, but he could not himself be everywhere at once. Even his presence was not so effective as it used to be. Formerly he had only to appear in person, and the waverers became loyal again; a few days or weeks of office-work and personal rounds of inspection had always put things to rights. Now, however, there were intrigues against him personally. That, perhaps, was natural with a dictator; and in Peru, too, they had insisted on his assuming dictatorial powers. The stigma of dictatorship never left him, and his personal intervention in any question was branded by his enemies as dictatorial. The plot in Bogotá was

---

[5]Páez was the president of Venezuela.—Ed.

[6]Santander was the vice president of Colombia.—Ed.

against his dictatorial power. Though the organizers were middle-aged intriguers and wire-pullers, the actual executants were mainly young men, with the fanatical faith of storm-troopers, relying on methods of terrorism. "We could not flatter ourselves with the thought of success, except by the impression of terror which the news of Bolívar's death would produce on our opponents." One of the assassins is speaking. Vice-President Santander, without being directly implicated himself, seems to have known that a new attempt was to be made; yet he gave Bolívar no warning, and did nothing to check the movement. He too had been intriguing against the Liberator, as intercepted letters showed. Bolívar had good reason to be discouraged.

On the night of the attempt the conspirators hid in the cathedral till midnight. It had been raining—the climate of Bogotá has been compared to a cold spring in Paris—but there was bright moonlight. One brigade of artillery had been won over by the conspirators; each knew exactly what he had to do, and they felt confident of success. The clock struck 12. They came out of the cathedral and got to work.

In his depression, and the rain, and the chilly afternoon, Bolívar had sent for Manuela Saenz.[7] She grumbled at having to go out just then, but duly came to the Palace. Bolívar was having a hot bath. She read to him while he lay in it, and then put him to bed. He seemed to have a feverish cold, and she stayed with him.

Manuela described what happened next:

"It was about 12 when the Liberator's dogs began to bark; and there was a peculiar noise which must have been the fight with the sentries, but no shooting. I woke the Liberator, and the first thing he did was to pick up a sword and a pistol and try to open the door. I stopped him and made him dress, which he did quite calmly but quickly. He said: 'Bravo! Well, here I am dressed; what do we do now? Barricade ourselves in?' He tried to open the door again, but I prevented him. Then I remembered something I had once heard the General say. 'Didn't you tell Pepe Paris,' I said, 'that that window would do for an occasion like this?' 'You're right,' he answered and went over to the window. I prevented him getting out at first, because there were people passing; but he managed it when they had gone, just as the door was being broken open [in the next room]. I went to meet them, to give him time to get away; but I didn't have time to see him jump, or to shut the window. As soon as they saw me, they seized me and said: 'Where's Bolívar?' I told them he was at a meeting, which was the first thing that occurred to me. They searched the outer room carefully and went on

---

[7]Since 1822 and their meeting during Bolívar's conquest of Peru, she had been Bolívar's mistress and the passion of his life.—ED.

to the second, and when they saw the window open, they exclaimed: 'He's got away! He's escaped.' I said: 'No, *sēnores*, he has not got away: he's at a meeting' . . . I said I knew there was a meeting, and that the Liberator went to it every night, but I didn't know where it was. At this they grew very angry, and dragged me away with them until we found Ibarra [an A.D.C.] lying wounded on the floor. 'So they've killed the Liberator?' he asked. 'No, Ibarra,' I said, 'the Liberator's alive.' I know it was stupid of us to talk, and I began to bandage him with a handkerchief. They asked me more questions; but as they couldn't get anything more they took me back to the room where they found me, and I brought the wounded man along too.

"Suddenly I heard the sound of heavy boots. I looked out of the window and saw Colonel Ferguson, running along from the house where he had been in bed with a sore throat. He saw me in the moonlight, which was bright just then. He asked for the Liberator, but I said I didn't know; and I couldn't tell him because of the guards they had left there, but I warned him not to come in because they would kill him. He answered that he would die doing his duty. In a moment I heard a shot . . . and then the blow on the head with a sabre which left him dead. . . .

"The Liberator had taken a pistol, and a sword which someone or other had given him in Europe. When he jumped into the street, his cook happened to be passing and went along with him. The General stood in the river [under a bridge] for some time; and then sent the man to see what was happening at the barracks. . . . I went as far as the cathedral, and there I saw the Liberator on a horse, talking to Santander and Padilla, with a crowd of soldiers cheering."

The rising was over in a few hours. By 4 a.m., Bolívar was back in the Presidential Palace. The conspiracy was crushed, but he had caught a chill from which he never recovered. It went to his lungs, and the effects of this attack of pleurisy never left him. The conspirators were rounded up, except for two or three who lived to conspire another day: one to write an impenitent account of the affair many years afterwards in Europe, and another to return and even become President of the Republic. Bolívar's first thought was to pardon them all; but the decision did not rest with him, and the faithful General Urdaneta had them dealt with summarily. Fourteen were shot. Santander was condemned to death, as accessory; but the sentence was commuted to one of banishment and loss of military rank, though he, too, eventually returned to be President of the Republic.

Bolívar was overwhelmed mentally and physically. He never recovered from the shock, and the tuberculosis made rapid strides. His letters, more voluble than ever, are sometimes incoherent, and his postscripts illegible.

"I am so worried," he wrote on November 15th, 1828, "that I shall go away to the country for several months, to a place where there are nothing but Indians. . . . I can't put up any longer with such ingratitude. I'm not a saint, I've no wish to suffer martyrdom. Only the luck of having a few good friends keeps me going in this torture."

The dictatorship continued, either under Bolívar personally, or exercised by others in his name. Reaction was energetically pursued, centralism accentuated. "The Liberator," a Venezuelan historian has remarked, "in spite of his understanding of the French Revolution, and his knowledge of British constitutional practice, had become a doctrinaire administrator of the Latin type. He thought in 1828 as if he were living in ancient Rome—the ancient Rome of the eighteenth-century *philosophes*. He still believed in political 'virtue' and held that dictatorship was a sovereign remedy in times of emergency; but in this way he fell into what seem to us now the greatest errors of his public life." He did not pretend that dictatorship could be a permanent system of government; "his good intentions are as evident as the error in his calculations." His reliance on the army and the church, and his persecution of liberalism, have already been referred to. Like most dictators since his time, he found himself obliged to interfere with the text-books read in schools and colleges. The books to which his attention was specially drawn were written by an Englishman—Bentham—who had personally sent Bolívar some of his writings, translated into Spanish by a liberal Catalan exile in London. They were removed from the list of works prescribed for study, although afterwards they were reinstated, and held their place for nearly a hundred years.

Other repressive measures against liberalism followed, and by 1829 very few of the liberal principles remained which had inspired the declaration of Venezuelan independence—indeed, throughout the length and breadth of Great Colombia the only revolutionary idea which was still intact was the firm resolve never to return to the domination of Spain.

Review and Study Questions

1. Given his background and heritage, why, in your opinion, did Bolívar finally join the revolution?

2. How do you account for the adulatory tone of so much of the Latin American Bolivarian literature?

3. Was Bolívar a true dictator or only a conservative advocate of strong central government? Discuss.

4. How well-taken does Trend's revisionism seem to be? Discuss.

Suggestions for Further Reading

The bibliography on Simón Bolívar is enormous, the great bulk of it in Spanish. The source materials have been collected by the great Venezuelan Bolívar scholar, Vicente Lecuna in *Cartas de Libertador*, 12 vols. But a two-volume selection from that collection has been translated and is the standard English source, *Selected Writings of Bolivar*, compiled by Vicente Lecuna, ed. Harold A. Bierck, tr. Lewis Bertrand, vol. I (1810–1822), vol. II (1823–1830) (New York: The Colonial Press, Inc., 1951), largely comprising letters and a few public documents. Other contemporary sources include General H. L. V. Ducoudray Holstein, *Memoirs of Simón Bolívar . . .* (Boston: S. G. Goodrich and Co., 1829), excerpted in this chapter; and a similar collection of memorials by another close friend and associate, the Irish volunteer officer General Daniel Florencio O'Leary, abridged from O'Leary's much longer work under the title *Bolivar and the War of Independence*, tr. and ed. Robert F. McNerney, Jr. (Austin and London: University of Texas Press, 1970). There is, in addition, a further collection of *The 'Detached Recollection' of General D. F. O'Leary*, ed. R. A. Humphreys (London: The Athlone Press, 1969). There are several useful collections from Bolívar and his contemporaries as well as from some later scholars of Bolívar in *The Liberator, Simón Bolívar, Man and Image,* ed. David Bushnell (New York: Knopf, 1970), excerpted in this chapter. *Simon Bolivar, The Hope of the Universe,* intro. and notes J. L. Salcedo-Bastardo (Paris: UNESCO, 1983) is a series of edited selections from Bolívar's own writings. A selection of his political writings are available in *The Political Thought of Bolivar, Selected Writings,* ed. Gerald E. Fitzgerald (The Hague: Nijhoff, 1971). A useful, though badly outdated guide not only to these materials but a much larger selection is R. A. Humphreys, *Latin American History: A Guide to the Literature in English* (London and New York: Oxford University Press, 1958).

There are more than 5,000 biographies of Bolívar. The best in English is still Gerhard Masur, *Simón Bolívar* (Albuquerque, N.M.: University of New Mexico Press, 1969), although Donald E. Worcester, *Bolivar* (Boston and Toronto: Little, Brown and Co., 1977) is a good, balanced, straightforward account, as is J. B. Trend, *Bolívar and the Independence of Spanish America* (New York: Harper, 1968), excerpted for this chapter. Waldo Frank, *Birth of a World, Bolivar in Terms of his Peoples* (Boston: Houghton Mifflin, 1951) presents Bolívar in somewhat broader terms, as does J. L. Calcedo-Bastardo, *Bolivar, A Continent and its Destiny*, ed. and tr. Annella McDermot (Atlantic Highlands, N.J.: Humanities Press, 1977). The intellectual setting for Bolívar's revolution is dealt with in Víctor Andrés Belaunde, *Bolivar and the Political Thought of the Spanish American Revolution* (Baltimore: The Johns Hopkins Press, 1938), the standard work, and Bernard Moses, *The Intellectual Background of the Revolution in South America* (New York: Russell and Russell, 1966 [1926]).

Salvador de Madariaga, *Bolivar* (Coral Gables, Florida: University of Miami Press, 1952) is a massive revisionist biography of Bolívar in which the great Spanish scholar is somewhat hostile to Bolívar and defensive of the Spanish colonial system. Irene Nicholson, *The Liberators, A Study of Independence Movements in Spanish America* (New York and Washington: Praeger, 1969) deals also with the Spanish colonial system and its opponents, including Bolívar. This is a competent survey of the existing research on the subject. Victor W. von Hagen, *The Four Seasons of Manuela, A Biography, The Love Story of Manuela Sáenz and Simón Bolívar* (Boston and New York: Duell, Sloan, and Pierce and Little, Brown and Co., 1952) is the best biography of Bolívar's fascinating mistress.

SHAKA ZULU: "BLACK NAPOLEON"

1787	Born
1810–16	Served under Dingiswayo
1816	Became chief of the Zulus
1817–23	Conquest of Natal
1828	Died

To a remarkable extent the Zulus dominated and defined the history of southern Africa in the nineteenth century. And the man who brought this about was the warrior-chief of the Zulu nation, Shaka the father of his people.

The Zulus belonged to a large ethnic conglomerate, the Bantu. A migratory, cattle-keeping people composed of many subgroups and speaking some two hundred related languages, the Bantu had gradually moved from the north into the eastern portion of southern Africa. A large subgroup of the Bantu, the Nguni, settled in the pleasant coastal strip of rich grazing land between the Drakenberg Mountains and the Indian Ocean, between Cape Colony to the southwest and what would be the Transvaal to the north. One of the Nguni clans was the Zulu, "the people of the Heavens." But they were neither numerous nor powerful, the entire clan probably numbering fewer than two thousand people in the last years of the eighteenth century.

It was into this setting that Shaka was born about 1787. By the end of his reign Zululand had been extended over an area of eighty thousand square miles, containing nearly half a million people. The slaughter of his enemies and the magnification of his own people were the two parallel accomplishments of Shaka, "the great elephant."

From Folklore to History

E. A. RITTER

The central problem of any history of the sub-Saharan African tribal peoples is the absence of written sources. This is the case with the Zulus and their leader, Shaka. These were preliterate people and, like most such people, they preserved their history and their lore, their religion and their magic in an oral tradition scrupulously passed down from generation to generation. Even today that lore has never been systematically written down. But bits and pieces of it have found their way into white people's accounts. One of these is E. A. Ritter's *Shaka Zulu: The Rise of the Zulu Empire,* excerpted below. This is a pivotal work in South African history precisely because Ritter has, as the *Manchester Guardian* reviewer wrote, "amalgamated, as perhaps no one else could have done, the printed records and the Zulu oral tradition."[1]

Ritter was born in 1890 and raised in South Africa, where his father was a magistrate in Natal, in the heart of Zululand. The father's chief court orderly was a Zulu named Njenga-bantu Ema-Bomvini, then almost seventy. His father Mahola had been one of Shaka's fellow-soldiers in Dingiswayo's army, and Mahola had passed down to his son his own recollections of Shaka. Young Ritter's first language was Zulu, which he learned from his nurses. As a boy he was a nearly daily listener to Njenga-bantu's recitals of Shaka's deeds, "taking in every word with the same rapt attention as the other listeners. Thus was laid the foundation of his being able to see Shaka as the Zulus saw him."[2]

Ritter also had access to another aged Zulu, Chief Sigananda Cube, who, as a boy, had been a personal servant of Shaka. At the time of Sigananda's death, about 1906, he had been recognized by Pika Zulu, Shaka's great-nephew and custodian of the Zulu royal family's unwritten history, as the leading exponent of that history.

As Ritter observed, however, "when Zulus give an account of an historical event their method is not dry reportage, it is more akin to drama, and the feelings and words of all protagonists are recounted as in epic poetry."[3] This is clearly evident in Ritter's work, especially

---

[1]*Manchester Guardian,* August 19, 1955.

[2]Ritter, *Shaka Zulu,* p. xi.

[3]*Ibid.,* p. xiv.

in the early part of his account of Shaka, where there are no reliable non-Zulu sources. We start there.

Shaka's father, Senzangakona, a young Chieftain of the Zulu clan, is said by the Zulu tradition to have come upon his mother, Nandi, while she was bathing in a woodland pool and, fired by her beauty, to have boldly asked for the privilege of *ama hlay endlela*.[4] To this, after some banter and mutual teasing, she consented, both parties lost their heads, broke the rules governing casual intercourse, with the result that three months later Nandi realised that she was pregnant.

As soon as Nandi's pregnancy was discovered, a messenger was rushed off bearing a formal indictment against the young Zulu chief. But Mudli, Ndaba's grandson and chief elder of the clan, indignantly denied the charge. 'Impossible,' said he, 'go back home and inform them the girl is but harbouring *I-Shaka*.'[5] But in due course Nandi became a mother. 'There now!' they sent word to the Zulu people over the hills; 'there is your beetle' (*I-Shaka*). 'Come and fetch it for it is yours.'

And reluctantly they came, and deposited Nandi, unwedded, in the hut of Senzangakona; and the child was named U-SHAKA—the year 1787.

The unhappy Nandi was now not only illicitly a mother but, what was worse, within the forbidden degrees of kindred—her mother being Mfunda, daughter of Kondlo, the Qwabe chief, with whose clan intermarriage with the Zulus was taboo. But Senzangakona, being a chief, 'could do no wrong', and without the wedding-feast— there being no ceremonial celebration of the coming of a bride already with child—Nandi, doubly dishonoured, was quietly installed as the chief's third wife. . . . Shaka's first six years were overshadowed by the unhappiness of a mother he adored. At the age of six he went out to care for his father's sheep, with the other herd-boys; in a moment of negligence he allowed a dog to kill a sheep, his father was angry, his mother defended him, and they were dismissed from Senzangakona's kraal.

Shaka now became a herd-boy at his mother's I-Nguga kraal in E-Langeni-land, twenty miles away from his father's kraal. He was immediately subjected to much bullying by the elder boys, and what hurt him more deeply still was that his dear mother felt herself to be disgraced through the dismissal by her husband, and tongues were

---

[4]A form of mock, external intercourse called "the pleasures of the road."—ED.
[5]An intestinal beetle thought to cause interruption of menstruation.—ED.

not wanting to rub this in. Thus, his years of childhood in E-Langeni-land were not happy. . . .

Modern psychology has enabled us to understand the importance in after life, of a child's unhappiness. Perhaps we may trace Shaka's subsequent lust for power to the fact that his little crinkled ears and the marked stumpiness of his genital organ were ever the source of persistent ridicule among Shaka's companions, and their taunts in this regard so rankled that he grew up harbouring a deadly hatred against all and everything E-Langeni. . . .

'Never mind, my *Um-Lilwane* (Little Fire), you have got the *isibindi* (liver, meaning courage) of a lion and one day you will be the greatest chief in the land,' Nandi would tell him. 'I can see it in your eyes. When you are angry they shine like the sun, and yet no eyes can be more tender when you speak comforting words to me in my misery.' So the Zulu chroniclers give her words. . . .

In due course Shaka went to Senzangakona's kraal and went through the ceremonial rites of puberty. But when his Royal father presented him with his *umutsha*[6] he rejected it with disdain, and otherwise succeeded in getting himself so generally disliked that his early return to his mother became imperative.

Shaka had a very definite reason for deciding to continue living unclothed. He wished it to be known that he was now physically adequate. In particular he wanted all his associates of the E-Langeni tribe to see and know this, and especially his former tormentors, who would now, if anything, be envious of him. . . .

Nandi now sent the boy to her father's sister, in Mtetwa-land, near the coast. Neither Shaka nor his mother was a person of any consequence at this period; indeed, as destitute vagrants, they were everywhere despised. But the headman, under King Jobe, in charge of the district in which they settled was Ngomane, son of Mqombolo, of the Dletsheni clan, and with him they soon became acquainted. He treated Nandi and her son with a kindness which Shaka never forgot, and there in a 'real home' surrounded by sympathy Shaka at last had come to rest. . . .

The Chief of the Mtetwa tribe, with whom Shaka dwelt, had been Jobe. His sons had conspired against him, one had been put to death and the other, Godongwana, had fled. He changed his name to Dingiswayo (The Wanderer). When Jobe died, Dingiswayo returned and became chief in 1809. He revived the *Izi-cwe* (Bushmen) regiment by calling-up Shaka's age-group, including Shaka. Thus Shaka became a soldier. . . .

Shaka's commander, Buza, and in fact the whole regiment, did not fail to note the prowess of the young warrior; he was allowed to lead the

---

[6]The ceremonial loincloth or apron worn by adult Zulu men.—ED.

giya or victory dance. Shaka was pleased with his progress, but pondered deeply over the fact that he constantly broke the light throwing assegais with his mighty stabs into the opposing warriors' bodies. But the custom of hurling an assegai,[7] mostly without any effect, at a distant foe, was to him as though merely throwing one's weapon away. According to the chronicle, it was then that he conceived the idea of a single, massive-bladed assegai with a stout, short handle. This would mean fighting at close quarters, with deadly physical and psychological effect. . . .

Like other great conquerors, Shaka began his career by reforming not only tactics, but weapons. His own prowess as an infighter had shown him what was needed, but, as we have seen, he had found the throwing spear dangerously fragile when used as a striking or thrusting weapon. He was determined to get his stabbing blade which, however, had to conform with the very definite specifications formulated in his mind. . . .

The Mbonambi clan, south-eastern neighbours of the Mtetwas, were the most renowned blacksmiths and one of their best craftsmen was Ngonyama (Lion), and to him Shaka went with his problem. . . . Shaka now told him exactly what he wanted, and why, and his fervour soon infected the old 'Lion', who agreed that none of the existing blades would quite answer Shaka's purpose. . . .

'What you want, Zulu, you shall have,' responded the 'Lion' at last. 'But it will take time, for we might as well start at the very beginning. A new furnace shall be equipped with new bellows to ensure that the iron is of the best. The blade will be tempered with the strongest fats, and in your hands it will ever be victorious. It will cost me a lot, but for you I will do it for the price of one heifer, and that you may send to me when you are satisfied with my work, and in your own good time.' . . .

With the magic rites completed, Ngonyama once more became a practical and ardent blacksmith, and again the forest resounded to his hammer blows as he put all his craftsmanship into finishing and refining the blade. . . .

Thus was born the blade which was the model of others which were destined to sweep irresistibly over half a continent. As Shaka held it in his hand and gazed at it with admiration his eyes shone, but not yet had he finished with his tests. He tried it for its 'ring' and vibration, and its resiliency, and, as it had not yet been sharpened he gave a part of its forward edge a good rub on a hard sandstone provided for that purpose. It took a lot of rubbing before it became sharp, razor sharp, as Shaka demonstrated by shaving a few of the sparse hairs which grew on his arm. Then at last he was satisfied and expressed his gratitude to the smith. . . .

---

[7]The traditional Zulu spear or lance.—ED.

Very soon the *Izi-cwe* regiment was doctored again for war. . . . In the following campaign Dingiswayo took personal command of the *Izi-cwe* regiment, brigaded with the *Yengondlovu* regiment. The year was 1810 and Shaka twenty-three years old. . . .

In the ensuing battle Dingiswayo's forces are victorious.

After some twenty head of cattle had been killed for the victors and the vanquished, Dingiswayo told Buza, the commander of the Izi-cwe regiment, to present Shaka to him. He had already had a very favourable report on his first battle, and was greatly impressed by what he had seen that day.

At his first glance into the sharp and intelligent eyes of the huge young warrior, he instantly recognized a leader. After putting a number of questions to him, he was agreeably surprised at the prompt and clever replies. He then questioned Shaka on the matter of fighting without sandals, and with a single stabbing assegai, and conceded that Shaka was right as far as war only was concerned, but for the time being he was content to fight in a less sanguinary way, and to achieve his aims by persuasion with the minimum employment of force. However, after conferring with Buza and Ngomane, he there and then promoted Shaka to Captain of 'one hundred', or the equivalent of a leader of two 'guilds', and also presented him with ten head of cattle. . . .

Shaka now joined the other two regimental commanders and the headmen who were in attendance on Dingiswayo, and the heads of the contingents supplied by allied tribes. Presently the campaign was discussed and Shaka remained silent whilst his seniors gave their opinions. In fact he said nothing until he was invited by Dingiswayo to speak.

Shaka then said that in the next battle the army should be drawn up with a central head and chest, with half a regiment on each side thrown out as enveloping horns to ensure the complete annihilation of the enemy force. Only thus would they gain the complete submission of the remnants of the tribe, and do away with the periodical reconquests necessitated by the present easygoing methods which had proved to be so futile and inconclusive. Moreover, in future campaigns the broad-bladed, stout stabbing assegai should replace the light throwing spears, and sandals should be discarded to increase the mobility of the warriors.

Dingiswayo conceded the advantages in an *impi ebomvu* (red war, or war to a finish), but emphasized again that he did not wish to destroy, but merely to teach a lesson, whereupon Shaka sharply rejoined, 'Which will never be learned'. . . .

Nevertheless, Shaka continued to be a successful war leader and to be advanced by Dingiswayo.

Shaka was now promoted to Commander-in-Chief of all Dingiswayo's armed forces, and a member of the inner Council. As such, he insisted on visiting each military kraal in rotation to tighten up the discipline and extend the drill with rapid forced route marches. In fact he constituted himself an Inspector-General of the Forces. . . .

Towards the end of 1815 Senzangakona's health rapidly declined, and early in 1816 he died. Weak and wasted, he had in the end given way to the incessant importuning of his eighth wife, Bibi, to appoint her son Sigujana as his successor. . . . When Shaka and Dingiswayo heard that Sigujana had appropriated the chieftaincy by prevailing upon the dying Senzangakona to nominate him, the former was furious, and the latter much annoyed, as he had not been advised or consulted. . . .

Dingiswayo now summoned Shaka and told him to take over the chieftaincy of the Zulu clan. He put at his disposal the 2nd Izi-cwe regiment (subsequently known as 'Ngomane's Own'), which had recently been formed under Shaka's energetic recruiting policy for the expansion of Dingiswayo's armed forces. He also provided him with an imposing staff, headed by Ngomane and Dingiswayo's own nephew, Siwangu of Mbikwane. At the head of this triumphal and irresistible force Shaka entered his father's Esi-Klebeni kraal—the home of his childhood days.

With his immense size—perfectly proportioned—and in his full gala dress, his regal, dignified bearing, the easy grace of all his movements, his piercing eyes set in a strong, stern face, and the general look of authority, made plain to all that here was a warrior-king indeed. . . .

Ngomane now advanced to address the headmen of the Zulu clan, who, each with their following, had been assembled for the occasion.

'Children of Zulu! To-day I present to you Shaka, son of Senzangakona, son of Jama, descended from Zulu, as your lawful chief. So says the "Great One" (Dingiswayo) whose mouth I am. Is there anyone here who can contest the righteousness of this decision? If so, let him stand forth and speak now, or hereafter be silent.' . . .

'No one speaks,' said Ngomane, 'then salute your chief.' . . .

Finding that he had no army, Shaka at once called up the whole manhood of the Zulus, capable of bearing arms. . . . Shaka was tireless in getting his little army into shape. Nearly every day he visited one of his two other military kraals and woe betide the defaulters. His kingdom was so small—a paltry ten miles by ten—that from his central position he could reach any of its confines within an hour. . . .

Shaka, having effected all his reforms in his own tribe, proposed to extend his reformative and retributive activities. He had dealt with individuals; now he would deal with clans, beginning with the E-Langeni, of which his own mother was a daughter, in which he and she had spent those first hideous years of exile and sorrow, and where they had been so cruelly treated. His army was now a war machine indeed. He marshalled it and made a night march of twenty-five miles over the Mtonjaneni Heights to E-Langeni-land. Before dawn he had silently surrounded the Esiweni kraal, the capital of Makedama, the E-Langeni chief. As soon as it became light the chief was summoned to surrender, and he did so without any waste of time.

Shaka ordered all the inhabitants to be brought before him, and singled out all those who, so many years before, had inflicted untold misery on his mother and himself. Some other kraals which harboured his youthful tormentors had also been surrounded by detachments of the army, and their inhabitants were also brought up for scrutiny and judgment. . . .

Whilst this was being done Shaka called for two bowls of water, and then deliberately disrobed in front of all the gathering. The bound men on the left were ordered to approach and squat on their haunches. Shaka then arose and towered over them.

'You will all die,' he roared. Then after a dreadful pause he resumed in deep, even tones, 'Before I tell you the manner of your going there are some things I have to say to you. You are such a filthy collection of *utuvi* (excrement) that the very sight of you contaminates me, and I must wash before I proceed.' Very deliberately he now poured water over his head, and rinsed his whole body carefully, until the first bowl was empty. Then he reminded them of how they had sneered at his bodily inadequacy and bade them note that they had lied. . . .

'This is the death I have in mind for you. The slayers will sharpen the projecting upright poles in this cattle-kraal—one for each of you. They will then lead you there, and four of them will pick you up singly and impale you on each of the sharpened poles. There you will stay till you die, and your bodies, or what will be left of them by the birds, will stay there as a testimony to all, what punishment awaits those who slander me and my mother.' As the anguished victims were led away Shaka taunted them with 'Hlalani gahle' ('Sit you well!' not the customary 'Salani gahle!' i.e. 'Stay you well'). Then he ordered the second bowl of water, and again washed his whole body to 'cleanse it from the last defiling look' of those he had sent to their doom. . . .

After a time Shaka sent orders to the slayers to end the death agonies of the victims by placing bundles of grass under them and firing them. As the flames licked about them, those who were still conscious shrieked out in their death agonies, which were now short-lived.

The White Man's History of Shaka

HENRY FRANCIS FYNN

White people first came to Zululand in 1824. Francis George Farewell, a Capetown businessman; James Saunders King, the captain of a coastal brig; and several other investors formed the Farewell Trading Company at Port Natal, a harbor about a hundred miles south of Shaka's home kraal. Shortly the company was joined by a young Englishman, Henry Francis Fynn, who had been educated at Christ's Hospital in London and had worked for a while as a surgeon's assistant, but had decided to come to South Africa looking for adventure. He had already learned some African dialects when he joined the Farewell Trading Company. He discovered from the natives near Port Natal that the land they had settled on—indeed all of Natal—was Shaka's personal domain. Fynn decided to visit the great Zulu chief. On his first venture to the north along the coast he came across one of Shaka's military parties and watched in amazement as some 20,000 warriors tramped past him. Fynn sent word ahead that he wanted to meet with the chief, but Shaka was not ready, and bade him return to Port Natal; he did send him a gift of ivory and forty head of cattle.

Later that summer of 1824 Shaka invited the white men to visit his kraal. Farewell and Fynn and several others mounted their horses, packed an assortment of gifts, and set out in mid-July. Fynn, of course, took his medical kit. After meeting Shaka and exchanging gifts, the party returned to Port Natal, but Fynn stayed on. He quickly became fluent in Zulu and was to be in more or less constant contact with Shaka for the next four years. He would later write his account of his adventures, based on his diary, from which the following excerpt is taken.

On entering the great cattle kraal we found drawn up within it about 80,000 natives in their war attire. Mbikwana[8] requested me to gallop within the circle, and immediately on my starting to do so one general

---

[8]The leader of their native servants, who served as interpreter.—ED.

shout broke forth from the whole mass, all pointing at me with their sticks. I was asked to gallop round the circle two or three times in the midst of tremendous shouting. . . .

Mbikwana, standing in our midst, addressed some unseen individual in a long speech, in the course of which we were frequently called upon by him to answer "*Yebo*," that is to affirm as being true all he was saying, though perfectly ignorant of what was being said.

While the speech was being made I caught sight of an individual in the background whom I concluded to be Shaka, and, turning to Farewell, pointed out and said: "Farewell, there is Shaka." This was sufficiently audible for him to hear and perceive that I had recognised him. He immediately held up his hand, shaking his finger at me approvingly. Farewell, being near-sighted and using an eye-glass, could not distinguish him.

Elephant tusks were then brought forward. One was laid before Farewell and another before me. Shaka then raised the stick in his hand and after striking with it right and left, the whole mass broke from their position and formed up into regiments. Portions of each of these rushed to the river and the surrounding hills, while the remainder, forming themselves into a circle, commenced dancing with Shaka in their midst.

It was a most exciting scene, surprising to us, who could not have imagined that a nation termed "savages" could be so disciplined and kept in order.

Regiments of girls, headed by officers of their own sex, then entered the centre of the arena to the number of 8,000–10,000, each holding a slight staff in her hand. They joined in the dance, which continued for about two hours. . . .

The people now dispersed, and he directed a chief to lead us to a kraal where we could pitch our tents. He sent us a sheep, a basket of corn, an ox, and a pot of beer, about three gallons. At seven o'clock, we sent up four rockets and fired off eight guns. He sent people to look at these, but from fear did not show himself out of his hut. The following morning we were requested to mount our horses and proceed to the King's quarters. We found him sitting under a tree at the upper end of the kraal decorating himself and surrounded by about 200 people. . . .

While he was dressing himself, his people proceeded, as on the day before, to show droves of cattle, which were still flocking in, repeatedly varying the scene with singing and dancing. In the meantime, we observed Shaka gave orders for a man standing close to us to be killed, for what crime we could not learn, but we soon found this to be a very common occurrence.

Mr. Petersen, unfortunately, at this moment placed a musical box on the ground, and, striking it with a switch, moved the stop. Shaka heard the music. It seemed to produce in him a superstitious feeling.

He turned away with evident displeasure and went back immediately to the dance.

Those portions of regiments which had separated prior to the dance now returned from the river and from behind the adjoining hills, driving before them immense herds of cattle. A grand cattle show was now being arranged. Each regiment drove towards us thousands of cattle that had been allotted to their respective barracks, the colour of each regiment's cattle corresponding with that of the shield the men carried, which, in turn, served to distinguish one regiment from another. No cattle of differing colour from those allotted to a given regiment were allowed to intermix. . . .

Two oxen were slaughtered for us. After dinner we prepared to retire, but messengers from Shaka requested us to go to him, with Jacob the interpreter. I was then led into the seraglio, where I found him seated in a carved wooden chair and surrounded by about 400 girls, two or three chiefs and two servants in attendance.

My name Fynn had been converted into Sofili by the people in general; by this, after desiring me to sit in front of him, he several times accosted me in the course of the following dialogue:

"I hear you have come from umGeorge, is it so? Is he as great a king as I am?"

Fynn: "Yes; King George is one of the greatest kings in the world."

Shaka: "I am very angry with you," said while putting on a severe countenance. "I shall send a messenger to umGeorge and request him to kill you. He sent you to me not to give medicine to my dogs." All present immediately applauded what Shaka had said. "Why did you give my dogs medicine?" (in allusion to the woman I was said to have brought back to life after death).[9]

Fynn: "It is a practice of our country to help those who are in need, if able to do so."

Shaka: "Are you then the doctor of dogs? You were sent here to be my doctor."

Fynn: "I am not a doctor and not considered by my countrymen to be one."

Shaka: "Have you medicine by you?"

Fynn: "Yes."

Shaka: "Then cure me, or I will have you sent to umGeorge to have you killed."

Fynn: "What is the matter with you?"

Shaka: "That is your business to find out."

---

[9]Some time had passed and this was an incident which had occurred several days before.—ED.

Fynn: "Stand up and let me see your person."

Shaka: "Why should I stand up?"

Fynn: "That I may see if I can find out what ails you."

Shaka stood up but evidently disliked my approaching him closely. A number of girls held up lighted torches. I looked about his person and, after reflecting on the great activity he had shown during the day, was satisfied he had not much the matter with him. I, however, observed numerous black marks on his loins where native doctors had scarified him, and at once said he had pains in his loins. He held his hand before his mouth in astonishment, upon which my wisdom was applauded by all present. Shaka then strictly charged me not to give medicine to his dogs, and, after a few commonplace questions in which he showed good humour, I was permitted to retire for the night. . . .

The following day had been appointed by Shaka for receiving our present, which, fortunately, had been well chosen by Farewell for presentation to so superior a chief as Shaka. It consisted of every description of beads at that time procurable in Cape Town, and far superior to those Shaka had previously obtained from the Portuguese at Delagoa. There was a great variety of woollen blankets, a large quantity of brass bars, turned and lacquered, and sheets of copper, also pigeons, a pig, cats and dogs. There was, moreover, a full-dress military coat, with epaulettes covered with gold lace. Though Shaka showed no open gratitude, we saw clearly that he was satisfied. He was very interested in the live animals, especially the pig, until it got into his milk stores where it committed great havoc, and set all the women in the seraglio screaming for assistance. All this ended in the pig being killed.

The showing of cattle and dancing continued during the day, whilst other regiments, which had come from a great distance, arrived and took part in the festivities. . . .

In conversation on our object in coming to Natal, this part of South Africa, Shaka showed great desire that we should live at the port. Each evening he sent for me and conversed with me through the Kaffir Jacob, the interpreter, for three or four hours.

On the first day of our visit we had seen no less than ten men carried off to death. On a mere sign by Shaka, viz: the pointing of his finger, the victim would be seized by his nearest neighbours; his neck would be twisted, and his head and body beaten with sticks, the nobs of some of these being as large as a man's fist. On each succeeding day, too, numbers of others were killed; their bodies would then be carried to an adjoining hill and there impaled. We visited this spot on the fourth day. It was truly a Golgotha, swarming with hundreds of vultures. The effects of this together with the scenes of death made Mr. Petersen decide at once to dissolve the partnership and leave for the Cape. . . .

During Fynn's visit an assassination attempt is made on Shaka's life,
apparently at the insistance of a distant rival chief. Fynn is summoned.

I immediately washed the wound with camomile tea and bound it up
with linen. He had been stabbed with an assegai through the left arm,
and the blade had passed through the ribs under the left breast. It had
made the King spit blood. I could not account for the assegai not
entering the lungs; it must have been due to mere accident; I was for
some time in doubt. His own doctor, who seemed to have a good
knowledge of that nature, also attended him. He gave the King a vomit
and afterwards administered purges and continually washed the
wound with decoctions of cooling roots. He also probed the wound to
ascertain if any poison had been used on the assegai.

Shaka cried nearly the whole night, expecting that only fatal consequences would ensue. The crowd had now increased so much that the
noise of their shrieks became unbearable, and this noise continued
throughout the night. Morning showed a horrid sight in a clear light. I
am satisfied I cannot describe the horrid scene in language powerful
enough to enable the reader, who has never been similarly situated, to
appreciate it aright. The immense crowds of people that arrived hour
after hour from every direction began their shouting on coming in sight
of the kraal, running and exerting their utmost powers of voice as they
entered it and joined those who had got there before them. They then
pulled one another about, men and women throwing themselves down
in every direction without taking care how they fell. Great numbers
fainted from over exertion and excessive heat. The females of the seraglio, more particularly, were in very great distress, having overtaxed
themselves during the night. They suffered from the excessive heat and
from want of nourishment, which no one dared to touch, whilst the
four brass collars each had, fitting so tightly round the neck as to make it
impossible for the wearer to turn her head, nearly suffocated them. Several of them died. Finding their situation so distressing, and there being no one to afford them relief, I poured a quantity of water and threw
it over them as they fell; this went on till I was myself so tired as to be
obliged to desist. They then made some attempt to help one another.

All this time I had been so busily employed as not to see the most
sickening part of this tragical scene. They had now begun to kill one
another. Some were put to death because they did not cry, others for
putting spittle into their eyes, others for sitting down to cry, although
strength and tears, after such continuous mourning and exertion,
were quite exhausted. No such limits were taken into account.

We then understood that six men had been wounded by the assassins
who wounded Shaka. From the road they took, it was supposed that

they had been sent by Zwide, King of the Ndwandwes (Ndwandwe tribe), who was Shaka's only powerful enemy. Two regiments were accordingly sent off at once in search of the aggressors.

In the meantime the medicines which, on his leaving, Mr. Farewell had promised to send were received. They came very opportunely, and Shaka was much gratified. I now washed his wounds frequently, and gave him mild purgatives. I, moreover, dressed his wounds with ointment. The King was in a hopeless condition for four days. During all that time people were continuing to flock in from the outskirts of his country and joining in the general tumult. It was not till the fourth day that cattle were killed for the sustenance of the multitude. Many had died in the interval, and many had been killed for not mourning, or for having gone to their kraals for food.

On the fifth day there were symptoms of improvement in the King's condition; these favourable indications were also noticeable on the day following.

At noon on that day the party sent out in search of the would-be murderers returned, bringing with them the dead bodies of three men whom they had killed in the bush (jungle). These were the supposed assassins. The bodies, having been carried off, were laid on the ground in a roadway about a mile from the kraal. Their right ears were then cut off and the two pursuing regiments sat down on either side of the road, while the whole of the people, men and women, who had assembled at the kraal, probably exceeding 30,000, passed up the road crying and yelling. Each one, on coming up to the bodies, struck them several blows with a stick, which was then left at the spot, so that nothing more of these was to be seen; only an immense pile of sticks remained, but the formal ceremony still went on. The whole body now collecting, and three men walking in advance with sticks on which were the ears of the dead and now shattered bodies, the procession moved to Shaka's kraal. The King now made his appearance. The national mourning song was chanted. After this a fire was made in the centre of the cattle kraal where the ears were burnt to ashes. . . .

Early in 1828 Shaka sent his army south to raid clear to the Cape Colony border. When they returned he sent them far to the north. Such random, irrational behavior apparently gave his two brothers their long-awaited opportunity to assassinate Shaka.

During the life of Shaka his despotic sway was so feared that his name was seldom mentioned but as the form of an oath, and much more dangerous was the attempt to trace in any way the particulars of his family, who were not permitted publicly to be known as his relatives. His brothers, though numerous, were not allowed to call themselves so, except Ngwadi, brother on his mother's side. Dingane and Mhlangana were only partially known, the former much resembling Shaka in person. Their apparent fondness was so great that one was seldom seen without the other. In the same house lived M6opha, son of Sithayi, a Zulu chief and principal servant of Shaka. These were the three conspirators who put Shaka to death. . . .

On the 24th September, 1828, Shaka, while taking his usual sleep at midday, dreamt he was killed and M6opha's sister, one of the seraglio, knowing the result would be likely to prove her brother's death, told him what had transpired, to give him an opportunity of killing a cow as soon as possible, to invoke his spirit. This information induced M6opha to urge his accomplices. Some Bechuanas arriving with crane feathers, which Shaka had long expected, these people were brought to him, he being in a small kraal he had built about 50 yards from Dukuza, calling it Nyakomu6i or Ugly Year. There he went to receive them. The two brothers, being informed of it by M6opha, took a circuitous route to come in at the back of the kraal, having concealed assegais under their karosses, and sat behind the fence. Shaka asked the Bechuanas what had detained them so long, in a harsh tone. M6opha immediately threw a stick at them. They ran away instantly, supposing it the signal for their death, which had been given to M6opha by Shaka unperceived by them, as was his custom in those cases. Shaka asking why he had struck them, Mhlangana embraced the opportunity and, from behind the fence, stabbed at the back of his left shoulder. Shaka had only time to look round and, seeing the two brothers, exclaim: "What is the matter, children of my father?" when Dingane stabbed him. He then threw the blanket from him and, taking the assegai from his side with which Dingane had stabbed him, fell dead near the kraal gate.

A Modern Shaka

BRIAN ROBERTS

The Zulu Kings, by Brian Roberts, from which the following excerpt is taken, has been called "the first tempered account we have of Shaka and the rise of the Zulu nation."[10] He presents us with a healthy skepticism

---

[10]*New York Times Book Review,* July 20, 1975, p. 20.

about the reports of Europeans such as Fynn. Like E. A. Ritter, Roberts relied on records derived from Zulu oral tradition. But where Ritter tended to reflect the colonial attitudes of the turn of the century, Roberts reflects careful modern research and a skillful reading of both Zulu and non-Zulu sources. He has created both a "plausible" and a "not unsympathetic picture"[11] of Shaka. His assessment follows.

As far as is known, Shaka was forty-one when he died. If he had come to power in 1817—the year Dingiswayo is said to have died—he had been the effective ruler of Zululand for eleven years. In that time he had forged one of the mightiest empires the African continent has ever known. Under his leadership, his small insignificant clan had risen from obscurity and given their name to an all-powerful nation. During his lifetime the Zulu army had been organised into a fearsome military machine which had transformed the age-old pattern of southern African society. The Nguni system of clanships and petty chieftainships had been replaced by a single, authoritarian state, feared by its neighbours and acknowledged far beyond its borders. Few leaders in history have accomplished so much, so quickly. Shaka not only established Zulu supremacy but ensured the lasting renown of his nation. For generations to come the word Zulu was to be synonymous with might. It was an awe-inspiring achievement.

But, like all such achievements, it was not come by gently. Shaka was a tyrant; he could have been nothing else. He rose amid appalling bloodshed. It has been estimated that no less than two million people died as a result of the upheavals created by Shaka. When the white men first arrived in Natal, they found the country desolate, the landscape littered with skeletons. Shaka reigned supreme because he had obliterated all semblance of opposition. He took no advice, he demanded blind obedience; he was intolerant, ruthless and inflexible. He knew nothing of the softer virtues, had he done so he would not have achieved what he did: his strength was derived from his callousness.

Living as he did, in the first quarter of the nineteenth century, it was inevitable that he should be compared with a contemporary despot: he has been called the Black Napoleon. But the comparison is more romantic than real. The system instigated by Shaka was unique. To compare it, even superficially, with that of a European power is misleading. The aims, methods and values of the white men were unknown to Shaka. The society he ruled and the opponents he

---

[11]*Atlantic*, June 1975 (235), p. 95.

fought were so far removed from the regimes of nineteenth-century Europe that to set his achievements against those of a sophisticated conqueror like Napoleon is meaningless. Shaka had no set objectives and was uninfluenced by political and moral considerations. He was guided by intuition; he learned from his own experience. It is necessary to realise this to appreciate his extraordinary genius.

Shocking as was his apparent cruelty, this also must be judged in isolation. The ethics of the white man meant nothing to him. He relied on his own interpretation of humanity. Treachery, disobedience and cowardice were, for him, the cardinal sins; he did not regard life as sacred—any more than did most of his subjects. When white men, fresh from Regency England, were plunged into a society that recognised none of their values, they were appalled. The fact that that society was rigidly organised only increased their horror: the frightful punishments inflicted by Shaka appeared to them all the more cold blooded. It was difficult to reconcile fine discipline with primitive values. But there was nothing so exceptional about the grim Zulu penal code. Shaka was by no means the only African ruler to order summary executions; he was, however, one of the few whose activities have been reported in vivid detail.

One must accept that European and African values were often irreconcilable. Nowhere was this divergence more apparent than in an early conversation between Fynn and Shaka. The Zulu King was flabbergasted to learn that the white men imprisoned offenders for months, even years. Such punishment seemed to him far more sadistic than the tortures he inflicted. To kill a man, however painfully, was preferable to the living death of confinement. As a warrior he could imagine nothing worse than a long, meaningless captivity. . . .

Reports of Shaka spread by the traders, make him appear an unnatural fiend whose activities went far beyond the dictates of even the most primitive code. He is shown as a mass murderer, a depraved ogre who revelled in the tortures he devised and drooled over his victims. 'History,' said James Saunders King, 'perhaps does not furnish an instance of a more despotic and cruel monster than Chaka.' . . . Anyone wishing to present a lively picture of the monster Shaka can find plenty of material in *Travels and Adventures in Eastern Africa* by Nathaniel Isaacs.[12] It does not do, however, to enquire too deeply into the authenticity of Isaacs's account. Many of his observations on Natal and Zulu customs are undoubtedly accurate and will be of lasting value. But when he

---

[12]Nathaniel Isaacs came to Port Natal somewhat later than Fynn and only knew Shaka at the very end of his reign. His work, however, is second only to Fynn's in value as a contemporary account.—ED.

comes to deal with the terrible Shaka his comments are, to say the least, suspect. . . .

Fynn was more honest, less sensational. His account is far more factual; it contains none of the purple patches Isaacs delighted in. . . . [Nevertheless he] had some covering up to do. What is more, his so-called 'diary' was written many years after the events it describes. He is said to have lost the original notes he was collecting for his book when they were mistakenly buried with his brother Frank and he thus had 'to rewrite the whole of the contents from memory as well as he could'. Unfortunately his memory was not all that reliable. The re-written notes were fragmentary; often he gives more than one version of a single incident; invariably the versions differ. It is possible that, when recalling some events, he was influenced by Isaac's *Travels and Adventures in Eastern Africa*.

Fynn does not dwell on Shaka's sadism to the same extent as does Isaacs. Nevertheless he gives many examples of torture and executions. The executions mostly result from some offence to Shaka, often a trivial offence. Fynn says, for instance: 'On one occasion I witnessed 60 boys under 12 years of age despatched before he had breakfasted.' Precisely why these boys were killed he does not say. The implication would seem to be that Shaka did not require a reason for butchery. . . .

What is difficult to understand is the reaction of the traders. If they really believed that Shaka was a capricious, indiscriminate killer, then why did they remain in Natal? They were given repeated opportunities to leave but they refused them all. One would have thought that, with a monster like Shaka breathing down their necks, there would have been a mad scramble to board the first ship that called at Port Natal. Yet Farewell, Fynn, Cane and Ogle stayed for four years under Shaka; King, Isaacs, Hutton and the seamen were there three years. Young boys like Thomas Halstead and John Ross wandered about the country, apparently without fear. King even brought Farewell's wife to Natal.

Did they really think they would be protected by their white skins and magic medicines? Or were they so self-seeking that they were willing to risk their necks for a haul of ivory? Given their picture of Shaka, neither explanation is particularly convincing. A man who murdered his own family and wilfully massacred his own people could hardly be relied upon to respect a difference in skin colour indefinitely. Their medicines were limited and by no means infallible. Shaka is said to have commanded an army of 30,000; if, in one of his unpredictable moods, he had turned against the traders, their firearms would have counted for nothing. The chance of a fortune might have inspired them to take a reasonable risk, but it does not explain why they—down to the last seaman—willingly remained at the uncertain mercy of a savage extremist. . . .

But the undeniable fact is that the traders did not recoil 'at the serpent's hiss or the lion's growl'. They stayed on for years with this terrifying fiend who, according to Isaacs, was continually threatening their lives. James Saunders King tried desperately to force the British to occupy Port Natal and thus provide the traders with protection, but his failure to achieve this did not prevent him, or the others, from returning to the Zulu territory. Just how afraid of Shaka were the traders?

There can be little doubt that the tortures and executions described by Isaacs and Fynn did take place. This was part of the Zulu system and was to be observed, independently, by others who later visited those Zulu rulers trained at Shaka's court. Painful death was the inevitable punishment for those who offended the King: and the King was easily offended. An ill-suppressed cough, sneeze or fart in the royal presence could result in a menacing finger being raised and the executioners moving in. The sixty boys whom Fynn says were put to death before breakfast might have done no more than titter at a serious gathering. Immediate death was the only punishment allowed for such offence. Was this, as Isaacs suggests, simply the means by which Shaka indulged a sadistic whim? If it was, then the traders had good reasons for their professed fears.

But it seems more likely that Shaka's behaviour was not as erratic as they pretended. The Zulu system was based on a harsh, rigid, but recognisable discipline. By means of this discipline Shaka had made his army invincible; in the same way he had ensured his supremacy. From Fynn's description of the mass hysteria which was so easily generated among Shaka's subjects, it is obvious that the Zulu nation could never have reached the heights it did under a ruler less severe and determined than Shaka. To say this is not to excuse a cruel despotism, but to understand the motivations of an intelligent but barbarous ruler. Only by resorting to the abnormal could Shaka—like many another tyrant—retain his hold over his people.

The traders must have recognised this. They, as well as Shaka's subjects, must have been aware of the disciplinary code laid down by the King. They must have realised that, as long as they observed that code, they were safe. Safer in fact than a more ignorant and emotional Zulu. . . .

The only first-hand, detailed reports of Shaka are those given by his white visitors. Knowledge of the first Zulu King depends entirely on the biased observations of Isaacs and Fynn. Stripped of their subjective judgements, the few facts to emerge from these accounts are not entirely to Shaka's detriment. Confronted by a group of strange white men, with seemingly mysterious powers, the King offered them friendship when he might have destroyed them from fear. He not only welcomed them but gave every indication of wishing to meet their fellows. He granted them land, he supplied them with ivory, he fell in with their schemes. He stood between them and the wrath of his people. While Shaka lived no white man in Natal was harmed.

It is unfortunate that no contemporary Zulu account of Shaka exists. Did his people loath him as his enemies—both white and black—later maintained? There seems little evidence to support such a claim. Not even Fynn and Isaacs suggest the possibility of a popular rising against Shaka. The only recorded assassination attempt on the King, apart from that which killed him, was, as far as one can tell, that of an enemy agent. This might be explained, in part, by Shaka's iron-handed rule. Nevertheless, the Zulu were a warrior race, by no means servile, and when Shaka's brothers decided to strike they did so with relative ease. If discontent under Shaka was widespread, it was certainly not apparent.

But there is further evidence in Shaka's favour. Zulu sources are not entirely silent on the founder of their nation. Far from it. For generations oral tradition has hailed Shaka as the greatest of Zulu heroes. His name is frequently invoked in Zulu councils, his example is cited as a supreme authority. Any criticism of Shaka can, and often does, earn a sharp rebuke from Zulu elders and statesmen. He is the subject of eulogistic praise chants and poems; the hero of more than one African novel. The Zulu people have erected a monument in his honour at the site of his Dukuza kraal. When, in 1972, the Zulu Territorial Authority nominated a national day for the newly created kwaZulu, they chose the anniversary of their founder's assassination: Shaka's Day.

Review and Study Questions

1. Can the unwritten, oral tradition of such a preliterate people as the Zulus serve as an authentic source for their history?

2. What reforms did Shaka undertake to turn his army into a superb fighting force?

3. Why, do you imagine, did Shaka receive the white men so favorably?

4. How do you assess the nature of Shaka's accomplishments? Were they important in the history of southern Africa?

5. Could Shaka be described as "the Black Napoleon"?

Suggestions for Further Reading

No written Zulu account of the oral tradition about Shaka exists. We have already noted the skillful and sympathetic use of portions of that tradition by E. A. Ritter, *Shaka Zulu: The Rise of the Zulu Empire* (London: Longmans, Green and Co., 1965), excerpted for this chapter. Probably the closest thing we have to an authentic ethno-history of the Zulus is in two works by A. T. Bryant, *The Zulu People as They Were Before the White Man Came* (New York: Negro Universities Press, 1970 [1948]) and *Olden Times in Zululand and Natal* (London and New York: Longmans, Green and Co., 1929), both compendia of Zulu customs and behavior written by a missionary and the most credible Zulu scholar and linguist of the early part of this century.

Of the two important European contemporary accounts of Shaka, the best is *The Diary of Henry Francis Fynn,* ed. James Stuart and D. McK. Malcolm (Pietermaritzburg: Shuter and Shooter, 1950), excerpted for this chapter. But Nathaniel Isaacs, *Travels and Adventures in Eastern Africa . . .* ed. Louis Herman and Percival R. Kirby (Cape Town: C. Struik, 1970) is worthwhile too.

Ritter's book, *Shaka Zulu,* is the only biography of Shaka. But there are several good works on Zulu history that treat him very fully. One of the best is Brian Roberts, *The Zulu Kings* (New York: Charles Scribner's Sons, 1974), excerpted for this chapter. Two excellent ones are also Donald R. Morris, *The Washing of the Spears: A History of the Rise of the Zulu Nation under Shaka and Its Fall in the Zulu War of 1879* (New York: Simon & Schuster, 1965) and T. V. Bulpin, *Natal and the Zulu Country* (Cape Town: Books of Africa, Ltd., 1969).

Some of the more general works on African history are useful in providing a context within which to understand particular leaders and peoples, like Shaka and the Zulus. One of the best and most comprehensive is *The Cambridge History of Africa,* vol. 5, from c. 1790 to c. 1870, ed. John E. Flint (Cambridge et al.: Cambridge University Press, 1976). Though smaller in scope, two other good general African histories are Robert W. July, *A History of the African People,* 3rd ed. (New York: Scribner, 1980) and Robin Hallett, *Africa to 1875: A Modern History* (Ann Arbor: University of Michigan Press, 1970). An elegant and handsome book, though not as useful as the two preceeding ones, is *The Horizon History of Africa* (New York: American Heritage Publishing Co., 1971). Finally, there is an interesting work by the French anthropologist Jacques Maquet, *Civilizations of Black Africa,* tr. and rev. Joan Rayfield (New York: Oxford University Press, 1972) which presents a series of typologies, e.g., "The Civilization of the Bow," "The Civilization of the Granaries," and, including the Zulus, "The Civilization of the Spear."

MAHATMA GANDHI: SOLDIER OF NONVIOLENCE

1869	Born
1888–91	Studied law in England
1893–1914	Lived in South Africa
1915–20	Leader of the Indian National Congress
1922–24	Imprisoned for sedition
1928–34	Leader of the cause of Indian independence
1947	Indian independence achieved
1948	Died

Mahatma Gandhi was one of the best-known people in the world in the 1930s and 1940s, instantly recognizable from the pictures of him in newspapers, magazines, and newsreels—a frail little brown man in a loincloth, swathed in a shawl that he had woven himself out of yarn he had spun himself on a hand spinning wheel. He had no wealth and, for most of his life, no official political position. He was not an intellectual nor a political theorist. He was a moral leader, for millions in his native India and for millions more throughout the world. The American general and secretary of state George C. Marshall called him "the spokesman for the conscience of all mankind."[1] But it was not the whole world where he chose to play out the drama of his life. It was India. And his cause was Indian independence from the British Empire. Gandhi became the driving force in its final achievement in 1947, after two centuries of colonial rule. In that process he became a world figure.

Mohandas K. Gandhi was born in 1869, the fourth and youngest child of his father's fourth wife. He was born in the poor little provincial capital of Porbandar on the west coast of India. His father was an

---

[1]Louis Fischer, *The Life of Mahatma Gandhi* (New York: Harper, 1950), p. 10.

official in the state administration of the Indian ruling prince, and by native standards the family was reasonably well off. His mother was a deeply religious woman and Gandhi was raised as a devout Hindu.

After completing grammar school Gandhi, following his father's wishes, traveled to England to study law in 1888. He was enrolled in the Inner Temple and was called to the bar in 1891. He immediately returned to India. He had made an unimpressive record as a law student; he was even less impressive as a struggling young lawyer in Porbandar. In 1893 a business firm in the city offered to send him to South Africa for a year as its representative, and he accepted.

In South Africa Gandhi came face to face with the racial segregation policies of the government. He was a "colored," hence an inferior person. The indignities he suffered there—and more, the indignities suffered by his fellow Indians—galvanized Gandhi and started him on his life's work. He did not return to India after his year's contract was up. Instead he stayed in South Africa, opened a law office in Durban, and quickly became the spokesman for the rights of the many Indians there. He organized the Natal Indian Congress; he wrote dozens of eloquent petitions to the government on behalf of Indian rights; he wrote pamphlets to the same purpose. His activities and his views gained him wide coverage in the press in India and in Britain; at the same time, these activities and views—and their coverage in the foreign press—infuriated South African white extremists. He was threatened, even assaulted. He neither resisted nor brought charges against his attackers.

Then in 1899 the Boer War broke out and Gandhi, to the consternation of many of his fellow Indians, organized and led an Indian Ambulance Corps of over a thousand volunteers. Gandhi argued that if they claimed the right to be treated as subjects of the British Empire, they incurred the obligation of defending the Empire.

The Origin of Nonviolence

M. K. GANDHI

In spite of the most heroic service in the war, at its conclusion the Indians of South Africa found their status not at all improved, either with the Boers or with the British. Indeed, the situation deteriorated. In the late summer of 1906 an ordinance was proposed by the Transvaal government that would require all Indians to register with the authorities and to carry a certificate at all times on penalty of imprisonment or deportation. Gandhi, along with most of the Indian leaders, was convinced that this "Black Act" would mean absolute ruin for the Indians of South Africa. After a preliminary strategy session among the leaders, a public meeting was called. In the course of it Gandhi discovered the tactic that would be the fundamental center of his life's work—nonviolence, or as he called it, *Satyagraha*.

Here is his own account of the event.

The meeting was duly held on the 11th September 1906. It was attended by delegates from various places in the Transvaal. But I must confess that even I myself had not then understood all the implications of the resolutions I had helped to frame; nor had I gauged all the possible conclusions to which they might lead. The old Empire Theatre was packed from floor to ceiling. I could read in every face the expectation of something strange to be done or to happen. Mr. Abdul Gani, Chairman of the Transvaal British Indian Association, presided. He was one of the oldest Indian residents of the Transvaal, and partner and manager of the Johannesburg branch of the well-known firm of Mamad Kasam Kamrudin. The most important among the resolutions passed by the meeting was the famous Fourth Resolution, by which the Indians solemnly determined not to submit to the Ordinance in the event of its becoming law in the teeth of their opposition and to suffer all the penalties attaching to such non-submission.

I fully explained this resolution to the meeting and received a patient hearing. . . . The resolution was duly proposed, seconded and supported by several speakers one of whom was Sheth Haji Habib. He too was a very old and experienced resident of South Africa and made an impassioned speech. He was deeply moved and went so far as to say that we must pass this resolution with God as witness and must never yield a cowardly submission to such degrading legislation. He then went on solemnly to declare in the name of God that he would never submit to that law, and advised all present to do likewise. Others also delivered powerful and angry speeches in supporting the resolution.

When in the course of his speech Sheth Haji Habib came to the solemn declaration, I was at once startled and put on my guard. Only then did I fully realize my own responsibility and the responsibility of the community. The community had passed many a resolution before and amended such resolutions in the light of further reflection or fresh experience. There were cases in which resolutions passed had not been observed by all concerned. Amendments in resolutions and failure to observe resolutions on the part of persons agreeing thereto are ordinary experiences of public life all the world over. But no one ever imports the name of God into such resolutions. In the abstract there should not be any distinction between a resolution and an oath taken in the name of God. When an intelligent man makes a resolution deliberately he never swerves from it by a hair's breadth. With him his resolution carries as much weight as a declaration made with God as witness does. . . .

Full of these thoughts as I was, possessing as I did much experience of solemn pledges, having profited by them, I was simply taken aback by Sheth Haji Habib's suggestion of an oath. I thought out the possible consequences of it in a single moment. My perplexity gave place to enthusiasm. And although I had no intention of taking an oath or inviting others to do so when I went to the meeting, I warmly approved of the Sheth's suggestion. But at the same time it seemed to me that the people should be apprised of all the consequences and should have explained to them clearly the meaning of a pledge. And if even then they were prepared to pledge themselves, they should be encouraged to do so; otherwise I must understand that they were not still ready to stand the final test. I therefore asked the President for permission to explain to the meeting the implications of Sheth Haji Habib's suggestion. The President readily granted it and I rose to address the meeting. I give below a summary of my remarks just as I can recall them now:

"I wish to explain to this meeting that there is a vast difference between this resolution and every other resolution we have passed up to date and that there is a wide divergence also in the manner of making it. It is a very grave resolution we are making, as our existence in South Africa depends upon our fully observing it. The manner of making the resolution suggested by our friend is as much of a novelty as of a solemnity. I did not come to the meeting with a view to getting the resolution passed in that manner, which redounds to the credit of Sheth Haji Habib as well as it lays a burden of responsibility upon him. I tender my congratulations to him. I deeply appreciate his suggestion, but if you adopt it you too will share his responsibility. You must understand what is this responsibility, and as an adviser and servant of the community, it is my duty fully to explain it to you.

"We all believe in one and the same God, the differences of nomenclature in Hinduism and Islam notwithstanding. To pledge ourselves or to take an oath in the name of that God or with Him as witness is not something to be trifled with. If having taken such an oath we violate our pledge we are guilty before God and man. Personally I hold that a man, who deliberately and intelligently takes a pledge and then breaks it, forfeits his manhood. . . .

"I know that pledges and vows are, and should be, taken on rare occasions. A man who takes a vow every now and then is sure to stumble. But if I can imagine a crisis in the history of the Indian community of South Africa when it would be in the fitness of things to take pledges that crisis is surely now. There is wisdom in taking serious steps with great caution and hesitation. But caution and hesitation have their limits, which we have now passed. The Government have taken leave of all sense of decency. We would only be betraying our unworthiness and cowardice, if we cannot stake our all in the face of the conflagration which envelopes us and sit watching it with folded hands. There is no doubt, therefore, that the present is a proper occasion for taking pledges. But every one of us must think out for himself if he has the will and the ability to pledge himself. Resolutions of this nature cannot be passed by a majority vote. Only those who take a pledge can be bound by it. This pledge must not be taken with a view to produce an effect on outsiders. No one should trouble to consider what impression it might have upon the Local Government, the Imperial Government, or the Government of India. Every one must only search his own heart, and if the inner voice assures him that he has the requisite strength to carry him through, then only should he pledge himself and then only would his pledge bear fruit.

"A few words now as to the consequences. . . .

"We might have to go to jail, where we might be insulted. We might have to go hungry and suffer extreme heat or cold. Hard labor might be imposed upon us. We might be flogged by rude warders. We might be fined heavily and our property might be attached and held up to auction if there are only a few resisters left. Opulent today we might be reduced to abject poverty tomorrow. We might be deported. Suffering from starvation and similar hardships in jail, some of us might fall ill and even die. In short, therefore, it is not at all impossible that we might have to endure every hardship that we can imagine, and wisdom lies in pledging ourselves on the understanding that we shall have to suffer all that and worse. If some one asks me when and how the struggle may end, I may say that if the entire community manfully stands the test, the end will be near. If many of us fall back under storm and stress, the struggle will be prolonged. But I can boldly declare, and with certainty, that so long as there is even a handful of men true to their pledge, there can only be one end to the struggle, and that is victory.

"A word about my personal responsibility. If I am warning you of the risks attendant upon the pledge, I am at the same time inviting you to pledge yourselves, and I am fully conscious of my responsibility in the matter. It is possible that a majority of those present here might take the pledge in a fit of enthusiasm or indignation but might weaken under the ordeal, and only a handful might be left to face the final test. Even then there is only one course open to the like of me, to die but not to submit to the law. . . . Although we are going to take the pledge in a body, no one should imagine that default on the part of one or many can absolve the rest from their obligation. Everyone should fully realize his responsibility, then only pledge himself independently of others and understand that he himself must be true to his pledge even unto death, no matter what others do."

I spoke to this effect and resumed my seat. The meeting heard me word by word in perfect quiet. Other leaders too spoke. All dwelt upon their own responsibility and the responsibility of the audience. The President rose. He too made the situation clear, and at last all present, standing with unraised hands, took an oath with God as witness not to submit to the Ordinance if it became law. I can never forget the scene, which is present before my mind's eye as I write. The community's enthusiasm knew no bounds.

None of us knew what name to give to our movement. I then used the term "passive resistance" in describing it. I did not quite understand the implications of "passive resistance" as I called it. I only knew that some new principle had come into being. As the struggle advanced, the phrase "passive resistance" gave rise to confusion and it appeared shameful to permit this great struggle to be known only by an English name. Again, that foreign phrase could hardly pass as current coin among the community. A small prize was therefore announced in *Indian Opinion*[2] to be awarded to the reader who invented the best designation for our struggle. We thus received a number of

---

[2]A journal founded by Gandhi for which he often wrote.—ED.

suggestions. The meaning of the struggle had been then fully discussed in *Indian Opinion* and the competitors for the prize had fairly sufficient material to serve as a basis for their exploration. Sr. Maganlal Gandhi[3] was one of the competitors and he suggested the word "Sadagraha," meaning "firmness in a good cause." I liked the word, but it did not fully represent the whole idea I wished it to connote. I therefore corrected it to "Satyagraha." Truth (Satya) implies love and firmness (Agraha) engenders and therefore serves as a synonym for force. I thus began to call the Indian movement "Satyagraha," that is to say, the Force which is born of Truth and Love or non-violence, and gave up the use of the phrase "passive resistance," in connection with it, so much so that even in English writing we often avoided it and used instead the word "Satyagraha" itself or some other equivalent English phrase. This then was the genesis of the movement which came to be known as Satyagraha, and of the word used as a designation for it. . . .

Gandhi and Civil Disobedience in India

JUDITH M. BROWN

For the next decade Gandhi's program of *Satyagraha* led thousands of Indians in South Africa to resist the government, to endure hardship and danger and deprivation, even imprisonment. Gandhi himself was jailed for two months in 1908, the first of several such terms of prison for him in South Africa. Thousands of Indians were deported with the loss of all their property, and thousands of Indian indentured servants and miners who remained went on strike. The government remained firm, although many liberal whites, including many clergymen, openly supported Gandhi and the cause of Indian justice in South Africa. Gandhi made two trips to England to appeal to the imperial government, but to no avail. In South Africa the government tightened its restrictions. By 1914, largely under the pressure of world opinion and in the face of even more massive resistance than it could handle, the government of what was by now

---

[3]A second cousin of Gandhi's who had joined him in his work in South Africa.—ED.

the Union of South Africa offered Gandhi a compromise. By its terms some of the most outrageous provisions against Indians were repudiated. It was no more than half a victory for Gandhi, but he accepted it as the best he could do. He shortly left South Africa for India.

When he arrived in Bombay on January 9, 1915, Gandhi already had a worldwide reputation as a nonviolent political activist because of his work in South Africa. He also had a considerable knowledge of Indian affairs, which he had followed closely during the years of his absence. There were programs being advocated by various factions for Indian self-rule, or *swaraj*. But Gandhi was reluctant to embrace any of them too quickly. He took the better part of a year to travel all over India—always by third-class rail—to get to know the people. He spoke, quietly but emphatically, whenever he was invited to do so, often on disturbing topics such as the shame of the untouchables or peasant poverty. He set up a headquarters in the form of a communal farm.

With allied victory in World War I, British repression in India tightened. In 1919 the government proposed a series of antisedition bills that were bitterly opposed by most Indians. It was at this point that Gandhi entered the battle for *swaraj*. In the spring of 1919 he announced a *Satyagraha* struggle. It swept the country, with work stoppages, boycotts, and nearly total noncooperation. Gandhi was its inspiration: he had begun to be called *Mahatma* or "great soul," a traditional Hindu title of respect. He had also become the spokesman of the Indian National Congress, which was rapidly becoming the political vehicle for his program of Indian independence. The British authorities reacted to Gandhi's campaign of nonviolent resistance with a proclamation of martial law and mass imprisonment for sedition. Gandhi himself was in prison from 1922 to 1924. In 1928 he formally proposed in the Congress a resolution calling for dominion status for India within a year. It was ignored, and repression continued.

Early in 1930 Gandhi led a *Satyagraha* against the salt tax, which was a longstanding burden on the poor. Again he was spectacularly successful. The British were forced to imprison more than 60,000 people. In the following year Gandhi was imprisoned again. The British had proposed a new constitution for India as an alternative to independence, but Gandhi found both the concept and its provisions unacceptable. While still in prison he took up a fast. The threat to the Mahatma's life quickly brought the cancellation of the most odious provisions of the constitution, but not of the proposal for the constitution itself. While Gandhi was still far from his goal of *purna swaraj* or "total independence," by the early 1930s he had attained a unique position of leadership in his nation.

The following excerpt is from the most detailed and authoritative history of this period of Gandhi's life and of the Indian struggle for independence, Judith M. Brown, *Gandhi and Civil Disobedience: The Mahatma in Indian Politics, 1928–34.*

In the 1920s and 1930s, despite and in a sense because of the growing experience of reformed political institutions in Delhi, the provincial capitals and the localities, India did not have a single well-defined political system in which Indians encountered their compatriots and their rulers, but a cluster of intermeshing systems in each of which ideals, strategies and alliances were being created. In this complicated environment of political interaction Gandhi played a crucial role for over a quarter of a century. He was for much of the period the figurehead of the Indian National Congress; and at particular times led agitations which constituted a serious challenge to the raj's moral authority and its power to control its subjects. He evoked popular adulation of a kind and to an extent never before enjoyed by an Indian politician; and he attracted the respect of numerous idealists outside India. Gandhi's role and standing in Indian politics were extraordinary phenomena when seen against the barriers to continental political leadership created by regional and social divisions and the limited development of mass media. . . .

At the level of conscious aspiration Gandhi was compelled into politics by a consuming vision of the nature of man and the type of society and government which permitted men to realize their true nature. He believed that in satyagraha he possessed the perfect mode of political action because he saw it as means and end, by its action producing the sort of people whose personal transformation was the foundation of the Indian society. . . . Here was an explosive political mixture: a man careless of the conventional trappings of power, with the iron will of a fanatic, who entered politics with a messianic zeal for the purification of individuals and their relations with each other, one who was willing to bend on many matters but refused to compromise on what he considered essentials though others considered them mere fads, one who would only participate in organized politics if he was undisputed leader. He claimed to be guided by an 'inner voice'; and his willingness to suffer privation and the prospect of death in the pursuit of what he perceived as Truth suggests that he was utterly convinced of the reality of his inner guidance and was neither charlatan nor humbug, covering the tracks of self-seeking ambition with the cloak of religion.

Gandhi's vision of the span of public work essential to his pursuit of swaraj was a significant aspect of his perception of his public role. His interest in health, diet, hygiene, clothing, social customs and religious practice was as strong as his concern for politics. Such activities contributed to Gandhi's continental and international reputation, generating respect for him among segments of Indian society which it was difficult to touch with a more conventional political appeal. They also gave him a flexibility which few other political leaders possessed. If he felt at a particular juncture that he could not act as a political leader without compromising his ideals, he could devote himself to these matters temporarily without a sense of defeat, secure in the belief that they were as important steps on the road to the final goal as promoting resistance to the raj through civil disobedience. The absence of any internal constraint of aspiration to a political career through office in Congress or the governmental structures gave the Mahatma a flexibility which paradoxically was vital in enabling his continued political importance in a period of rapid change. . . .

The most dramatic manifestations of public response to Gandhi were the crowds who flocked to see him and hailed him as a Mahatma. But theirs was not truly political support. Curiosity and veneration were rarely emotions which impelled men into following his exhortations, whether to wear *khadi*,[4] to abandon the observation of Untouchability or to join the ranks of the satyagrahis. Nonetheless Gandhi's public image across the land among vast multitudes was a factor which impinged on the attitudes towards Gandhi of men who were active in politics. The British acknowledged this in their agonized discussions on the time and place to jail him, and the need to avoid his death in prison. Responsivists became reluctant satyagrahis, and moderates refrained from public criticism, in deference to the Mahatma's unprecedented repute among their compatriots. . . .

It was in the all-India gatherings that Gandhi achieved his greatest prominence and influence because as all-India leader he performed a multiplicity of service roles in the particular context of 1928–31. He proved pre-eminent among Congressmen as an arranger of compromises because of his skill with words, his aloofness from factional strife and his ability to set a goal which could provide a focus of unity and a propaganda weapon. It was to achieve a vital unity that some of them deliberately called him back to Congress in 1928, and because of his success in satisfying this need that he was able to assert a new authority at the Calcutta session with the acquiescence of the majority.

Thereafter, as the civil disobedience 'expert', Gandhi was of extraordinary value to Congressmen in circumstances where a campaign of

---

[4]Homespun cloth.—ED.

opposition to parts of the imperial structure seemed the best tactic to exert pressure on the raj and to mask their own divisions. Satyagraha solved many of the dilemmas conflict posed in their relations with their rulers and their compatriots. It was a mode of direct action which permitted them temporarily to leave the paths of cooperation while avoiding the pitfalls of violent resistance, which they were ill equipped to organize, and would not only have threatened many of their vested interests but also alienated many Indians and foreign observers whose sympathy was important if they were to put pressure on the British. Civil disobedience provided an umbrella for a host of individual and corporate protest movements, as it coincided fortuitously with the onset of the depression. It helped them to cement local followings, to elicit support from businessmen, and to exert pressure on more moderate Hindu politicians who felt themselves isolated and their constitutional endeavours threatened by the evidence of widespread support for the movement. It also attracted considerable foreign sympathy. . . . Added to the advantages of placing Gandhi in a leadership position as civil disobedience 'expert' were his skill in fund-raising and his energy as an organizer, qualities which convinced Vallabhbhai Patel, for example, that the Mahatma was a man who meant business and was worth following.

Gandhi reached the peak of his influence early in 1931. His dominance was however only in the realm of all-India politics, because only in that context were his skills valued. Even in that arena the pressures to which he was subjected by those who looked to him for leadership, and his failures in asserting authority, most markedly among Muslims, showed the weakness inherent in a position which hinged on the ability to perform a lubricant function in the processes of political action rather than the capacity to forward the clear interests of a cohesive group. The nature of his leadership was even clearer in 1933–4, when his position of ascendancy was rapidly eroded. The civil disobedience campaign inaugurated in 1932 elicited far less popular support than the 1930 campaign, and was soon stifled by the government. Consequently it strengthened neither Congressmen's cross-regional alliances nor their links with those who should have been the rank and file. . . . It had far less influence than the 1930 campaign on moderate politicians who continued, though with considerable gloom, to cooperate in British reform plans. Ultimately it even alienated those Bombay businessmen who had financed it in the hope that it would assist them in gaining control over economic policy. The cumulative result was the campaign's failure to put pressure on the British and bring Congress into negotiations on the forthcoming constitution. Now Gandhi's tactic was a force isolating and dividing Congressmen instead of uniting them and integrating their different lev-

els of political activity. Moreover Gandhi's skills and potential as an
ally were judged of little use by the British. . . .

In 1934 Gandhi recognized that in the changing circumstances he
could no longer act as continental leader in the role of civil disobedience 'expert'. Such were his personal aspirations and priorities that
he preferred to solve the dilemma his presence and insistence on
satyagraha created for his Congress colleagues by liberating them
from a technique which for them was a mere tactic and so preserve it
and his own integrity, and 'retire' rather than retain an all-India leadership position by performing the functions they now desired of him.
However, these decisions did not mean the end of Gandhi as an all-
India political leader. Congressmen would not lightly ignore him; and
civil disobedience remained an important tactic for use when confrontation with the raj offered more benefits than cooperation, or when
no other programme could secure among them an essential unity.
Nor had Gandhi himself lost interest in politics: he had merely redi-
rected his energies to preserve himself and his technique from compromise. Ironically, by 'retiring' Gandhi did for himself what the British had done for him in 1922. He took time to review the changing
situation where the politics of elections, conciliar activity and even
acceptance of office would probably become Congressmen's primary
concerns. In this political context men like Vallabhbhai Patel who
could weld the disparate elements in the Congress movement into a
coherent and disciplined party would be of supreme importance. It
was a leadership function Gandhi was ill fitted to perform either by
inclination or by expertise. What his role might be in the new context
was unclear late in 1934; but by abandoning a role which had proved
redundant for his contemporaries he freed himself to adopt another
on which a new position of continental leadership could be based, if a
situation developed where his personal inclinations and expertise
dovetailed with the needs of contemporaries, and offered him a
sphere and mode of political action which could forward both their
aims and his vision of swaraj.

Nonetheless, Gandhi's civil disobedience campaigns between 1930
and 1934 were of lasting importance in the development of Indian
politics. Although civil disobedience neither led to *purna swaraj* nor
very significantly influenced the process of constitutional reform, it
proved a powerful bonding agent among Indians within and across
regions under the Congress banner. It gave many activists a new sense
of unity born of shared illegal activities and sojourns in jail. Participation in it became one qualification for political place and a source of
prestige in the years which followed. Moreover the campaigns were
recruiting grounds for Congress, involving younger people and numbers of women in Congress organizations and activities for the first

time and educating them for future positions in the Congress and state structures. The experience of running a continental campaign and Gandhi's emphasis on efficiency were also significant factors in Congress's success in turning itself into an all-India party geared to attract the votes of an enlarged electorate. The Congress name and organization, sketchy though the latter was, had been an important resource in politics in the 1920s. This importance was magnified as Congress emerged from civil disobedience into constitutional competition for power. Few Hindus would now lightly isolate themselves from it, and the influence of those who controlled its central organs was increased because they offered rewards and wielded sanctions which the Mahatma had never had at his command.

In less material ways civil disobedience also equipped Congress for a new political dispensation. It had been a remarkable publicity operation, demonstrating political ideas and actions throughout the land and generating political awareness even in remote villages. It convinced many Indians, and to a lesser extent their rulers, that Congress was a significant factor in political life which could not be ignored. Although its claims to be the people's intermediary with government had not received formal recognition, once Congress returned to constitutional politics most Hindus with political ambitions regarded it as the natural channel through which to pursue them, while the majority of the community who had no aspirations to political activism were sympathetic to its aims and claims. Gandhi's political activities had provided Congress with a pedigree. . . . This was soon clear, in the 1934 Assembly elections, when the poll was higher than in any previous Assembly election and Congress successes outstanding. No other group came near it in organization, resources and appeal. . . .

Gandhi and Indian Independence

JAWAHARLAL NEHRU

In 1934 Gandhi resigned completely from the Indian National Congress, convinced that the other leaders of the movement had adopted nonviolence only as a political tactic rather than as a fundamental political and philosophic commitment. He was disillusioned with politics. In the next few years he devoted himself to increasingly severe asceticism and to the advocacy of social reforms. He restricted his diet to a mere handful of vegetables a day. His personal possessions were reduced to little besides his spectacles, his food bowl, and his sandals, loincloth, and homespun shawl. He kept a small ivory carving of "The Three Wise Monkeys" given him by a friend in South Africa. Though his wife and family continued to live in the commune, Gandhi himself had long since renounced all sexual contact and stayed alone in a small cell where he slept, took his meals, worked and wrote.

He continued to defend the cause of the untouchables: he called them *Harijans* or "children of God." He was equally concerned about the vast number of Indian peasants, almost universally impoverished, ignorant, and hopeless. For them he prepared educational texts, proposed the teaching of a single language, and strongly advocated a return to Indian cottage industry—the making of *khadi* or homespun cloth, for example. This, of course, meant his rejection of industrialization, which the British had brought to India and which many progressive Indian leaders had welcomed.

With the outbreak of World War II the question of Indian independence became hopelessly mixed with that of India's role in the war. In 1942 the British cabinet minister Sir Stafford Cripps came to India with a proposal. The Cripps proposal called for complete British control of India as part of the allied war effort but held out the promise of full dominion status after the war. Gandhi said to Cripps, "Why did you come if this is what you have to offer? If this is your entire proposal to India, I would advise you to take the next plane home."[5] To Gandhi the plan was fatally flawed in that it called not for a united but a pluralistic India, with independence for Hindus and Muslims, even for the Indian princely states. The other congress leaders objected to the plan on other grounds.

Gandhi now reentered the political arena. Within months of the rejection of the Cripps proposal he demanded immediate British withdrawal from India. This became the famous "Quit India Resolution." The British reacted by jailing the entire leadership of the Congress, including Gandhi. Britain and India were now totally estranged.

With the end of the war it was clear that Indian independence, at long last, was at hand. There were intense negotiations over its terms. The stumbling block was the Muslim insistence on a separate state, an insistence underscored by widespread violence. Partition was finally accepted in the plan that Lord Louis Mountbatten, the last British viceroy, proposed in the early summer of 1947. This plan became the basis for independence and for the creation not of one India but of the two new nations of India and Pakistan, in August 1947.

---

[5]Louis Fischer, *The Life of Mahatma Gandhi*, p. 358.

Gandhi was brokenhearted at the failure to achieve a united independent India. Nevertheless, he worked unceasingly to heal the divisions between Hindus and Muslims and bring an end to the religious violence. On January 30, 1948, he died, a victim of that religious violence, shot to death by a Hindu fanatic on his way to his evening prayers.

Gandhi had been, unquestionably, the leading force in the independence movement. His role in the last years of the struggle is evaluated by his lifelong friend, fellow Congress leader, and the man who would become the first prime minister of India, Jawaharlal Nehru. The selection is taken from Nehru's biographical reflection on Gandhi's life, *Mahatma Gandhi*, written a few months after his assassination.

When Gandhiji[6] raised in 1940 the question of non-violence in relation to the war and the future of free India, the Congress Working Committee had to face the issue squarely. They made it clear to him that they were unable to go as far as he wanted them to go and could not possibly commit India or the Congress to future applications of this principle in the external domain. This led to a definite and public break with him on this issue. Two months later further discussions led to an agreed formula which was later adopted as part of a resolution by the All-India Congress Committee. That formula did not wholly represent Gandhiji's attitude; it represented what he agreed, perhaps rather unwillingly, for Congress to say on this subject. At that time the British Government had already rejected the latest offer made by the Congress for co-operation in the war on the basis of a national government. Some kind of conflict was approaching, and, as was inevitable, both Gandhiji and Congress looked toward each other and were impelled by a desire to find a way out of the deadlock between them. The formula did not refer to the war, as just previously our offer of co-operation had been unceremoniously and utterly rejected. It dealt theoretically with the Congress policy in regard to non-violence, and for the first time stated how, in the opinion of Congress, the free India of the future should apply it in its external relations. That part of the resolution ran thus:

> [The A.I.C.C.] firmly believes in the policy and practice of non-violence not only in the struggle for Swaraj, but also, in so far as this may be possible of application, in free India. The Committee is convinced, and recent world events have demonstrated, that complete

---

[6]The suffix is an indication of respect and affection.—ED.

world disarmament is necessary and the establishment of a new and juster political and economic order, if the world is not to destroy itself and revert to barbarism. A free India will, therefore, throw all her weight in favour of world disarmament and should herself be prepared to give a lead in this to the world. Such lead will inevitably depend on external factors and internal conditions, but the state would do its utmost to give effect to this policy of disarmament. Effective disarmament and the establishment of world peace by the ending of national wars depend ultimately on the removal of the causes of wars and national conflicts. These causes must be rooted out by the ending of the domination of one country over another and the exploitation of one people or group by another. To that end India will peacefully labour, and it is with this objective in view that the people of India desire to attain the status of a free and independent nation. Such freedom will be the prelude to the close association with other countries within a comity of free nations for the peace and progress of the world.

This declaration, it will be noticed, while strongly affirming the Congress wish for peaceful action and disarmament, also emphasized a number of qualifications and limitations.

The internal crisis within the Congress was resolved in 1940, and then came a year of prison for large numbers of us. In December 1941, however, the same crisis took shape again when Gandhiji insisted on complete non-violence. Again there was a split and public disagreement, and the president of the Congress, Maulana Abul Kalam Azad, and others were unable to accept Gandhiji's view. It became clear that the Congress as a whole, including some of the faithful followers of Gandhiji, disagreed with him in this matter. The force of circumstances and the rapid succession of dramatic events influenced all of us, including Gandhiji, and he refrained from pressing his view on the Congress, though he did not identify himself with the Congress view.

At no other time was this issue raised by Gandhiji in the Congress. When later Sir Stafford Cripps came with his proposals, there was no question of non-violence. His proposals were considered purely from the political point of view. In later months, leading up to August 1942, Gandhiji's nationalism and intense desire for freedom made him even agree to Congress participation in the war if India could function as a free country. For him this was a remarkable and astonishing change, involving suffering of the mind and pain of the spirit. In the conflict between that principle of non-violence, which had become his very lifeblood and meaning of existence, and India's freedom, which was a dominating and consuming passion for him, the scales inclined toward the latter. That did not mean, of course, that he weakened in his faith in non-violence. But it did mean that he was prepared to agree to the Congress not applying it in this war. The practical statesman took precedence over the uncompromising prophet.

The approach of the war to India disturbed Gandhiji greatly. It was not easy to fit in his policy and programme of non-violence with this new development. Obviously civil disobedience was out of the question in the face of an invading army or between two opposing armies. Passivity or acceptance of invasion were equally out of the question. What then? His own colleagues, and the Congress generally, had rejected non-violence for such an occasion or as an alternative to armed resistance to invasion, and he had at last agreed that they had a right to do so. But he was none the less troubled, and for his own part, as an individual, he could not join any violent course of action. But he was much more than an individual; whether he had any official status or not in the nationalist movement, he occupied an outstanding and dominating position, and his word carried weight with large numbers of people. . . .

While this struggle was going on in India's mind and a feeling of desperation was growing, Gandhiji wrote a number of articles which suddenly gave a new direction to people's thoughts, or, as often happens, gave shape to their vague ideas. Inaction at that critical stage and submission to all that was happening had become intolerable to him. The only way to meet that situation was for Indian freedom to be recognized and for a free India to meet aggression and invasion in co-operation with allied nations. If this recognition was not forthcoming then some action must be taken to challenge the existing system and wake up the people from the lethargy that was paralyzing them and making them easy prey for every kind of aggression. . . .

Some of us were disturbed and upset by this new development, for action was futile unless it was effective action, and any such effective action must necessarily come in the way of war effort at a time when India herself stood in peril of invasion. Gandhiji's general approach also seemed to ignore important international considerations and appeared to be based on a narrow view of nationalism. During the three years of war we had deliberately followed a policy of non-embarrassment, and such action as we had indulged in had been in the nature of symbolic protest. That symbolic protest had assumed huge dimensions when thirty thousand of our leading men and women were sent to prison in 1940–41. And yet even that prison-going was a selected individual affair and avoided any mass upheaval or any direct interference with the governmental apparatus. We could not repeat that, and if we did something else it had to be of a different kind and on a more effective scale. Was this not bound to interfere with the war on India's borders and encourage the enemy?

These were obvious difficulties, and we discussed them at length with Gandhiji without converting each other. The difficulties were there, and risks and perils seemed to follow any course of action or inaction. It became a question of balancing them and choosing the lesser evil. Our mutual discussions led to a clarification of much that had been vague and cloudy, and to Gandhiji's appreciating many international factors to which his attention had been drawn. His subsequent writings underwent a change, and he himself emphasized these international considerations and looked at India's problem in a wider perspective. But his fundamental attitude remained: his objection to a passive submission to British autocratic and repressive policy in India and his intense desire to do something to challenge this. Submission then, according to him, meant that India would be broken in spirit, and whatever shape the war might take, whatever its end might be, her people would act in a servile way and their freedom would not be achieved for a long time. It would mean also submission to an invader and not continuing resistance to him regardless even of temporary military defeat or withdrawal. It would mean the complete demoralization of our people and their losing all the strength that they had built up during a quarter of a century's unceasing struggle for freedom. It would mean that the world would forget India's demand for freedom and the postwar settlement would be governed by the old imperialist urges and ambitions. . . .

Gandhiji was getting on in years, he was in the seventies, and a long life of ceaseless activity, of hard toil, both physical and mental, had enfeebled his body. But he was still vigorous enough and he felt that all his lifework would be in vain if he submitted to circumstances then and took no action to vindicate what he prized most. His love of freedom for India and all other exploited nations and peoples overcame even his strong adherence to non-violence. He had previously given a grudging and rather reluctant consent to the Congress not adhering to this policy in regard to defence and the state's functions in an emergency, but he had kept himself aloof from this. He realized that his halfhearted attitude in this matter might well come in the way of a settlement with Britain and the United Nations. So he went further and himself sponsored a Congress resolution which declared that the primary function of the provisional government of free India would be to throw all her great resources in the struggle for freedom and against aggression and to co-operate fully with the United Nations in the defence of India with all the armed as well as other forces at her command. It was no easy matter for him to commit himself in this way, but he swallowed the bitter pill, so overpowering was his desire that some settlement should be arrived at to enable India to resist the aggressor as a free nation. . . .

While we were doubting and debating, the mood of the country changed and from a sullen passivity it rose to a pitch of excitement and expectation. Events were not waiting for a Congress decision or resolution; they had been pushed forward by Gandhiji's utterances, and now they were moving onward with their own momentum. It was clear that whether Gandhiji was right or wrong, he had crystallized the prevailing mood of the people. . . .

On August 7 and 8, 1942, in Bombay the All-India Congress Committee considered and debated in public the resolution which has since come to be known as the "Quit India Resolution." That resolution was a long and comprehensive one, a reasoned argument for the immediate recognition of Indian freedom and the ending of British rule in India "both for the sake of India and for the success of the cause of the United Nations. The continuation of that rule is degrading and enfeebling India and making her progressively less capable of defending herself and of contributing to the cause of world freedom. . . . The possession of empire, instead of adding to the strength of the ruling power, has become a burden and a curse. India, the classic land of modern imperialism, has become the crux of the question, for by the freedom of India will Britain and the United Nations be judged, and the peoples of Asia and Africa be filled with hope and enthusiasm." The resolution went on to suggest the formation of a provisional government which would be composite and would represent all important sections of the people, and whose "primary function must be to defend India and resist aggression with all the armed as well as the non-violent forces at its command, together with its Allied Powers." This government would evolve a scheme for a constituent assembly which would prepare a constitution for India acceptable to all sections of the people. The constitution would be a federal one, with the largest measure of autonomy for the federating units and with the residuary powers vesting in those units. "Freedom will enable India to resist aggression effectively with the people's united will and strength behind it."

This freedom of India must be the symbol of and prelude to the freedom of all other Asiatic nations. Further, a world federation of free nations was proposed, of which a beginning should be made with the United Nations.

The committee stated that it was "anxious not to embarrass in any way the defence of China and Russia, whose freedom is precious and must be preserved, or to jeopardize the defensive capacity of the United Nations." (At that time the dangers to China and Russia were the greatest.) "But the peril grows both to India and these nations, and inaction and submission to a foreign administration at this stage is not only degrading India and reducing her capacity to defend herself and resist aggression but is no answer to that growing peril and is no service to the peoples of the United Nations."

The Committee again appealed to Britain and the United Nations "in the interest of world freedom." But—and there came the sting of the resolution—"the Committee is no longer justified in holding the nation back from endeavouring to assert its will against an imperialist and authoritarian Government which dominates over it and prevents it from functioning in its own interest and in the interest of humanity. The Committee resolves therefore to sanction, for the vindication of India's inalienable right to freedom and independence, the starting of a mass struggle on non-violent lines" under the inevitable leadership of Gandhiji. That sanction was to take effect only when Gandhiji so decided. Finally, it was stated that the Committee had "no intention of gaining power for the Congress. The power, when it comes, will belong to the whole people of India."

The resolution was finally passed late in the evening of August 8, 1942. A few hours later, in the early morning of August 9, a large number of arrests were made in Bombay and all over the country.

Freedom came to us, our long-sought freedom, and it came with a minimum of violence. But immediately after, we had to wade through oceans of blood and tears. Worse than the blood and tears was the shame and disgrace that accompanied them.

Review and Study Questions

1. How did Gandhi's experiences in South Africa prepare him for his later work on behalf of Indian independence?

2. How important to his lifelong work was Gandhi's commitment to peaceful nonresistance?

3. How important to his lifelong work were Gandhi's spiritual and religious views?

4. How was the strident problem of the religious conflict between Hindus and Muslims dealt with in the struggle for Indian independence?

Suggestions for Further Reading

Gandhi himself was a prolific writer. The official collection of his works fills sixty-four volumes: Mahatma Gandhi, *Collected Works*

(Delhi: Publications Division, Ministry of Information and Broadcasting, Government of India, 1958–76). His autobiography, while it appears in the *Collected Works,* was originally written in Gujarati in 1927–29 but translated into English by Mahadev Desai and separately published as *Gandhi's Autobiography: The Story of My Experiments with Truth,* 2 vols. (Washington: Public Affairs Press, 1948). It was written very early in his life and is not very useful as a source of biographical information. There are, of course, many anthologies and collections of his works. Some of these reflect the adoring discipleship of his followers and emphasize his personal qualities and his philosophy: see, for example, *Gandhi's India: Unity in Diversity, Selections Prepared by the National Integration Sub-Committee of the National Committee for Gandhi Centenary* (New Delhi: National Book Trust, 1968) or *The Quintessence of Gandhi in His Own Words,* ed. Shakti Batra (New Delhi: Madhu Muskan, 1984). Others contain more substantial selections dealing with his political career as well as with his life and philosophic concerns. These include *The Gandhi Reader: A Source Book of His Life and Writings,* ed. Homer A. Jack (Bloomington: Indiana University Press, 1956), excerpted for this chapter; *The Essential Gandhi, An Anthology: His Life, Work, and Ideals,* ed. Louis Fischer (New York: Vintage, 1963); *Gandhi in India in His Own Words,* ed. Martin Green (Hanover and London: University Press of New England, 1987). Of rather special interest is a series of selections collected and translated by Professor Nirmal Kumar Bose, *Selections from Gandhi* (Ahmedabad: Navajivan, 1968 [1948]), endorsed in a Foreword by Gandhi himself just a year before his death.

There are a number of biographical reminiscences of Gandhi by people who knew him well. One of the most valuable of these is Jawaharlal Nehru, *Mahatma Gandhi* (Bombay et al.: Asia Publishing House, 1966 [1949]), excerpted for this chapter—not only because of Nehru's lifelong friendship with Gandhi but because of his central position in Indian affairs. An equally useful work devoted to Gandhi's early years was written by his personal secretary and is rich in detail: Pyarelal Nair, *Mahatma Gandhi—The Early Phase,* 2 vols., 2nd ed. (Ahmedabad: Navajivan Publishing House, 1965). Of the same sort is Nirmal Kumar Bose, *My Days with Gandhi* (Bombay: Orient Longman, 1953).

There are several works by western journalists who knew Gandhi and spent time with him. Vincent Sheean, *Lead, Kindly Light* (New York: Random House, 1949) is a luminous appreciation of Gandhi as a philosophical, and especially religious, figure. More gritty and realistic are William L. Shirer, *Gandhi: A Memoir* (New York: Simon & Schuster, 1979), based on Shirer's acquaintance with Gandhi in the early 1930s, and Louis Fischer, *The Life of Mahatma Gandhi* (New York:

Harper, 1950), based on Fischer's close association with Gandhi through the crucial 1940s. The latter is also a full-scale biography, the first to appear after Gandhi's assassination.

There are a number of other excellent biographies: the two best are Geoffrey Ashe, *Gandhi* (New York: Stein and Day, 1968), and Robert Payne, *The Life and Death of Mahatma Gandhi* (New York: Dutton, 1969). And there are a number of important scholarly books on specialized topics. One of the best of these is Judith M. Brown, *Gandhi and Civil Disobedience: The Mahatma in Indian Politics, 1928–34* (Cambridge et al.: Cambridge University Press, 1977), excerpted for this chapter. Equally good is her earlier book, *Gandhi's Rise to Power: Indian Politics 1915–1922* (Cambridge: Cambridge University Press, 1972). Two other excellent studies of yet other periods of Gandhi's life are Robert A. Huttenback, *Gandhi in South Africa: British Imperialism and the Indian Question, 1860–1914* (Ithaca and London: Cornell University Press, 1971), and Francis G. Hutchins, *India's Revolution: Gandhi and the Quit India Movement* (Cambridge: Harvard University Press, 1973).

Two books can be recommended among the many devoted to aspects of Gandhi's political and philosophic views: Jayantanuja Bandyopadhyaya, *Social and Political Thought of Gandhi* (Bombay et al.: Allied Publishers, 1969), and H. J. N. Horsburgh, *Non-Violence and Aggression: A Study of Gandhi's Moral Equivalent of War* (London: Oxford University Press, 1968).

MAO TSE-TUNG:
THE PEOPLE'S EMPEROR

1893	Born
1912	Formation of the Republic of China
1921	Joined Communist Party
1934–35	The Long March
1937–45	The Japanese War
1949	Formation of People's Republic of China
1966–69	The Cultural Revolution
1976	Died

Mao Tse-tung, the man who was to become China's great proletarian revolutionary, was born into a well-to-do peasant family in Hunan province, in central China, in 1893. As a boy he received a traditional Confucian education in the local primary school. At sixteen he went to a neighboring town to attend a "radical" new, Western-style school, teaching such things as foreign history and geography. He went on to secondary school in the provincial capital of Chang-sha.

But his education was overwhelmed by the rush of political events. Sun Yat-sen was preaching cultural and political revolution. In 1911 the revolution actually broke out against the Manchu dynasty. Mao joined the army. His military service was brief and unimpressive. In the spring of 1912 the Republic of China was proclaimed and he was mustered out of the army.

After trying several kinds of schools Mao finally graduated from the First Provincial Normal School of Chang-sha in 1918. He then enrolled at Peking University. The six months he spent there were to turn his life around. He was exposed to the radical new doctrines of Marxism-Leninism. In 1921 he was one of the founders of the Chinese Communist Party.

The fledgling Communist Party joined with Sun Yat-sen's Nationalist Party (Kuomintang) against the imperial government in Peking. With the death of Sun Yat-sen in 1925, Chiang Kai-shek became head of the Kuomintang and broke with the Communists. The Chinese civil war had begun. Mao was one of the organizers of the Chinese Red Army and emerged as its leader in the Long March—a harrowing retreat from Chiang Kai-shek's forces. But the war against Japan brought Communists and Nationalists together against their common enemy. In the course of the war Mao Tse-tung became the leader of the spreading Communist movement throughout China.

With the end of the war the old rivalry between the Communists and the Kuomintang resurfaced, but with far different results this time. In the spring of 1949 the People's Liberation Army, as the Red Army was now called, forced Chiang out of the country, eventually to rule Nationalist China on the island of Taiwan. Mao was the master of mainland China. For a while he followed the lead of Stalin's Soviet Union. But he was increasingly disillusioned both with the Soviet leadership of world communism and with the Soviet model of socialist development that had been promoted in China.

In 1955 he vigorously stepped forward with a program of his own for China. He advocated the abandonment of the emphasis on heavy industry and capital production and the classical Soviet preference for central planning in agriculture. He announced instead a nationwide program of cooperative agricultural communes. Further, he encouraged Chinese intellectuals and technical and managerial experts to speak out in criticism of the party's failures and the defects of the system. "Let a hundred flowers bloom," he declared in early 1956. But the intellectuals and specialists not only criticized the failures of the system, they criticized the system itself—and its leadership under Chairman Mao. At this point things changed abruptly. Writers who had been too outspoken found themselves cleaning toilets or scrubbing floors; indiscreet managers of plants and businesses were reassigned as laborers on distant farm communes. From the disappointing intellectuals, administrators, and specialists Mao turned to the unlettered masses, the peasants. If China was to be changed, let them change it. These new policies, begun in the fall of 1957, were to be called the Great Leap Forward. Not only agriculture but all forms of economic activity were organized at the grass roots in small communal units, relying on local initiative. Equally important, there was a decentralizing of political power into the hands of communal party secretaries.

The Great Leap Forward turned out to be a dismal failure: the economy was disrupted and there were severe food shortages. Mao's policies were reversed. He retired as chairman of the Chinese People's Republic and settled into a period of reflection and inactivity. But he retained the chairmanship of the Communist Party and he retained his popularity with the People's Liberation Army.

Differences grew between Mao and his chief rival in the party, Liu Shao-ch'i, who had replaced him as chairman of the People's Republic. In 1966 Mao once more seized control of the party and of the nation in the most radical experiment in the history of Communist China, the Great Proletarian Cultural Revolution.

The Great Proletarian Cultural Revolution

CHAIRMAN MAO

The Great Proletarian Cultural Revolution was, in part, a substantive program that grew naturally out of much that Mao had thought and advocated—in particular his suspicion of intellectuals and his almost mystical bond with the Chinese peasants. But it was also powerfully motivated by Mao's bitterness toward Liu and his faction in the Central Committee of the party, his conviction that the party was moving in the wrong direction, and his consequent intention of regaining undisputed control over it. As early as 1962–63 he and Liu had clashed over party objectives. Then in the late summer of 1966 Mao, through his great personal prestige, convinced the Central Committee to adopt his bold new scheme.

Mao proclaimed a new stage in China's socialist revolution that would reclaim the leadership in education, literature, and the arts from the "bourgeois" corruption of experts and authorities and restore it to the true proletariat, the Chinese masses. It is essential, Mao argued, to trust the masses and not to fear disorder or disruption. They can educate themselves. Schools must be reformed according to the aims of Chairman Mao; in order to serve the needs of the proletariat, education must be combined with productive labor to teach students not only their academic subjects but farming, military affairs, and industrial work. If this program is followed the people will achieve greater, faster, better, and more economical results in all fields of work. In all this the guide is to be Mao Tse-tung's thought.

Mao himself traveled widely through China to assess the progress of the Cultural Revolution, and from the fall of 1967 to the summer of 1969 he issued a series of "directives" that appeared in the major Chinese newspapers. They analyzed the results of the revolution and suggested some courses of action. The following are the most pertinent of those "directives."

April 19, 1968

The great proletarian cultural revolution is in essence a great political revolution made under the conditions of socialism by the proletariat against the bourgeoisie and all other exploiting classes; it is a continuation of the prolonged struggle between the Chinese Communist Party and the masses of revolutionary people under the Party's leadership on the one hand and the Kuomintang reactionaries on the other, a continuation of the class struggle between the proletariat and the bourgeoisie.

August 2, 1968

It is still necessary to have universities; here I refer mainly to colleges of science and engineering. However, it is essential to shorten the length of schooling, revolutionize education, put proletarian politics in command and take the road of the Shanghai Machine Tools Plant in training technicians from among the workers. Students should be selected from among workers and peasants with practical experience, and they should return to production after a few years' study.

August 23, 1968

Our country has 700 million people and the working class is the leading class. Its leading role in the great cultural revolution and in all fields of work should be brought into full play. The working class also should continuously enhance its political consciousness in the course of the struggle.

August 30, 1968

In carrying out the proletarian revolution in education, it is essential to have working-class leadership; it is essential for the masses of workers to take part and, in co-operation with Liberation Army fighters, bring about a revolutionary "three-in-one" combination, together with the activists among the students, teachers and workers in the schools who are determined to carry the proletarian revolution in education through to the end. The workers' propaganda teams should stay permanently in the schools and take part in fulfilling all the tasks of struggle-criticism-transformation in the schools, and they will always lead the schools. In the countryside, the schools should be managed by the poor and lower-middle peasants—the most reliable ally of the working class.

The struggle-criticism-transformation in a factory, on the whole, goes through the following stages: establishing a revolutionary committee based on the "three-in-one" combination, mass criticism and repudiation, purifying the class ranks, rectifying the Party organization, simplifying organizational structure, changing irrational rules and regulations and sending people who work in offices to grass-roots levels.

October 11, 1968
Sending the masses of cadres to do manual work gives them an excellent opportunity to study once again; this should be done by all cadres except those who are too old, weak, ill or disabled. Cadres at work should also go group by group to do manual work.

December 27, 1968
It is very necessary for educated young people to go to the countryside to be re-educated by the poor and lower-middle peasants. Cadres and other people in the cities should be persuaded to send their sons and daughters who have finished junior or senior middle school, college or university to the countryside. Let us mobilize. Comrades throughout the countryside should welcome them.

July 4, 1969
Every Party branch must reconsolidate itself in the midst of the masses. This must be done with the participation of the masses and not merely a few Party members; it is necessary to have the masses outside the Party attend the meetings and give comments.

In the Great Proletarian Cultural Revolution, some tasks have not yet been fulfilled and they should now be carried on, for instance, the tasks of struggle-criticism-transformation.

A Contemporary Analysis

STUART SCHRAM

The resolution adopted by the Central Committee of the Chinese Communist Party on August 8, 1966, giving authorization for the Cultural Revolution, was implemented immediately. The first agency was the People's Liberation Army. Since 1959 it had been headed by Lin Piao, a dedicated supporter of Chairman Mao. Under his leadership the army had become "a great school of Mao Tse-tung's thought." The official army newspaper carried the thoughts of the chairman on page one of every issue, and the *Quotations from Chairman Mao*, the famous "Little Red Book," was first published by the army in 1964. Each edition contained a foreword by Lin that began "Comrade Mao Tse-tung is the greatest Marxist-Leninist of our era." Clearly a part of the intent of the Cultural Revolution was to put forward a position favored by both Mao and the army, that China must be separated from Russia and Russian-style communism, and the parallel position that China was the natural leader of the Third World.

With the army benignly in the background, Mao pushed forward as the leading element in his Cultural Revolution a quasi-military group known as the Red Guards or, as he called them, the "little devils." They were young people, totally dedicated to Chairman Mao, guided by his thoughts in the "Little Red Book" and utterly contemptuous of both their cultural betters and the Communist Party leaders. They smashed temples and burned books and called party leaders to task before people's courts. Thousands of people were deprived of their livelihoods; thousands more were killed in the streets amid mindless riots.

In the confusion of the Cultural Revolution, and with the resulting paralysis of the Chinese Communist Party, Mao had little trouble dismissing Liu Shao-ch'i, his hated rival, from office and reasserting his own firm control of the party and the nation.

The excerpt presented below deals with the onset and early course of the Cultural Revolution. It is from a biography of Mao written by Stuart Schram. Schram is not only a distinguished international authority on Communist China; he was in China at the beginning of the Cultural Revolution and his knowledge of it is first hand. Because the Cultural Revolution was still going on at the time the book was written, his conclusions about it are very cautious. But his analysis of the forces that set it moving and, in particular, his analysis of Mao's motives are extremely interesting and germane to our understanding of Mao Tse-tung.

If Mao no doubt sincerely identifies himself with the anti-imperialist struggles of other peoples, his primary concern remains, as it has always been, the fate of China. At the same time, it must be added that in his eyes China's internal evolution has now taken on decisive international importance. For to the extent that he sees China as the only genuinely socialist great power—the Soviet Union having definitively taken the road of revisionism and the restoration of capitalism—the ideological purity and firmness of will of the Chinese revolutionaries is henceforth the principal guarantee of ultimate victory on a world scale.

It is therefore of the utmost importance that China, in Mao's phrase, should not "change color"—i.e., alter her political character. In order to guard against this danger, the hard lessons of past struggles must be brought home to the young people who have grown to maturity since the victory of 1949.

This preoccupation with training succeeding generations of revolutionaries, in order that China may continue to play her role as the vanguard of the world revolution, lies at the heart of the "Great Proletarian Cultural Revolution" that has swept across China during the past year. . . .

The problem of "revolutionizing" young people, in order to make of them revolutionaries forever, both at home and abroad, was the central theme of the Ninth Chinese Communist Youth League Congress in June 1964. It figures extensively in the last and most remarkable of the nine Chinese replies to the Soviet blast of July 14, 1963, entitled "On Khrushchev's Phony Communism and Its Historical Lessons for the World," issued on the first anniversary of the Soviet article. In this text Mao is credited with the view that a very long period of time is necessary to decide the issue of the struggle between capitalism and socialism. "Several decades won't do it; success requires anywhere from one to several centuries." During this period, the proletarian dictatorship must be maintained and strengthened. . . .

The most important factor in these developments was the growing rôle of the army. Early in 1964, a campaign was launched to "learn from the People's Liberation Army." The army was held up as a model of political loyalty and political consciousness, and "political departments" similar to those in the army were set up in the organizations responsible for administering economic enterprises. . . . Mao regards the army as the natural repository of the ethos of struggle and sacrifice which is for him the hallmark of every true revolutionary movement. The army also tends naturally toward the combination of discipline and initiative which is Mao Tse-tung's constant preoccupation. It is thus not surprising that the heroes recommended as models to Chinese youth in the last few years have been soldiers.

The campaign launched in 1964 did not appear to involve the modification of the Chinese political system by the transfer of political authority to the army. It was, however, a portent of such developments in the future. How much so has only recently been revealed, as the Red Guards' bible, *Quotations from Chairman Mao . . .* , has become available outside China. For the first edition of this book, we now learn, was published in May, 1964, on the eve of the Chinese Communist Youth League Congress, and thereafter it was distributed widely as a reward for the meritorious study of Chairman Mao's works. And this volume, which was thus to play a key role in the ideological training of cadres of the party and other organizations, was published by the Political Department of the Army.

It is clear today that the Army was also involved in two other trends which emerged during 1964, and which are central to the current "Great Proletarian Cultural Revolution": the attack on tradition, and the increasingly extravagant cult of Mao Tse-tung and his thought. . . . Developments since 1964, and especially in the course of 1966, have none the less lifted the Mao cult to a completely new level as regards its intensity and all-pervasiveness, and have also brought striking changes in the nature of that cult. To understand the significance and function of these tendencies, it is necessary to put them in the context of the current political situation as a whole.

Before reviewing the extraordinary events in China since the spring of 1966, it will be well to pause and ask ourselves who launched this movement, and why. There is no doubt that it corresponds to Mao's temperament and political style, and that he fully supports it and gives his approval to all major decisions. . . .

If the current Great Proletarian Cultural Revolution is to a considerable extent stage-managed for Mao by someone else, a large part of the responsibility obviously rests on Lin Piao. . . .

Although it is clear that the army is not entirely united behind Lin Piao, he does speak, of course, for the group now in control of the military establishment. Thus, it is surely no accident that Lin's ascension into public view should have begun immediately after the issuance of the current edition of *Quotations from Chairman Mao*, the preface of which is dated August 1, 1965—August 1st, the anniversary of the Nanchang Uprising, being Army Day in China.

Another key figure in the events of 1966, who also emerged from semiretirement to play a leading role in the Great Proletarian Cultural Revolution, is none other than Mao's wife, today known not under her stage name of Lan-p'ing, but as Comrade Chiang Ch'ing. Since her marriage to Mao in Yenan she had played no open political role whatever, though according to some reports she persistently endeavored to intervene in cultural affairs. . . .

Chiang Ch'ing's rise to eminence found its culmination in her appointment as adviser on cultural work to the People's Liberation Army, which was announced on November 28, 1966, at a meeting celebrating the mass induction into the army of the Peking opera troupe and several other musical and theatrical organizations. In her speech on that occasion—which was greeted by a "thunderous ovation"—Chiang Ch'ing revealed that her "fairly systematic contact with certain sections of literature and art" had begun "a few years" previously. We may assume that one of the first episodes in her intervention in this field was precisely the reform of the Peking opera beginning in 1964. As regards the substance of cultural policy, she affirmed flatly that the "critical assimilation" of the Chinese heritage was "impossible," thus completely reversing the position of her husband, who in the past had come out repeatedly in favor of the selective assimilation of all that was precious in China's past. She also displayed her discriminating knowledge of Western culture by lumping together "rock-and-roll, jazz, strip-tease, impressionism, symbolism, abstractionism, fauvism, modernism" as things "intended to poison and paralyze the minds of the people."

Assuming that leadership in the Great Proletarian Cultural Revolution belongs largely to the trio Mao Tse-tung–Lin Piao–Chiang Ch'ing, why did they decide to launch this movement? Fairly obviously, it was in order to deal with opposition within the Chinese Communist Party toward the radical policies they favor.

If I am correct in assuming that for the past five years Mao has been waiting until the time was ripe to impose a new leap forward, economic policy must have been a major issue. This time Mao was resolved to eliminate opposition *before* launching a new leap, and his suspicion undoubtedly fell on all those who had shown a lack of enthusiasm for his policies in 1958–59, of whom Liu Shao-ch'i was evidently one. These skeptics perhaps also ventured to think that "Mao Tse-tung's thought" placed too heavy an accent on the omnipotence of the human will, as compared to the rational elements in Marxism, and was better adapted to inspiring guerrilla fighters than to building a modern economy.

Undoubtedly the war in Vietnam and the possibility of an American attack against China herself were also subjects of discussion. Some observers of the Chinese scene have made of this the central point and have suggested that the Great Proletarian Cultural Revolution as a whole should be viewed primarily as an attempt to prepare for a war with the United States, which Mao regards as henceforth inevitable. I cannot subscribe to this view. The events of the past year appear to me to be above all an attempt to reshape China and the Chinese people. But it is very likely that the anxiety inspired in Peking by events in Southeast Asia helped Mao and Lin Piao to impose their radical and uncompromising line on the Central Committee.

Whatever the issues in the debate, it is clear from the events since the spring of 1966 that Mao's position by no means won universal acceptance throughout the party apparatus. For if it had, Mao would hardly have embarked on the extraordinary and perilous adventure of creating an entirely new organization, the "Red Guards," which is beyond the control of the party officials except Mao and his henchmen. This enterprise is, of course, entirely without precedent in the forty-nine-year history of Communist regimes, which have always taken as their most fundamental axiom the predominance of the party over all other forms of political and social organization. It is also in contradiction to Mao's own principle, laid down in 1938: "The party commands the gun; the gun must never be allowed to command the party." For the Red Guards, although they harness the enthusiasm of adolescents delighted to occupy the center of the stage, were created and guided by the army, and continue to take the army as their model and inspiration. . . .

At first glance it appears exceedingly singular that Mao should encourage young people to revolt in a country which has been under communist rule for seventeen years, especially as this revolt is directed against "persons within the party who have been in authority, and have taken the capitalist road." To be sure, these persons are said to be only a handful, but in fact the resistance of the party apparatus is obviously much greater than these optimistic official statements would imply, and Mao's aim is not merely to eliminate a few individuals. He is bent on nothing less than smashing the entire party organization as it now exists, and building it up again from the bottom—no doubt incorporating into it in the process a great many revolutionary cadres and militants drawn from the Red Guards and others who have come to the fore in the course of the Great Proletarian Cultural Revolution. In order to attain this end, he has not shrunk back from the possible consequences of a period of disorganization. As the Red Guards of the Middle School attached to Tsinghua University wrote in their first poster, the aim is to "turn the old world upside down, smash it to pieces, pulverize it, and create chaos—the greater the confusion the better!"

What does Mao want to bring out of this chaos? His ambition is apparently to create a party organization of a new type, with built-in safeguards against "bureaucracy." In particular, the "Cultural Revolution Groups" which emerged during the spring and summer of 1966 are to be made permanent. . . . A careful reading of the innumerable "philosophical" articles by workers and peasants published in the Chinese press revealed that what their authors had learned from the study of Mao's thought was to be resourceful, to look at all sides of a problem, to test their ideas by experiment, and to work hard for the sake of the common good.

This rational kernel in the Great Proletarian Cultural Revolution, while it has not entirely disappeared from view, has been largely swallowed up in a mass movement which has attained levels—or at least forms—of irrationality previously unknown even in Stalin's Russia. In essence, this trend, which emerged in the middle of August, combines a cult of Mao's person of an entirely new type with the transformation of the "Thought of Mao Tse-tung" from an ideology into a kind of Marxist Koran endowed with magical virtues. . . .

This development is intimately linked with the growth and transformation of the Mao cult, which has attained in the past few months a level which leaves that of Stalin completely in the shade. This is true, first of all, in simple quantitative terms. Mao's photo and Mao's name are far more ubiquitously and insistently present in the Chinese press than were Stalin's in the Soviet press fifteen years ago. But qualitatively the difference is even more striking.

Until very recently, although Mao and his thought were the object of the highest respect, his physical presence as such did not play any great role in his leadership style. With the exception of the banquet and parade on the occasion of the Chinese national day, he seldom appeared in public. Though he was not obliged, like Stalin, to avoid crowds for the sake of security, he preferred to make known his views either through written statements or through speeches before closed groups for the party or state apparatus, and leave the mass meetings to others. A certain element of mystery and withdrawal was apparently thought desirable to enhance his prestige. . . . But it was the rally of August 18 in T'ien An Men Square, the first of several such gatherings, that marked the veritable starting point for the singular developments we are now witnessing in China.

It was on this occasion that the Red Guards made their first official appearance, though they had been seen on the streets of Peking for several days previously. In the course of the afternoon's proceedings, a girl student placed a Red Guard armband on Mao's arm, thus symbolizing the personal union between the "great teacher, great leader, great supreme commander, and great helmsman" (as Mao is henceforth called) and the young activists who are his instrument in carrying out the "cultural revolution." The Red Guards waved in the air their red-bound volumes of *Quotations from Chairman Mao,* thus producing a characteristic effect which has been repeated and amplified on each subsequent occasion. . . .

It is not easy to pass judgment on a phenomenon of this magnitude. Clearly more is involved than an artificially created mass hysteria. Although there is undoubtedly deep and widespread dissent both within the party and outside it, Mao probably still enjoys a degree of popular adhesion substantially greater than that in the Soviet Union under Stalin, who ruled by sheer police terror. At the same time, there is reason to wonder whether Mao's popularity has not already been gravely undermined by the massive use of violence in recent months. During the wave of terror unleashed by the Red Guards in August and September 1966, the number of people savagely beaten was probably several tens of thousands, of whom several thousand were actually beaten to death. And back of the Red Guards stands, as everyone knows, Lin Piao with his army. This situation is hardly calculated to encourage the public expression of dissent, but neither is it likely to strengthen the citizen's feeling of identification with his government. . . .

Understandably the most enthusiastic support comes from youth. The great majority of the Red Guards were born after 1949, and all of them have been taught during the whole of their conscious lives to regard Chairman Mao as the savior of China and a kind and solicitous father figure. Moreover, they have not been steeped like their elders in the culture of the past, and this, joined to youthful exuberance, makes them the natural and enthusiastic instruments of the smashing of statues, burning of books, and defacing of pictures which occurred in Peking and other cities in August and September of 1966. Quantitatively, this vandalism probably has been less than in France at the time of the revolution, or in England at the time of the dissolution of the monasteries by Henry VIII. But given the profound respect for the heritage of the past which undoubtedly still exists among many older Chinese, the psychological shock may be even greater. The numerous suicides among the elite of China's writers and artists may well be the result not merely of the harassment to which they have been subjected by the Red Guards, but of despair at the wanton destruction of elements in China's literary and artistic heritage which only primitive-minded fanatics can regard as reactionary.

A More Distant Perspective

ROSS TERRILL

By 1967 Mao himself was tired of the Cultural Revolution and the increasing arrogance and excesses of the Red Guards. Moreover, it had served his purposes. It had reminded China and the Communist Party of Mao's deepest revolutionary theories—that people are more important than things, that purge and renewal are necessary for a continuing revolution, that revolution is best left to the proletarian/peasant masses, and that China rather than Russia is the inevitable leader of world communism—that "yellow and brown are the colors of the future." Moreover, he had used the Cultural Revolution to overcome those who opposed him in the Chinese Communist Party and Politburo. But most of all, the Cultural Revolution had reasserted Mao's position as the embodiment of the Chinese Communist revolution. Mao's "cult of personality" was so firmly in place that he was, in fact, "the people's emperor" right up to the time of his death in 1976.

The true dimensions of the Cultural Revolution and its significance have become considerably clearer since Schram wrote of it in 1966. This is revealed in the excerpt that follows, from Ross Terrill, *Mao: A Biography*. This book, published in 1980, is the best full-scale contemporary biography of Chairman Mao. Ross Terrill is a distinguished authority and a prolific writer on contemporary China, and positions his account of Mao firmly in the setting of recent Chinese history.

In the 1940s and 1950s it would not have been apt to speak of "Maoism" or "Maoists." While collegial authority endured in the CCP, *every* Party member was to a large degree a Maoist. Maoism was pretty much the Chinese Communist Way.

Now things were different. Mao's following had shrunk from almost the whole, in the 1950s, to merely one part, in the 1960s. In a split Party he was reduced to latching on to one wedge.

But he did have a substantial wedge. Its color was khaki. Mao launched a drive for all of China to "Learn from the PLA [People's Liberation Army]."

What exactly would China learn from the PLA? First signs were odd. "Comrade Jiang Qing talked with me yesterday," Lin Biao told a group in Shanghai. "She is very sharp politically on questions of literature and art."

For years Jiang Qing's health had been spotty and her mood brittle. Mostly she had stayed home and looked after the two daughters. Mao had spent much time away from her. "A man with few words," was how she found him even when they were together.

But her topic—culture—was Mao's chosen weapon for the first round of the fight he was preparing for. "Green Waters"[1] plunged into art and literature circles with a heavy baggage of resentment at her long exclusion from them.

Soon soldiers were doing songs and dances at her behest. Her terrible crusade to put China's artistic life into a straitjacket had begun. . . .

Mao left Peking for Shanghai in the autumn of 1965. Jiang Qing was with him. . . .

The spell away from Peking was one more of his retreats, prior to a

---

[1]The English translation of Jiang Qing's name.—ED.

strong return with batteries recharged. He came to Shanghai to re-cruit some bright young intellectuals as political tools.

One day the Shanghai daily *Literary Currents* carried a heavy piece of drama criticism. That at least is what the strollers on the Shanghai Bund, opening their papers after work on November 10, thought it was.

The article was the first shot in the most amazing gunfire that any Marxist government has ever inflicted upon itself.

The Cultural Revolution had begun. Only in China could an epic of political theater begin with a dry slice of real theater.

The author of the drama column was Yao Wenyuan, a 44-year-old Shanghai essayist with a moon face and sly eyes. As drama criticism his review was stale stuff. For the play that he damned was none other than *Hai Rui Dismissed from Office*, the 1961 work by the vice-mayor of Peking.

Wu Han's play was a cunning allegory that protested Mao's own dismissal of Peng from the defense ministry. Mao had seen the barb behind it four years before. Now he felt he could hit back. . . .

Only Mao would have made a big issue of Wu Han's play—because Mao was its target. In remarking to some Albanian visitors that the Cultural Revolution began with the *Literary Currents* article, Mao admit-ted that his own role in Chinese politics was its first bone of contention.

Yet Mao did have some broad and even noble motives for his "Great Proletarian Cultural Revolution." Villagers so wretched that they ate bark, he told Malraux, made better fighters than glib chauffeurs from Shanghai. He was worried about the softness of the 300 million young people born since 1949. They must be put through a struggle of their own.

Mao was also reasserting his belief that people count more than things. "Should we attach more importance to men, to things, or to both?" he asked in a directive on labor reform. It was a question that Chinese tradition had long concerned itself with and Mao gave an answer that was very Confucian. "If we do our work on men well," he concluded, "we shall have things as well." Mao was trying to reestab-lish, amid the shifting sands of the Chinese Revolution, a priority for social relations over economic output.

The man believed deeply in purge and renewal. "If you have to fart, fart!" he once cried out at a Party meeting. "You will feel much better for it." As in the past, it was nature that lent him the patterns of thought he felt comfortable with.

"Don't peasants weed several times a year? The weeds removed can be used as fertilizer." The sentiment was macabre in its implications. Yet Mao was rousing himself not without hope.

He was in search of immortality for Mao Zedong—but also for the Chinese Revolution.

Mao started with a shot at *Hai Rui Dismissed from Office* for reasons beyond mere wounded vanity. Like any Chinese leader, he had a healthy regard for the role of literature in cementing, or undermining, the legitimacy of a political dynasty.

Being a semi-intellectual himself, he did not quite trust the species, yet he was fascinated by it too. He had come to believe—and told an audience of economic planners so in mid-1964—that in Russia the new privileged elite had sprung first from literary and artistic circles.

"Why are there so many literary and artistic associations in Peking?" he inquired in irritation. "They have nothing to do." At the festivals, "army performances are always the best, local troupes rank second, and those from Peking are the worst."

His obsession with Russia, his chauvinism, his craving for immortality, all tumbled out before the same group of economic planners. "You have this association, that organization—it's all just a transplant from the Soviet Union . . . all ruled by foreigners and dead men. . . ."

If Mao was furious with Peking cultural officials, he also had bigger fish to fry. Shooting at the vice-mayor, he hoped to splatter some blood of accusation on the mayor.

Peng Zhen was a man of taste and stature. In some eyes he was a possible successor to Mao. His urbane, routinized ways turned Peking into a city that Mao found as soulless and self-important as some Deep Southerners find Washington.

Mao angrily refused to read *People's Daily* during these years. He preferred the army paper *Liberation Army Daily.* . . .

Two outlooks were about to collide.

Using a crablike technique to bring pressure to bear on Peng Zhen and the Peking establishment, Mao appointed a group that included the mayor himself to guide what he had already labeled a Cultural Revolution. Nothing could come of that, except a fight.

The mayor tried to limit the Yao article to the realm of academic debate. Mao was bent on far-reaching political change. The first wave of the Cultural Revolution was against those officials who had come to regard the edifice of PRC rule as an end in itself. A fight was just what Mao had in mind.

He watched it brew during the spring of 1966 from the vantage point of Shanghai. . . .

Mao had made a new analysis of international relations which put Russia and America theoretically on a par as class enemies of China. It was a confused analysis—gaily mixing up national and class factors, arbitrarily reclassifying Russia as capitalist—yet it carried the seed of a coherent new foreign policy line for China.

Mao's problem in calling a plague on both superpowers was that most of the Politburo disagreed with him.

It was clear to everyone in Peking that the U.S. was still a threat to China. Mao did not deny it. The novelty of Mao's position was that he asserted *Russia could be no help* to China in this predicament. Liu and many PLA leaders, on the other hand, still believed in the possibility of "joint action" with Moscow in the face of the American threat. . . .

Mao's strategic view was not changed by the outcome of the Vietnam War. He had already decided by the mid-1960s that Russia was a rising menace and the U.S. a falling one. The U.S. failure in the rice paddies of Indochina merely gave a delayed illustration to his thesis. . . .

While in retreat from Peking, Mao reread *Journey to the West*. The hero of the novel is a monkey with a red ass named Sun. He performs wonderful feats.

Sun steals and eats the peaches of immortality in the gardens of paradise. He storms the gates of hell in order to strike his name off the cosmic blacklist. He covers 180,000 leagues in one bound to reach the pillars that mark the boundary of the world, and once there pisses on a pillar to show his independent spirit.

Daring fate, Sun the monkey king has a trick for coping with adversity. He plucks hair from his body—the term for "hair" happens to be the same Chinese character as Mao's name—bites it into fragments and cries "Change!" Each piece then turns into a small monkey and he has at his side an army of supporters.

"We must overcome the king of hell and liberate the little devils," Mao remarked to a Politburo colleague in March 1966. "We need more Suns from the various local areas to go and disrupt the heavenly palace."

He—and Peking—got them before the year was out. . . .

By mid-1966 Mao was ready to spring back in person to the public arena and he did so clutching a packet of surprises worthy of Sun the monkey king.

He let China know he was alive (but not where he was sojourning) by receiving the premier of faithful Albania at an undisclosed location. Then he offered proof of his physical vigor. He went to Wuhan and swam the Yangze before a battery of TV cameras.

People's Daily reported—perhaps in the spirit of the monkey king legend—that Mao covered fifteen kilometers in sixty-five minutes and showed no sign of fatigue afterward.

Mao returned to Peking to summon some real-life "little devils" to his cause, and to write in his own hand a wall poster that asked the whole nation to revolt.

So the Cultural Revolution really began.

"We need," Mao ruminated of China's future, "determined people who are young, have little education, a firm attitude, and the political experience to take over the work."

His own experience was his guide. "When we started to make revolution we were mere 23-year-old boys," he pointed out, "while the rulers of that time . . . were old and experienced. *They had more learning but we had more truth.*"

The Cultural Revolution put this idea to the test. Young people were supposed to be untainted with old ways. Their education had been purely Chinese and without distortions from the non-Chinese world. As pristine products of new China, would they not prove to have "more truth"?

In that sense the Cultural Revolution was a fresh effort to do what the Hundred Flowers had failed to do: crystallize a moral consensus.

In another sense the Cultural Revolution was a departure from anything Mao had tried before. The "political experience" that Mao wished youth to have was to be gained by a *struggle against the Party!*

This gamble, too, stemmed from the shocks of 1956–1957. At that time Mao lost his faith in the established doctrines of Marxism-Leninism. Truth and the authority of the Party were thereafter quite separable in Mao's mind. So much so that by 1966 he believed that truth could be established *over against* the authority of the Party.

For the Great Leap Forward Mao trusted the Party as vehicle. For the Cultural Revolution he did not. He called in the little devils to assault the Party.

Mao set the Red Guards loose by assuring them that "To rebel is justified" is the gist of Marxism. He invited them to "Knock down the old."

At first their targets were cultural. They smashed temples. They ransacked the homes of intellectuals and better-to-do folk for items that seemed "bourgeois" or "revisionist."

Sunglasses were unacceptable on the first score; chess was too Russian to pass the second test. Almost all books other than those of Marxist doctrine were suspect. Burning them made rousing bonfires which were fun to watch.

If the Red Guards seemed at times like religious zealots, Mao had handed them an apt doctrine. His line of thought was reminiscent of the maxim "Love God and do what you like," which some Christians down the ages have believed in.

If the heart is in the right place, it presumes, then good conduct will flow as naturally as water down a slope.

Mao in 1966 gave Marxism a similar twist. He put "rebellion" in the center, where the Protestant sectarian put "love." If youth has the spirit of rebellion, the Mao of 1966 and 1967 believed, then it will do good deeds for China.

It was a mindless theory and it issued in mindless practice.

The Red Guards had their own reasons to find satisfaction in rebellion. They were a lost generation who suddenly had a sense of being found. They had been to high school, but the expectations aroused there could not be fulfilled. Neither college places nor city jobs existed for them.

A generation that had never had the chance to let its hair down now did so to an extreme. High school kids, who would not have known a capitalist if they saw one, accused veterans who had battled against capitalism for decades of being fingers on capitalism's black hand!

A group of Red Guards broke into Peng Zhen's home in the middle of the night, switched on the light in his bedroom and ordered the mayor to rise and come downtown to be criticized. "Peng Zhen's face turned ashen out of surprise," the young zealots wrote in a breathless report, "and he could not even dress himself properly." . . .

The Red Guards seemed to be devoted to Mao as believers to a prophet. It was in some cases a sincere devotion. But a student of seventeen could not really share Mao's perspective on the Cultural Revolution. For him or her it was exciting to shout insults at "evil ones." It lent self-importance to travel up to Peking by special train to see Chairman Mao and "take part in revolution."

The mechanics probably meant more than the message.

"The Central authorities constantly urged us," one Cantonese youth who eventually swam to Hong Kong recalled, "to take along Mao's *Quotations* and study them whenever there was time. What we did was take along a pack of cards and play whenever there was time."

It seemed that Mao had forgotten the difference between student politics, with all its instability and mixed motives, and the politics of administering a country of 700 million people. . . .

At first the Red Guards wrote posters that merely criticized everything old. But in late 1966, Mao handed graver tasks to the little devils. He asked them to knock power from the hands of half of the Politburo. As if to anoint them for their labors, Mao met eleven million of them at ten sunrise rallies by the Gate of Heavenly Peace.

The young people wore khaki—what did the seasoned veterans of the PLA think of that?—with a red armband and the white words "Red Guard." Each one clutched a copy of *Quotations*. Waved in the air, the red covers made the square resemble a field ablaze with butterflies.

Mao contributed to the rather forced military atmosphere by wearing his PLA fatigues and cap with the red star. The floppy green garments hid a figure that was by now pear-shaped.

At none of the rallies did Mao make any kind of speech (it was frequently Lin Biao who spoke). He merely stood on top of the gate, Jiang Qing beside him (also in PLA uniform), and raised an arm. Yet hundreds of thousands wept from joy, biting their sleeves and jumping up and down in response to his mere presence.

The Cultural Revolution brought all kinds of formalization of self-expression. In a weird way, Mao revived old China's ritual in his waning years.

The philosopher who had written books wrote 200-word posters instead.

The leader who used to lecture for hours to persuade his followers of the merits of a new policy now merely appeared before them with an upraised hand and a glassy smile.

The teacher who always wanted his students to think for themselves seemed content to have them chant a phrase of adoration which they no more understood than does a child understand the catechism it repeats.

Artists signed their paintings, during the mad months of late 1966 and 1967, not with their own name—not with any name—but with the sycophantic phrase: "Ten Thousand Years to Chairman Mao."

How could Mao look at himself in the mirror each morning amid such disgusting nonsense? Had he not asked in his 1949 speech on "Methods of Work" for a "stop to flattery and exaggerated praise"? Had he not forbidden even the naming of a street after a Party leader?

Yet now his own statue stared down over every lobby, his phrases were treated like magic charms, and urban China had come to resemble the interior of a Catholic cathedral with Mao as a red Mary.

Why had Mao changed? Because in his old age he did not any longer believe in the collegial authority of the Communist Party, and his own self-image reverted toward that of a traditional Chinese ruler. . . .

Because Lin Biao was pushing the Mao cult, for his own purposes, and a mixture of lack of energy and lack of will prevented Mao from scotching it.

"You should be concerned about the national crisis," he told a throng outside the Central Committee building one day, "and you should carry out the Great Proletarian Cultural Revolution to the end." He needed more turmoil, for inside the building he was in danger of being outvoted. . . .

The Mao-Liu split began to open up at the time of de-Stalinization. Mao's eventual response to the shock from Moscow—a decision to find a Chinese Way to socialism even if it was not still a Marxist way—left Liu behind in dogged orthodoxy and sheer incomprehension at the pranks of the monkey king. . . .

Liu proved obdurate. The split might have been arrested if Liu had the willow's suppleness, as Zhou had, but he did not. Speaking to an Albanian group in late April 1966, when Mao was starting to crack the whip for his new adventure, Liu did not once mention the words "Cultural Revolution" or even "Mao"!

Liu's most drastic step of resistance was typical of his organization-mindedness: he tried to summon a full Central Committee meeting and have Mao's Cultural Revolution reviewed. But 1966 was not a moment for the triumph of the letter of Party law; a Caesar had much of the nation mesmerized. . . .

Mao's responses grew more and more anti-leftist. The opening stage of the Cultural Revolution, 1965–1966, had been directed against those "veteran cadres encountering new problems" (the code word was "capitalist roaders").

The next stage, from 1967, was directed against young firebrands who proved less good at building than at smashing (the code word was "ultra-leftists").

The wind shifted. *People's Daily* still managed to urge rebellion. Yet between the lines was a very different admonition to law and order. Well before Liu was formally dismissed from office, in October 1968, Mao's focus of anxiety had switched from Liu's errors to the errors of the "little devils" who had attacked Liu and who wanted "communism now."

The turning point came in Shanghai. Militant leftists "seized power" as Mao had invited them to. They proclaimed a "Shanghai Commune" along the lines of the utopian Paris Commune of 1871. Mao did not approve.

He summoned to his office in February 1967 the two leaders of the Cultural Revolution in Shanghai: Zhang Chunqiao, a former journalist whose career was closely linked with Mao's patronage; and Yao Wenyuan, the moon-faced propagandist who had written the critique of *Hai Rui Dismissed from Office*.

Mao could hardly wait to see them. As their plane flew up from Shanghai he kept asking his secretary if it had arrived at Peking airport yet. The supreme leader ended up waiting in the doorway for the two firebrands to enter his quarters.

He poured cold water on them. Anarchism should be avoided, he said. Organizations must have someone in charge of them.

Shanghai leftists had been quoting a statement of Mao's from the May Fourth period. "The world is ours," ran this cry of youth, "the nation is ours, society is ours." Don't quote it anymore, Mao said, murmuring that he didn't "altogether recall" using those exact words.

As for a Shanghai Commune, Mao backed out of it with a curiously thin objection. If all China's cities set up communes would China's name not have to be changed from PRC to something else? Would foreign countries grant recognition to a "People's Commune of China"?

Zhang and Yao went back to Shanghai and turned down the thermostat of the Cultural Revolution from hot to lukewarm. The Shanghai Commune lasted just nineteen days.

The reason for Mao's change of heart was his dismay at the factionalism of the leftists. They had excelled at knocking down. But when it came to building, there were hundreds of supervisors and no bricklayers.

Mao took trips around China. He did not like what he saw. Not only were Red Guards fighting among themselves, but Red Guards as a whole were coming into bitter conflict with industrial workers. Rumblings of discontent could be heard in the army. . . .

By late 1967 Mao was in favor of law and order. The "little devils" were ordered back to school. They were still to "make revolution," but in practice the reopening of the schools rendered that impracticable.

"If leftists remain uneducated," he murmured in Jiangxi, "they will become ultra-leftists." . . .

Mao scolded the Red Guard leaders for using violence in the factional struggles. . . .

He tried to switch the Cultural Revolution back to its academic beginnings: "We want cultural struggle, not armed struggle."

Mao dealt with the Red Guard leaders bluntly as a veteran politician talking to neophytes. "I am the black hand that suppressed the Red Guards," he said to these young people who had expected that "seizing power" would lead to a new political system. . . .

Was the Cultural Revolution the culmination of Maoism? By no means. It was a charade in a hothouse.

Mao wanted a new society. But in the Cultural Revolution he was driven less by a vision of the future than by a flight from a recent past that he did not like. . . .

Mao also entered on the Cultural Revolution determined to establish more deeply his long-standing socialist values.

- Relations between people are more important than production of things.

- Struggle has a therapeutic benefit that goes beyond attaining the object of the struggle.

- Life is a battleground on which few victories are final and the low and the high change places often.

Here Mao had *some* success. He reminded China of the Maoist faith, even if he did not convert China to it.

The Cultural Revolution did not produce a new type of rule—only some new assistants to the ruler and, for a season, a new social atmosphere. It did, though, put untrammeled power back in Mao's pale and aging hands.

Review and Study Questions

1. In what fundamental ways did Chinese communism under Mao Tse-tung differ from Soviet communism?

2. What prompted Mao to take such radical measures as the Great Proletarian Cultural Revolution? How successful was it?

3. What role did Mao see for China in the so-called Third World?

4. To what extent was the Great Proletarian Cultural Revolution a means to greater power for Mao and the perpetuation of his cult of personality?

5. To what extent was the Great Proletarian Cultural Revolution a genuine effort on the part of Chairman Mao to reenergize and reinvigorate the Chinese Communist revolution?

Suggestions for Further Reading

Mao Tse-tung was a prolific writer, but the entire corpus of his works is not available in English. There are two "official" collections: Mao Tse-tung, *Selected Works,* 5 vols. (New York: International Publishers, 1954) and a British edition of the same collection; and *Selected Works of Mao Tse-tung,* 5 vols. (Oxford and New York: Pergamon Press, 1977), prepared by the Foreign Languages Press in Peking and authorized by the Central Committee of the Chinese Communist Party. Both these editions are devoted to public documents, proclamations, position papers, and the like. Neither contains a shred of biographical material. And further, both editions have been heavily edited and revised by the Communist authorities. To an extent the same is the case with *Selected Military Writings of Mao Tse-tung* (Peking: Foreign Languages Press, 1966). The first of a projected six-volume set of *The Writings of Mao Zedong, 1949–1976,* vol. I, *September 1949–December 1955,* ed. Michael Y. M. Kau and John K. Leung (Armonk, N. Y.: M. E. Sharpe, 1986) has appeared.

There are two English-language versions of Mao's writings in *Mao Tse-tung's Quotations: The Red Guard's Handbook,* ed. Stewart Fraser (Nashville: George Peabody College for Teachers, 1967) and *Quotations from Chairman Mao Tse-tung,* ed. Stuart R. Schram (New York et al.: Praeger, 1967). Somewhat more useful are two carefully edited and selected collections, *The Political Thought of Mao Tse-tung,* ed. Stuart R. Schram (New York et al.: Praeger, 1963) and *Chairman Mao Talks to the People, Talks and Letters: 1956–1971,* ed. and intro. Stuart Schram, tr. John Chinnery and Tieyun (New York: Pantheon, 1974). Of a similar sort are *Mao Tse-tung on Revolution and War,* ed. M. Rejai

(Garden City, N. Y.: Doubleday, 1969), and Philippe Devillers, *Mao*, tr. Tony White (New York: Schocken Books, 1969), in the "What They *Really* Said" series. There is no autobiography as such. There is, however, a work that has been used as a substitute for an autobiography for Mao's early career: Edgar Snow, *Red Star over China*, rev. ed. (New York: Garden City Publishing Co., 1939), in which Snow reports a long series of private conversations with Mao about his childhood and early life. There are two books that present selections from Mao's works in a chronological order and hence are biographical or autobiographical in structure: *Mao Papers: Anthology and Bibliography*, ed. Jerome Ch'en (London: Oxford University Press, 1970), and *Mao*, ed. Jerome Ch'en (Englewood Cliffs, N.J.: Prentice-Hall, 1969). The latter of these, part of the series "Great Lives Observed," is the most useful; it not only presents Mao in his own words but has a section called "Mao Viewed by His Contemporaries" and one called "Mao in History." Another book by Jerome Ch'en, *Mao and the Chinese Revolution*, has an interesting section consisting of "Thirty-seven Poems by Mao Tse-tung," tr. Michael Bullock and Jerome Ch'en (London et al.: Oxford University Press, 1965). Mao was famous as a poet in China.

There is no end of books analyzing Mao's thought. One of the best of them is Arthur A. Cohen, *The Communism of Mao Tse-tung* (Chicago and London: University of Chicago Press, 1964). Cohen's book deflates the exaggerated Chinese representation of Mao as a political philosopher and makes the case for his being simply a skillful revolutionary strategist. There is still no better guide to Mao's thought than this one, in spite of such later books as Alain Bouc, *Mao Tse-tung: A Guide to His Thought*, tr. Paul Auster and Lydia Davis (New York: St. Martin's, 1977) and Frederic Wakeman, Jr., *History and Will: Philosophical Perspectives of Mao Tse-tung's Thought* (Berkeley et al.: University of California Press, 1973).

In general, with the conspicuous exceptions of Stuart Schram's *Mao Tse-tung* (New York: Simon & Schuster, 1966), excerpted for this chapter, and Edgar Snow's *Red Star over China*, the older biographies of Mao can be dismissed in favor of those written in the decade following his death. The best of these is Ross Terrill, *Mao: A Biography* (New York et al.: Harper & Row, 1980), excerpted for this chapter. Two others can also be recommended: Dick Wilson, *The People's Emperor: Mao, A Biography of Mao Tse-tung* (Garden City, N.Y.: Doubleday, 1980), stresses the earthy, peasant quality of Mao and his preoccupation with the traditional Chinese cult of the ruler rather than his Marxism or his higher political skills. It is impressionistic and anecdotal and very readable, as is the work by an able Chinese-American journalist, Eric Chou: *Mao Tse-tung: The Man and the Myth* (New York: Stein and Day, 1982). Two books can be recommended that deal specifically with the Great Cultural Revolution. Roderick Macfarquhar, *The Origins of the Cultural Revolution*, vol. I, *Contradictions among the People 1956–1957;* vol. II, *The Great Leap Forward 1958–1960* (New York: Columbia University Press, 1974, 1983), with a third volume to come, is a definitive, detailed, and altogether convincing analysis of the origins of the Cultural Revolution in the failure of the Great Leap Forward. A less demanding but satisfactory work that also focuses on the Cultural Revolution is Stanley Karnow, *Mao and China: From Revolution to Revolution* (New York: Viking, 1972).

Two books attempt to assess the place of Chairman Mao in modern history: Stuart R. Schram, *Mao Zedong: A Preliminary Reassessment* (New York: St. Martin's, 1983), and *Mao Tse-tung in the Scales of History: A Preliminary Assessment,* organized by the *Chinese Quarterly,* ed. Dick Wilson (Cambridge et al.: Cambridge University Press, 1977).

Of the many books on the history of revolutionary China, there are two that can be especially recommended: Chalmer A. Johnson, *Peasant Nationalism and Communist Power: The Emergence of Revolutionary China* (Stanford: Stanford University Press, 1962), and John King Fairbank, *The Great Chinese Revolution, 1800–1985* (New York: Harper & Row, 1986).

UPI/Bettmann

GOLDA MEIR: MOTHER OF ISRAEL

1898	Born in Kiev
1906	Emigrated to Milwaukee
1921	Emigrated to Palestine
1948	Signatory to Israel's declaration of independence
1949–56	Minister of Labor
1956–66	Foreign Minister
1969	Prime Minister
1973	Yom Kippur War
1974	Resigned as Prime Minister
1978	Died

Golda Meir was born Goldie Mabovitch, in 1898, in Kiev in the Ukraine, the daughter of a Russian-Jewish family. Among her earliest memories was that of her father and his neighbors nailing boards across the doorway to guard against a cossack raid.[1] At the age of eight she and her family emigrated to the United States and settled in Milwaukee.

She grew up in that city, studied education, and entered upon a career as a teacher. As a young woman, Golda became passionately committed to the Zionist movement—the drive to create a Jewish homeland in Israel—and was one of the leaders of the Milwaukee Labor Zionist Party. She married Morris Myerson, and in 1921 they emigrated to Palestine, where they joined a Jewish agricultural commune (kibbutz). In Palestine she adopted the Hebrew version of her last name, "Meir."

Meir soon plunged into Israeli politics. She represented her kibbutz in the Histardruth, the General Federation of Labor, and later became secretary to its Women's Labor Council. During World War II she continued to be a spokesperson for the Zionist cause and, in the years immediately following the war, she worked tirelessly for Zion-

---

[1]Golda Meir, *A Land of Our Own, An Oral Autobiography* (New York: Putnam, 1973), p. 15.

ism. On May 14, 1948, she was a signatory to Israel's declaration of independence and, in that same year, she was appointed the new state's minister to Moscow. The following year Meir was elected to the Israeli parliament, the Knesset, where she served until 1974. In 1956 she was appointed foreign minister and, in 1967, became one of the founders of the Israel Labor Party. In 1969 Meir was elected prime minister upon the death of Levi Eshkol.

Despite her commitment to peace with Israel's Arab neighbors she lived during a period of four wars between Israel and those neighboring Arab states. The last and most serious of them, the so-called Yom Kippur War, broke out in October 1973 with a sudden attack on two fronts from Egypt and Syria.

The Yom Kippur War

GOLDA MEIR

Golda Meir had been, in some considerable part, responsible for the worldwide support that had come to the new state of Israel. She traveled widely encouraging and promoting that support, which was crucial in enabling Israel to survive in the hostile environment of the Arab Middle East. She was, as prime minister in 1973, responsible for the conduct of the Yom Kippur War, which began on that most holy of Jewish holy days.

In her autobiography Meir writes of the war, not as a military narrative, but as an account of the political events that led up to it, the policy considerations of the Israeli state, and her own reactions to it.

The following excerpt is from that account.

Of all the events upon which I have touched in this book, none is so hard for me to write about as the war of October, 1973, the Yom Kippur War. But it happened, and so it belongs here—not as a military account, because that I leave to others, but as a near disaster, a nightmare that I myself experienced and which will always be with me.

Even as a personal story, there is still a great deal that cannot be told, and what I write is far from being definitive. But it is the truth as I felt and knew it in the course of that war, which was the fifth to be forced on Israel in the twenty-seven years that have passed since the state was founded.

There are two points I should like to make at once. The first is that we won the Yom Kippur War, and I am convinced that in their heart of hearts the political and military leaders of both Syria and Egypt know that they were defeated again, despite their initial gains. The other is that the world in general and Israel's enemies in particular should know that the circumstances which took the lives of the more than 2,500 Israelis who were killed in the Yom Kippur War will never ever recur.

The war began on October 6, but when I think about it now, my mind goes back to May, when we received information about the reinforcement of Syrian and Egyptian troops on the borders. Our intelligence people thought that it was most unlikely that war would break out; nonetheless, we decided to treat the matter seriously. At that time I went to general headquarters myself. Both the minister of defense and the chief of staff, David Elazar (who is known throughout the country by his nickname, Dado) briefed me thoroughly on the armed forces' state of preparedness, and I was convinced that the army was ready for any contingency—even for full-scale war. Also, my mind was put at rest about the question of a sufficiently early warning. Then, for whatever reason, the tension relaxed.

In September we started to receive information about a buildup of Syrian troops on the Golan Heights, and on the thirteenth of that month an air battle took place with the Syrians, which ended in the downing of thirteen Syrian MIGs. Despite this, our intelligence people were very reassuring: It was most unlikely they said, that there would be any major Syrian reaction. But this time, the tension remained, and what's more, it had spread to the Egyptians. Still our intelligence assessment remained the same. The continued Syrian reinforcement of troops was, they explained, caused by the Syrians' fear that *we* would attack, and throughout the month, including on the eve of my departure to Europe, this explanation for the Syrian move was repeated again and again.

On Monday, October 1, Yisrael Galili called me in Strasbourg. Among other things, he told me that he had talked to Dayan and that they both felt that as soon as I got back, we should have a serious discussion about the situation in the Golan Heights. I told him that I would definitely return the next day and that we should meet the day after.

Late on Wednesday morning I met with Dayan, Allon, Galili, the commander of the air force, the chief of staff and, because the head of intelligence was sick that day, the head of military intelligence research. Dayan opened the meeting, and the chief of staff and the head of intelligence research described the situation on both fronts in great detail. There were things that disturbed them, but the military evaluation was still that we were in no danger of facing a joint Syrian-Egyptian attack and, what's more, that it was very unlikely that Syria would attack us alone. The buildup and movement of Egyptian forces in the south was probably due to the maneuvers that were always held around this time of year, and in the north the bolstering and new deployment of forces were still explained as they had been before. The fact that several Syrian army units had been transferred only a week before from the Syrian-Jordanian border was interpreted as part of a recent détente between the two countries and as a Syrian gesture of goodwill toward Jordan. Nobody at the meeting thought that it was necessary to call up the reserves, and nobody thought that war was imminent. But it was decided to put a further discussion of the situation on the agenda for Sunday's cabinet meeting.

On Thursday, as usual, I went to Tel Aviv. For years I had been spending Thursdays and Fridays in my Tel Aviv office, Saturdays at my house in Ramat Aviv and returning to Jerusalem either late Saturday evening or early Sunday morning, and there seemed to be no reason for changing the pattern that week. In fact, it was a short week in any case, because Yom Kippur (the Day of Atonement) was to begin on Friday evening, and most people in Israel were taking a long weekend. . . .

On Friday, October 5, we received a report that worried me. The families of the Russian advisers in Syria were packing up and leaving in a hurry. It reminded me of what had happened prior to the Six-Day War, and I didn't like it at all. Why the haste? What did those Russian families know that we didn't know? Was it possible that they were being evacuated? In all the welter of information pouring into my office that one little detail had taken root in my mind, and I couldn't shake myself free of it. But since no one around me seemed very perturbed about it, I tried not to become obsessive. Besides, intuition is a very tricky thing; sometimes it must be acted upon at once, but sometimes it is merely a symptom of anxiety and then it can be very misleading indeed.

I asked the minister of defense, the chief of staff and the head of intelligence whether they thought this piece of information was very important. No, it hadn't in any way changed their assessment of the situation. I was assured that we would get adequate warning of any real trouble, and anyway, sufficient reinforcements were being sent to the fronts to carry out any holding operation that might be required. Everything that was necessary had been done, and the army was placed on high alert, particularly the air force and the armored corps. When he left me, the head of intelligence met Lou Kaddar in the corridor. Later she told me that he had patted her shoulder, smiled and said, "Don't worry. There won't be a war." But I was worried; furthermore, I couldn't understand his certainty that all was well. What if he were wrong? If there was even the slightest chance of war, we should at least call up the reserves. At any rate, I wanted a meeting at least of those cabinet ministers who would be spending the Yom Kippur weekend in Tel Aviv. It turned out that very few of them were around. I was reluctant to ask the two National Religious Party ministers who lived in Jerusalem to come to a meeting in Tel Aviv on the eve of Yom Kippur, and several other ministers had already left for their kibbutzim, which were all fairly far away. Still, nine ministers were in town, and I told my military secretary to schedule an emergency meeting for Friday noon.

We gathered in my Tel Aviv office. In addition to the cabinet members, the meeting was attended by the chief of staff and the head of intelligence. We heard all the reports again, including the one that concerned the rushed—and to me still inexplicable—departure of the Russian families from Syria, but again, no one seemed very alarmed. Nevertheless, I decided to speak my mind. "Look," I said, "I have a terrible feeling that this has all happened before. It reminds me of 1967, when we were accused of massing troops against Syria, which is exactly what the Arab press is saying now. And I think that it all means something." As a result, although as a rule a cabinet decision is required for a full-scale callup, that Friday we passed a resolution, suggested by Galili, that if necessary, the minister of defense and I could do so by ourselves. I also said that we should get in touch with the Americans so that they could get in touch with the Russians and tell them in no uncertain terms that the United States was not in the mood for trouble. The meeting broke up, but I stayed on at the office for a while, thinking.

How could it be that I was still so terrified of war breaking out when the present chief of staff, two former chiefs of staff (Dayan and Chaim Bar-Lev, who was my minister of commerce and industry) and the head of intelligence were far from sure that it would? After all, they weren't just ordinary soldiers. They were all highly experienced generals, men who had fought and led other men in spectacularly victorious battles. Each one of them had an outstanding military record, and as for our intelligence services, they were known to be among the best in the world. Not only that, but foreign sources with whom we were in constant touch agreed absolutely with the assessment of our experts. So why was it that I was still so ill at ease? Was I perhaps talking myself into something? I couldn't answer my own questions.

Today I know what I should have done. I should have overcome my hesitations. I knew as well as anyone else [what] full-scale mobilization meant and how much money it would cost, and I also knew that only a few months before, in May, we had had an alert and the reserves had been called up; but nothing had happened. But I also understood that perhaps there had been no war in May exactly because the reserves had been called up. That Friday morning I should have listened to the warnings of my own heart and ordered a callup. For me, that fact cannot and never will be erased, and there can be no consolation in anything that anyone else has to say or in all of the commonsense rationalizations with which my colleagues have tried to comfort me.

It doesn't matter what logic dictated. It matters only that I, who was so accustomed to making decisions—and who did make them throughout the war—failed to make that one decision. It isn't a question of feeling guilty. I, too, can rationalize and tell myself that in the face of such total certainty on the part of our military intelligence—and the almost equally total acceptance of its evaluations on the part of our foremost military men—it would have been unreasonable of me to have insisted on a callup. But I know that I should have done so, and I shall live with that terrible knowledge for the rest of my life. I will never again be the person I was before the Yom Kippur War.

Then, however, I sat in the office, thinking and agonizing until I just couldn't sit there anymore and I went home. Menachem and Aya had invited a few friends to drop in after dinner. Jews eat dinner early on the eve of Yom Kippur because traditionally it is their last meal for twenty-four hours, and by the time the stars are out the fast has begun. We sat down to eat; but I was very restless and had no appetite at all, and although they wanted me to stay on with their friends, I excused myself and went to bed. But I couldn't sleep.

It was a still, hot night, and through the open window I could hear the voices of Menachem and Aya's friends talking quietly in the garden below. Once or twice the children's dog barked, but otherwise it was a typically silent Yom Kippur night. I lay awake for hours, unable to sleep. Eventually I must have dozed off. Then, at about 4 A.M., the phone next to my bed rang. It was my military secretary. Information had been received that the Egyptians and the Syrians would launch a joint attack on Israel "late in the afternoon." There was no doubt anymore. The intelligence source was authoritative. I told Lior to ask Dayan, Dado, Allon and Galili to be in my office before 7 A.M. On the way there, I caught sight of an old man going to synagogue, his prayer shawl over his shoulders holding the hand of a small child. They looked like symbols of Judaism itself, and I remember thinking sorrowfully that all over Israel, young men were fasting in synagogues today and that it was from their prayers that they would soon be called to arms.

By eight o'clock the meeting had begun. Dayan and Dado differed as to the scale of the callup. The chief of staff recommended the mobilization of the entire air force and four divisions and said that if they were called up at once, they could go into action the next day— that is, Sunday. Dayan, on the other hand, was in favor of calling up the air force and only two divisions (one for the north and one for the south), and he argued that if we had a full mobilization before a single shot was fired, the world would have an excuse for calling us the "aggressors." Besides, he thought that the air force plus two divisions could handle the situation, and if toward evening the situation worsened, we could always call up more within a few hours. "That's my suggestion," he said, "but I won't resign if you decide against me."

"My God," I thought, "*I* have to decide which of them is right?" But what I said was that I had only one criterion: If there really was a war, then we had to be in the best position possible. "The callup should be as Dado suggested." But, of course, it was the one day of the year that even our legendary ability to mobilize rapidly partly failed us.

Dado was in favor of a preemptive strike since it was clear that war was inevitable in any case. "I want you to know," he said, "that our air force can be ready to strike at noon, but you must give me the green light now. If we can make that first strike, it will be greatly to our advantage." But I had already made up my mind. "Dado," I said, "I know all the arguments in favor of a preemptive strike, but I am against it. We don't know now, any of us, what the future will hold, but there is always the possibility that we will need help, and if we strike first, we will get nothing from anyone. I would like to say yes because I know what it would mean, but with a heavy heart I am going to say no." Then Dayan and Dado went to their offices and I told Simcha Dinitz (now our ambassador to Washington, who happened to be in Israel that week) to fly back to the States immediately and I called in Menachem Begin to tell him what was happening. I also asked for a cabinet meeting for noon and called the then U.S. ambassador, Kenneth Keating, and asked him to come and see me. I told him two things: that according to our intelligence, the attacks would start late in the afternoon and that we would not strike first. Maybe something could still be done to avert the war by U.S. intervention with the Russians or maybe even directly with the Syrians and the Egyptians. At all events, we would not make a preemptive strike. I wanted him to know that and to relay that information as soon as possible to Washington. Ambassador Keating had been a very good friend to Israel for many years, both in the U.S. Senate and in Israel itself. He was a man I liked and trusted and on that dreadful morning I was grateful to him for his assistance and understanding.

When the cabinet met at noon, it heard a full description of the situation, including the decision to mobilize the reserves and also my decision regarding a preemptive strike. Nobody raised any objections whatsoever. Then, while we were meeting, my military secretary burst into the room with the news that the shooting had started, and almost at once we heard the wailing of the first air-raid sirens in Tel Aviv. The war had begun. . . .

What those days were like for me I shall not even try to describe. It is enough, I think, to say that I couldn't even cry when I was alone. But I was very rarely alone. I stayed in the office most of the time, although now and then I went to the war room and sometimes Lou made me go home and lie down until the phone summoned me back. There were meetings all through the day and all through the night, incessantly interrupted by phone calls from Washington and bad news from the front. Plans were presented, analyzed and debated. I couldn't bear to be away from the office for more than an hour at a time because Dayan, Dado, Foreign Office people and various ministers were constantly coming in either to report to me on the most recent developments or to ask my advice on various matters.

But even on the worst of those early days, when we already knew what losses we were sustaining, I had complete faith in our soldiers and officers, in the spirit of the Israel Defense Forces and their ability to face any challenge, and I never lost faith in our ultimate victory. I knew we would win sooner or later; but each report of the price we were paying in human lives was like a knife being turned in my heart, and I shall never forget the day when I listened to the most pessimistic prediction I had yet heard.

On the afternoon of October 7 Dayan returned from one of his tours at the front and asked to see me at once. He told me that in his opinion the situation in the south was so bad that we should pull back substantially and establish a new defensive line. I listened to him in horror. Allon, Galili and my military secretary were in the room. Then I asked Dado to come in too. He had another suggestion—that we should go on with the offensive in the south. He asked if he could go to the southern front to supervise things himself and for permission to make whatever decisions might have to be made on the spot. Dayan agreed and Dado left. That night I called a cabinet meeting and got the ministers' approval for us to launch a counterattack against the Egyptians on October 8. When I was alone in the room, I closed my eyes and sat perfectly still for a minute. I think that if I hadn't learned, during all those years, how to be strong, I would have gone to pieces then. But I didn't.

The Canal had been crossed by the Egyptians, and our forces in the Sinai had been battered. The Syrians had penetrated in depth on the Golan Heights. On both fronts the casualties were already very high. One burning question was whether at this point we should tell the nation how bad the situation really was, and I felt very strongly that we should wait for a while. The very least we could do for our soldiers, and for their families, was to keep the truth to ourselves for a few more days. Nonetheless, some kind of statement had to be made at once, so on that first day of the war I addressed the citizens of Israel. It was one of the most difficult assignments of my life because I knew that, for everyone's sake, I could not tell all the facts.

Talking to a nation that had no idea yet of the terrible toll being taken in the north and in the south or of the peril that Israel faced until the reserves were fully mobilized and in action, I said, "We are in no doubt that we shall prevail. But we are also convinced that this renewal of Egyptian and Syrian aggression is an act of madness. We did our best to prevent the outbreak. We appealed to quarters with political influence to use it in order to frustrate this infamous move of the Egyptian and Syrian leaders. While there was still time, we informed friendly countries of the confirmed information that we had of the plans for an offensive against Israel. We called on them to do their utmost to prevent war, but the Egyptian and Syrian attack had started."

On Sunday Dayan came in to my office. He closed the door and stood in front of me. "Do you want me to resign?" he asked. "I am prepared to do so if you think I should. Unless I have your confidence, I can't go on." I told him—and I have never regretted this—that he had to stay on as minister of defense. We decided to send Bar-Lev to the north for a personal assessment of the situation. Then we began our negotiations to get military aid from the United States. Decisions had to be taken very quickly—and they had to be the right ones. There was no time nor any margin for mistakes.

By Wednesday, the fifth day of the war, we had pushed the Syrians back across the 1967 cease-fire line and begun our attack into Syria, while in Sinai the situation was sufficiently static for the cabinet to consider our crossing of the Canal. But what if our troops crossed and then were trapped? I also had to consider the possibility that the war would not be a short one and that we might find ourselves without the planes, tanks and ammunition we needed. We needed arms desperately, and, in the beginning they were slow in coming.

I talked to Dinitz in Washington at all hours of the day and the night. Where was the airlift? Why wasn't it under way yet? I remember calling him once at 3 A.M., Washington time, and he said, "I can't speak to anyone now, Golda. It is much too early." But I couldn't listen to reason. I knew that President Nixon had promised to help us, and I knew from my past experience with him that he would not let us down. Let me, at this point, repeat something that I have said often before (usually to the extreme annoyance of many of my American friends). However history judges Richard Nixon—and it is probable that the verdict will be very harsh—it must also be put on the record forever that he did not break a single one of the promises he made to us. So why was there a delay? "I don't care what time it is," I raged at Dinitz. "Call Kissinger now. In the middle of the night. We need the help today because tomorrow it may be too late.". . . Each hour of waiting that passed was like a century for me, but there was no alternative other than to hold on tight and hope that the next hour would bring better news. I phoned Dinitz and told him that I was ready to fly to Washington incognito to meet with Nixon if he thought it could be arranged. "Find out immediately," I said. "I want to go as soon as possible." But it wasn't necessary. At last Nixon himself ordered the giant C-5 Galaxies to be sent, and the first flight arrived on the ninth day of the war, on October 14. The airlift was invaluable. It not only lifted our spirits, but also served to make the American position clear to the Soviet Union, and it undoubtedly served to make our victory possible. When I heard that the planes had touched down in Lydda, I cried for the first time since the war had begun, though not for the last. That was also the day on which we published the first casualty list—656 Israelis had already died in battle.

But even the Galaxies that brought us tanks, ammunition, clothing, medical supplies and air-to-air rockets couldn't bring all that was required. What about the planes? The Phantoms and Skyhawks had to be refueled en route, so they were refueled in the air. But they came—and so did the Galaxies that landed in Lydda, sometimes at the rate of one every fifteen minutes.

When it was all over, in the spring, the U.S. colonel who had been in charge of the airlift came back to visit Israel with his wife, and they came to see me. They were lovely young people, filled with enthusiasm for the country and with admiration for our ground crews, who had learned, almost overnight, to use the special equipment for unloading those giants. I remember going out to Lydda once to watch the Galaxies come in. They looked like some kind of immense prehistoric flying monsters, and I thought to myself, "Thank God I was right to reject the idea of a preemptive strike! It might have saved lives in the beginning, but I am sure that we would not have had that airlift, which is now saving so many lives."

In the meantime, Dado shuttled from one front to the other. Bar-Lev returned from the north, and we sent him to the south to straighten out the confusion that had arisen there because the generals on the spot had such critical differences of opinion about the tactics to be employed. He was asked to stay there as long as necessary. On Wednesday he phoned me from the Sinai. It was right after a colossal tank battle in which our forces had smashed the Egyptian armored advance. Dado has a slow, very deliberate way of speaking, and when I heard him say, "G-o-l-d-a, it will be all right. We are back to being ourselves and they are back to being themselves." I knew that the tide had turned, although there were still bloody battles ahead in which hundreds of young men, and older ones too, lost their lives. It was not for nothing that people bitterly suggested later that this war should be known, not as the Yom Kippur War, but as the War of the Fathers and Sons, for all too often they fought side by side on both fronts. . . .

The next day I addressed the Knesset. I was very tired, but I spoke for forty minutes because I had a lot to say, although most of it didn't make pleasant hearing. But at least I could tell the Knesset that, as I was speaking, a task force was already operating on the west bank of the Canal. I wanted also to make public our gratitude to the president and the people of America, and, equally clear, our rage at those governments, notably the French and British, that had chosen to impose an embargo on the shipments of arms to us when we were fighting for our very lives. And most of all, I wanted the world to know what would have happened to us had we withdrawn before the war to pre-Six-Day War lines of 1967—the very same lines, incidentally, that had not prevented the Six-Day War itself from breaking out, although no one seems to remember that. . . .

Also, I wanted to put on record the culpability of the Soviet Union and to stress the evil role Russia was once again playing in the Middle East. . . .

The Yom Kippur War: The Aftermath

HOWARD M. SACHAR

Howard M. Sachar is not only an American academic historian but an established authority on Israel and the contemporary Middle East. Among his many books is *A History of Israel from the Rise of Zionism to our Time.* In this book he gives a very detailed and analytical account of the Yom Kippur War that parallels the highly personal account of Mrs. Meir. He goes on to deal then with the implications of the war for Israel's search for security.

And so the familiar ritual was to begin once more: the protracted diplomatic stalemate, the quest for at least an intermediate security in the wake of a dearly achieved military triumph. Under American pressure, Israel reluctantly had allowed a Red Cross supply convoy to pass through its lines to the beleaguered Egyptian Third Army. But thereafter the Meir government was unprepared to offer further concessions until the Egyptians made available a list of Israeli prisoners of war. Nor could there be any question of Israeli forces returning to their October 22 positions on the west bank of the Canal, as the Egyptians demanded. Concessions had to be mutual, Mrs. Meir insisted. As it turned out, the prime minister's difficulties henceforth were to be less with the Arabs than with the Americans. On October 27, Secretary of State Kissinger was visited in Washington by Ismail Fahmi, a genial and resourceful Egyptian diplomat who was shortly to become his country's foreign minister. Kissinger was impressed by the Egyptian's seeming moderation, his professed wish for renewed ties with the United States, and his avowed interest in peace. The secretary therefore assured Fahmi that he would do his utmost not merely to negotiate a permanent supply corridor to the Third Army—in effect, to secure Israeli withdrawal to the October 22 cease-fire line—but to persuade Israel gradually to evacuate the Sinai altogether in return for a stable peace treaty. As the initial step in fulfillment of this pledge, Kissinger requested Jerusalem to evince "flexibility" on the supply corridor.

By then, Mrs. Meir recognized that there was no further time to be lost in achieving clarification with the Americans. On October 31 she flew to Washington to meet personally with Kissinger and Nixon. In her discussions with the secretary, the prime minister expressed her government's basic reservations. By what moral obligation, she asked, was Israel to pay a higher price than Egypt for accommodation, since the Egyptians had launched the war and had failed subsequently to win it? Kissinger appreciated Mrs. Meir's reasoning. Yet his own arguments were not less compelling. It was true that Israel had won the war on the battlefield. Its army had penetrated deep into Arab territory and its casualties were less than one-fifth of those sustained by the Arabs. But the secretary knew, too, that the victory had left the Israelis with ashes in their mouths. The cost in blood and treasure had been far too high. Moreover, Israel now found itself in a state of virtual diplomatic isolation. . . .

These were the circumstances under which Kissinger sought, and achieved, a more flexible Israeli bargaining position from Mrs. Meir. The secretary then pursued the opportunity for a Middle East accommodation in a five-nation swing through the Arab capitals between November 5 and 9, while en route to the Far East. He was well received by the Arab leaders as a "messenger of peace," the only man, after all, who could persuade the Israelis to disgorge occupied land. In a cordial meeting with Sadat on November 7, Kissinger persuaded the Egyptian leader to modify his demand for an immediate Israeli withdrawal to the October 22 cease-fire line, and instead to put this narrow issue into the broader context of a general disengagement of Israeli and Egyptian troops. Both sides, in any event, recognized that the current cease-fire lines were too precariously entwined to survive. Kissinger meanwhile assured Sadat that, at a peace conference later, he, the secretary, would exert his influence on the Israelis to achieve a more generous withdrawal in the Sinai. . . .

By then also, Kissinger was known in both Egypt and Israel as a "miracle man." It was indeed his success in mediating the disengagement, and his promise to undertake a similar effort between Israel and Syria, that persuaded the Arab oil-producing nations on March 18 to end their embargo, although not their continuing price hikes. Factories in Europe and the United States gradually resumed production; traffic began to move freely again. The atmosphere seemingly was conducive for a parallel Syrian-Israeli disengagement. Both Sadat and Feisal of Saudi Arabia were appealing now to Damascus to rely on Kissinger's good offices. Admittedly, the task of negotiating an accord on the Golan would not be easy. The Syrians had earned a reputation as the most uncompromising nationalists in the Arab world. Their hostility toward Israel was more deeply rooted and implacable than that of any other Arab people. Worse yet, the Assad government remained a minority cabal, largely Alawite in membership, and widely distrusted by the public at large; it enjoyed little political elbow-room for compromise. Nor were matters helped by the personality of Assad himself. Kissinger's conversations with the forty-eight-year-old ex-air force general proved to be the most exasperating of his diplomatic career. The man was apparently immovable, Kissinger confided to intimates, and given to disconcerting intervals of crooning in the midst of negotiations. Not least of all, the Assad regime was receiving powerful encouragement from Moscow to hold firm. Fearful of losing Syria altogether to American influence, the Soviets were determined to coalesce a hard-line Syrian-Iraqi-Libyan-Palestinian "rejection front." With Soviet backing, then, the Damascus government continued to insist that part of the Golan be returned immediately, with an advance commitment from Israel to evacuate the entire plateau in final negotiations.

The Israelis at first appeared equally unbudging. If the war had taught them anything, it was not merely the incorrigible brutality of their northern enemy, but the absence of territorial leeway for concessions on the Golan. From the western edge of this highland, it was a descent of only 60 miles to the Haifa-Acre enclave, the industrial heartland of the Jewish state; and the Israelis had learned the hard way that without at least a substantial foothold on the Golan, including the "eyes" of the Mount Hermon range, their warning time and defense buffer area were critically reduced. Nevertheless, the Meir cabinet understood that some small accommodation would have to be offered even on this northern front. American pressure was not the only factor here. The Syrians evidently intended to maintain the state of tension along the cease-fire line. Throughout March and April they fired repeated artillery salvos at Israeli emplacements and launched occasional commando raids behind the Israeli front lines. The rising scale of violence imposed a daily attrition that the nation was no longer prepared to endure. In the new round of fighting between March and May 1974, the Israelis suffered an additional 37 soldiers killed and 158 wounded.

Even more decisive in altering the government's stance was the issue of prisoners of war. The Israelis counted over 200 troops missing on the northern front, and possessed no way of determining how many of these were alive; Damascus refused to supply a list of Israeli POWs or to allow Red Cross inspection. From the trussed and bullet-riddled Israeli corpses retrieved on the Golan, however, little imagination was needed to assess the fate of those troops remaining in Syrian hands. Each additional day of their captivity was a nightmare for the Israeli people. The families of missing troops already were demonstrating before the Knesset and the prime minister's office. If the Syrians could be persuaded to display even the meagerest evidence of flexibility, Israel would respond. . . .

In the 1949 Israeli-Syrian armistice agreement, both parties had agreed that no "paramilitary forces" would be allowed to commit any "warlike or hostile" act against the other. This time Damascus refused to make a similar commitment: it would not publicly disown activities by the various guerrilla organizations. On the other hand, the United States reassured Israel. "Raids by armed groups or individuals across the demarcation line are contrary to the cease-fire," said Kissinger's letter. "Israel, in the exercise of its rights of self-defense, may act to prevent such actions by all available means." Presumably the veiled warning would inhibit fedayun attacks directly from the Syrian territory (for several years it did). On this basis the Israeli Knesset voted to approve the agreement, 73 to 35. Almost immediately afterward prisoners of war were exchanged; many of the Israelis among them were human wrecks. In the next three weeks the troop disengagement was carried out on schedule. Although the Syrians ominously took no steps to rebuild or repopulate al-Quneitra—flattened by Israel as a "precautionary measure" before withdrawal—it appeared nevertheless that the likelihood of renewed hostilities in the north had faded for the time being.

Meanwhile, the elections for Israel's Eighth Knesset, postponed for two months due to the war and afterward rescheduled for December 31, were held under the shadow of the nation's heavy manpower losses and the perennial threat of renewed fighting. The Labor Alignment undoubtedly would have suffered a limited erosion in any case as a result of scandals in government and class inequities in society. But in the wake of the recent conflict, military-territorial issues were to take precedence once more. The fall of the Bar-Lev Line and the pulverizing Syrian offensive had thrown the nation into shock. Whatever the complaints against the Alignment, no one had ever doubted that a regime headed by Golda Meir and Moshe Dayan could be relied on to maintain the invincibility of the near-sacred defense forces. Now that assurance had been undermined. So had confidence in the nation's security altogether. Israel's first three wars had not ended in peace treaties; but they had at least produced extended interludes of comparative stability. No longer, evidently. In 1973–74, Soviet pressure, with American acquiescence, had compelled the army to halt short of final victory and of logical strategic goals. The implications for the future were grave.

The trauma of the war, the specter of possibly bloodier and even more open-ended conflicts, profoundly altered national attitudes toward the occupied territories as well. On November 12–13, a poll conducted by the Israel Institute of Social Research found that three-fourths of the citizens interviewed were prepared, in exchange for peace, to give up all or nearly all of the land taken in 1967. This attitude in turn forced a certain revision of party platforms for the impending elections. As we recall, the Labor Alignment on November 28 sharply modified the original Galili plan, and implied compromise on the "administered" areas. Likud took a more adamant stance, insisting on "direct negotiations" with the Arabs. To be sure, rather than express unqualified opposition to withdrawal Likud simply demanded a "rejection of withdrawals that would endanger the peace and security of the nation." Yet in the case of Begin, Sharon, and other rightist leaders, the alteration in language effected no change in image. While many citizens would vote for Likud to punish the Meir government for the blunders of the recent war, the majority of the nation was not prepared to swing to the Right. Few Israelis believed that Likud's hard-line spokesmen could be trusted to explore all opportunities for peace.

Golda

THE NEW REPUBLIC

On April 10, 1974, with the end of the Yom Kippur War, Golda Meir resigned as prime minister. Four years later she died. This was the occasion for newspapers and magazines all over the world to take stock of her and her achievements. One such was the American magazine *The New Republic.* Following is its appraisal.

Her life reads like a Hollywood script composed by an overzealous screenwriter bent on producing a spectacular on great moments in contemporary Jewish history. To provide unity the major character, preferably a woman for added poignancy, is placed at the center of all key events. All the required scenes are available: a child cowering in fear of a pogrom in czarist Russia; a girl enjoying the freedom and opportunities of the United States yet determined to become a socialist pioneer in the wastes of Palestine; a young woman suffering extreme poverty and personal hardship in the barren homeland. The heroine of this increasingly improbable scenario—she scrubs laundry by hand to pay for the schooling of her children—is a woman torn by the conventional feminist conflict between the duties of wife and mother and a compelling ideological commitment. Nor is melodrama missing: there is the perilous journey to Amman in 1948, unconvincingly disguised as an Arab woman though she knows no Arabic, when she tries to persuade King Abdullah not to join the Arab attack on Israel. Then there is the incredible shot showing the newly appointed Israeli minister to the Soviet Union engulfed by a mass of supposedly assimilated Russian Jews, who defy the authorities to greet the emissary of the Jewish state in front of a Moscow synagogue. Is this a bit much, perhaps? Later, in depicting the Jewish heroine's audience with the pope, shouldn't the writer have hesitated before giving his heroine the haunting utterance, "I am the daughter of a carpenter?" Finally, why, as a climax, did he present an old, sick woman, now prime minister of the embattled state, in the role of arbiter, obliged to make crucial political and military decisions when her male cabinet ministers and generals were in disarray during the onslaught of the Yom Kippur War? The plot seems extravagant; judicious bluepencilling clearly would be in order. Yet that's how it was. So obituary comment on Golda Meir runs the danger of indulgence in superlatives made hollow by repetition. But a cautious reduction of her stature would not be closer to the truth.

The line from childhood in Kiev to fulfillment in Jerusalem was direct. There were no deviations in plan or purpose. From the beginning to the end, her convictions had a disarming, and sometimes disconcerting, slogan-like clarity: a persecuted people must be emancipated. Having learned the meaning of independence in the United States, she herself took part in this emancipation. And being a socialist, she strove to build a just society in a Jewish homeland. This terrifying, unswerving simplicity in thought and feeling—her detractors would call it simplistic—was a prime source of Golda Meir's strength. She was spared the doubts and hesitations of more complex or timid natures. In every crisis she refused to be deflected by considerations she dismissed as rationalizations for an unwillingness to face the consequences of a basic belief. No amount of acquired sophistication or temptation to disenchantment could shake her assurance in the purity of her goal and the possibility of its realization. The assurance, allied to shrewd competence, made it possible for her to become both a combative, sometimes ruthless, politician in Israel and a moral force for the Jewish people. She knew not only what she wanted but what should be wanted, and she had a unique power to communicate this knowledge.

At her best she was a remarkably effective speaker. Her best was not on most occasions at the United Nations or on other formal occasions when she had to deliver a carefully prepared address. Then she spoke like her diplomatic colleagues. But when she cast away the prepared text, as she once did at the UN to appeal directly to the Arabs, or in times of peril or triumph when she spoke impromptu to the Israeli multitudes, she had no peer. There were more brilliant stylists among Zionist orators—some deplored her poor Hebrew and elementary English—but her audience was more concerned with her message than with her oratory style. Those who heard her became for a moment selflessly involved in her emotion and her cause.

In the 1940s, when the struggle of Jewish Palestine against the British Mandatory Power was launched, she was the most moving exponent of what seemed a desperate gamble. How could an ill-armed community of 600,000 venture to challenge the British Empire to "open the gates" of Palestine to Jewish survivors? The policy of resistance was formulated by Ben-Gurion, but Golda became its voice. When she declared at village meetings or at kibbutz funerals, "we have no alternative," she meant that people of a given commitment had no alternative. Less dangerous courses could be pursued, such as settling for a modest immigration quota and a permanent minority status for the Jewish community of Palestine. Similarly, when Ben-Gurion advocated the declaration of a state after the passage of the Partition Resolution, though all knew that Arab armies were poised for the invasion of the fledgling country, Golda was among the chief activists. Many devoted Zionists counselled prudence, to avoid imperiling all that had been achieved by four decades of Jewish settlement in a confrontation either with England or the Arab states. Such prudence was alien to both her convictions and her temperament, not because she was foolhardy and ignorant of the immense risk but because the risk to the Jewish people—the betrayal of the Jewish refugees and the Zionist dream—was greater. This attitude dictated her course in the coming decades of struggle.

As a leader of the Histadrut, the Israeli labor federation, she was at first uncompromising in her egalitarian vision. She insisted on the principle of equal pay in the Histadrut regardless of the nature of the work. At one time, the nurses of the federation's health plan, who wanted to receive more pay than charwomen, viewed her as their antagonist. When she was minister to Moscow, she tried to run her office in keeping with the austere principles of the kibbutz tradition. Inevitably these Utopian efforts foundered. In Israel and abroad, outside the kibbutz enclaves, individuals sought rewards in accordance with their skills and their positions. Impassioned but no fanatic, Golda bowed to realism. Yet all her life, the kibbutz cooperative remained her image of the ideal society. That her daughter and grandchildren worked in a Negev desert kibbutz was her special pride. And at international socialist conferences, she appeared to the end as the representative of a progressive trade union movement and of a labor party that, despite the imperfections and concessions of the present, still cherished the dream of a socialist society with a human face.

The idealistic girl matured into an adroit stateswoman, skilled in negotiation, temperate in argument and wonderfully persuasive with the great of the earth. But the granite core remained. Her critics called her short-sighted and inflexible in her insistence on "secure borders" when she became prime minister. They called her indifferent to the plight of the Palestinians—an accusation that she rejected. Her policy was shaped not only by an ideological conviction of the justice of Israel's cause, but by her own experiences. She knew that when she had worked in a malaria-infested kibbutz in the valley of the Jordan, she had made Palestine more habitable for Arabs as well as Jews. She knew that she had called herself a Palestinian at a time when Arabs disdained the designation.And she knew that from 1947 on, she had repeatedly and vainly pleaded for cooperation between Arabs and Jews. Her scepticism about the value of international guarantees derived from the abandonment of Israel by the powers pledged to the state's safety in 1948 and in 1967. Therefore "secure borders" became for her synonymous with Israel's survival.

The Yom Kippur War was the bitterest experience of her long life. This was not only because of Israel's peril, but because for the first time she was made the butt of her people's agony. Her associates were aware of the letters she received from parents blaming her and her ministers for the deaths of their sons. No suffering in her personal life could have equalled her pain at these charges, because in each instance she sorrowed with the bereaved. But the measure of her influence with the Israeli people is that she surmounted the grimness of this period and became revered again in the years before her death.

In a speech she gave before the Six Day War, she declared that her life had been blessed. She enumerated the blessings: the child fearful of pogroms had lived to be the free citizen of an independent Jewish state. Her own children took part in the just society of a kibbutz. Her national and social visions were on the way to fulfillment.

Dying as she did before the hoped-for peace with the Arabs has been achieved, it is hard to be confident that the optimism of this earlier summation of her life had been sustained. And there is the added irony that the peace, if achieved, will be attained by the man against whose social and political policies she fought all her days. But she had too much wry humor not to appreciate the tricks of history, and too much magnanimity where the fate of her people was involved for any personal disappointment to be more than slight.

For many who shared her beliefs but lacked her courage, she was a gadfly. In an intimate sense she was the conscience of the Jewish people. Those who loved her will long remember the deep, firm voice that called to action and the searching eyes that demanded, "where are you?" In 1967, when she saw many young American Jews thronging to help in Israel's defense, she said forthrightly, "You are ready to die with us. Why do you not remain to live with us?" This question tormented her with increasing intensity. Not too long before her death she spoke of plans to come to the United States in behalf of *aliyah*, immigration to Israel. In any case, it is doubtful if even she would have achieved the miracle of stimulating large-scale immigration of American Jews to Israel.

Women throughout the world viewed Golda Meir as an example of what women might accomplish. Americans responded to her homespun, earthy directness. For Israel and the Jewish people she became a mother figure—wise, compassionate and stern when need be. The shrinking pantheon of great national leaders has been further diminished by her passing.

Review and Study Questions

1. What is Zionism?
2. What are kibbutzim and why were they important in the early settlement of Israel?
3. Discuss the Yom Kippur War. How did Meir assess her role and responsibility in the war?
4. What was the role of the United States in the Yom Kippur War? Discuss.

Suggestions for Further Reading

There are several sources of Golda Meir's own writings. Her autobiography, *My Life* (New York: Putnam, 1975) is excerpted in this chapter. Her selected official papers are collected in *This is Our Strength, Selected Papers of Golda Meir,* ed. and intro. Henry M. Christman, foreword Eleanor Roosevelt (New York and London: The Macmillan Co., 1962). There are two editions of *Golda Meir Speaks Out,* ed. Marie Syrkin (London: Weidenfeld and Nicolson, 1973) and Golda Meir, *A Land of Our Own, An Oral Autobiography,* ed. Marie Syrkin (New York: Putnam, 1973).

There are several biographies of Meir, widely varying in their sympathy and point of view. Robert I. Friedman, *Zealots for Zion, Inside Israel's West Bank Settlement Movement* (New York: Random House, 1992) is not quite a biography but it does deal with Meir's part in the rancorous West Bank settlement; it is also highly critical. Ralph G. Martin, *Golda: Golda Meir, The Romantic Years* (New York: Scribner, 1988) is an account only through 1948. Thus it is not complete, nor is it a very good account. Peggy Mann, *Golda, The Life of Israel's Prime Minister* (New York: Coward, McCann and Geoghegan, 1971), though it covers events only before 1971, is scrupulously honest and historically accurate. Also limited to events before 1971 is Terry Morris, *Shalom Golda* (New York: Hawthorn Books, 1971), an admiring, brief popular biography. Eliyahu Agress, *Golda Meir, Portrait of a Prime Minister,* tr. Israel I. Taslitt (New York: Sabra Books, n.d.) is a picture book compiled under the auspices of the Israeli government.

To compensate for the lack of treatment of the 1970s in the available biographies there are a number of books on the Arab-Israeli wars, especially the Yom Kippur War. The best is *The Yom Kippur War,* by The Insight Team of the London *Sunday Times* (New York: Doubleday, 1974). Of almost equal authority, and equally well researched is Edgar O'Ballance, *No Victor, No Vanquished, The Yom Kippur War* (San Rafael, Ca., and London: Presidio Press, 1978). *The Yom Kippur War, Israel and the Jewish People,* ed. Moshe Davis (New York: Arno Press, 1974) is a collection of authoritative essays and articles on the war from all over the world. Peter Allen, *The Yom Kippur War* (New York: Scribner, 1982) is a popular book but highly favorable to Israel. Of somewhat larger scope is Trevor N. Dupuy, *Elusive Victory, The Arab-Israeli Wars, 1947–1974* (New York et al.: Harper and Row, 1978), by an established military historian.

There are any number of good general histories of modern Israel. We have excerpted one of them for this chapter, Howard M. Sachar, *A History of Israel, From the Rise of Zionism to our Time* (New York: Knopf, 1976). Amos Perlmutter, *Israel, The Partitioned State, A Political History since 1900* (New York: 1985) is also an authoritative work, as is Terence Prittie, *Israel, Miracle in the Desert,* rev. ed. (New York et al.: Praeger, 1968), though it stops short of the topic in this chapter. Lawrence Meyer, *Israel Now: Portrait of a Troubled Land* (New York: Delacorte Press, 1982) is a good, readable general treatment by an experienced journalist.

Useful also are the several biographies and autobiographies of Meir's leading colleagues and fellow Israeli officials. Moshe Dayan, *Story of My Life* (New York: Morrow, 1976) is a case in point. See also the work of his daughter, Yael Dayan, *My Father, His Daughter* (New York: Farrar, Straus and Giroux, 1985) and Shahtai Teveth, *Moshe Dayan* (London and Jerusalem: Weidenfeld and Nicolson, 1972). See also Abba Eban, *Personal Witness, Israel Through My Eyes* (New York: Putnam, 1992). For America's important role in these events a useful source is the writings of Henry Kissinger, secretary of state under President Nixon. See Henry Kissinger, *Years of Upheaval* (Boston and Toronto: Little, Brown and Co., 1982) and Henry Kissinger, *American Foreign Policy,* 3rd ed. (New York: Norton, 1977).

JOMO KENYATTA: "THE BURNING SPEAR"

c. 1894	Born
1914	Joined a Church of Scotland mission and was baptized
1922	Joined the East Africa Association political protest movement
1928	General secretary of the Kikuyu Central Association
1929	Went to London to protest white domination of East Africa
1936–38	Studied anthropology at London School of Economics
1946	Returned to Kenya to become president of the Kenya African Union
1952–53	Arrested and tried as the "manager" of the Mau Mau organization
1961	Released from prison
1963–64	Became prime minister, then president of Kenya
1978	Died

Jomo Kenyatta of Kenya was the most widely known and charismatic of the leaders of the several African peoples who were clamoring for independence from colonial rule in the 1950s. He was a large, powerfully built man, with a commanding presence, a penetrating, transfixing gaze, and a deep, kettle-drum voice. He was a spell-binding orator, well educated, and an experienced political leader and consensus builder among the many factions of his people. He was clearly a danger to continued white supremacy in Kenya. He knew it and the white settlers knew it.

He was born about 1894, near Mount Kenya, the grandson of a Kikuyu witch doctor. His life coincided with the period of white penetration of East Africa. He later recalled, as a boy, seeing the first white men to reach the interior. He was fascinated by them, by their bustling progress and their literacy. At about the age of twelve he presented himself at a Church of Scotland mission school, clad only in three wire bracelets and a strip of cloth around his neck. He became a student and a Christian. He took the baptismal name Johnstone, from his admiration for the Apostles John and Peter (the "rock" or "stone" of the early church), adding it to his tribal name Kamau.

After five years in the mission school he went to Nairobi, the rapidly growing political and economic hub of East Africa. Here he held a succession of jobs that provided him with a living and the ability to buy fancy clothes, including a decorated belt which in the Kikuyu language is called *kenyatta*. He took this as a new name symbolizing his new life of affluence.

In 1922 Kenyatta joined the fledgling East Africa Association, the first political protest movement in Kenya against white domination. Government pressure forced this organization to disband, but its members shortly reorganized as the Kikuyu Central Association. Kenyatta became its general secretary in 1928. That same year a British colonial commission recommended a union of Kenya with Uganda and Tanganyika, with the prospect of self-government. Such a prospect spelled ruin for native Kikuyu interests, and the following year Kenyatta went to London to work against the scheme.

He made no progress at all with British authorities, but he and his cause were championed by various radical groups and individuals in England, including Fenner Brockway, a socialist member of parliament who was an outspoken critic of imperialism. Under the sponsorship of radical groups, Kenyatta traveled to Moscow and to the International Negro Workers' Conference in Hamburg. He was becoming identified with European radical politics—but he was radical only in the interests of his own people. In 1932 he was finally permitted to testify on behalf of Kikuyu land claims before a British government commission, but his testimony was generally ignored. He continued to travel on the Continent, visiting the Soviet Union again, where he studied at Moscow University for a year. Returning to England, he worked as a phonetic informant at University College, London, and from 1936 to 1938 studied anthropology at the London School of Economics. His thesis, *Facing Mount Kenya*, a study of Kikuyu tribal life, was published in 1938. For that book he took yet another name, Jomo "Burning Spear."

After the start of World War II Kenyatta was unable to return to Kenya. In England he lectured on African affairs for the Workers Educational Association and continued to write pamphlets advocating African rights. With the end of the war he helped organize the Fifth Pan-African Congress, which met, not in Africa, but in Manchester. Resolutions were passed demanding African independence from colonial rule. Shortly thereafter, he was able to return to Kenya, where, in 1947, he was elected president of the newly formed Kenya African Union. Under his leadership the union grew into an enormous, mass nationalist party, with an increasingly insistent agenda for self-government.

Suffering without Bitterness

JOMO KENYATTA

In the face of the intransigence of the white settler government of Kenya, some sort of violent reaction was nearly inevitable. It came in 1952 with the outbreak of the black terrorist movement called Mau Mau. It was a widespread secret society, its members pledged, by the most gruesome oath-taking ceremonies, to violence against both whites and temporizing fellow blacks.

The Mau Mau created a nationwide panic. White settlers barricaded themselves in their farm compounds, fearing even their most faithful native retainers. Black tribal leaders who advocated anything short of violent solutions were in danger of their lives. A climax was reached with the murder of a revered senior chief of the Kikuyu, Chief Waruhiu, in the fall of 1952. On October 20, at the request of the newly appointed governor, Sir Evelyn Baring, the British government issued an Emergency Proclamation. Jomo Kenyatta was widely perceived among the white settlers to be the leader of the Mau Mau. Under the Emergency Proclamation he was arrested, along with nearly two hundred other African leaders. Kenyatta was immediately flown to a remote northern village, Kapenguria, where he was charged with "management" of the Mau Mau and brought to trial.

The book from which the following excerpt is taken, *Suffering without Bitterness,* was published under the name of Jomo Kenyatta. While it does contain substantial excerpts from his speeches and writings, it was actually written by two close associates of Kenyatta, his former secretary Duncan Nderitu Ndegwa, and Anthony Cullen, a member of his personal staff. Kenyatta himself read and contributed to the manuscript as it took shape. It is thus an "official biography." It deals with the famous Kapenguria trial, with Kenyatta's subsequent imprisonment, and with his eventual release and triumphant return to Kenyan national leadership.

The excerpt selected is a refutation of the charge against Kenyatta that he was the leader of the Mau Mau. Quite the reverse: it depicts him as an opponent of the movement and the leading advocate of Kenyan nationalism by peaceful, constitutional means.

The record of evidence at this point illustrates beyond rational doubt that, far from being a catalyst of disaster, Kenyatta was an implacable opponent of lawlessness and violence. By all his words, and by his very presence, he stood unyieldingly for nationalist demands, to be secured by the forces of peace.

He risked his life, before he was arrested, to strengthen his national Party. His principles, rooted in personal philosophy tempered by wide experience, were those of constitutional means. Beyond this, he could envisage how terrorism must provoke such reprisals, and permit such propaganda, as to undo—or set right back—the effect of solid preparation and persuasion over thirty years.

It seems remarkable in retrospect that, in 1952, men of ingrained honesty, and often of undoubted brilliance, should have stifled or have found themselves deserted by such attributes. . . . All were caught up in a monstrous lie.

The national Swahili newspaper *Baraza*—one of the *East African Standard* group of publications—covered a meeting at Muguga, about fifteen miles from Nairobi, in its issue of April 12, 1952. This account was quoted in evidence, incidentally, during the Kapenguria trial.

Baraza was staffed by professional journalists, who reported that: "Mr. Jomo Kenyatta, the President of the KAU, said last Saturday that, because of the rumours that had spread everywhere that KAU is connected with an Association which was proscribed—that is, Mau Mau—there should be no other meetings after the close of KAU meetings". . . .

Also quoted in the Court records was a report in the newspaper *Sauti ya Mwafrika* of June 20, 1952, in reference to a speech by Jomo Kenyatta at Naivasha at that time. In this speech, he emphasized that demands must be pursued peacefully, and warned against racial intolerance. This—be it noted—was not a subtle or strategic address to a select group of intelligentsia, but one of a series of orations to the ordinary people who gathered in thousands to hear him, standing in groups or perched in trees or seated on the ground. . . .

Then came two enormous mass meetings, of the greatest possible significance to any appraisal of Mzee[1] Kenyatta's activities and objectives over this period. The first of these was a KAU meeting at Nyeri on July 26, 1952, with an attendance of at least 50,000 people.

There is an official record of his words at this meeting. As an orator on such occasions, Kenyatta had—and indeed still has—a magic touch and a capability without peer. He could have inflamed this crowd and turned the country onto any chosen path, bending the

---

[1]*Mzee* is a Kikuyu term of respect.—ED.

future to his will. In the event, this was the occasion when he called for national unity rather than subversion, and for the faithful pursuit of democratic principles. He proclaimed that violence and thuggery could only delay Kenya's independence. Denouncing Mau Mau and lawlessness, he urged this vast assembly, and through them the millions to whom his words would gradually seep, to renounce force and rely instead on the supreme power of justice and brains. . . .

The second of these equally large mass meetings was held at Kiambu on August 24, 1952. . . .

Jomo Kenyatta started his speech with these words—"Many people were asked what this meeting is about and who the organizers are. The meeting is of the Kikuyu elders and leaders, who have decided to address a public meeting and see what the disease in Kikuyuland is, and how this disease can be cured. We are being harmed by a thing which some people seem to call Mau Mau."

Kenyatta went on to ask all those who were against Mau Mau to raise their hands. Response was immediate and unanimous. He then went on to talk about the objects of the KAU, and to disclaim any association between the Union and Mau Mau activities. He ended his speech with these words—"Let us agree not to engage in crime. We have pleaded for more land for many years. A Commission will soon be coming out to look into the land question. If you do not stop crime, those people who come out on the Land Commission will be told that we are thieves, that we are this, that we are that, which would do us immeasurable harm. We must now work together". . . .

He went on: "Mau Mau has spoiled the country. Let Mau Mau perish for ever. All people should search for Mau Mau and kill it. . . ."

Only 57 days elapsed after these declarations before Kenyatta was arrested. It is possible to ascribe motivation, not with the assurance of testimony, but at least with the confidence that has to emerge from the absence of alternative assumption. It must have been thought, by those responsible, that here was a man drawing inconveniently near to the attainment of at least some legitimate demands, by lawful means. It must have been thought that here was the one mature and powerful leader, in whose absence ambition—or even rebellion— could speedily be crushed. But whatever the composite of motives and emotions, Kenya was plunged into disaster. And those annals of justice to which the British people cling, with such modest and seemingly-casual devotion, were made to look shoddy, by the work of frightened servants of the Crown. . . .

After Kenyatta's arrest the Mau Mau violence grew worse. But the trial hastened on. In the course of the trial, Kenyatta made the following statement during testimony as a witness, called by his leading defense council, Mr. D. N. Pritt.

'I blame the Government because—knowing that the Africans have grievances—they did not go into these grievances: shortage of houses in places like Nairobi, land shortage, and poverty of the African people both in the towns and in the Reserves. I believe if the Government had looked into the economic and social conditions of the people, they could have done much good.

'And instead of joining with us to fight Mau Mau, the Government arrested all the leading members of the Kenya African Union, accusing them of being Mau Mau. It should have been the Government's duty to co-operate with KAU to stamp out anything that was bad, such as Mau Mau. Instead of doing that, they have arrested thousands and thousands of people who would have been useful in helping to put things right in this country. It is on these points that I blame the Government; they did not tackle the business in the right way.

'They wanted—I think—not to eliminate Mau Mau, but to eliminate the only political organization, the KAU, which fights constitutionally for the rights of the African people, just as the Electors Union fights for the rights of the Europeans and the Indian National Congress for the rights of the Asians. I think and believe that the activity of Government in arresting all the leading members of KAU, who are innocent people engaged in ordinary business, is not the right way of combatting Mau Mau. Most of the people behind bars today are people who would be helping to adjust things and eliminate Mau Mau from the country.

'We know pretty well that the reason for our arrest was not Mau Mau, but because we were going ahead uniting our people to demand our rights. The Government arrested us simply because, when they saw we could have an organization of 30,000 or 40,000 or more Africans demanding their rights here, they said: we have an excuse to stop this—Mau Mau.'

This clearly went to the root of the matter, and the presentation of this truth has been curiously hushed up—or simply unseen by superficial observers of Africa—in almost all subsequent literature and discussion.

But what of the trial itself? How was this conducted, and what was the calculated arrangement of the Prosecution case?

This may be gauged from Mr. Pritt's final address, spread over two days beginning on March 2, 1953. . . .

What follows now is an accurate precis, employing a selection of Mr. Pritt's unaltered words, of the case as he saw it at that stage:

'The prosecution case in this very serious litigation was scarcely properly prepared at any stage, either in the weeks or months preceding the charges, or in the weeks or months when the accused were already in detention, or during the period of the case itself.

'It does not seem that the prosecution has ever made up its mind on what is the essence of its case against the accused.

'I could understand the prosecution attitude if some political or other pressure had brought about the launching of a case that never should have been launched, but in no other way can I understand it.

'Some of the witnesses we wanted to call were in England, and the Government of Kenya refused to give us any safe conduct for them to come here.

'I have constantly wondered why so much of the prosecution evidence, and so much of their examination of the accused and witnesses, has seemed so remote from the allegations contained in the charges, which relate to management and membership of Mau Mau.

'Managing Mau Mau? Well, where? In what fashion, with what assistance, in what office, with what policy, with what documents? There was never anything.

'In order to convict Mr. Kenyatta of managing, the evidence would have to show that he is the manager, that is to say the one person who is at the head of the management, and not just one of a number of persons taking part in management. Therefore I would submit that Mr. Kenyatta not only cannot be convicted of being a manager, as a matter of law, because there is no evidence of his management in that sense of the word, but that he cannot be convicted of assisting in the management, since he is not charged with assisting in the management.

'The prosecution's case is sought to be built up out of all sorts of little bits and pieces, and little items on the periphery, and never any real evidence of anything seriously connected with Mau Mau. . . .

'You have to prove something grave and terrible, that the accused participated in a terrorist organization, whereas there is very substantial evidence that the body in which they are most prominent—the Kenya African Union—is a plain and outspoken enemy of that organization'. . . .

On April 8, 1953, the 58th day of the Kapenguria trial, judgment was delivered by the magistrate, Mr. R. S. Thacker, Q.C. The record shows that Kenyatta was convicted on both counts, sentenced to seven years imprisonment, with a recommendation that he be confined thereafter.

In all the history of legal process, there can hardly have been a more astounding verdict as an outcome of trial proceedings. It caricatured—rather than echoed—those farcical performances of law

in Police States which, before and since, have been widely condemned
by humanists and liberal-minded men. . . .

Mau Mau from Within

DONALD L. BARNETT AND KARARI NJAMA

In spite of the government's best efforts to keep Kenyatta's trial secret,
it quickly became an international event. India's Premier Pandit Nehru
sent a team of Indian lawyers to defend him; he had the best available
Kenyan lawyers; and his English radical friends secured the services of
D. N. Pritt, one of Britain's most famous defense attorneys and a noted
advocate of minority and subversive causes.

But the government pressed on with its case. The main charge was
that Kenyatta was the active, managing leader of the Mau Mau. Despite
the most blatant lapses in judicial process and the witch-hunt atmosphere of the trial, despite the perjured testimony of the leading prosecution witness (to which he later admitted), the presiding judge found
Kenyatta guilty as charged. It was a judgment thoroughly approved by
the Kenyan white settler community, who were unanimous in their
belief that Kenyatta was indeed the leader of the Mau Mau. This was a
belief shared by many native blacks, perhaps even a majority.

The following account is excerpted from a sensational book, *Mau
Mau from Within,* the recollections of a Kikuyu teacher named
Karari Njama, who joined the movement and whose book is a defense of it. In the account of his oath-taking it is clear that Kenyatta
was regarded as the leader of the movement. It is equally clear that
the distinction between Mau Mau tactics and legitimate protest—
which was the heart of Kenyatta's defense—was totally ignored by
Njama and the Mau Mau. Njama explicitly identifies Mau Mau with
the Kikuyu Central Association (KCA), the radical political movement Kenyatta had once headed.

Njama had been persuaded by a friend to attend a feast at a neigh-
bor's house. Only after he arrived did he begin to suspect that it was actually to be a Mau Mau initiation. Here is his account of his oath-taking.

Groups of men and women continued to come until there was very
little room for anyone to sit. A few persons would be called by names
and moved in the next hut. When I was called to go to the next hut, I

was very pleased, but arriving outside in a clear moonshine, I could see hundreds of people standing some armed with *pangas, simis* (swords) and clubs. They formed a path on both sides leading to the door of the next hut. I became certain that the day had arrived for me to take the oath, and I had to face it manly, I thought.

As I led my group marching in the cordoned path, they waved their *pangas* and swords over our heads and I heard one of them asking whether there was an informer to be 'eaten.' With a reply that we were all good people from another person, we entered the next hut.

By the light of a hurricane lamp, I could see the furious guards who stood armed with *pangas* and *simis*. Right in front of us stood an arch of banana and maize stalks and sugar cane stems tied by a forest creeping and climbing plant. We were harassed to take out our coats, money, watches, shoes and any other European metal we had in our possession. Then the oath administrator, Githinji Mwarari— who had painted his fat face with white chalk—put a band of raw goat's skin on the right hand wrist of each one of the seven persons who were to be initiated. We were then surrounded [bound together] by goats' small intestines on our shoulders and feet. Another person then sprayed us with some beer from his mouth as a blessing at the same time throwing a mixture of the finger millet with other cereals on us. Then Githinji pricked our right hand middle finger with a needle until it bled. He then brought the chest of a billy goat and its heart still attached to the lungs and smeared them with our blood. He then took a Kikuyu gourd containing blood and with it made a cross on our foreheads and on all important joints saying, 'May this blood mark the faithful and brave members of the Gikuyu and Mumbi Unity; may this same blood warn you that if you betray our secrets or violate the oath, our members will come and cut you into pieces at the joints marked by this blood.'

We were then asked to lick each others blood from our middle fingers and vowed after the administrator: 'If I reveal this secret of Gikuyu and Mumbi to a person not a member, may this blood kill me. If I violate any of the rules of the oath may this blood kill me. If I lie, may this blood kill me.'

We were then ordered to hold each others right hand and in that position, making a line, passed through the arch seven times. Each time the oath administrator cut off a piece of the goat's small intestine, breaking it into pieces, while all the rest in the hut repeated a curse on us: '*T'athu! Ugotuika uguo ungiaria maheni! Muma uroria muria ma!*' ('Slash! may you be cut like this! Let the oath kill he who lies!').

We were then made to stand facing Mt. Kenya, encircled by

intestines, and given two dampened soil balls and ordered to hold the left hand soil ball against our navels. We then swore: 'I, (Karari Njama), swear before God and before all the people present here that. . . .

(1) I shall never reveal this secret of the KCA oath—which is of Gikuyu and Mumbi and which demands land and freedom—to any person who is not a member of our society. If I ever reveal it, may this oath kill me! ([Repeated after each vow while] biting the chest meat of a billy goat held together with the heart and lungs.)

(2) I shall always help any member of our society who is in difficulty or need of help.

(3) If I am ever called, during the day or night, to do any work for this society, I shall obey.

(4) I shall on no account ever disobey the leaders of this society.

(5) If I am ever given firearms or ammunition to hide, I shall do so.

(6) I shall always give money or goods to this society whenever called upon to do so.

(7) I shall never sell land to a European or an Asian.

(8) I shall not permit intermarriage between Africans and the white community.

(9) I will never go with a prostitute.

(10) I shall never cause a girl to become pregnant and leave her unmarried.

(11) I will never marry and then seek a divorce.

(12) I shall never allow any daughter to remain uncircumcised.[2]

(13) I shall never drink European manufactured beer or cigarettes.

(14) I shall never spy on or otherwise sell my people to Government.

(15) I shall never help the missionaries in their Christian faith to ruin our traditional and cultural customs.

(16) I will never accept the Beecher Report.[3]

(17) I shall never steal any property belonging to a member of our society.

(18) I shall obey any strike call, whenever notified.

(19) I will never retreat or abandon any of our mentioned demands but will daily increase more and stronger demands until we achieve our goals.

(20) I shall pay 62/50s. and a ram as assessed by this society as soon as I am able.

---

[2]Female circumcision had been opposed by white missionaries and, to some extent, whites generally, as a cruel and dangerous practice—but it had become one of the nationalistic issues to the Kikuyu.—ED.

[3]A report on public education in 1949, seen as inimical to black interests.—ED.

(21) I shall always follow the leadership of Jomo Kenyatta and Mbiyu Koinange.'

We repeated the oath while pricking the eye of a goat with a kei-apple thorn seven times and then ended the vows by pricking seven times some seven sodom apples. To end the ceremony, blood mixed with some good smelling oil was used to make a cross on our foreheads indicating our reception as members of Gikuyu and Mumbi [while] warning us: 'Forward ever and backward never!' . . .

After we had all been sworn, the house was very crowded that contained about 80 people; nearly all of whom were initiated on that night. About the same number of old members were working outside as guards. A speech was made by the oath administrator, Githinji Mwarari, and his assistant Kariuki King'ori, who told us that they had been sent from the Head Office in Nairobi to give people an oath that could create a real unity among all the Africans which would make it easier for the African to gain his land and freedom. . . .

When he sat down, his assistant administrator, Kariuki King'ori, stood and taught us greetings—the old Kikuyu greetings rarely used due to changes brought about by the European civilization—such as the shaking of hands and the terminology. 'If any person wants to refer to the society he would not say "Mau Mau" as you have already been warned, but he would refer to the society as *Muhimu* (a Swahili word meaning "Most Important"), *Muingi* (meaning "The Community" in Kikuyu) or *Gikuyu na Mumbi*.' . . .

It was about four o'clock in the morning, the cocks were crowing, the moon and the stars were brightly shining. The footpaths were wet and muddy as it had rained sometime before midnight. I quickly and quietly went home and called my wife to open the door for me. Without talking to her I went straight to my bed.

I spent the whole day in bed, partly asleep, as I had not slept the night before, and partly reciting and reasoning my vows. Reflecting on the crowd at the KAU rally held one and a half months ago at Nyeri Showgrounds supporting national demands under the national leader Jomo Kenyatta assisted by Peter Mbiyu Koinange, the cleverest Africans in Kenya—whose leadership was advertised in Mathenge's song book where Jesus Christ's name has been substituted for by Jomo Kenyatta's—and whereas the Government had taken no action against them proved to me that our true and just grievances were led by powerful and honoured men. I believed that it was an all Kenya African national movement and not a tribal one. With the understanding that African labour is the whole backbone of Kenya's economy, I believed that if all Kenya Africans went on a labour strike we would paralyse the country's economy and the white community who holds the most of it would suffer most and recognize our demands. Furthermore, our national leader, Jomo Kenyatta, had lived in England for 17 years and must have during his stay convinced the British Government of our claims.

Rush to Judgment

JEREMY MURRAY-BROWN

Was the Kapenguria trial and conviction of Jomo Kenyatta a disgraceful and cynical rush to judgment? Kenyatta's assertions that he was never associated with the Mau Mau, but that he sought only the rights of his people under a constitutional government, seem to be borne out by the subsequent course of events.

After the trial and a series of fruitless appeals, Kenyatta was imprisoned in 1954, at Lokitaung. But African independence was on the march. There was a continuous clamor for his release. In 1960 he was elected *in absentia* as president of the Kenya African National Union, the leading native independence party. He was finally released in the summer of 1961, and he immediately began a speaking tour that brought out throngs wherever he went. Within the next two years he was elected president of KANU and a member of the Legislative Assembly. He was clearly the only black leader of Kenya with a substantial following. Under an agreement reached with the British, the last governor of Kenya, Malcolm Macdonald, invited Kenyatta to form a government on June 1, 1963, and he became the first Prime Minister of a self-governing Kenya. In the following year Kenya became a republic with Kenyatta as its president. In his triumph Kenyatta did not seek vengeance. Instead, he became the most pro-British of African leaders, and generally the most pro-Western, pro-white. He even reached an accommodation with the white settlers. This situation lasted until his death in 1978.

Were his moderation and statesmanlike policies as head of state indicative that he had been innocent of the charges brought against him in the trial at Kapenguria? Most of his detractors have said no, and have continued to characterize Kenyatta as, at best, an adroit politician who permitted his name to be used by the Mau Mau, and allowed himself and his party to profit from their violent tactics.

In the excerpt that follows from Jeremy Murray-Brown's *Kenyatta*, the most authoritative biography of Jomo Kenyatta, the author treats the trial at Kapenguria in great detail and proves conclusively that it was indeed a rush to judgment, a cynical pretext for removing Kenyatta as a dangerous political influence, and that the Mau Mau charge was a total fabrication.

The account begins with the appointment of the new governor of Kenya, Sir Evelyn Baring, and the proclamation of a state of emergency.

On taking up his appointment as Governor, Baring took the view that it would be a mistake for him to meet Kenyatta formally since if he then had to arrest him he would appear to have double-crossed the Africans. The first assumption of the Emergency operation was that once the nationalist leaders were out of the way, peace would return among the normally law-abiding natives of the colony.

The government was as shaken as everyone else by the Kikuyu reaction to the loss of their leaders, once the initial numbness wore off. It left them with the problem of having to decide what to do with Kenyatta. In London questions were raised in Parliament where Kenyatta had powerful friends in Fenner Brockway and Leslie Hale. Peter Mbiyu Koinange was also at large and able to denounce the Emergency measures. The confusion of thinking that led to Kenyatta's arrest compelled the government to find some pretext for his detention. Perhaps the most obvious solution was to bring him to trial and to try to make him out to be a common criminal. But of what offence should it accuse him? And how could they make the charge stick?

They made vigorous efforts to find something. A ton and a half of documents, books and papers had been removed from Kenyatta's house at Gatundu the night of his arrest, and a senior police officer was immediately detailed to go through these and prepare a case against him. He was given three weeks to complete his enquiries. It is fair to say he found nothing. . . . As Kenyatta's alleged crimes and the place of his arrest both lay in the Kiambu district of Kikuyuland, the natural and proper course would have been to try him in Nairobi. But the government feared the attention and demonstrations which this would attract and wanted to carry the case through as quietly as possible, at some remote spot.

Kapenguria was ideal for this purpose. It lay in a restricted area, to which no one could go without a permit; the scanty local population was backward and uninterested; it had never had a resident magistrate, so that the government could pick someone on whom it could rely. Had the prosecution been decided on from the start, the accused could have been sent straight to one of the prisons at Kapenguria where it would be simple to 'apprehend' them and give some plausibility to the holding of the trial there. But, as it was, the government had to go through a legal farce. On 18 November Kenyatta and his colleagues Kaggia, Kubai, Ngei and Oneko, all of whom were also executive members of KAU, and Kunga Karumba, who was chairman of an important regional branch of the party, were brought down to Kapenguria, technically released from custody and immediately rearrested, thus creating jurisdiction for trial in Kapenguria. They were now charged with the management of Mau Mau, which was a proscribed society. The offence carried a maximum penalty of seven years' imprisonment. Their trial was set for 24 November.

This was apparently the first Kenyatta heard of the government's intentions towards him. He managed to get a message out requesting that defence lawyers be briefed on his behalf. Within Kenya, feeling among the European community was running so high that no white man in the colony dared join in the defence, which was now being handled from Nairobi by the Indian supporters of the nationalist movement, led by a young barrister, A. R. Kapila. But immediate offers of help came from elsewhere, and soon an impressive international team of counsel was assembled, including Chaman Lall, a member of the Upper House of the Indian Parliament and friend of Nehru, H. O. Davies from Lagos, and Dudley Thompson, a West Indian practising in Tanganyika. Two Kenya residents also took part, a Goan, Fitzwell de Souza and a Sikh, Jaswant Singh.

To lead this team, Koinange, Brockway and Hale invited the services of D. N. Pritt QC, one of the ablest advocates at the English Bar. On 24 November the six accused were again brought down to Kapenguria where a judge recently retired from the Supreme Court of Kenya, R. S. Thacker, had been specially appointed to hear the case. He adjourned proceedings until 3 December to allow the defence team time to come together.

D. N. Pritt QC had as great an experience of political trials as anyone in the British Commonwealth. A Member of Parliament for fifteen years and known for pro-Soviet views, he had long been an opponent of imperialism. In the Parliament of 1945–50 he had sat as an independent Socialist. His acceptance of the Kapenguria brief made it certain that Kenyatta's case would receive wide publicity. If the Kenya Government hoped to get away with a hole-and-corner affair to cover their blunder in arresting Kenyatta, they badly miscalculated. Their attempt to make Kenyatta out to be an ordinary criminal came unstuck the moment Pritt arrived on the scene. As became clear during the trial itself, the prosecution soon shifted the base of its attack from Kenyatta's alleged criminal activities as manager of Mau Mau to the politics of African Nationalism. . . .

On 3 December 1952, all was ready for the trial proper to begin. The government provided window-dressing in the form of armoured cars,

barbed wire and helicopters circling overhead. Troops were everywhere in evidence. The six accused men were brought from their
prison a mile away by army truck and marched in handcuffs by armed
askaris to the door of the court. Only then were the handcuffs removed.
The 'public' consisted of wives of settlers and of government officers
who applauded every point which seemed to go against Kenyatta. But
Nairobi journalists and half a dozen of the best foreign correspondents
of the English Press were there, along with government photographers. The government intended, no doubt, to humiliate Kenyatta
and impress such Africans as were present with the power of the colonial regime. In the long run the steps taken to destroy him in the eyes
of his people ensured his resurrection as their suffering servant.

Kenyatta still wore the clothes in which he had been arrested. The
police had removed his stick and ring. He was to spend fifty-eight
days in court before judgement was passed, but everyone who was
present at the trial felt that his was the dominating personality at
Kapenguria.

On 3 December 1952, then, Deputy Public Prosecutor Somer-
hough opened for the Crown:

> 'May it please your Honour. The charge is that of managing an unlawful
> society. . . . The Crown cannot bind themselves to any particular place
> in the Colony where this society was managed. The Society is Mau Mau.
> It is a Society which has no records. It appears to have no official list of
> members. It does not carry banners. Some details of its meetings and
> rites, the instrument of which are got from the local bush, will be heard
> later in the proceedings. Arches of banana leaves, the African fruit
> known as the Apple of Sodom, eyes of sheep, blood and earth—these
> are all gathered together when ceremonies take place. . . .
>
> The Crown case is going to be that Mau Mau is part of KAU—a
> militant part, a sort of Stern gang, if I may borrow a phrase from
> another country. It is possible to be a member of KAU and have noth-
> ing to do with Mau Mau; yet Mau Mau itself is a definite limb or part of
> KAU as it existed in 1952 when all the accused were closely connected
> with KAU as high office bearers.'

The Crown proceeded confidently to its first witness, a certain
Rawson Macharia. Rawson Macharia was a young man still in his thir-
ties and Kenyatta's neighbour at Gatundu. His evidence contained
obvious untruths which the defence exposed, but its main significance
was that it was the strongest of only three statements that implicated
Kenyatta directly with oath-giving ceremonies. Macharia claimed to be
a drinking friend of Kenyatta's, and to have been present when
Kenyatta personally administered a 'Mau Mau' oath to several people
and tried to make Macharia take it also. He gave convincing details—a

goat's head from which the eyes had been removed and placed on thorns and the tongue cut out, ceremonial arches, a brew of blood and earth. Kenyatta, he alleged, made the oath-takers repeat the words:

"When we agree to drive Europeans away you must take an active part in driving them away or killing them."

MAGISTRATE: Jomo Kenyatta said this?
MACHARIA: Yes, Mr. Kenyatta said this: "If you see any African killing anyone, you must not disclose it or tell anyone. If you shall see an African stealing, you must help him. You must pay sixty-two shillings and fifty cents to this society." Then he said: "And that is Mau Mau, and you must not ask how this money is used, and if you shall be asked whether you are a member of this society you must say you are a member of KAU."

Macharia said this incident took place on 16 March 1950, which was before Mau Mau was proscribed and so, even if proved, it was not an offence in itself. Pritt argued that the evidence should be disallowed. Thacker, however, accepted it on the grounds that it was a strong indication that Kenyatta must also have engaged in similar oath-giving ceremonies after the banning of Mau Mau. But the prosecution could produce nothing to substantiate this. . . . In the tensions of the Emergency any hint that a man might have links with Mau Mau was enough to condemn him. At Kapenguria Kenyatta was already cast as the villain by the government, and anything he had done or had said, anything which he now said in court, took on sinister meaning in the eyes of the Europeans.

It was for this reason that Rawson Macharia's evidence was so significant. It set the tone for the prosecution case, and put the judge in a receptive frame of mind. Despite the fact that Macharia's story was refuted by no less than nine witnesses whom the defence were able to bring to Kapenguria, as well as being denied by Kenyatta himself, the judge in his summing up said: 'Although my finding of fact means that I disbelieve ten witnesses for the Defence and believe one for the Prosecution, I have no hesitation in doing so. Rawson Macharia gave his evidence well.'

Rawson Macharia had reason to do so, knowledge of which was denied to Pritt at the time, though not to the government. The reader should now be made aware of it, as it is an important illustration of the peculiar circumstances in which Kenyatta's trial was held.

Almost six years later, towards the end of 1958, Macharia signed an affidavit swearing that his evidence against Kenyatta was false. He was then prosecuted himself for perjury—but for what the government said was a perjured affidavit, not for the perjury at Kapenguria to which he confessed. At his trial in 1959 a copy of a letter was produced which purported to emanate from the office of Kenya's Attorney-General and in which were set out the terms of a government offer to Macharia to pay for his air fare to England, for a two years' course at an English University and two years' subsistence for himself and his family, and a government post on his return. The value of the offer amounted to over £2,500. The letter included the sentence: 'In the event of the above named [Rawson Macharia] being murdered for providing evidence, Government will undertake the maintenance of his family and the education of his two sons.' It carried the date 19 November 1952. . . .

It was not until 19 January 1953 that the prosecution completed its evidence. Pritt then argued at length that there was no case to answer: 'I would submit that it is the most childishly weak case made against any man in any important trial in the history of the British Empire.' The Crown disagreed and Thacker adjourned for a weekend to ponder the arguments in Nairobi. He ran into the most dramatic confrontation between the settlers and the colonial government of the whole Emergency.

On the evening of Saturday 24 January occurred the murder of the Ruck family. The Europeans heard the news on the Sunday and at once gave vent to their feelings. On Monday several hundred of them gathered in Nairobi and marched in a body to Government House brandishing their weapons and shouting for the Governor. They demanded a greater say in the running of affairs; the government seemed on the verge of collapse. . . .

Thacker returned from Nairobi to rule that there was a case to answer. The trial resumed under the shadow of increasing settler discontent. A Kenya newspaper warned the judge against acquitting Kenyatta. An article by Elspeth Huxley comparing him with Hitler was reprinted in a settler periodical. Inaccurate information about his life was circulated by men like W. O. Tait who had known him in the past. Kenyatta was the universal scapegoat.

After lunch that Monday, 26 January 1953, Kenyatta at last entered the witness-box himself. . . .

There follows a grueling cross-examination of Kenyatta.

In the interval the situation with Mau Mau underwent a dramatic deterioration. Two incidents, both on the night of 26 March, shocked all races in the colony.

The first was a daring raid on Naivasha police station, in the Rift Valley. With only five guns between them, the attackers rushed the post in the dark and got away with weapons and ammunition which they loaded on to government trucks and drove off to the forests. It showed the Mau Mau bands were capable of military planning and discipline, and it gave them essential supplies for guerrilla warfare. . . .

The second incident had greater repercussions. For reasons which in part stretched back into the troubled history of the Tigoni removal, all the villagers of a location called Lari who were loyal to their government-appointed chiefs were marked for destruction by rivals. On the night of 26 March some 3,000 embittered men, most of whom had taken the stiffest Mau Mau oaths, swept through the location burning huts and hacking wildly at humans and animals. At least ninety-seven men, women and children in the village died.

Lari and the beginnings of this spiralling descent into nightmare coincided with the closing stages of Kenyatta's trial. They placed him in an impossible situation. The leader of a nationalist movement must always expect to find himself in the dock sooner or later. What he then says will decide his future standing with his people. For Kenyatta to deny the springs of nationalism would have been to deny his whole political life. The judge at Kapenguria could only sentence him to a term of imprisonment; but if he said anything against his own people, who could say what might happen to him. Some of the other accused who played such a subordinate role at Kapenguria were not above murder for their cause.

On 8 April 1953, the court reassembled at Kapenguria for the last time. In the situation just described, an acquittal was politically unthinkable. The judge duly found them all guilty. He dwelt upon Kenyatta's evasive attitude, implying that Kenyatta had virtually condemned himself. Kenyatta then addressed the court. For all he knew it was to be his political testament. In the circumstances it was a remarkable statement.

'May it please Your Honour. On behalf of my colleagues I wish to say that we are not guilty and we do not accept your findings and that during the hearing of this trial which has been so arranged as to place us in difficulties and inconvenience in preparing our cases, we do not feel that we have received the justice or hearing which we would have liked.

'I would like also to tell Your Honour that we feel that this case, from our point of view, has been so arranged as to make scapegoats of us in order to strangle the Kenya African Union, the only African political organisation which fights for the rights of the African people. We wish to say that what we have done in our activities has been to try our level best to find ways and means by which the community in this country can live in harmony. But what we have objected to—and we shall continue to object—are the discriminations in the government of this country. We shall not accept that, whether we are in gaol or out of it, sir, because we find that this world has been made for human beings to live in happily, to enjoy the good things and the produce of the country equally, and to enjoy the opportunities that this country has to offer. Therefore, Your Honour, I will not say that you have been misled or influenced, but the point that you have made is that we have been against the Europeans, and sir, you being a European, it is only natural that perhaps you should feel more that way. I am not accusing you of being prejudiced, but I feel that you should not stress so much the fact that we have been entirely motivated by hatred of Europeans. We ask you to remove that from your mind and to take this line: that our activities have been against the injustices that have been suffered by the African people and if in trying to establish the rights of the African people we have turned out to be what you say, Mau Mau, we are very sorry that you have been misled in that direction. What we have done, and what we shall continue to do, is to demand the rights of the African people as human beings that they may enjoy the facilities and privileges in the same way as other people.

'We look forward to the day when peace shall come to this land and that the truth shall be known that we, as African leaders, have stood for peace. None of us would be happy or would condone the mutilation of human beings. We are humans and we have families and none of us will ever condone such activities as arson that we have been guilty of. . . .

'I do not want to take up more of your time, Your Honour. All that I wish to tell you is that we feel strongly that at this time the Government of this country should try to strangle the only organization, that is the Kenya African Union, of which we are the leaders, who have been working for the betterment of the African people and who are seeking harmonious relations between the races. To these few remarks, Your Honour, I may say that we do not accept your finding of guilty. It will be our duty to instruct our lawyer to take this matter up and we intend to appeal to a higher Court. We believe that the Supreme Court of Kenya will give us justice because we stand for peace; we stand for the rights of the African people, that Africans may find a place among the nations.

'That, in short, is all that I shall say on behalf of my colleagues; that we hope that you and the rest of those who are in authority will seek ways and means by which we can bring harmony and peace to this country, because we do believe that peace by force from any section is impossible, and that violence of any kind, either from Europeans or from Africans, cannot bring any peace at all.'

Thacker turned to sentence him.

'You, Jomo Kenyatta, stand convicted of managing Mau Mau and being a member of that society. You have protested that your object has always been to pursue constitutional methods on the way to self government for the African people, and for the return of land which you say belongs to the African people. I do not believe you. It is my belief that soon after your long stay in Europe and when you came back to this Colony you commenced to organise this Mau Mau society, the object of which was to drive out from Kenya all Europeans, and in doing so to kill them if necessary. I am satisfied that the master mind behind this plan was yours. . . .

You have much to answer for and for that you will be punished. The maximum sentences which this Court is empowered to pass are the sentences which I do pass, and I can only comment that in my opinion they are inadequate for what you have done. Under Section 70 and on the first charge the sentence of the Court is that you be imprisoned for seven years with hard labour, and under Section 71 and on the third charge for three years with hard labour, both sentences to run concurrently, and I shall also recommend that you be restricted.'

Thacker was immediately flown out of Kenya. The settlers were satisfied. Kenyatta was out of the way.

Review and Study Questions

1. In your view, is Jomo Kenyatta's account of his own trial a valid historical document?

2. What were the government's motives in pressing the trial of Kenyatta?

3. Was Mau Mau ever a really serious nationwide problem in Kenya?

4. In your view, was Kenyatta the manager of Mau Mau?

5. To what extent was Kenyatta's trial and imprisonment the springboard to his political success and Kenyan independence?

Suggestions for Further Reading

Jomo Kenyatta himself wrote extensively. We have excerpted, for this chapter, his authorized "official biography," *Suffering without Bitterness: The Founding of the Kenya Nation* (Nairobi: East African Publishing

House, 1968). His anthropology thesis is a substantial and respected work: *Facing Mount Kenya: The Tribal Life of the Gikuyu* (London: Secker and Warburg, 1939). Some of his speeches have been collected in *Harembee!: The Prime Minister of Kenya's Speeches, 1963–1964* (New York: Oxford University Press, 1965).

There are several books by contemporaries dealing with Kenya during the early years of Kenyatta's life: for example, Elspeth Huxley, *The Flame Trees of Thika: Memories of an African Childhood* (New York: William Morrow, 1959), and Karen Blixen, *Out of Africa* (New York: Random House, 1970). There are several more dealing with the years of the Mau Mau crisis in the early 1950s. One is excerpted for this chapter: Donald L. Barnett and Karari Njama, *Mau Mau from Within: Autobiography and Analysis of Kenya's Peasant Revolt* (New York and London: Modern Reader Paperbacks, 1966). Barnett is an American anthropologist who annotates and interprets the account of Njama. A similar account is Josiah Mwangi Kariuki, *"Mau Mau" Detainee: The Account by a Kenyan African of His Experiences in Detention Camps, 1953–1960* (London and Nairobi: Oxford University Press, 1963). Another book of the same type is J. Wamweya, *Freedom Fighter* (Nairobi: East African Publishing House, 1971). The story is told from a white perspective in *So Rough a Wind: The Kenya Memoirs of Sir Michael Blundell* (London: Weidenfeld and Nicholson, 1964). There are two other worthwhile books representing the colonialist viewpoint—one by a former civil servant, N. S. Carey Jones, *The Anatomy of Uhuru: Dynamics and Problems of African Independence in an Age of Conflict* (New York and Washington: Praeger, 1966), the other by a journalist whom President Kenyatta personally had escorted out of the country, Richard Cox, *Kenyatta's Country* (New York and Washington: Praeger, 1965).

There are several biographies of Kenyatta. By far the best is Jeremy Murray-Brown, *Kenyatta*, 2nd ed. (London: George Allen and Unwin, 1979), excerpted for this chapter. George Delf, *Jomo Kenyatta: Towards Truth about "The Light of Kenya"* (Garden City, N.Y.: Doubleday, 1961), is limited since it was written in 1960 while Kenyatta was still in prison, his future uncertain. There are two somewhat laudatory and superficial illustrated biographies: Anthony Howarth, *Kenyatta: A Photographic Biography* (Nairobi: East African Publishing House, 1967) and Mohamed Amin and Peter Moll, *Mzee Jomo Kenyatta: A Photobiography* (Nairobi: Trans Africa Publishers, 1973). A good political biography is Guy Arnold, *Kenyatta and the Politics of Kenya* (London: J. M. Dent, 1974). An excellent straightforward account of Kenyatta's trial is Montague Slater, *The Trial of Jomo Kenyatta* (London: Secker and Warburg, 1955).

There is a useful assessment of the Mau Mau movement in Carl G.

Rosberg, Jr. and John Nottingham, *The Myth of "Mau Mau": Nationalism in Kenya,* Hoover Institution Publications (New York and Washington: Praeger, 1966). There are two useful works on the Kenyan economy under Kenyatta: Arthur Hazlewood, *The Economy of Kenya: The Kenyatta Era* (New York: Oxford University Press, 1979) and Norman N. Miller, *Kenya: The Quest for Prosperity* (Boulder, Colo. and London: Westview Press, 1984).

There is a specialized historical study of Kenya's fight for independence following World War II in David F. Gordon, *Decolonization and the State in Kenya* (Boulder, Colo. and London: Westview Press, 1986). A good, even-handed one-volume history of Kenya is A. Marshall Macphee, *Kenya* (New York and Washington: Praeger, 1968). Also useful is *The Oxford History of East Africa,* especially vol. 3, ed. D. A. Low and Alison Smith (Oxford: Clarendon, 1976).

Acknowledgments (continued from copyright page)

Elizabeth I: From *Our Fortunate Memory of Queen Elizabeth of England* by Sir Francis Bacon.

From *History of England from the Fall of Wolsey to the Defeat of the Armada* by James Anthony Froude.

From *The Invincible Armada and Elizabethan England* by Garrett Mattingly. Copyright © 1963 by the Folger Shakespeare Library. Reprinted by permission of Associated University Press.

Akbar: From *The Akbar Nama* by Abul Fazl, translated by H. Beveridge, 1972; Volume 2, pp. 246–247, 294–296, 316–317, 421; Volume 3, 2–3, 157–158, 364–366. Reprinted by permission of Atlantic Publishers, 4346/4C Ansari Road, Darya Ganj, New Delhi 110002, India.

From *Muntakhabu-T-Tawarikh, Abstract of Histories* by Al-Badaoni, translated by W. H. Lowe, revised edition, 1973, Volume 2, pp. 262–265, 267–269, 272, 277–280. APT Books, New York.

From *The Great Moghuls* by Bamber and Christina Gascoigne, pp. 107–118. (Rainbird/ Jonathan Cape, 1971) Copyright © 1971 Bamber and Christina Gascoigne. Reproduced by permission of Penguin Books Ltd.

Tokugawa Ieyasu Shogun: From *The Makers of Modern Japan: The Life of Tokugawa Ieyasu* by A. L. Sadler, pp. 387–389. Copyright © 1977 Allen and Unwin. Reprinted by permission of Routledge.

Reprinted from *A History of Japan, 1334–1615* by George Sansom with the permission of the publishers, Stanford University Press. Copyright © 1961 by the Board of Trustees of the Leland Stanford Junior University.

From *Japan: The Story of a Nation* by Edwin O. Reischauer. Copyright © 1970 by Edwin O. Reischauer. Reprinted by permission of Alfred A. Knopf, Inc.

Galileo: From *Dialogue Concerning the Two Chief World Systems: The Ptolemaic and Copernican*, 2nd revised edition, trans. and edited by Stillman Drake, pp. 5–6, 338–342, 463–464. Copyright © 1952, 1962, 1967 Regents of the University of California. Reprinted by permission.

From *The Crime of Galileo* by Giorgio de Santillana, pp. 261–267, 270–271, 273. Copyright © 1955 by The University of Chicago Press. Reprinted by permission.

From *Galileo Galilei*, Appendix A, by Ludovico Geymonat, translated by Stillman Drake, 1963. Reprinted by permission of Giullo Einaudi editore S. P. A., Turin, Italy.

Clive of India: From *A Letter to the Proprietors of the East India Stock* by Lord Clive. (London: J. Nourse, 1764), pp. 1–63.

From *Critical and Historical Essays*, Vol. IV of *Works* by Thomas Babington Macaulay. (Boston and New York: Houghton Mifflin & Co., 1900), pp. 362–404.

From "Clive's Parliamentary Hearing" from *Clive of India* by Mark Bence-Jones, 1974, pp. 287–302. Reprinted by permission of Constable Publishers, UK.

Catherine the Great: From *Memoirs of Catherine the Great* by Katherine Anthony, translator and editor. Copyright © 1927 by Alfred A. Knopf, Inc., and renewed 1955 by Katherine Anthony. Reprinted by permission of the publisher.

From *The Modernization of Russia Under Peter I and Catherine II*, by Prince M. M. Shcherbatov, edited and translated by Basil Dmytryshyn, 1974. Copyright © 1974 Basil Dmytryshyn. Reprinted by permission of John Wiley & Sons, Inc.

From *Catherine the Great: A Short History* by Isabel de Madariaga. Copyright © 1990 Yale University Press. Reprinted by permission.

Napoleon: From *Memoirs of the Life, Exile, and Conversations of the Emperor Napoleon* by the Marquis de Las Cases.

From *Madame de Stael on Politics, Literature, and National Character*, translated and edited by Monroe Berger, 1964.

From *Napoleon: From 18 Brumaire to Tilsit* by George Lefebvre, translated by Henry F. Stockhold. Copyright © 1969 Columbia University Press, New York. Reprinted with permission of the publisher.

Simon Bolivar: From *Memoirs of Simon Bolivar, President and Liberator of the Republic of Columbia* by General Ducoudray Holstein (Boston: S.G. Goodrich & Co., 1829), pp. 3–45.

From a portion of Larrazabal's work translated and excerpted in *The Liberator, Simon Bolivar, Man and Image*, ed. by David Bushnell (New York: Knopf, 1970), pp. 122–126.

From *Bolivar and the Independence of Spanish America* by J. B. Trend.

Shaka Zulu: From *Shaka Zulu* by E. A. Ritter, pp. 12–18, 21–26, 30–32, 34–35, 44–47, 55, 57–61, 71. (Penguin Books 1978, first published by Longmans). Copyright © 1955 by E. A. Ritter. Reproduced by permission of Penguin Books Ltd.

From *The Diary of Henry Francis Fynn* edited by James Stuart and D. Malcolm. (London: Longman Group Ltd.), pp. 28–30, 71–79, 84–86, 132–136, 156–157.

From *The Zulu Kings* by Brian Roberts. Copyright © 1974 by Brian Roberts. Reprinted by permission of Brandt & Brandt Literary Agents, Inc.

Mahatma Gandhi: From *The Origin of Nonviolence* by M. K. Gandhi.

From *Gandhi and Civil Disobedience: The Mahatma in Indian Politics* by Judith M. Brown. Copyright © 1977 Judith M. Brown. Reprinted with the permission of Cambridge University Press, North American Branch.

From *Mahatma Gandhi* by Jawaharlal Nehru. Asia Publishing Co., A-32 College Street, Market, Calcutta 700007, India.

Mao Tse-Tung: From *Post Revolutionary Writing* by Mao Tse-tung and Lin Piao. Copyright © 1972 by K. H. Fan. Used by permission of Doubleday, a division of Bantam Doubleday Dell Publishing Group, Inc.

From *Mao Tse-tung* (1966), pp. 298, 312–315, 317–320. Stuart Schram, England.

From *Mao: A Biography* by Ross Terrill, 1980. Reprinted by permission of the author and the author's agents, Scott Meredith Literary Agency, L. P., 845 Third Avenue, New York, New York 10022.

Golda Meir: Reprinted by permission of The Putnam Publishing Group from *My Life* by Golda Meir, pages 420–434. Copyright © 1975 by Golda Meir.

From *A History of Israel* by Howard M. Sachar. Copyright © 1976 by Howard M. Sachar. Reprinted by permission of Alfred A. Knopf, Inc.

From "Golda," by editors of *The New Republic*, December 23–30, 1978. Reprinted by permission of *The New Republic*. Copyright © 1978 The New Republic, Inc.

Jomo Kenyatta: From *Suffering Without Bitterness: The Founding of the Kenya Nation* by Jomo Kenyatta (1968), pp. 46–63. East African Publishing House, P.O. Box 3209, Dar es Saalam, Tanzania.

From *Mau Mau From Within: Autobiography and Analysis of Kenya's Peasant Revolt* by Donald L. Barnett and Karari Njama. Copyright © 1966 by Donald L. Barnett and Karari Njama. Reprinted by permission of Monthly Review Foundation.

From *Kenyatta*, second edition, by Jeremy Murray-Brown. Copyright © 1979 Allen and Unwin. Reprinted by permission of Routledge UK and E. P. Dutton USA.